ZHOU HISTORY UNEARTHED

Zhou History Unearthed

THE BAMBOO MANUSCRIPT *XINIAN* AND
EARLY CHINESE HISTORIOGRAPHY

Yuri Pines

Columbia University Press
New York

Columbia University Press wishes to express its appreciation for assistance given by the Chiang Ching-kuo Foundation for International Scholarly Exchange and Council for Cultural Affairs in the publication of this book.

Columbia University Press
Publishers Since 1893
New York   Chichester, West Sussex
cup.columbia.edu
Copyright © 2020 Columbia University Press
All rights reserved

Library of Congress Cataloging-in-Publication Data
Names: Pines, Yuri, author.
Title: Zhou History Unearthed : The Bamboo Manuscript Xinian and Early Chinese Historiography / Yuri Pines.
Other titles: Bamboo manuscript Xinian and early Chinese historiography | Xi nian. English.
Description: New York : Columbia University Press, [2020] | Includes bibliographical references and index.
Identifiers: LCCN 2020009651 (print) | LCCN 2020009652 (ebook) | ISBN 9780231196628 (cloth) | ISBN 9780231196635 (paperback) | ISBN 9780231551755 (ebook)
Subjects: LCSH: China—History—To 221 B.C.—Historiography. | Zuoqiu, Ming. Zuo zhuan. | China—History—Zhou dynasty, 1122-221 B.C.—Historiography. | China—History—Warring States, 403-221 B.C.—Sources.
Classification: LCC DS741.25 .P56 2020 (print) | LCC DS741.25 (ebook) | DDC 931/.03072—dc23
LC record available at https://lccn.loc.gov/2020009651
LC ebook record available at https://lccn.loc.gov/2020009652

Cover design: Julia Kushnirsky
Cover image: Courtesy of Tsinghua University, Research and Conservation Center for Excavated Texts
清华大学出土文献研究与保护中心

Contents

Preface   vii
Note on Translations, References, and Dates   ix
Maps   xi

INTRODUCTION   The Riddle of Zhou Historiography   1

PART I   Rethinking Early Chinese History Writing

1   Zhou Historiography as Seen from the Transmitted Texts   11

2   *Xinian* and Zhou Historiography   37

3   Zhou Historiography in Other Newly Discovered Sources   68

4   Beyond Sima Qian: Zhou History Revisited   95

5   Chu Historiography and Chu Cultural Identity   122

PART II   *Xinian* Translation and Commentary

XINIAN 1   151

XINIAN 2   155

XINIAN 3   161

[v]

XINIAN 4   165
XINIAN 5   169
XINIAN 6   173
XINIAN 7   178
XINIAN 8   181
XINIAN 9   184
XINIAN 10   186
XINIAN 11   188
XINIAN 12   192
XINIAN 13   194
XINIAN 14   196
XINIAN 15   200
XINIAN 16   206
XINIAN 17   210
XINIAN 18   214
XINIAN 19   220
XINIAN 20   223
XINIAN 21   227
XINIAN 22   231
XINIAN 23   235

Notes   243
Bibliography   277
Index   307

Preface

In the 1990s, when working on my dissertation on the intellectual contents of *Zuo zhuan* 左傳—the major historical text from China's preimperial period—I became engaged in manifold scholarly controversies concerning that text's nature, date of composition, and historical reliability. Whereas those debates and the colleagues' subsequent publications caused me to modify some of my views, I did not feel it appropriate to engage anew the topic on which so much has already been written. Recently, however, the publication of a series of newly discovered historical and quasi-historical texts—most notably *Xinian* 繫年 from the Tsinghua (Qinghua) University collection of bamboo slips—spurred a renewed interest in the origins of China's historiographic tradition and its immense complexity. My new understandings are presented in this monograph.

In preparing this book I have benefited immensely from discussions with colleagues and friends, whose views helped me tremendously in modifying my conclusions and avoiding some embarrassing mistakes. I want to thank first and foremost Chen Minzhen, Steve Durrant, Paul R. Goldin, Martin Kern, Li Wai-yee, Edward L. Shaughnessy, and the reviewers of the manuscript and of my earlier related articles. I want to thank also the participants of the May 2019 symposium "Rethinking Early Chinese Historiography" (Institute for Advanced Study, Hebrew

University of Jerusalem), whose ideas were particularly enriching. Needless to say, any lingering mistakes and inaccuracies are mine.

In undertaking the research for this book, I was supported by the Israel Science Foundation (Grant 240/15) and the Michael William Lipson Chair in Chinese Studies. This work was published with the support of the Israel Science Foundation (Grant 6/20).

Note on Translations, References, and Dates

All translations in the text are mine unless otherwise indicated.
    In translating passages from the *Spring and Autumn Annals* and *Zuozhuan*, I borrow from the recent translation by Stephen Durrant, Li Wai-yee, and David Schaberg (2016), modifying when necessary.

Whenever I refer to a transmitted text that has a stable division into chapters (*pian* 篇) and sections/paragraphs (*zhang* 章), I refer only to the number of a chapter and a section/paragraph separated by a period. Whenever such a division does not exist, I identify, whenever relevant, the scroll (*juan* 卷, indicated by Roman numerals) and the chapter (*pian* 篇); they are separated by a period and are followed by the page number of the modern edition, separated by a colon.

Whenever I cite a recently unearthed text, I indicate the slip number according to the sequence proposed by the original publishers; the characters are normally written in their modern form according to the editors' or other scholars' suggestions. In a few cases of debatable characters, I provide their image as published by the texts' editors or an alternative reading.

In translating *Xinian* and other unearthed texts I add missing words in square brackets. In parentheses I add short explanations that should facilitate reading: mostly the names under which historical personages are more commonly known and years of the events according to the common chronology. In Chinese text in bold square brackets I add the number of the bamboo slip.

Throughout this monograph I mark with an asterisk the titles of unearthed manuscripts if they were given by the contemporary editors. To avoid alienating the reader with too many asterisks, I do this only at the first occurrence of the manuscript's name.

One of the thorniest questions for a translator of terminology related to the Spring and Autumn period is dealing with the aristocratic ranks of that age. The problem is aggravated by the fact that a single Chinese word can have multiple meanings. Thus whenever a five-grade division of regional lords (and of the leading nobles from the Zhou royal domain and from the state of Chu) is concerned, it makes sense to translate *gong* 公 as "duke," *hou* 侯 as "marquis," *bo* 伯 as "earl," *zi* 子 as "viscount," and *nan* 男 as "baron."[1] But note that most regional rulers were posthumously referred as X + *gong*, in which case a neutral "lord" is preferable. Hence, I normally translate YX + *gong* as Lord X of Y when X stands for a posthumous name and Y for the state; however, I translate Duke of Y or Marquis of Y when the text refers to the person's status. I invariably translate Gongzi 公子 as "Ducal Son" and Gongsun 公孫 as "Ducal Grandson." *Bo* 伯 also has different meanings: it can refer to one's birth sequence (the elder), to one's rank (earl), or to one's position as a regional "overlord." The term *zi* 子 is even more confusing, because, aside from being a designation of one's rank (viscount), it served as a common polite designation of persons of noble status. As such it could be added to a personal name (*ming* 名), to one's appellative (*zi* 字), to a posthumous name (*shi* 謚) (in all these cases I simply transliterate), or to a surname, in which case I adopt "Sir so-and-so." Finally, in translating heads of local administration in the state of Chu, I distinguish between *gong* 公 (duke), *jun* 君 (lord) and *yin* 尹 (governor).

Most of the reign dates in this book are given according to the chronological tables composed by Fang Shiming (1991); for the Western Zhou period, I follow the reconstruction of the Xia-Shang-Zhou chronological project (Xia-Shang-Zhou duandai gongcheng zhuanjia zu 2000). In both cases not a few dates appear to be wrong, but I use them for heuristic convenience, adding "ca." whenever the dates are disputable. In reconstructing the reign dates of Chu kings of the fifth to early fourth centuries BCE, I relied on Li Rui 2013 and on the tentative reconstructions scattered through Su, Wu, and Lai 2013. Whenever relevant I utilized also the suggestions of Xiong Xianpin (2017).

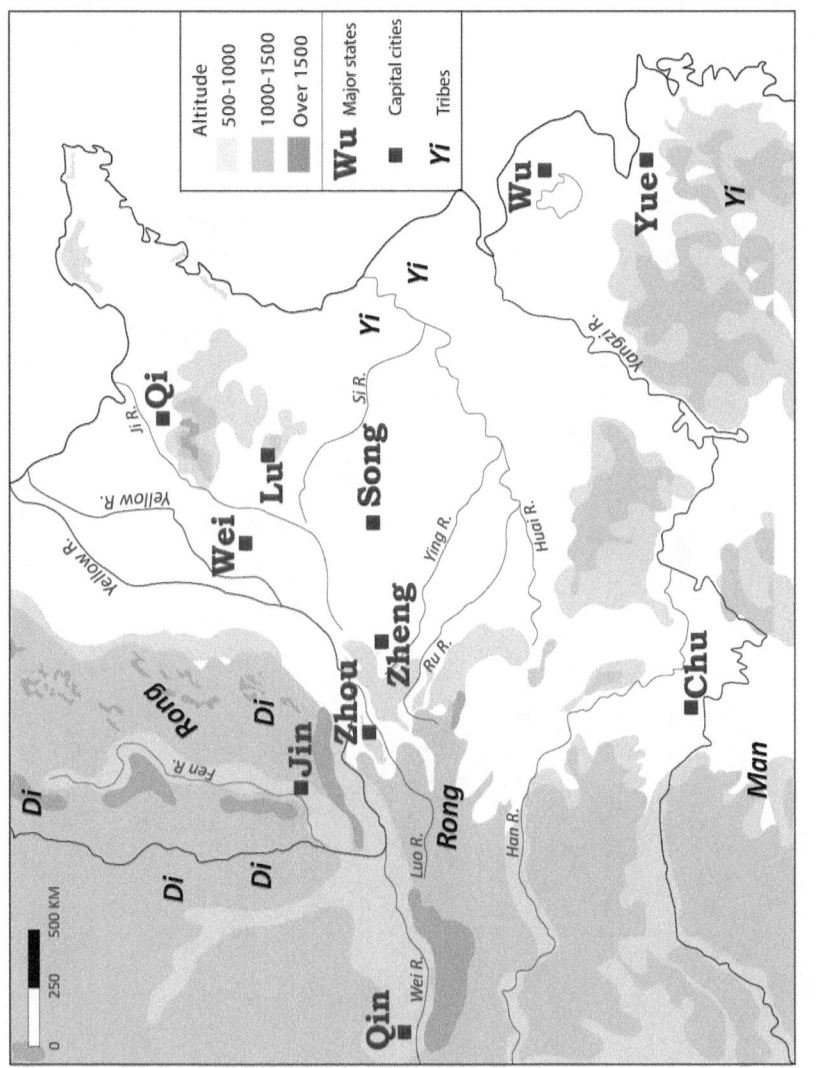

Map 1. The Zhou World ca. 600 CE

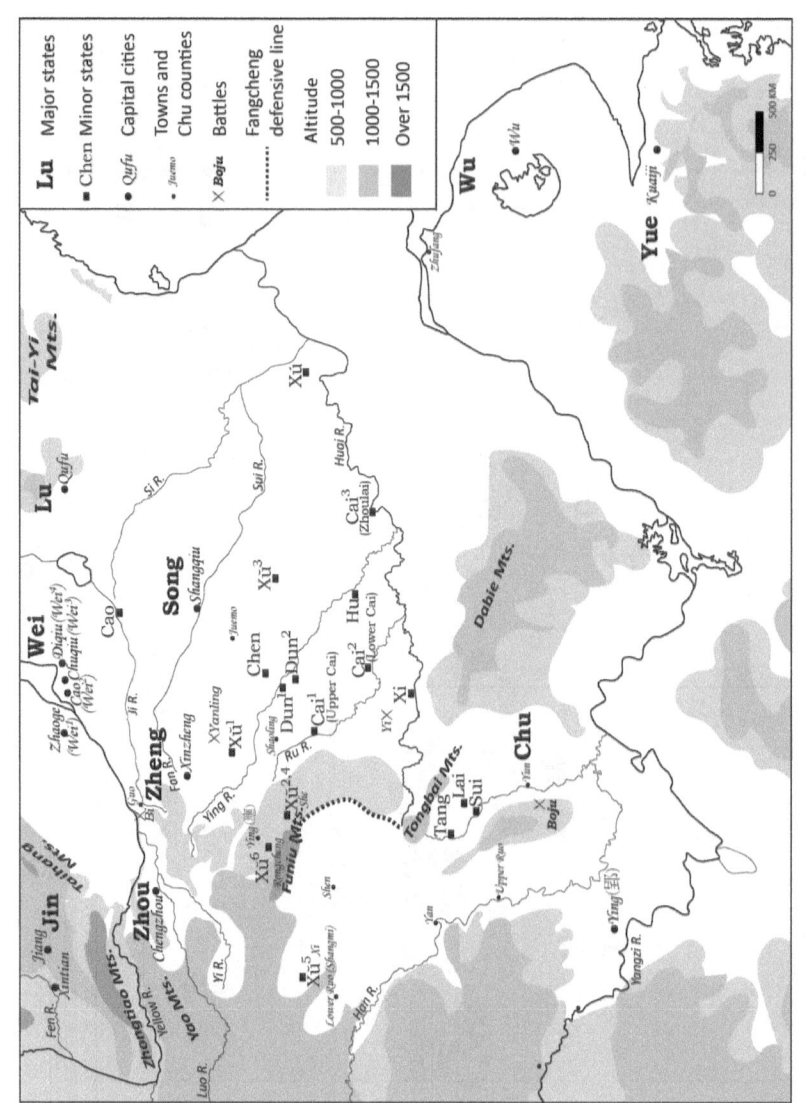

Map 2. Chu and Its Neighbors, 670–470 BCE

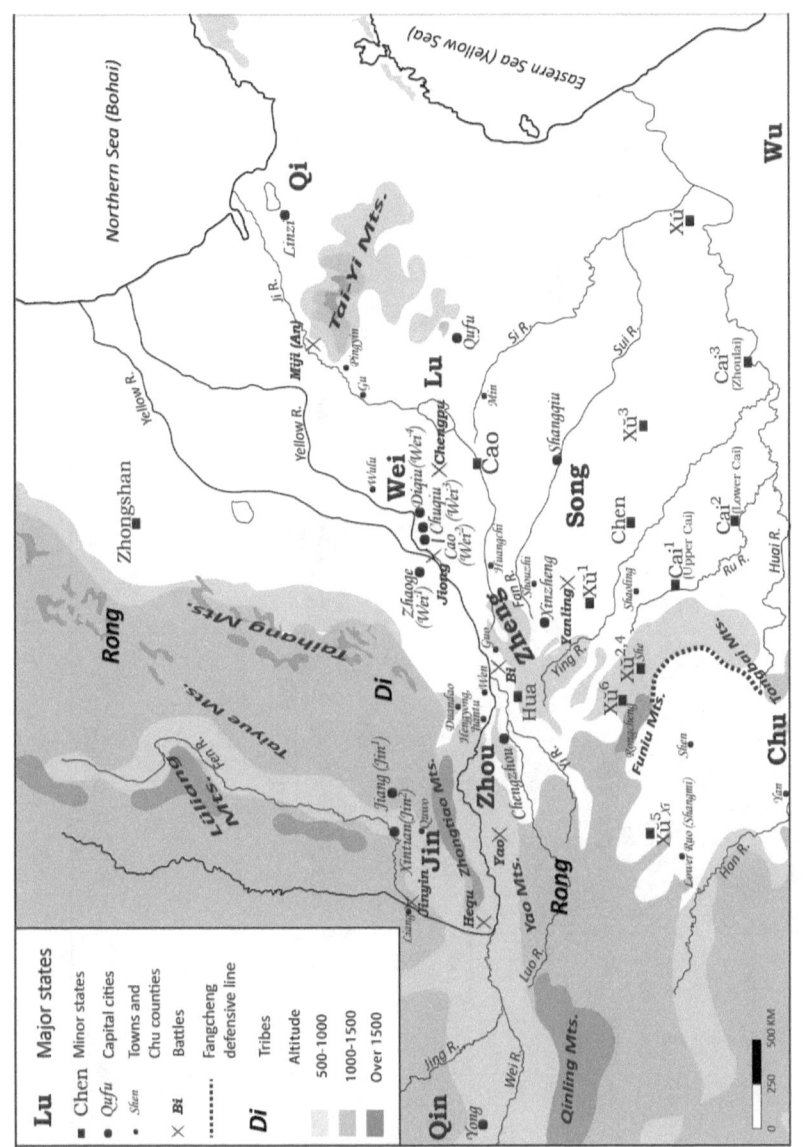

Map 3. Jin and Its Neighbors, 650–470 BCE

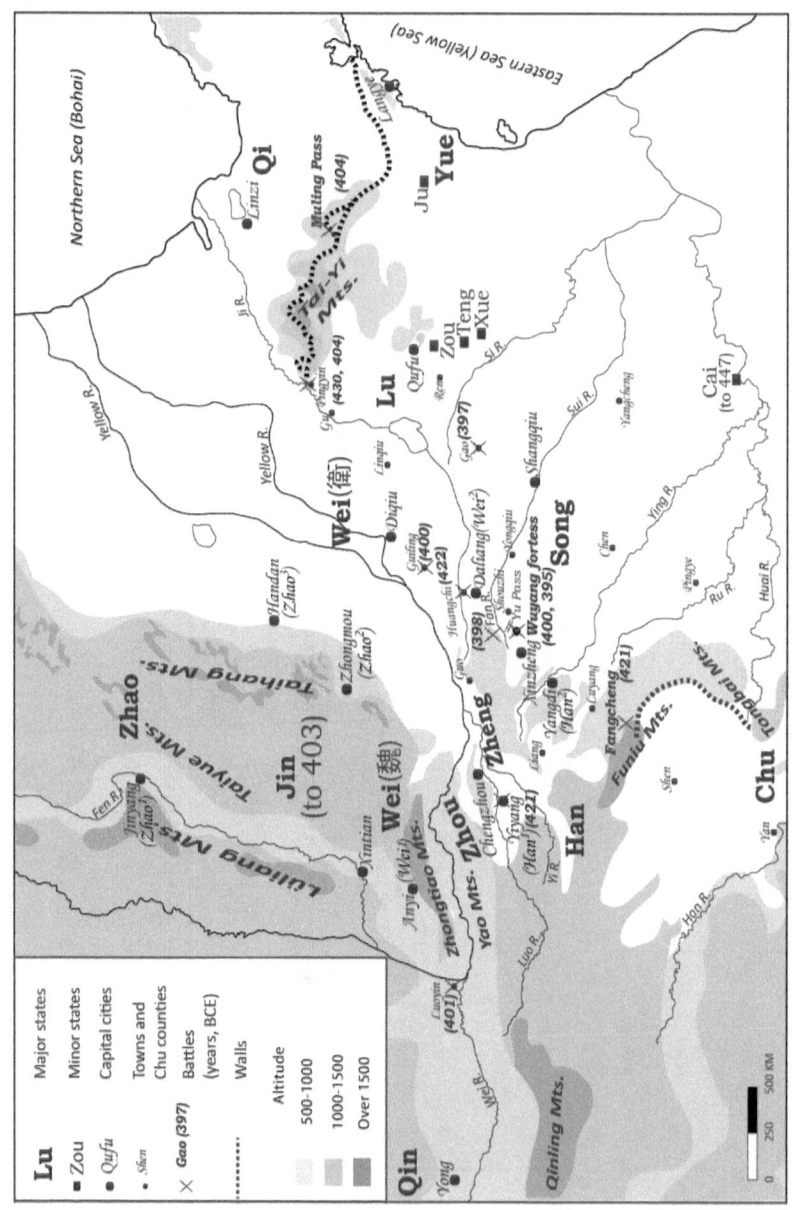

Map 3. Chu, Jin, Qi, and Yue 470–370 BCE

Introduction

The Riddle of Zhou Historiography

Liang Qichao 梁啟超 (1873–1929), one of the most eminent Chinese intellectuals active at the turn of the twentieth century, claimed once that "among all fields of learning in China, historiography is the most developed, and Chinese historiography is the most developed worldwide." Elsewhere he added, though, that prior to Sima Qian 司馬遷 (ca. 145–90 BCE), "China had no historiography per se."[1] Although each of these statements, particularly the latter, is debatable, they can serve as a useful point of departure for a discussion of early Chinese historiography. Indeed, the contrast between the richness of the historical production of the imperial age (221 BCE–1912 CE) and its meagerness in the preceding centuries is striking.

To demonstrate this contrast, it is useful to recall briefly the extraordinary place of history writing in China's imperial polity. Whether or not Chinese historiography was "the most developed worldwide," that few if any civilizations could compete with China in terms of the overarching importance of history writing is beyond doubt. Compiling histories was considered a highly prestigious occupation for a man of letters and was also an important political undertaking. Every major dynasty ordered the composing of an official version of its predecessors' history and simultaneously prepared documentation for its own history that would be written by its successors.[2] Many more studies of the past were composed by private individuals. As a result, each year in the history of imperial China is thickly covered in official dynastic histories as well as in a variety of officially and privately produced local histories, institutional histories, biographies, and the like. Despite the eventual loss of many of these works, particularly from the early imperial period, the richness of the remaining materials defies the imagination.

China's imperial historiography has been well studied. What helps researchers to understand its nuances is its relative transparency. We know the authors of all but a very few historical works. These authors—starting with Sima Qian—identify themselves, often tell us of their motivations and some of their agendas, and from time to time inform us of their sources.[3] We know the political and ideological context in which most works were produced, and we can evaluate the works' intended audience and their reception by the educated elite. Often, we are in a position to compare between two or more accounts of the same event (e.g., those by Sima Qian and those by the second major imperial historian, Ban Gu 班固 [32–92]); and these comparisons greatly enhance our understanding of the subtleties of the historical genre.[4] For scholars dealing with imperial-period historiography, often the most challenging task is processing a huge amount of information rather than discovering new evidence.

This richness contrasts dramatically with the dearth of known historical works from the lengthy Zhou 周 age (ca. 1046–255 BCE). With the major exception of *Zuozhuan* 左傳 (the *Zuo Tradition* or *Zuo Commentary*)—arguably the only preimperial text that is comparable with later dynastic histories in terms of systematic coverage of major events—transmitted literature preserves only a tiny sample of historical and quasi-historical texts. These include one example of annalistic writings; namely, the canonized *Spring and Autumn Annals* (*Chunqiu* 春秋) of the state of Lu 魯;[5] a corpus of important speeches attributed to the former paragons (collected in the *Canon of Documents* [*Shujing* 書經 or *Shangshu* 尚書] and in the *Remainder of Zhou Documents* [*Yizhoushu* 逸周書]); and a variety of historical anecdotes, by far the richest source of our knowledge of the preimperial past. The number of these anecdotes is impressive, but it should be remembered that they stand at the nexus of history, philosophy, literature, and rhetoric rather than belonging to the historiographic genre per se. The didactic message is much more important to their authors than historical accuracy.[6]

Yet the dearth of sources is just the tip of the iceberg of problems faced by scholars of preimperial (i.e., pre-221 BCE) historiography. What is even more frustrating is that we know all too little about our texts and their background. We do know—as discussed in chapter 1—that routine records of certain events started as early as the Shang 商 dynasty (ca. 1600–1046 BCE). We also know that exceptionally significant events—such as the overthrow of the Shang dynasty by the Zhou circa 1046 BCE—were commemorated in written and oral forms, as well as through ritual performances. We know, too, that already in the Western Zhou 西周 period (ca. 1046–771 BCE) certain thinkers and statesmen were willing to turn to the past for guidance to the present, and that appeals to the past become ubiquitous in the texts of the competing Hundred Schools of Thought of the Warring States (Zhanguo 戰國) period (453–221 BCE). But we do not know when and how these three strands of early historiography interacted. We do not know, for instance, whether or not factual accuracy mattered to those who sought to deduce proper lessons from past events. We do not know by whom, when, and under what circumstances extant historical and quasi-historical texts were composed. The authors of our sources prefer to remain hidden; if they interact at all with their readers, it is done through a neutral self-identification as a "noble man."[7] The dates of the composition of almost every known text are hotly contested, which poses great difficulties in attempting to compare two or more texts.[8] More broadly, we know very little about how historical knowledge was produced and how it was disseminated. The contrast with the situation for the imperial era could not be stronger.

In the past whenever scholars tried to answer the foregoing questions, the lion's share of the answers revolved around conflicting interpretations of *Zuozhuan*. This text is indeed exceptionally rich, but it is also among the most controversial in the entire corpus of preimperial literature. The ongoing heated debates about its nature, dates, and reliability (for which see chapter 1) have greatly hindered its utilization as a source for the early historiographic tradition. Nor could infrequent consultations with other texts—be they anecdotal collections, such as *Discourses of the States* (*Guoyu* 國語), or chronicles such as the *Spring and Autumn Annals*—advance our research considerably. The general picture of early Chinese historiography remained elusive. To reconstruct it, one needed sufficient evidence for historiographic production outside the *Zuozhuan* narratives, and this evidence remained lacking. The debates seemed to reach an impasse.

It is against this backdrop that we can understand the revolutionary impact of the new paleographic discoveries, which enable us to dramatically expand our understanding of preimperial Chinese historiography. The earliest of these discoveries was made more than seventeen centuries ago. In 279 or 280 CE, robbers who plundered the tomb identified as that of King Xiang of Wei 魏襄王 (r. 318–296 BCE) at Ji 汲 Commandery, Henan, brought to light numerous bamboo manuscripts, the most prominent of which was a chronicle named by its editors *Bamboo Annals* (*Zhushu jinian* 竹書紀年). This chronicle not only allowed the correction of a few inaccuracies in Sima Qian's *Records of the Historian* (*Shiji* 史記) but also contributed toward the emergence of the genre of historical criticism in general.[9] Then came a long lull in the discovery of early historical texts. The paleographic revolution of the twentieth century, with its profound impact on almost every aspect of early China studies, was quite disappointing from the point of view of historiography. Only a few unearthed manuscripts could be associated with the historical genre, and none of these were particularly exciting.[10] Yet from the beginning of the twenty-first century, a series of newly unearthed texts has profoundly changed this trend. These texts provide us with an entirely new perspective on the history of Zhou historiography.

The most valuable of these discoveries is the bamboo manuscript ★*Xinian* 繫年 ("String of years" or "Linked years") from the collection of Tsinghua (Qinghua) University. This relatively short but exceptionally informative manuscript stands at the center of the present study. Other relevant discoveries include a text that focuses on relocations of the Chu royal palaces, ★*Chu ju* 楚居 (Chu dwellings), dozens of new historical anecdotes, and several highly informative bronze inscriptions. When read together with the received texts, the new manuscripts provide us with a wealth of fresh information and, of particular importance, allow us to ask novel questions and seek new answers about early Chinese historiography.

There are three major fields in which the new manuscripts can have a considerable impact on our research. The first and most obvious one is the possibility of correcting and expanding our knowledge of China's preimperial history. This pertains not only to the essential—but hardly exciting—work of correcting wrong dates, place-names, and personal names known from the received texts but also to providing highly interesting information on the periods that are not adequately covered in our sources, most notably those that precede and postdate the *Zuozhuan* narrative (i.e., pre-722 BCE and post-468 BCE). For instance, *Xinian* provides fascinating new details about the early years of the Eastern Zhou (traditionally 770–255 BCE) and about the interstate dynamics of the fifth century BCE. Such topics as the near demise of the Zhou dynasty circa 750 BCE, the history of the state of Yue 越 in the fifth century BCE, and the background for the de jure dissolution of the state of Jin 晉 in 403 BCE—all can be now addressed anew, as demonstrated in chapter 4.

Second, the unearthed manuscripts allow us to profoundly revise our understanding of the received texts, primarily (but by no means exclusively) *Zuozhuan*. As I have mentioned (and discuss in detail in chapter 1), this text generated heated controversies, especially throughout much of the twentieth century. Some of these controversies—especially about the reliability of *Zuozhuan* as a source for the history of the Spring and Autumn period (Chunqiu 春秋, 770–453 BCE)—could have been partly resolved had we better understood the source materials that were utilized in the composition of *Zuozhuan*. However, insofar as debates about these source materials revolved around internal evidence from *Zuozhuan* itself, the answers remained tentative at best. Now, with the publication of *Xinian* and other texts, including a few bronze inscriptions, the nature of these source materials can be understood much better than previously, as I hope to demonstrate in chapters 2 and 3. This in turn enhances our understanding of the reliability (or its lack) of *Zuozhuan* and of other received texts, such as *Records of the Historian* (for which see chapter 4).

The third contribution of the new materials is that they allow us to start recharting the picture of preimperial Chinese historiography. We can now observe for the first time a great variety of previously unknown historical and quasi-historical genres. We can analyze with greater precision than before who composed historical writings and for which audience. We can discern multiple usages of history in the political discourse of that age beyond the immediately observable cliché of providing edifying and moralizing examples from the past. We can ask how the historical texts circulated and what happened to them in the process of circulation, including how the transmitters intervened in their source materials and for what purposes. And above all, we can ask how the historical genre contributed to broad cultural and intellectual developments throughout the centuries preceding the imperial unification. The answers will often remain partial and at times speculative. Yet the very possibility of asking these questions and advancing toward answering them is thrilling for historians of early China.

A word of caution is needed here. My discussion is based on a series of accidental discoveries that by no means represent the entire breadth of early Chinese historiography. A large portion of manuscripts discussed in this book come from the single state of Chu 楚, and whereas they definitely incorporate materials from other states, a broader sample would certainly be helpful. The time scope covered in those of the unearthed texts that have been published heretofore is limited to roughly 800–380 BCE, which means that many questions regarding the last century and a half of the Warring States period cannot be fully answered. Moreover, most of the manuscripts with which I operate were not scientifically excavated but supposedly looted from Chu tombs and then acquired by Chinese institutions at the Hong Kong antiquity market. This poses a series of challenging questions, in particular regarding these materials' authenticity (as discussed in chapter 2). Besides, some of the recently unearthed manuscripts have not yet been published. Needless to say, any new publication—not to mention a new discovery—may require revision of some of my conjectures and conclusions.[11] Nonetheless, I believe the scope of the heretofore published manuscripts is sufficiently large to allow us considerable advancement en route to reconstruction of early Chinese historiography.

The present book is divided into two parts. The first is analytical: it introduces the new materials and their potential impact on the ongoing debates about early Chinese historiography. I start with a brief survey of the state of the field as reflected from the received texts. Chapter 1 traces the evolution of early Chinese historiography from its beginnings to the fourth century BCE, with a specific focus on *Zuozhuan*. The goal of this discussion is to highlight the points on which the unearthed materials may be conducive for resolving debates about *Zuozhuan* and related texts. In chapter 2, I introduce *Xinian*, the single most important of the unearthed texts in terms of its historiographic value. Chapter 3 introduces other relevant sources—from the Chu manuscripts to several bronze inscriptions—showing their role in expanding the horizons of our understanding of the preimperial historiographic tradition. Chapter 4 analyzes the new information provided in *Xinian* (and other sources, when relevant) on the historical periods that are not covered in *Zuozhuan*, placing this information in the context of broader discussions of Zhou history, as understood from Sima Qian's *Records of the Historian*. Chapter 5 focuses on the history and historiography of the state of Chu and asks what we can learn from the newly discovered manuscripts about Chu's cultural identity.

The second part of the book provides a full annotated translation of *Xinian*. Each of the sections of the text is preceded by a brief introduction highlighting the section's contents and its importance in the broader context of Zhou history and historiography. I hope that this effort will be my modest addendum to the translation of *Zuozhuan* recently produced by Stephen Durrant, Li Wai-yee, and David Schaberg (2016). Their translation, I believe, will have a lasting and tremendously important impact on studies of early Chinese history and historiography in the Anglophone community. By providing a small extension to their work, I hope to contribute further to their great endeavor.

PART I

Rethinking Early Chinese History Writing

CHAPTER 1

Zhou Historiography as Seen from the Transmitted Texts

Before we can evaluate the impact of the new paleographic discoveries on our understanding of early Chinese historiography, it is appropriate to start with a brief summary of the picture that can be retrieved from the transmitted (or previously unearthed) texts. My goal in what follows is not to present a systematic view of the evolution of history writing in early China—a topic that would require an entire monograph of its own—but just to focus on selected aspects of this evolution, with the aim of highlighting the issues at stake for my subsequent discussion of the unearthed manuscripts. What can be deduced from the transmitted literature about the authors of early historical texts, their audience, and the goals of these texts' composition? And how do the answers to these questions influence our assessment of the historical reliability of the received texts?

My discussion in this chapter is divided into three parts. I start with outlining the evolution of nascent historical thinking and the earliest examples of recording events in the Western Zhou 西周 (ca. 1046–771 BCE) period and their impact on the subsequent Chinese historiographic tradition. I then move to the canonical *Spring and Autumn Annals* of the state of Lu, which, as I shall try to demonstrate, represents an important genre of ritualistic historiography. The largest section focuses on *Zuozhuan* and the multiple debates that this text generates, with a special emphasis on the question of the nature of its primary sources. Finally I briefly outline what I consider as major changes in the attitudes toward history writing in the Warring States period. This last topic is addressed more systematically in chapter 3.

Origins of History Writing: From Shang to Western Zhou

When did history writing start in China? Some scholars are eager to place it at the earliest known stages of Chinese civilization. For instance, Du Weiyun identified history writing with the appearance of the scribal office (*shi* 史).[1] This line of argument does not appear convincing: the term *shi* referred to a broad range of officials, including record makers and record-keepers, but also to a variety of clerks, cultic functionaries, astrologers, and officeholders whose responsibilities had little or nothing to do with history writing. It would take many centuries before the term *shi* acquired its predominant meaning of "history" and "historian." An attempt to transpose this meaning to the remote past is anachronistic.[2]

For the sake of my discussion it may be useful to distinguish between mature history writing and related practices that could precede it by many centuries. One such practice is the commemoration of meritorious ancestors and cultural heroes. This commemoration is fairly widespread throughout human cultures and it may be plausibly inferred that in China, as elsewhere, it started long before the advent of writing.[3] Another relevant practice, which is more closely related to history writing, is the habit of recording important events. As I try to demonstrate in the following, these records became the skeleton of future histories, providing their writers with crucial information about who did what, when, and where. However, the recording of events does not necessarily mean the emergence of full-scale history writing, for which the critical question is why—that is, explaining the reasons behind important events and learning from them.

The earliest surviving examples of writing on Chinese soil—the oracle-bone inscriptions of the Shang 商 dynasty (ca. 1600–ca.1046 BCE)—can be viewed as the nascent form of historical records. The inscriptions were made on the bones (bovine scapulae and turtle plastrons) that were used for divining the future in continental East Asia beginning in the late Neolithic period. The Shang innovation was recording the charge, the deities' answer, and, infrequently, the verification of this answer on the scapula itself.[4] These inscriptions were by no means intended to be historical accounts directed at posterity; rather, they were in all likelihood prepared to train the kings (who acted as chief diviners) in the arts of discerning the ancestors' answers. Yet some of the inscriptions' features—such as meticulous recording of the events' dates (perhaps important for hemerological reasons)—would remain the hallmark of subsequent historical records.

We do not know whether or not the Shang dynasty had a more developed tradition of history writing. A statement attributed to the Zhou vanquishers of the Shang, which reminds the officers of the defeated dynasty that Shang possessed records about the overthrow of the preceding Xia 夏 dynasty, cannot be considered a reliable source for Shang historiography.[5] What is more likely is that the Shang developed a tradition of recording the genealogy of the royal lineage (and possibly of other noble lineages as well). These genealogical records, incorporated in the late Warring States–period text *Roots of Generations* (*Shi ben* 世本), may have served Sima Qian in his—more or less accurate—reconstruction of the sequence of the Shang rulers.[6] Whether or not these genealogical records were accompanied with other materials, such as accounts of the ancestors' merits, is currently unverifiable.

The overthrow of the Shang by the Zhou dynasty circa 1046 BCE was a momentous event in China's history. Zhou's surprisingly swift subjugation of the polity that was the center of gravity in the middle Yellow River basin for many centuries was an astounding success, and so was the subsequent dramatic expansion of Zhou's control over vast areas from the Huai River basin in the south to the vicinity of modern Beijing in the north.[7] Yet almost simultaneously with this success came a warning: the rebellion of Shang loyalists, joined by disgruntled members of the Zhou royal family itself circa 1042 BCE, almost toppled the new dynasty. The subsequent rationalization of Zhou's successes and challenges gave rise to the peculiar concept of Heaven's Mandate. This concept in turn profoundly influenced the formation of Chinese historiographic tradition.

In the nutshell, the idea of the mandate was that Heaven, the supreme deity, is in charge of proper order on earth. When the ruler behaves violently and oppressively—as was allegedly the case of the last king of Shang, Zhòu 紂 (d. ca. 1046 BCE; hereafter Zhouxin 紂辛)[8]—Heaven, out of concern for the people below, transfers its mandate to a better incumbent. It was through his utmost morality and concern for the weakest members of society that King Wen of Zhou 文王 (d. ca. 1047 BCE) attained the mandate, allowing his son, King Wu 武王 (d. ca. 1042 BCE), to overthrow the Shang and establish the new dynasty. But the mandate is "not constant." Should the future generations of Zhou kings lose their *de* 德 ("moral virtue," but also "charisma," "mana"), "merciless Heaven" will withhold the mandate and transfer it to a better candidate.[9]

The idea that the ruler acts on behalf of the supreme deity and is scrutinized by it was not peculiar to China. Yet the Zhou religion had one feature that strongly distinguished it from, for example, Near Eastern religious traditions—namely, the difficulty of communicating with Heaven. No prophets spoke on Heaven's behalf, no scriptures enshrined its instructions, no priests interpreted its will. And, although the Zhou kings in their capacity as Sons of Heaven (*tianzi* 天子) enjoyed preferential access to the supreme deity, this did not turn them into speakers on Heaven's behalf. Mantic practices, of which our sources are conspicuously silent, were certainly employed to assess Heaven's immediate intent,[10] but they were of little value in understanding Heaven's abstract moral requirements. The only secure way of understanding Heaven's guiding principles was through analyzing the past manifestations of its will, most specifically the mandate transfer from Shang to Zhou. Not surprisingly, commemorating this event—in sacrificial hymns, model speeches attributed to the dynasty's founders, and a variety of performances in the ancestral temples of Zhou kings—became the focal concern of nascent Zhou historical thought.[11]

The *Canon of Poems* (*Shijing* 詩經) and *Canon of Documents* are the major repository of early Zhou cultural memory, political thought, and also nascent historical thinking. Putting aside for the time being the debates about the formation of these corpuses and the dating of individual odes and documents, we can surmise that the earliest layers of both canonical collections do reflect Western Zhou perceptions, even though they may well postdate their alleged authors, such as the Duke of Zhou 周公 (d. ca. 1035 BCE), by more than a century.[12] Insofar as historical thought is concerned, what matters is an observable bifurcation of these texts into what can be called prescriptive and descriptive history. The former was mostly concerned with validation of the Heaven's Mandate theory. This validation—which became ever more urgent in the generations after the establishment of the dynasty, when the memories of its glorious past were fading away, whereas new manifestations of Heaven's guidance were nowhere to be seen—could be achieved through a variety of means. The most widespread was a repeated glorification of the Zhou overthrow of the Shang, as performed for instance in the ode "King Wen" (Wen wang 文王), the first in the so-called "Great Odes" (Da ya 大雅) section of the *Canon of Poems*.[13] Other texts—such as, for example, the "Duo fang" 多方 (Many regions) and "Duo shi" 多士 (Many officers) chapters of the *Canon of Documents*—expanded the story of the mandate transfer back to the putative overthrow of the Xia by the Shang, making it part of a constant historical pattern rather than a singular event.[14] Yet other documents, such as "Wu yi" 無逸 (Do not be idle), put forward a distinct "just deserts" theory, according to which good rulers were blessed by Heaven with considerable longevity and lengthy tenure in office, whereas the bad ones all died prematurely. Needless to say, the historical foundation for the latter argument was extremely weak, to put it mildly.[15] Differences aside, all three types of texts share one common feature: what mattered for their authors was not how things happened in the past but how they should have happened and which moral lessons should be gleaned from these events.

Yet preoccupation with moral lessons aside, early Zhou historical thought seems to have developed a different, descriptive rather than prescriptive, attitude to the past. This attitude can be related to the repeated exhortation to treat the Shang as a "mirror" to the Zhou.[16] If Zhou rulers wanted to avoid the loss of the mandate, they should learn from the Shang experience. This learning is supposed to be earnest: in "Declaration to Kang" (Kang gao 康誥, one of the earliest documents in the canonical collection), the speaker (presumably the Duke of Zhou) urges his younger brother who was appointed to govern Shang's subjects: "Seek the traces of the former wise kings of Yin [Shang] so as to protect and regulate the people. . . . Search out about the wise former kings [of Shang] of antiquity, and employ [their experience] in tranquilizing and protecting the people."[17] Here what matters are not the abstractions of the mandate transfer but the real achievements and governance modes of the Shang kings. This line of argumentation was conducive for creating more or less accurate accounts of the past so as to serve current and future policy makers.

We cannot determine with certainty when detailed narrative accounts of the past emerged. What is clear is that the Western Zhou age witnessed further expansion of the tradition of recording major events. These records could be used for the commemoration of exceptional occurrences. For example, the "Shi fu" 世俘 (The great capture)—an early Zhou text that is currently assimilated into the *Remainder of Zhou Documents* but possibly originally was part of the *Canon of Documents*—is likely to incorporate an earlier chronicle of the Zhou conquest of the Shang.[18] Yet even less-dramatic episodes seem to be regularly recorded. In general, recording one's merit on the battlefield and elsewhere would be significant for the meritorious servant himself (whose merits could bring about lavish reward and possibly promotion), for his descendants, who would inherit his position, and for his superiors (the Zhou king or other dynastic leaders), who should maintain accounts of their servants' former achievements. These "records of merit" duly appear in many of the inscriptions on ritual bronze vessels, and some of them contain precious information about early Zhou history.[19]

Since I discuss the peculiarity of the inscriptions as a genre in chapter 3, here I confine myself to a single point. Some of the inscriptions contain what appears to be a more or less verbatim reproduction of the documentary records related to events in the life of the vessel's donor. In a few cases they contain a relatively lengthy historical narrative. One of the most interesting examples of these narratives is the inscription on the Jin Hou Su-*bianzhong* 晉侯穌編鐘 chime bells. The inscription, carved on the bells that were partly looted, partly archaeologically discovered at the tomb of a Marquis of Jin named Su 穌, tells of a campaign fought by the Zhou royal troops against the Su Yi 蘇夷 polity in southwestern Shandong. Putting aside complexities of the inscription's precise dating and the correlation between its information and that in the transmitted texts,[20] it is clear that it is based on a detailed account of the military campaign. The campaign lasted for several months, and the inscription records minute details, such as dates, place-names, and even minor skirmishes. Certainly it is based on a larger and even more detailed account of the campaign that was prepared more or less simultaneously with its enfolding.

It is possible that maintaining detailed records of major campaigns and of the ensuing rewards meted out to meritorious officers was originally done primarily for archival purposes, although the "Shi fu" chapter shows that records could be used for commemorative activities as well. What is clear is that in due time these detailed records of important events became the raw material for lengthier historical accounts. Whether or not these long accounts already appeared during the Western Zhou period is not clear. Yet these accounts undoubtedly existed during the subsequent Spring and Autumn period. Let us now turn to the historiography of that age.

The *Spring and Autumn Annals*

The Spring and Autumn period is the only era in Chinese history named after a text, the *Spring and Autumn Annals* of the state of Lu. These *Annals*, one of the most enigmatic texts in the entire corpus of early Chinese writings, had a profound impact on China's historiographic tradition. Understanding this impact—and understanding the *Annals* in their immediate context—is crucial for proper analysis of the subsequent development of history writing.

The canonical position of the *Spring and Autumn Annals* derives from the tradition that associates this text with Confucius (Kongzi 孔子, 551–479 BCE), the single most influential thinker in China's history. Confucius's devoted follower Mengzi 孟子 (ca. 380–304 BCE), famously proclaimed,

> When the world declined and the Way fell into obscurity, heresies and violence again arose. There were instances of regicides and patricides. Confucius was apprehensive and created [*zuo* 作] the *Spring and Autumn Annals*. The *Spring and Autumn Annals* are the matter of the Son of Heaven. That is why Confucius said, "Those who understand me will do so through the *Spring and Autumn Annals*; those who condemn me will also do so because of the *Spring and Autumn Annals*." . . . Confucius created the *Spring and Autumn Annals*, and rebellious ministers and murderous sons were all overawed.[21]

This is a very peculiar passage. First, it attributes Confucius with no less than the "creation" of the *Annals*. The verb *zuo* has manifold meanings, and it can be interpreted as "boosting" or "giving rise" to a certain tradition, but its association with an active power of "creation" is most notable, and this meaning comes first in interpreting this passage.[22] Second, Mengzi assumes that the *Annals* are not just a dry account of political events but a very special political text, and its promulgation (or composition?) was an exclusive prerogative of the Son of Heaven (the Zhou king). Third, the impact of the *Annals* is enormous: their publication allegedly overawed the "rebellious ministers and murderous sons." This exceptional political potency of the *Annals* is hinted at also in the final words of one of their major commentaries, the *Gongyang zhuan* 公羊傳, which asserts, "To eradicate generations of disorder and return to the right there is nothing like the *Spring and Autumn Annals*."[23]

Putting aside for the time being the alleged political potency of the *Annals*, we should immediately ask, what was the relation of Confucius to this text? Was he an author, as is possibly hinted in *Mengzi*; an editor, as implied, for instance, in the *Gongyang Commentary*;[24] or just a promulgator (a publisher?) of this text? The first of these assertions can be safely rejected: certainly Confucius did not author the meticulous chronicle of 242 (or 244) years,[25] but, if anything, based his work on a preexisting text. We cannot know whether or not he revised this text in the process of its transmission to his disciples. Yet the third assertion—that Confucius promulgated this text and attributed important meaning to it—is fairly plausible. Otherwise it would be very difficult to understand why the dry *Annals* attracted sufficient attention to merit no fewer than five distinct commentaries as early as during the Warring States period.[26] Whether or not the text reflects the "great meaning in subtle words" (*wei yan dayi* 微言大義) allegedly inserted in it by Confucius is a different question, though, and the answer to that is much more equivocal. For the purposes of the current discussion, I prefer to treat the *Annals* as overwhelmingly reflecting the scribal norms of the Spring and Autumn period, without ruling out the possibility that certain entries were modified by Confucius or by another later editor.[27]

Who made the records that were incorporated into the *Annals*, and who was the audience? The answer to the first question is relatively easy: from *Zuozhuan*, as well as other texts, it is clear that the records were made by court scribes (*shi* 史). As noted earlier, *shi* were not pure historians but also astrologers, recordkeepers, religious functionaries in charge of communicating with the deities, and responsible for a variety of other tasks, from advice on ritual matters to diplomatic missions. This multiplicity of functions should be taken into account when we consider the composition of the *Annals* and their audience. Specifically, I believe that the *Annals* were prepared by the scribes as part of their religious function of maintaining communications with the ancestral spirits.

In an earlier study I tried to demonstrate that the *Annals* originated in the seasonal records prepared for the ancestors of the ruling house and displayed in the ancestral temple.²⁸ Whether that assertion is correct or not is of little importance for the present discussion. What matters is that the *Annals* were doubtless not designed as a historical text directed at posterity. Their extreme laconism, highly formulaic language, absence of any interest in causality, abundance of "empty" records (i.e., records that indicate only a season and a month without providing any other information), and the like—all these make them barely understandable for a reader lacking scribal education. To demonstrate this point, suffice it to cite the *Annals*' entries for the first year of the text, the first reign year of Lord Yin of Lu:

1. 元年,春,王正月。 The first year, spring, the royal first month.
2. 三月,公及邾儀父盟于蔑。 In the third month, our lord and Zhu Yifu swore a covenant at Mie.
3. 夏,五月,鄭伯克段于鄢。 In summer, in the fifth month, the Earl of Zheng overcame Duan at Yan.
4. 秋,七月,天王使宰咺來歸惠公、仲子之賵。 In autumn, in the seventh month, the Heaven-appointed king sent his steward Xuan to us to present the funeral equipment for Lord Hui and Zhongzi.
5. 九月,及宋人盟于宿。 In the ninth month, we swore a covenant with a Song leader at Su.
6. 冬,十有二月,祭伯來。 In winter, in the twelfth month, the Zhai Earl came.
7. 公子益師卒。 Ducal Son Yishi died.

These entries make little sense for an average reader. The commentaries help us to discern the "great meaning" behind some of them. For instance, the first entry of the year should have contained the record "our lord acceded to his position" (公即位). That this phrase is omitted implies irregularity in succession procedure in the state of Lu.²⁹ The third entry, as is painstakingly explained in *Zuozhuan*, is formulated so as to mildly criticize the ruler of Zheng 鄭 as well as to condemn his rebellious brother Duan 段.³⁰ Yet this meaning remains obscure unless one consults the commentaries. Other entries are even more puzzling. Who would grasp, for example, the meaning of the second entry, in which the Viscount of Zhu is referred to not by his title but, exceptionally, by his appellative (zi 字)? Or what does the Zhai Earl's visit (entry 6) mean? Who are the protagonists and how are they related to each other? These—and hundreds of other entries in the *Annals*—cannot be understood by a layman. Not incidentally, the Han man of letters Huan Tan 桓譚 (ca. 20 BCE–56 CE), exclaimed, "Should the [*Spring and Autumn Annals*] classic lack the [*Zuozhuan*] commentary, the sage would close the door, ponder over it for ten years, and even then he would not understand it!"[31]

The commentarial tradition of the *Annals* bifurcates into what I have dubbed elsewhere the sacred and the profane reading of the text.[32] The first is represented by the *Gongyang Commentary* and the parallel *Guliang Commentary* (*Guliang zhuan* 穀梁傳) (in what follows I focus only on the former).[33] The adherents of these traditions read the *Annals* not as a historical but as a political text, which embeds, first, the superior ritual norms bequeathed by the Zhou founder, King Wen, and, second, the hidden praise and blame of historical personages by Confucius, the utmost sage. The latter's judgments are concealed behind the text's formulaic language. Having been understood through the proper commentary, King Wen's rules and Confucius's judgments provide a blueprint for the ideal monarchic system. Real historical facts are of little concern for the creators of this blueprint: hence from time to time the two commentaries provide fancy or even overtly weird interpretations of events of the Spring and Autumn-period so as to fit their ideological agenda.[34] History matters for the commentators only insofar as it tests the applicability of ritual norms in highly complex situations, providing a reader with the ability to "weigh" (*quan* 權) different ways of action and choose an appropriate one.[35]

In contrast, *Zuozhuan* proposes a much more down-to-earth reading of the *Annals*. Whereas the text does praise the *Annals*' subtle words, which can "encourage the good and frighten the licentious,"[36] it does not necessarily present the *Annals* as epitomizing the supreme truth. First, the *Annals* are implicitly dissociated from Confucius. The very fact that the *Zuozhuan* version of the *Annals* ends with Confucius's death in 479 BCE and not with the capture of the "unicorn" (*lin* 麟) in 481 BCE, as in two other commentaries, implies that Confucius simply could not author the text, nor edit its final version. Second, far from treating the *Annals* as infallible, *Zuozhuan* provides several explicit and many implicit cases that show how the text of the *Annals* was modified not out of commitment to moral and ritual values but rather because of political expediency in the state of Lu and elsewhere.[37] Third, aside from providing many examples of "praise and blame" in the *Annals*, *Zuozhuan* overwhelmingly treats the *Annals* as a peculiar historical record that requires contextualization in contemporaneous historical developments rather than ideological exegesis. This historicism of the *Zuozhuan* approach, which raised indignation among some of the *Annals*' later exegetes,[38] is the key for understanding the *Annals*' place in early Chinese historiography.

Two points concerning the *Annals* are of crucial importance for understanding their historiographic value: what is their historical reliability and who were their audience prior to their canonization? With regard to the first point the answer is not simple. On the one hand, judging from *Zuozhuan*, the *Annals*' entries were never whimsical. They invariably derived from the records of the Lu scribes or from reports from other polities, which routinely updated the Lu court about major events in the lives of their states, such as wars, covenants, rulers' successions, or cases of domestic turmoil.[39] Some of these records—for instance, those concerned with solar eclipses—can be independently verified, and from these verifications it is clear that the bulk of the information in the *Annals* is reliable, minor inaccuracies and scribal errors notwithstanding.[40] On the other hand, annoyingly for modern historians, the *Annals* were subjected to the "rules of recording" (*shu fa* 書法), which at times aimed to conceal no less than to reveal. For example, whenever rulers or crown princes of the state of Lu were assassinated, the *Annals* invariably reported these assassinations using the neutral term "to die" (*hong* 薨 for the ruler, *cu* 卒 for the crown prince).[41] The rules of concealment (*hui* 諱) were applied to other cases—when, for instance, the lord of Lu was detained or otherwise humiliated by foreign powers.[42] Similarly, when in 517 BCE the rebellious ministers expelled Lord Zhao of Lu 魯昭公 (r. 541–510 BCE) from his state, the *Annals* concealed this by a neutral record: "Ninth month; on [the day] *jihai*, the lord left for Qi."[43] There are many similar instances.[44]

The rules of concealment are part of a broader tendency in the *Annals* to present the ritually appropriate picture of events rather than mere facts. This insistence on "ritual reality"[45] is reflected on many levels. For instance, the *Annals* stubbornly refuse to recognize the appropriation of the royal title by the rulers of the powerful southern polities of Chu, Wu 吳, and Yue, consistently referring to them as "viscounts" (*zi* 子). The semblance of Zhou royal superiority over the regional lords is buttressed by the uniform placing of royal envoys above the rulers of even the most powerful regional states—including Jin and Qi 齊—whenever the text reports on an interstate assembly or a covenant. And—again annoyingly to modern historians—in certain cases the record in the *Annals* is supposed to reflect a legal and moral judgment rather than pure facts. The most famous and frequently discussed case is that of Zhao Dun 趙盾, a powerful prime minister of the state of Jin. In 607 BCE, Zhao Dun orchestrated the assassination of his ruler, Lord Ling 晉靈公 (r. 620–607 BCE), while pretending to flee the state. The court scribe, Dong Hu 董狐, nevertheless recorded for the Jin annals (and for publication in the annals of other states): "Zhao Dun assassinated his ruler." Zhao protested, but Dong Hu explained that as Zhao neither left the state at the time of the murder nor punished the criminals thereafter, the legal responsibility was his.[46] *Zuozhuan* tells us that courageous Dong Hu was eventually praised as a model scribe by Confucius himself—precisely because he understood that the function of the annals is not to record events as such but to present a ritually correct judgment of the rulers and their ministers.

Zhao Dun's case brings us to the next point: the role of the *Annals* in their contemporaneous world. Whereas in my opinion the initial addressees of the *Annals* were ancestral spirits, it is clear that their content was known to the top aristocrats as well. To understand the *Annals*' "secular" function, we should recall, first, that the Lu *Annals* were not an exceptional text. Similar court chronicles were prepared in other states, such as Jin and Qi (and in Chu as well, as chapter 2 discusses).[47] Second, these chronicles (i.e., other annals) were part of the web of interstate connections: the states routinely reported to each other about major events in their lives, and those were duly recorded in other states' annals. Thus, Dong Hu's record is duly reproduced in the *Spring and Autumn Annals* of the state of Lu.[48] Third, the annals could serve as a source of public shaming of the culprit. Although their text was not supposed to circulate broadly—a *Zuozhuan* anecdote dated to 540 BCE speaks of a Lu scribe who had shown the local *Annals* to a visiting Jin dignitary as a gesture of extraordinary favor[49]—their content was sufficiently known to chief political actors to make condemnation in the annals a source of grave concern. Several anecdotes in *Zuozhuan* tell of powerful ministers expressing remorse over their ancestors' shameful acts "recorded on the bamboo tablets of the regional lords" (i.e., in the court annals).[50] It is possibly in light of this impact of the annals that Confucius may have hoped to overawe "rebellious ministers and murderous sons" by encouraging the circulation of the *Spring and Autumn Annals* of the state of Lu.

If my analysis is correct, Confucius had radically altered the usage of the Lu *Annals* by redirecting them from the ancestors (who were the main, even if not necessarily the only, readers of this text) to the members of the educated elite. However, the *Annals* could not easily be understood as a stand-alone text. It is highly likely that from the very beginning of their circulation in their current form (i.e., as a text that covers 242/244 years and not as a small selection of records) they were accompanied by oral and written commentaries. One of these commentaries—*Zuozhuan*—is the richest repository of historical information about the Spring and Autumn period. It is also the richest source for exploring the early historiographic tradition. It is to this latter function of *Zuozhuan* that I turn now.

Zuozhuan and Its Sources

Zuozhuan is by far the longest and one of the best studied texts in the entire corpus of preimperial writings. It is also among the most controversial. The text has merited dozens of monographs and many hundreds of articles in Chinese and Japanese. In English, after a long lull of publications during most of the twentieth century, interest in *Zuozhuan* has resurfaced in recent decades, yielding three monographs in addition to numerous scholarly articles.[51] The recent state-of-the art translation of *Zuozhuan,* accompanied by an excellent introduction by Stephen Durrant, Li Wai-yee, and David Schaberg, marks a new stage in the studies of this text.[52] My goal in what follows is not to reopen the entire scope of discussions about *Zuozhuan* but to briefly introduce the text and then move to the crucial question of its primary sources. It is with regard to the latter that unearthed materials provide a variety of new clues.

Nature and Dates of Zuozhuan

The debates about *Zuozhuan* started in the last years of the first century BCE with the attempts of the Han librarian Liu Xin 劉歆 (46 BCE–23 CE) to establish an office of a court erudite (*boshi* 博士) for the *Zuo Tradition* (or *Commentary*) of the *Spring and Autumn Annals* on a par with the offices for adherents of the *Gongyang* and *Guliang* traditions. The controversy back then revolved around the question of whether or not *Zuozhuan* is a real commentary on the *Annals*.[53] Much later (starting in the eighth century CE), the debates shifted to the question of the text's authorship and dating.[54] These debates accelerated at the very end of the nineteenth century when the famous reformer Kang Youwei 康有爲 (1859–1927) utilized earlier criticisms of *Zuozhuan* to claim that the text in its entirety was Liu Xin's forgery.[55] These accusations were reinforced in the early twentieth century when "doubters of antiquity" (*yigupai* 疑古派) centered around Gu Jiegang 顧頡剛 (1893–1980) dismissed the historical reliability of *Zuozhuan*, relegating it to no more than a literary work akin to the *Romance of the Three Kingdoms* (*Sanguo yanyi* 三國演義).[56] Since then, and throughout much of the twentieth century and beyond, scholars have continued to debate the nature, authorship, dating, authenticity, and historical reliability of *Zuozhuan*.

After more than a century of debates, some of the questions have been partly resolved or lost their relevance, yet others continue to haunt the scholarly community. Few if any today would subscribe to the theory that *Zuozhuan* is a Han forgery or a "historical romance." To refute these dismissive views, suffice it to mention that significant portions of the text's information can be corroborated by unearthed materials (some of which are surveyed in chapters 2 and 3). Alternatively, the question of authorship has lost much of its relevance. The notion of an active author who is engaged in a dialogue with his readers, expresses his personal feelings, and hints at his hidden or overt agendas started in China only in the Han dynasty, most notably with Sima Qian.[57] Prior to his appearance, the authors, particularly in historical texts, preferred to remain hidden and speak, if at all, through the neutral voice of a "noble man."[58] Hence, whether or not *Zuozhuan* was composed by its putative author, Zuo Qiuming 左丘明, of whom we know next to nothing, does not matter much. An answer will not advance our understanding of the text, in which there was no place for an author as an individual creator.

The question of *Zuozhuan*'s relationship to the *Spring and Autumn Annals* is more complicated. Two reasons may explain scholars' ongoing dismissal of *Zuozhuan* as a commentary. One, which was prominent (even if not explicitly stated) in traditional scholarship, is ideological: as earlier argued, a historical reading of the *Spring and Autumn Annals* in *Zuozhuan* may undermine the perception of the *Annals* as a sacred text that contains

Confucius's utmost wisdom.[59] The second, which is common in the twentieth-century debates, is more concerned with the nature of *Zuozhuan* as a narrative. Many scholars argue that originally *Zuozhuan* was a pure historical text, which only later acquired exegetical layers, such as explicit references to the *Spring and Autumn Annals*, explanations of the *Annals*' "rules of recording," and, possibly, other interpretative devices, such as the "noble man's" comments.[60] This is an ostensibly reasonable scenario, but it fails to answer one major question: why should anybody invest considerable efforts in creating an unprecedentedly long pre–*Zuozhuan* historical text, which, quite incidentally, happened to cover exactly the same period as the *Annals*? Moreover, the overlap is not just in terms of the period covered. The absolute majority of *Zuozhuan* entries—including hundreds of those that do not directly comment upon the *Annals*—is closely related to the *Annals*' text, providing either the direct historical setting of the recorded event or its background, or, less frequently, the long-term outcome of a narrated story.[61] To dismiss these manifold explicit and implicit ties between the historical narrative in *Zuozhuan* and that in the *Spring and Autumn Annals* as a mere coincidence strikes me as a very unconvincing argument.

To resolve the riddle of the relations between the historical narrative and the exegetical layers in *Zuozhuan*, I propose a different scenario. The formation of *Zuozhuan* was based primarily on the amalgamation of local histories from the polities of the Spring and Autumn period. These histories, the nature of which I discuss later in this and the subsequent chapters, were in all likelihood local compilations: they used different calendars and were primarily focused on a single state. The compiler (or compilers) of *Zuozhuan* selected those sections of these histories that were relevant to the *Spring and Autumn Annals*, merged them, and arranged them chronologically so as to fit the *Annals*' structure. Despite these editorial efforts, some of the local flavor (i.e., usage of different calendric systems) is still visible in the *Zuozhuan* narrative.[62] If my scenario is correct, then it would suggest that *Zuozhuan* was prepared from the beginning as a commentary on the *Annals*, and that at least some of its commentarial layers were amalgamated with the historical narratives at the moment of its composition. Of course, it is plausible that additional interpretative passages and exegetical parts were added to *Zuozhuan* in the process of its formation before it took final shape in the third century CE. But these do not invalidate the intrinsic link between *Zuozhuan* and the *Annals*.

This observation also explains why it is so difficult to speak of the dates of *Zuozhuan*'s composition. This topic was hotly debated throughout most of the twentieth century. Scholars proposed almost any date from the fifth century BCE (the ending years of the *Zuozhuan* narrative) to Liu Xin's time.[63] To demonstrate the difficulty of arriving at a convincing answer, it suffices to consider a single example of an irresolvable contradiction. *Zuozhuan* contains no fewer than five predictions that were based on calculations of Jupiter's position. As paleo-astronomers had demonstrated, these calculations were retroactively produced after 375 or 365 BCE and then incorporated into the text.[64] On the other hand, *Zuozhuan* contains a famous prediction by the "noble man" according to which "Qin will never again march eastward." This prediction was probably made in the fifth century BCE, when Qin power reached its lowest point; it could not have been made after the 360s BCE, when Qin renewed its eastward expansion.[65] These examples of mutually contradictory dates can easily be multiplied. How can we understand them?

The riddle of the text's dating is resolved once we dismiss the erroneous (even if popular) idea according to which a single date can be offered for *Zuozhuan*'s composition. Actually, there are at least four or five dates for the materials in *Zuozhuan*. The earliest is the date of the composition of its component materials, the local histories, some of which were evidently composed very close to the depicted events—that is, in the late sixth or early fifth century BCE (and which, in turn, contained earlier materials, as specified in what follows). Then at a certain point (in my view in the fifth century BCE, but in that of many colleagues in the fourth) these histories were put together, arranged chronologically, and probably supplemented with the commentarial layer, providing the earliest version of the *Zuo* commentary on the *Annals*. Then came a lengthy period of transmission, during which unknown redactors of the text may have intervened in its content by, for example, inserting favorable accounts about their patrons' ancestors.[66] Then came the efforts of later editors, including (but not confined to) Liu Xin and Du Yu, who finally shaped the text in its current form.[67] Whereas the bulk of the historical information in *Zuozhuan* was fixed more or less at the time of the original compilation of the text, important additions and modifications occurred for centuries to come. Distinguishing later additions, interpolations, scribal errors, and the like (including early glosses that were inadvertently incorporated into the main text) from earlier layers of the text is an arduous task, even though much progress has been made in this direction.[68]

Zuozhuan *Sources*

Debates over *Zuozhuan*'s nature and dating aside, let us move to what in my view constitutes the single most important question related to *Zuozhuan*—its primary sources. What did they look like? What information did they contain? Which segments of the *Zuozhuan* text can be assumed to derive from its primary sources and which were added later by the text compiler(s), transmitters, and editors? Answering these questions is crucial for understanding *Zuozhuan*'s historical reliability. The answers may also considerably advance our understanding of early Chinese historiography in general.

That *Zuozhuan* incorporates distinct primary sources can easily be observed even from a cursory review of its narratives. Some textual segments of *Zuozhuan* comprise dry accounts of events; others include lengthy literary digressions. Some are rich in interpretative devices (speeches, evaluations by the "noble man" and Confucius, and the like), whereas others appear devoid of any moral or political judgments. The extent of coverage of states, events, and personalities varies dramatically from one textual segment to another. It is incongruent to attribute these differences to changes in the personal style of the author(s) or compiler(s) of *Zuozhuan*. Rather, it is highly likely that they reflect the intrinsic heterogeneity of the text's primary sources. The question is, can we discern these sources' original appearance? Can we understand who composed these sources and for which audience? Let us start this discussion with a few short entries from the first year of *Zuozhuan* (Yin 1):

1.3: 夏，四月，費伯帥師城郎。不書，非公命也。 In summer, in the fourth month, the Elder of Bi led troops to fortify Lang. This was not recorded because it was not by our lord's command.

1.6: 八月，紀人伐夷。夷不告，故不書。 In the eighth month, the men of Ji attacked Yi.[69] Yi did not report the attack, and that is why it was not recorded.

1.7: 有蜚。不為災，亦不書。 There were locusts. It did not become a disaster, so it also was not recorded.

1.9: 冬，十月庚申，改葬惠公。公弗臨，故不書。惠公之薨也，有宋師，太子少，葬故有闕，是以改葬。 In winter, in the tenth month, on the *gengshen* day [fourteenth day of the month], Lord Hui [the former ruler of the state of Lu] was reburied. Our lord [Lord Yin] did not attend, and that is why it was not recorded. When Lord Hui expired, there was [conflict with] Song troops, and the heir apparent was still young, so there were omissions in the burial protocol. It was for this reason that he was reburied.

1.10: 衛侯來會葬，不見公，亦不書。 The Marquis of Wei came to participate in the burial ceremony, but he did not meet with our lord, so it also was not recorded.

1.11: 鄭共叔之亂，公孫滑出奔衛。衛人為之伐鄭，取廩延。鄭人以王師、虢師伐衛南鄙。請師於邾，邾子使私於公子豫。豫請往，公弗許，遂行，及邾人、鄭人盟于翼。不書，非公命也。 During the rebellion of Gongshu [Duan] in Zheng, Ducal Grandson Hua left Zheng and fled to Wei. For his sake the Wei leaders attacked Zheng and seized Linyan. The Zheng leaders, assisted by the troops from the king and from the state of Guo, attacked Wei's southern marches. [Zheng] requested troops from Zhu, and the Viscount of Zhu sent a private message to Ducal Son Yu. Yu asked permission to go, but our lord would not allow it. Yu subsequently departed and swore a covenant with a Zhu leader and a Zheng leader at Yi. This was not recorded because it was not by our lord's command.

1.12: 新作南門，不書，亦非公命也。 The southern gate was built anew. This was not recorded because it also was not by our lord's command.

These seven entries (half of the entries for the first year of Lord Yin) have one thing in common: they all explain why certain events were *not* recorded in the *Spring and Autumn Annals*. Most of these events are very minor: unauthorized fortification and construction activities by the Lu nobles (1.3 and 1.12), a clash between two tiny neighboring polities (1.6), or an inconsequential appearance of locusts (1.7). Other entries refer to ritually important events related to the burial of the former Lord Hui of Lu (1.9 and 1.10). One entry provides a detailed account of the evolving conflict between two important polities, Zheng and Wei 衛, which caused a Lu prince to lead his troops to support Zheng without Lord Yin's authorization (1.11). In each of the cases, the compiler explains why a certain event that could otherwise have merited inclusion in the *Spring and Autumn Annals* was not recorded there.

What was the source of these records, which allowed the *Zuozhuan* compiler to reproduce minute details (including precise dating in 1.9) of relatively minor events that had taken place more than two centuries before the composition of *Zuozhuan* had started? Who would preserve these records and for what audience? I think the answer is implied in the explanation "this was not recorded." We have here a sample of training materials for a Lu scribe. In all likelihood, the scribal office kept much more extensive records than those that appear in the *Spring and Autumn Annals*. The *Annals*' entries were selected from these original records, whereas other records were provided with an explanation of the reason for their eventual omission from the *Annals*. Without this information, a future scribe would not be able to decide which events should merit inclusion in the court chronicles and which should not. These explanations may have been the foundation of the earliest exegetical layer of *Zuozhuan* itself.[70]

Zuozhuan notifications about the events omitted from the *Spring and Autumn Annals* are concentrated primarily in the first year of Lord Yin and recur only infrequently thereafter. Perhaps for the compiler(s) of *Zuozhuan* this initial sample sufficed to illustrate the principles of exclusion from the *Annals*. Yet there is no doubt that records of events as preparatory materials for the composition of local court chronicles were undertaken not only in Lu but also in the courts of other major polities of the Spring and-Autumn period.[71] In chapter 2, I point to traits of similar records from the state of Chu. For the current discussion, what matters is that these draft records could become parts of a larger historical text. *Zuozhuan* contains not a few segments of these texts, which are characterized by highly detailed information. Look, for instance, at a short extract from the *Zuozhuan* account of the rebellion of Prince Zhao 王子朝 in the Zhou royal domain. The rebellion itself lasted from 521 to 516 BCE, and it is extensively covered in *Zuozhuan*. Here is a small section from the narrative of the rebellion from its last year, 516 BCE:

四月，單子如晉告急。五月戊午，劉人敗王城之師于尸氏。戊辰，王城人、劉人戰于施穀，劉師敗績。...七月己巳，劉子以王出。庚午，次于渠。王城人焚劉。丙子，王宿于褚氏。丁丑，王次于萑穀。庚辰，王入于胥靡。辛巳，王次于滑。晉知躒、趙鞅帥師納王，使汝寬守闕塞。

In the fourth month, the Viscount of Shan visited Jin to report the crisis. In the fifth month, on *wuwu* [day 5], the Liu [lineage] troops defeated the Wangcheng [Prince Zhao's] army at the [settlement of the] Shi lineage. On *wuchen* [day 15], the men of Wangcheng did battle with the men of Liu at Shigu. The Liu army was completely defeated.... In the seventh month, on *jisi* [day 17], the Viscount of Liu fled together with the [incumbent] king. On *gengwu* [day 18], [they] camped at Qu. The Wangcheng troops set fire to [the settlement of] Liu. On *bingzi* [day 24], the king lodged at the [settlement of the] Chu lineage. On *dingchou* [day 25], the king camped at Wangu. On *gengchen* [day 28], the king entered Xumi. On *xinsi* [day 29], the king camped at Hua. Zhi Li and Zhao Yang of Jin led an army to reinstate the king. They ordered Ru Kuan to guard the Que Pass.[72]

This narrative abounds with details and there is no doubt that it derives from a meticulous written record, akin to the one that was inscribed on the Jin Hou Su bells. For whom was it prepared? I assume that such an exhaustively detailed narrative could interest only a very small group of readers: members of the noble lineages in the Zhou royal domain who would be able to apprehend the full meaning of personal and place-names, and for whom the dates of the events (i.e., the length of each minor campaign) would make sense. Such a detailed account would be attractive for the participants and their immediate offspring, whose destinies were deeply influenced by these dramatic events. For other readers, such a level of detail would probably bore them to death. I suspect that within a generation or two such a meticulous account would lose its appeal and be replaced by a shorter summary of major events (akin to the accounts discussed in chapter 2). The survival of several similarly detailed accounts in Lord Zhao's section of *Zuozhuan* (541–510 BCE) allows us a rare glimpse into the text's original sources before those underwent major editing.[73]

The preceding discussion suffices to demonstrate that detailed historical records, probably prepared by court scribes in their capacities as annalists, constitute the skeleton of *Zuozhuan* narrative. Yet it would be grossly inaccurate to reduce *Zuozhuan*'s sources just to these short annalistic-style units. First, the text contains numerous stories that are highly unlikely to be based on the scribes' records. Consider, for example, mentions of vengeful ghosts and descending deities, speaking stones and fighting dragons. Certainly these stories originate in oral lore or in somebody's imagination.[74] Second, and more important, *Zuozhuan* clearly incorporated much larger textual units than the short entries cited here. Some of these units, which span a few years, are easily identifiable. For instance, the foregoing excerpt, about troubles in the Zhou royal domain, belongs to the story about the rebellion of Prince Zhao (521–516 BCE, with some entries predating or postdating this time span). This story was obviously a coherent narrative unit that was disjoined by the *Zuozhuan* compilers to fit the rigid chronological framework of the text. Yet relatively short stories aside, there are also much longer narrative units in *Zuozhuan*, some of which span decades and even more than a century. It is to these units that I now turn.

The larger textual units are less apparent in *Zuozhuan* than those units that focus on a single event or a chain of closely related events, but they are nonetheless discernible. Take, for instance, the recurrence of certain narration patterns in textual segments associated with a certain polity. The Tang scholar Dan Zhu 啖助 (724–770) noted that "whenever Jin dispatches an army, [*Zuozhuan*] records all its commanders and their assistants; whenever there are upheavals in the state of Song, it fully records the newly appointed six top ministers."[75] Interestingly, this highly detailed account of major appointments characterizes *Zuozhuan*'s narrative of a few states (Jin, Song, Zheng) but not of others (e.g., Qi, Chu, or even Lu). Alternatively, the external campaigns of the state of Chu are narrated in much greater detail than is true for most other states. It is conceivable that these differences reflect different habits of, say, Jin, Song, and Chu scribes. If this supposition is correct, then it can be plausibly assumed that local histories produced in different states served as the building blocks of *Zuozhuan*.

The differences in the mode of coverage of individual states are often too subtle to be easily discerned. But we have clearer indicators that hint at disjoined narratives actually being parts of a larger textual unit. Of these, predictions of future events and lengthy speeches that analyze the events post-factum are singularly important. These and related means (a variety of signs, omens, and portents) allow a perceptive reader to discover longer narratives that comprise dozens of ostensibly unrelated entries dispersed over many decades. These narratives tell of such long-term developments as the rise to power of the Ji 季 lineage in the state of Lu or the Tian 田 (Chen 陳) lineage in the state of Qi, or the eventful collision of the state of Chu with its powerful southeastern neighbor, the state of Wu. The existence of these lengthy disjoined narratives has been duly noted by *Zuozhuan* exegetes, eventually giving birth to the "topical arrangement" (*jishi benmo* 紀事本末) of *Zuozhuan*'s text. Yet whereas a full-scale topical rearrangement of *Zuozhuan* was performed only by Gao Shiqi 高士奇 (1645–1704), its antecedents can clearly be identified a full two millennia before Gao—that is, in the text of *Xinian* discussed in chapter 2. In my view, this is not a coincidence. Rather, Gao's rearrangement might have inadvertently brought the *Zuozhuan* narrative closer to that of its original sources, which, as I try to demonstrate in the next chapter, were also utilized by the *Xinian* compiler(s).

In the next two chapters I explore the long narrative units, which I consider the building blocks of *Zuozhuan*. Here I want to focus first on yet another major difference of *Zuozhuan* from the dry, annalistic reports discussed in the preceding: *Zuozhuan* is first and foremost an interpretative history. Actually, its lasting appeal among Chinese literati was precisely because aside from who, what, when, and where, it persistently addresses the question of why. This preoccupation with an event's causality is visible most immediately through the ubiquitous illative expressions *gu* 故 (because of, hence) and *shiyi* 是以 (therefore), which recur in the text well over eight hundred times. Another means of highlighting causality is by providing background information that is deemed essential to understanding some complex affair: when this information breaks the chronological framework of the text, it is introduced with the word *chu* 初 (earlier; ninety-nine times). Yet by far more important are speeches of wise statesmen and post-factum observations of the "noble man" and Confucius, which allow the reader to draw proper historical lessons. It is this explicit didacticism that distinguishes *Zuozhuan* dramatically from the *Spring and Autumn Annals*.[76]

On the matter of the lasting appeal of *Zuozhuan*, it is appropriate to remind the reader that aside from its richness as descriptive and interpretative history, it is also an engaging literary work. Some of its short vignettes and a few longer narratives—such as those that deal with the rise of Ducal Son Chong'er 公子重耳 from rags to riches as Lord Wen of Jin 晉文公

(r. 636–628 BCE), or those that tell of a ruthless and powerful leader, King Ling of Chu 楚靈王 (r. 540–529 BCE)—can be considered China's earliest literary masterpieces. Stories of scheming concubines and wise spouses, of treacherous plotters and loyal ministers, of cruel or magnanimous rulers, of eloquent diplomats, brave warriors, and clever strategists, of chivalry and perfidy on the battlefield—all these make *Zuozhuan* one of the foundational texts of China's literary tradition and not just of its historiography.[77] The contrast between these pieces and the aforementioned annalistic-style accounts could not be greater.

The question to be asked is, how much of this variety of interpretative and literary devices was introduced by the authors of *Zuozhuan*'s primary sources, and how much should be attributed to the text's compilers, editors, and transmitters? Who integrated annalistic textual records with the stories of vengeful ghosts or secretive plotters, which either derived from oral lore or were invented altogether, and at what stage did this happen? Who invented the predictions and edited (or invented outright) the speeches so as to fit the narrative development? That some of the text's edifying and entertaining devices derive from its original sources is undeniable: it suffices to note *Zuozhuan*'s ideological multivalence and marked differences among different textual segments in terms of their literary quality.[78] But what was the relative weight of these early sources in developing the *Zuozhuan*'s interpretative and literary apparatus? The answer is important not only for a better understanding of *Zuozhuan* and its reliability but also for understanding the nature of the historiographic tradition of the Spring and Autumn period. Was it as rich as is suggested by *Zuozhuan*'s narrative? Or does the didactic and entertaining richness of *Zuozhuan* derive primarily from the creativity of later (Warring States) editors?

From reading *Zuozhuan*, we can infer that the Spring and Autumn period had a well-developed historiographic tradition. At the very least, *Zuozhuan* tries to persuade that historical knowledge mattered a great deal to members of the aristocratic elite of the time. The text is self-referential in its insistence on the importance of mastering history. Its protagonists routinely invoke the past in a variety of court or interstate debates, and their superior knowledge of former events becomes a useful polemical weapon. References to successes and failures of previous rulers and ministers, analyses of historical developments in a rival state, or invocations of earlier precedents to justify a policy choice are recurrent rhetorical strategies in *Zuozhuan*. And, insofar as the past is a useful tool in the statesman's hands, gathering information about it is of utmost importance. If these passages reflect a genuine intellectual atmosphere of the Spring and Autumn period, we can indeed expect the existence of a well-developed tradition of history writing at that time. But again, it is equally possible that these repeated emphases on the importance of mastering the past are nothing but self-promotion on the part of *Zuozhuan*: the text's emphasis on its own usefulness.

The problem with our attempts to discern the nature of *Zuozhuan*'s sources is that until recently we had to do so exclusively through relying on internal evidence from *Zuozhuan* itself. Alas, even the tremendous progress in *Zuozhuan* studies has its limits. In the absence of any direct glimpse of the text's primary sources, and in the absence of any parallel text of similar historical complexity prior to the appearance of Sima Qian's *Records of the Historian*, our explorations of Spring and Autumn–period historiography could not advance much beyond the conflicting interpretation of some of *Zuozhuan* passages. Now for the first time we have a chance to address this issue anew through the utilization of newly available paleographic sources. The impact of these sources is addressed in chapters 2 and 3.

History Writing After *Zuozhuan*: The Didactic Turn

Zuozhuan is the only preimperial text that fully combines informative and interpretative aspects of history writing. It is full of historical detail on the one hand but, on the other, is also rich in edifying and entertaining content. This balance disappears from later texts. Most of the historical and quasi-historical texts from the Warring States period onward focus almost exclusively on interpreting the past but deal much less with the questions of who, what, when, and where.

Take, for instance, another major quasi-historical compilation, *Discourses of the States* (*Guoyu* 國語). This is a large collection of historical anecdotes, the overwhelming majority of which come from the Spring and Autumn period. Almost two-thirds of the *Discourses*' narratives have parallels in *Zuozhuan*, and some segments of both texts are almost identical. For centuries scholars have discussed the relation between the two texts: were they produced by the same author, as implied by Sima Qian?[79]

Or did one of them serve as source material for the other? Some of these speculations can now be dismissed: we speak of two different texts, which in all likelihood were not produced at the same time.⁸⁰ It is highly likely that whereas both texts may have shared common primary sources, the *Discourses* were composed later than *Zuozhuan*, and they contain clearer signs of editorial intervention in the content of the cited speeches.⁸¹ What matters for the present discussion, though, is how different both texts are in treating the history of the Spring and Autumn period.⁸²

The differences between the two texts are most striking in their treatment of historical events. *Zuozhuan* is preoccupied first of all with what happened. Speeches and other interpretative devices are important but are clearly secondary to the narrative: indeed, many narratives are not accompanied by long—or any—speeches at all. In the *Discourses*, in contrast, what matters is the speech of a wise minister. The historical narrative, in marked contrast to *Zuozhuan*, is condensed, sometimes to an absolute minimum of a few dozen characters. The details that are so richly provided in *Zuozhuan*—personal and place-names, dates, official titles, and the like—are dramatically reduced. For example, the *ganzhi* 干支 dates of the sexagenary cycle, which permeate *Zuozhuan*, recur in just a very few sections of the *Discourses*. Clearly, the goal of the text's composers was not to tell the story but to jump as soon as possible to the moralizing historical lessons.

This shift away from historical detail and toward edifying (or entertaining) aspects of history writing is not exceptional to *Discourses of the States* but rather represents a common feature of texts of the Warring States period. That such an attitude characterizes the texts associated with the Masters (*zi* 子, "philosophers") is probably not surprising; but this is the rule also in texts that are supposed to be more historically oriented. Take, for instance, *Stratagems of the Warring States* (*Zhanguo ce* 戰國策). This text was compiled by a Han librarian, Liu Xiang 劉向 (79–8 BCE), from no fewer than six smaller collections, at least two of which—judging by their titles—dealt with the affairs (*shi* 事) of the Warring States—that is, with the events proper.⁸³ However, a closer look reveals that the historical context appears to be of marginal importance to the authors of all but a very few of the *Stratagems'* anecdotes. For example, the text lacks not just the *ganzhi* dates but even a basic chronology (i.e., that the event occurred in such and such year of such and such ruler). Not a few anecdotes dispense with even such essential information as the speaker's identity: they just start with "[Someone] told the king of X."⁸⁴ Needless to say, other historical details, such as names, official titles, and the like, are usually reduced to an absolute minimum, even in those cases when an anecdote seems to be grounded in real events and not just in the author's imagination.

The turn away from informative history and, more broadly, from historical accuracy (discussed in chapter 3) appears as a sweeping and profound development of the Warring States period. Its impact on our understanding of preimperial historiography in general is tremendous. Having accepted the ubiquity of the ideological concerns of Warring States–period authors as reflecting the uniform approach of preimperial historians, not a few scholars tended to read *Zuozhuan* through the prism of later didactic stories, focusing on its edifying aspects and downplaying or ignoring its rich informative content altogether. The result was a self-fulfilling prophecy. Having postulated the ubiquitous didacticism of early Chinese historiography, not a few scholars opted to simply gloss over any aspect of *Zuozhuan* (or other historical texts) that did not comfortably fit this paradigm.⁸⁵

It is against the backdrop of this state of affairs that we can fully evaluate the impact of the recent paleographic discoveries. These discoveries provide us with new clues about the usages of history in the Spring and Autumn and early Warring States periods. They demonstrate the sophistication and richness of the early historiographic tradition. Read in tandem with *Zuozhuan* and other transmitted texts, the new manuscripts allow us to revise our views of early Chinese history writing. The following chapters look at these discoveries and assesses their nature and impact on a new understanding of China's past.

CHAPTER 2

Xinian and Zhou Historiography

In 2008, Tsinghua University acquired more than two thousand bamboo slips at the antiquity market of Hong Kong.[1] These slips, the publication of which is still ongoing (as of 2020), contain a great wealth of manuscripts, including documents and poems that parallel or mimic those of the *Canon of Documents* and *Canon of Poems*, anecdotes about historical personalities from the Spring and Autumn period, divination and mathematical texts, political, philosophical, and ethical writings, and so forth. The longest of these manuscripts, the historical text named by the editors *Xinian* 繫年 ("String of years" or "Linked years"), is the focus of this chapter.

Xinian is the longest and most detailed historical text unearthed since the discovery of the *Bamboo Annals* more than seventeen centuries ago. It comprises slightly more than five thousand characters, written on 138 bamboo slips of 44.6 to 45 centimeters in length. The text is divided into twenty-three sections (*zhang* 章). Each slip (except the last) is numbered on its verso, and every section starts on a separate slip.[2] The slips are generally well preserved and only in section 13 are parts of slips 63 to 65 missing. This convenient arrangement of the text by its Warring States editors facilitated its speedy publication in the second volume of Tsinghua slips.

Immediately upon its publication, *Xinian* attracted great scholarly attention. By 2019, it had merited no fewer than twelve monographs and more than two hundred articles (including very lengthy ones), written in China,

Japan, and the West. These studies, which have greatly advanced our understanding of this text, serve as the foundation of my own research.³ In what follows, I introduce the nature of *Xinian*, discuss its authenticity, then explore its relations with *Zuozhuan*, its sources, and its possible audience.

The Composition of *Xinian*

Xinian covers six hundred fifty years of Zhou history, from the foundation of the Zhou dynasty circa 1046 BCE to the wars between Chu and its foes waged between 400 and about 396 BCE. Its focus is primarily on the foreign relations of Chu and of its major allies and rivals, specifically the state of Jin. The domestic affairs of various states are narrated only in the context of their impact on interstate dynamics; in particular, any references to domestic troubles in the state of Chu are conspicuously absent.

The twenty-three sections of *Xinian* can be conveniently divided into three parts. Part 1 (section 1 to the middle of section 4) deals primarily with the affairs of the Western Zhou period and the immediate aftermath of the Western Zhou collapse in 771 BCE. Its content is discussed in chapter 4. Part 2 (to the middle of section 20) covers the Spring and Autumn period. The narrative in this part overlaps considerably with that in *Zuozhuan*, and the relationship between the two texts is discussed later in this chapter. Part 3 (to section 23) deals with affairs of the midfifth to early fourth centuries BCE. This last part is exceptionally rich in historical information that has no parallels in either received or unearthed texts, and its content is surveyed in chapters 4 and 5. In this chapter, I briefly address the last part of *Xinian* only in the context of the clues it provides about the Chu historiographic tradition.

Xinian's individual sections differ considerably in size: the shortest (10 and 12) comprise two bamboo slips only, whereas the longest (15 and 23) are written on, respectively, eleven and thirteen slips. The differences in terms of the time covered are even more pronounced: a few sections (9, 12, 13) deal with the events of a single year, whereas others cover several decades (2, 15, 20) or even several centuries (1, 3, 4). Most sections constitute a coherent narrative unit that focuses on either a single event or on a chain of related events. In a few cases the divisions adopted by the text's editors are of questionable logic; for instance, the short sections 9–10 and 12–13 could easily have been merged into one coherent unit each. My misgivings notwithstanding, it is clear that the division into sections was performed by a person with considerable historical sensitivity. For example, aside from one minor overlap between sections 15 and 20, the narration avoids repeated references to the same event, even though not a few sections cover overlapping periods.

Even a cursory look at *Xinian* shows that its narrative is based on earlier sources. The most immediate indication of this resort to earlier materials is the difference in chronologies applied throughout the text. The first four sections count years according to the regnal periods of Zhou kings, while the rest are divided between sections that employ the regnal years of the lords of Jin and those that use the chronology of the Chu kings (in section 18 both Jin and Chu chronologies are employed). Conceivably, the text's sections must have come from at least two to three different sources: those from Zhou, Jin, and Chu (or only Jin and Chu).[4] As I demonstrate in the following, there are other, grammatical indications of the heterogeneity of *Xinian*'s primary sources.

Immediately upon *Xinian*'s publication, scholars noticed the peculiarity of its structure. *Xinian* is neither arranged chronologically, as the canonical *Spring and Autumn Annals* and its commentaries, nor is it a collection of anecdotes akin to *Discourses of the States* or *Stratagems of the Warring States*, nor, pace Li Xueqin, does it appear to be related to the *Bamboo Annals*.[5] Rather, the text's focus on chains of events that shaped the geopolitical situation in the Zhou world—be it the rise and fall of individual states or changing patterns of conflicts and alliances among major powers—curiously resembles the *jishi benmo* 紀事本末 (topical arrangement) genre. Although this genre itself did not flourish until the Song 宋 dynasty (960–1279), *Xinian*'s similarities to it are remarkable. In a few places (such as section 15, discussed in the following), *Xinian* surprisingly resembles the topical arrangement of *Zuozhuan* performed by Gao Shiqi 高士奇 (1645–1704) two millennia later.[6]

Whatever the genre is, it is advisable to treat *Xinian*'s sections as separate narrative units. To facilitate further discussion, I summarize in table 2.1 information about the length of every section, its content, and the chronology it employs. Note that when the chronology is placed in brackets it means that no exact years have been provided in the section under discussion.

Table 2.1 allows a relatively easy division of *Xinian* into what I henceforth tentatively call the Zhou (sections 1–4), Jin (sections 6–10, 14, 17, 20),

TABLE 2.1
Xinian's sections

Section	Slips	Time span BCE	Chronology	Focus (state)	Content (summary)
1	1-4	ca. 1046-789	Zhou	Zhou	Rise and decline of the Western Zhou
2	5-12	ca. 780-678	Zhou	Zhou, Jin, Zheng	Fall of the Western Zhou; rise of Jin, Zheng, and Chu
3	13-16	ca. 1042-770	(Zhou)	Qin	Rise of Qin
4	17-22	ca. 1040-629	Zhou	Wei 衛	Early Wei history
5	23-30	684-680	(Chu)	Chu	Start of Chu's northward expansion
6	31-40	656-635	Jin	Jin	Jin domestic crises and formation of Jin-Qin alliance
7	41-44	633-632	Jin	Jin	Jin struggle against Chu
8	45-49	630-627	Jin	Jin	Dissolution of Jin-Qin alliance
9	50-53	620	Jin	Jin	Jin succession crisis and its impact on Jin-Qin relations
10	54-55	620-615	Jin	Jin	Jin-Qin conflict

11	56–60	617–594	Chu	Chu conflict with Song
12	61–62	600	Chu	Chu-Zheng-Jin struggle
13	[63–65]	597	Chu	Chu-Zheng-Jin struggle
14	66–73	592–589	Jin	Jin-Qi conflict
15	74–84	599–505	Chu	Chu conflict with Wu
16	85–90	584–574	Chu, Jin	Failure of Chu-Jin peace treaty
17	91–95	557–548	Jin	Jin-Qi conflict
18	96–103	546–491	Chu, Jin	Chu-Jin relations, and Jin's weakening
19	104–107	541–493	Chu	Chu's annexation of Chen and Cai
20	108–113	585–430	Jin	From Jin-Wu alliance to Jin-Yue alliance against Qi
21	114–118	421–420	Chu	Chu-Jin conflict
22	119–125	404–403	Chu	Jin and Yue conflict with Qi
23	126–138	400–396	Chu	Chu wars with Jin and Zheng

and Chu (sections 5, 11–13, 15–16, 19, 21–23) parts. Section 18 is labeled Chu-Jin, because it employs both countries' chronology and was possibly based on a merger of their primary sources. As I try to demonstrate, the conjecture that different sections have distinct geographic origins can be corroborated through a grammatical analysis of their content.

Before I move to the next part of the discussion, however, it is important to reiterate that *Xinian*, despite its composite nature, should be considered a product of Chu historiography. That it was written in what is identified as Chu script[7] and probably plundered from a Chu tomb do not suffice to identify it as a Chu text; but there are stronger internal indicators suggesting that the manuscript was composed in Chu and underwent Chu editing. First, each section of the text, except for the first, which narrates exclusively Zhou affairs, deals with the state of Chu either directly or through discussing its primary rivals or allies, such as the states of Jin, Qin, Qi, or Wu. Second, the geographical perspective of *Xinian* is obviously biased toward the western part of the Zhou world. For instance, the state of Qin—an important ally of Chu during much of the period under discussion—is covered more comprehensively than in other contemporaneous texts,[8] whereas eastern states, such as Lu and its neighbors, which had a lesser role in Chu's history, are less prominent.[9] Third, the Chu affiliation becomes more pronounced in the last sections of the text (e.g., section 22), which—uncharacteristically for the rest of *Xinian*—adopt the Chu chronology even when the narrative deals with Jin. Fourth, whereas the text readily acknowledges Chu military defeats (see chapter 5), it avoids any direct reference to domestic turmoil in Chu, such as the coups that first catapulted King Ling 楚靈王 (r. 540–529 BCE) into power and then caused his fall.[10] This distinguishes Chu from other states, where domestic turmoil is not concealed. Fifth, there are ritual indications of the text's respect toward the Chu kings: their deaths are invariably recorded as solemnly "passing away" (即世). This courtesy is not uniformly observed with regard to other regional lords.[11] All this suggests that the text was produced in Chu, although it clearly incorporated non-Chu materials.

One final question that should be considered in this preliminary introduction concerns *Xinian*'s dating. Since the last section of the text mentions the posthumous title of King Dao of Chu 楚悼王 (r. ca. 400–381 BCE), the year 381 BCE should serve as the *terminus ante quem non* for the text's composition. The *terminus ante quem* is the date of the manuscripts' internment in the tomb from which they were supposedly looted. The

Tsinghua University's own radiocarbon analysis of one of the collected slips suggests a date of 305±30 BCE for the cache of the collected manuscripts.[12] But can we establish a more accurate date for *Xinian*'s production? Here the evidence from the three last sections strongly suggests an earlier date, closer to King Dao's death. I analyze this evidence in detail later; here suffice it to say that a majority of scholars tend to date *Xinian* to around 370 BCE, and this dating is supported by Guo Yongbing's study of the text's orthography.[13] For the time being, I accept this date and subsequently provide further suggestions for a relatively early date of *Xinian*'s production. But before any further discussion, one crucial topic should be considered: *Xinian*'s authenticity.

The Question of Authenticity

The last decade of the twentieth century and the first decade of the twenty-first witnessed an explosion in looting of ancient tombs throughout China. It was during these decades that the looters seem to have learned the value of bamboo manuscripts, many of which survive in the Chu elite tombs of the Hubei-Hunan area. The first major cache of looted manuscripts was purchased by the Shanghai Museum (a few bamboo slips from this cache ended up in the possession of the Chinese University of Hong Kong). The spectacular success of the Shanghai Museum team in repatriating these slips and publishing their content thrilled the scholarly community; but most unfortunately it may also have contributed to the race of both looters and donors of China's top educational institutions toward looting, selling, and purchasing more and more manuscripts. Looted slips purchased at Hong Kong's antiquity market found their way to the collections of Peking University (which purchased one cache of Han slips and another of Qin slips), Tsinghua University, Yuelu Academy (Changsha, Hunan), Zhejiang University, the Chinese University of Hong Kong, and, most recently (2017), Anhui University. In just a few years the entire field of paleographic studies in China seems to have been submerged under the tsunami of looted manuscripts that now overshadow much of the no less spectacular scientific archaeological discoveries of texts written on bamboo, wood, and silk.

This rapid proliferation of manuscripts of dubious provenance caused many scholars to start rethinking the situation. Originally most of us, myself included, paid little if any attention to the way the manuscripts were obtained by China's leading academic and cultural institutions. Paul R. Goldin was the first to voice strong dissatisfaction with this situation back in 2013.[14] Since then, the issue has been addressed by more scholars.[15] The problem can be divided into two aspects: an ethical one and a practical one. Ethically speaking, working with looted manuscripts is considered by some scholars, such as Goldin, to be indirect encouragement of further looting. This is a strong point, but it may be counterbalanced by an equally strong argument: the crime of letting invaluable manuscripts rot in the hands of antiquity dealers is arguably even less pardonable than paying these dealers for their illicit purchases. And, once the manuscripts have been published and their authenticity confirmed, ignoring their content out of disapproval of the way they were acquired does not appear to me a feasible position.[16] This brings us to the second, practical consideration: authenticity. Is it possible that some of the recently acquired manuscripts come from the hands of forgers? The insufficient transparency that surrounds the acquisition and authentication of manuscripts acquired from antiquity dealers raises fears that a shrewd forger may dupe the purchasers and, through them, the entire scholarly community.

These fears are not ungrounded. Attempts to create fake manuscripts are traceable back to the 1980s, and whereas most were unsuccessful, at least in one case—the Zhejiang University collection, particularly the alleged *Zuozhuan* extract contained therein—scholars nowadays tend to dismiss these bamboo slips as a forgery.[17] In other cases, doubts continue to linger, either explicitly or implicitly (i.e., expressed in informal conversations during scholarly conferences rather than in official publications).[18] To aggravate matters, there is always the possibility that a smart forger in possession of a small collection of genuine slips would opt to expand this collection by producing fake slips in addition to genuine ones. The problem of the authenticity of any looted manuscript should not be glossed over; rather, it should be acknowledged and, whenever possible, dealt with.

In the case of *Xinian*, we are lucky to have what appear to be solid indications of its authenticity. One of these indicators is the verso lines on the slips. These were continuous lines cut by a knife on the verso of the slips to indicate their original position as part of the bamboo culm segment from which the manuscript was produced. *Xinian* is divided into seven sets of slips from the same culm, as indicated by those lines. The verso lines phenomenon, which was noticed by paleographers only in 2011, could not have been known to a forger back in 2007, hence it strongly indicates that *Xinian* is authentic material.[19]

An additional major indicator of the text's authenticity is the peculiar distribution of grammatical particles therein. Chen Minzhen was the first to notice one of these peculiarities; that is, the balanced usage of particles *ji* 及 and *yu* 與 in the meaning of "with" or "and."[20] As a rule, Chu paleographic materials clearly prefer *yu*, whereas Qin manuscripts, in contrast, overwhelmingly use *ji*.[21] Geography aside, *ji* in the meaning of "with," "and" seems to be favored by early texts, such as the canonical *Poems* and *Documents*, and, most notably, the *Spring and Autumn Annals* (in which *yu* does not appear at all).[22] In transmitted Eastern Zhou texts, *yu* overwhelmingly predominates, except for historical texts, such as *Zuozhuan* (218 *yu* vs. 124 *ji*) or *Discourses of the States* (50 *yu* vs. 29 *ji*), in which the usage is more balanced.[23] In *Xinian*, like in other historical texts, both particles are used in the meaning of "with" or "and" with similar frequency (15 *yu* vs. 14 *ji*).[24] Yet what is more interesting is that the particles are unevenly divided among the different sections of *Xinian*. In table 2.2, I calculate their distinct appearance in the meaning of "with" and "and" in the sections coming from Zhou, Jin, and Chu (in addition to the mixed Jin-Chu section 18).

TABLE 2.2
Distribution of *ji* and *yu* particles in *Xinian*

	Zhou	**Jin**	**Jin-Chu**	**Chu**
ji 及	1	9	3	1
yu 與	1	3	-	11

Leaving aside the mixed Chu-Jin section in which the origin of *Xinian* sources cannot be clearly established, we find that nine of eleven cases of *ji* come from the Jin sections, while eleven out of fifteen cases of *yu* come from the Chu sections. The similarity to the preponderance of *yu* in unearthed Chu manuscripts becomes obvious. It is highly likely that this peculiar distribution reflects to some extent the grammatical preferences of *Xinian*'s sources.

Another notable peculiarity of *Xinian*'s language is the usage of the three sequential particles *nai* 乃, *sui* 遂, and *yan* 焉 synonymously in the meaning of "then" or "thereupon." Of these three particles, *nai* (sometimes written 廼) appeared as a sequential particle as early as in the Shang oracle-bone inscriptions, although by the Warring States period its usage as a sequential particle had declined markedly.[25] *Yan* is less frequently used to indicate time sequence; Li Meiyan has even opined that it may reflect a peculiar Chu usage (although, in my view, Li's study does not prove this point).[26] *Sui* is the most common sequential particle from the Warring States period onward. In *Xinian* all three particles are used, with a slightly higher frequency of *nai* (thirty-eight occurrences) over *sui* and *yan* (fifteen and thirteen occurrences, respectively). In addition, *Xinian* contains the rather peculiar expression *yan shi* 焉始 (then, for the first time), which marks novel political developments; this compound is extremely rare in the transmitted texts but appears in *Xinian* no fewer than seven times.[27] Yet for my study the most significant point is that the usage of *nai* (if not of other sequential particles) appears to be related to the geographical provenance of each section.

TABLE 2.3
Geographic distribution of *nai*, *sui*, and *yan* particles in *Xinian*

	Zhou	**Jin**	**Jin-Chu**	**Chu**
nai 乃	14	17	–	7
sui 遂	1	5	2	7
yan 焉	2	3	–	8
yan shi 焉始	2	4	–	1

Once again the differences are marked. Of thirty-eight *nai* particles, thirty-one are used in the Zhou and Jin sections. In contrast, the *sui* and *yan* particles are more evenly distributed, although in both cases their frequency in Chu sections is higher than elsewhere. However, the different usage of both particles may be less related to the geographic provenance of the source materials and more related to their dating. Let us divide the text into two more more-or or-less even parts that narrate history before and after 600 BCE. Part 1 comprises sections 1–12 (sixty-two slips); a slightly larger part 2 contains sections 13–23 (seventy-six slips). The results are given in table 2.4.

TABLE 2.4
Temporal distribution of *nai*, *sui*, and *yan* particles in *Xinian*

	Sections 1-12	Sections 13-23
nai 乃	36	2
sui 遂	7	8
yan 焉	8	5
yan shi 焉始	4	3

The results are unequivocal for *nai*: it dominates the early sections of *Xinian*, but then it almost disappears. In the case of *yan* the contraction is relatively minor, whereas *sui* is distributed more or less evenly throughout the text. Notably, however, *sui* appears only once in the Western Zhou sections (1–4), which are overwhelmingly dominated by *nai* (fourteen occurrences). It is tempting to suggest that *sui* became a natural replacer for *nai* and *yan* (both of which may have become too diversified semantically to be employed usefully as sequential particles).[28] Whether or not this is the pattern remains to be discussed by specialists of ancient Chinese grammar; for the current discussion, suffice it to conclude that the distribution of the particles in *Xinian* does not appear to be haphazard.

Another interesting example of uneven temporal distribution of particles in *Xinian* is the usage of locative *yu* 于/於 particles in the text. In what resembles *Zuozhuan*'s usage, *Xinian* transcribes the locative *yu* both with a "solemn" 于 and with a more "colloquial" 於 (eighty vs. fifty-four times).[29] This again distinguishes *Xinian* markedly from both excavated Warring States manuscripts and transmitted texts of that period, which overwhelmingly prefer the "newer" 於.[30] Yet the most interesting aspect of these particles' distribution is that in a notable resemblance to *Zuozhuan*, the "older" *yu* 于 predominates in the earlier sections of *Xinian* (twenty-eight 于 versus one 於 in sections 1–4 that deal with the Western Zhou, twenty-two slips), whereas the "newer" 於 is much more visible in the later part of the text (nineteen 於 versus five 于 in sections 21–23, altogether twenty-five slips). Notably, the substitution takes place in grammatically identical structures such as "to do battle at" (戰于/於) or "to make a covenant at" (盟于/於); thus, the distinction between the two particles is clearly temporal. Moreover, when the "solemn" 于 appears in the latter sections of the text, it invariably comes from the segments that seem to quote Chu court chronicles or related sources; that is, precisely those materials that are prone to use more dignified and ritualized language.

The cumulative impact of these patterns cannot be ignored. The differences in the distribution of grammatical particles in *Xinian* unequivocally support the authenticity of the text. It is inconceivable that a forger—sophisticated as he or she might be—would be able to reconstruct linguistic changes or barely noticeable geographic differences in the Zhou language. Taken together with the verso lines phenomenon (which, again, could not have been known to a forger in 2006 or 2007 when the future Tsinghua University bamboo slips appeared on the antiquity market), it suggests that *Xinian* is an authentic Warring States–period text.

Preliminary as they inevitably are, these findings raise two important issues related to the nature of *Xinian*. First, they further confirm that the authors of *Xinian* compiled their narrative from earlier sources, which were written at different times and at different locations in the Zhou world. Whereas the authors conceivably unified the language of their sources to conform to contemporaneous norms, they may have left it unchanged whenever two or more usages were acceptable. Second, the differences in the particles' distribution suggest that *Xinian* was composed primarily from written sources. Although the text did incorporate oral materials as well, written transmission will have predominated; otherwise such peculiarities as temporal changes in identically used *yu* particles would be difficult to explain.[31] Note that paleographic observations lend further support to this conclusion. For instance, Li Shoukui observes clear differences between the characters' shape in the first four sections of *Xinian* (the Western Zhou sections) and their shape in the rest of the narrative. This peculiarity evidently reflects a different source material for the early sections. A similar observation, mutatis mutandis, may explain the relatively frequent occurrence of the so-called Jin-style characters in many other sections of *Xinian*.[32]

Xinian and *Zuozhuan*

One of the most notable features of *Xinian* is the considerable overlap between its narratives in sections 5–19 (and segments of sections 2, 4, and 20) and those in *Zuozhuan*. By comparing these two texts we can reach a better understanding of their primary sources and of the different utilization of these sources by the texts' authors. In what follows I compare three sections of *Xinian* with *Zuozhuan* narratives. For the comparison I have chosen one short, one medium, and one long section; two of the sections focus on the state of Chu, and one on Jin. The sections are 5, 6, and 15.

Xinian 5: *Chu, Cai, and Xi*

Let us start with a short one. Section 5 of *Xinian* is the first one in the text that focuses on the affairs of the state of Chu. It revolves around a short anecdote that tells about the quarrel between the leaders of two neighboring polities, Cai 蔡 and Xi 息, both of which belonged to the royal Ji 姬 clan. The quarrel between them, which started with Marquis Ai of Cai's 蔡哀侯 (r. 694–675 BCE) abuse of his sister-in-law, Xi Gui 息嬀, the Marquis of Xi's wife, gave King Wen of Chu 楚文王 (r. 689–675 BCE) the chance both to eliminate Xi and to attack Cai, triggering the lengthy process of Cai's subjugation to Chu. The *Zuozhuan* version comprises two parts (told under the years 684 and 680 BCE, Zhuang 10.3 and 14.3). For the sake of convenience, I divided the *Xinian* anecdote into two parallel parts as well, the first of which will be directly compared with *Zuozhuan*[33] (see table 2.5 on p. 50).

The similarity between the two narratives is obvious. The differences are minor: thus, *Xinian* indicates clearly that the Marquis of Cai "wived"—that is, committed adultery with his sister-in-law—whereas in *Zuozhuan*, it is replaced by the euphemism that the Marquis of Cai "did not treat her as a guest" (弗賓). Elsewhere, *Zuozhuan* tells of the Marquis of Xi being "angry" (怒) at his adulterous brother-in-law, whereas *Xinian* uses the peculiar term 弗順, "to consider somebody incompliant," or, more precisely, "to bear a grudge against somebody"; this usage is attested elsewhere in *Xinian* (section 15). Furthermore, echoing the *Spring and Autumn Annals*, *Zuozhuan* provides a date for Marquis Ai's capture and informs of his personal name; these details seem to be of little interest to the *Xinian* compilers, who, uncharacteristically, do not even provide a precise year for the depicted event. Yet minor discrepancies aside, it is clear that both narratives derive from a single source: otherwise, their similarities cannot be properly explained.

TABLE 2.5
Xinian 5 and *Zuozhuan* compared

Xinian 5, slips 23–26	Zuozhuan, Zhuang 10.3
蔡哀侯取妻於陳，息侯亦取妻於陳，是息媯。息媯將歸于息，過蔡，蔡哀侯命止之，曰：「以同姓之故，必入。」息媯乃入于蔡，蔡哀侯妻之。息侯弗順，乃使人于楚文王曰：「君來伐我，我將求救於蔡，君焉敗之。」文王起師伐息，息侯求救於蔡，蔡哀侯率師以救息，文王敗之於莘，獲哀侯以歸。	蔡哀侯娶于陳，息侯亦娶焉。息媯將歸，過蔡。蔡侯曰：「吾姨也。」止而見之，弗賓。息侯聞之，怒，使謂楚文王曰：「伐我，吾求救於蔡而伐之。」楚子從之。秋，九月，楚敗蔡師于莘，以蔡侯獻舞歸。
Marquis Ai of Cai took a wife in Chen. The Marquis of Xi also took a wife in Chen, who was Xi Gui. When Xi Gui was going to be married, she passed through Cai. Marquis Ai of Cai ordered her to be stopped, saying, "Since she is from the same family [as my wife], she must enter [the city]." Xi Gui then entered into Cai, and Marquis Ai of Cai "wived" her. The Marquis of Xi considered [Marquis Ai] incompliant; then he sent a messenger to King Wen of Chu, saying, "My lord should come and attack us; we shall seek help from Cai, and you can thereupon defeat them." King Wen raised an army and attacked Xi, and Marquis Ai of Cai led his army to save Xi. King Wen defeated him at Shen and captured Marquis Ai of Cai, returning with him.	Marquis Ai of Cai took a wife in Chen. The Marquis of Xi also took a wife there. When Xi Gui was going to be married, she passed through Cai. The Marquis of Cai said, "She is my sister-in-law." He stopped her and met with her, but he did not treat her as a guest. When the Marquis of Xi heard this, he was angry and sent someone to tell King Wen of Chu, "Attack us, and when we seek help from Cai, then attack them." The Viscount of Chu[1] acted accordingly. **In autumn, in the ninth month, Chu defeated the Cai troops at Shen. They captured Xianwu, Marquis of Cai, returning with him.**[2]

[1] Note that *Zuozhuan* refers to Chu kings variously by their native title, "king," and by their official title in the Zhou hierarchy, *zi* 子, "viscount."

[2] The sentences in boldface cite the *Spring and Autumn Annals* (*Chunqiu*, Zhuang 10.5). The only difference is that in the *Annals*, Chu is referred to by its alternative name, Jing 荊.

The second part of the *Xinian* story also parallels *Zuozhuan*, but the discrepancies here are much more visible, hence I focus on the *Xinian* text alone:

> King Wen was a guest at Xi, and the Marquis of Cai accompanied him. The Marquis of Xi was serving ale to King Wen. The Marquis of Cai knew that he had been lured by the Marquis of Xi; hence he told King Wen, "The wife of the Marquis of Xi is extraordinarily beautiful; my lord must demand to see her." King Wen ordered her to be shown to him. The Marquis of Xi refused, but the king insistently ordered her to be shown to him. Having seen her, he went back [to Chu]. The next year, he raised an army and invaded Xi. He overpowered it, killed the Marquis of Xi, and took Xi Gui with him to return. She [eventually] gave birth to Du'ao and [the future] King Cheng.
>
> Thanks to this, King Wen opened lands northward beyond Fangcheng, advanced, and acquired [territories up] to the Ru River, trained his armies near Chen, and thereupon seized Dun so as to overawe the Marquis of Chen.

The story in the first paragraph here parallels *Zuozhuan*, but it differs in one notable detail. Both texts agree that Marquis Ai of Cai instigated Chu's attack against Xi by enticing King Wen with the intention of obtaining Xi Gui. Yet in *Zuozhuan*, this was done during Marquis Ai's stay in Chu's custody, whereas in *Xinian* this happens immediately after Marquis Ai's capture. The difference is minor, but it has chronological ramifications: *Xinian* suggests that the attack on Xi took place a year after an attack on Cai (i.e., in 683 BCE), whereas *Zuozhuan* places it in the immediate vicinity of Chu's renewed attack on Cai in 680 BCE. This raises the interesting possibility that the *Zuozhuan* authors deliberately manipulated their sources, transposing the story of the elimination of Xi to the year 680 BCE so as to emphasize its connection with Chu's renewed incursion into Cai in that year.[34] This enabled them to make the two events closely related, strengthening thereby the didactic message, which criticized the Marquis of Cai's perfidy. This message is duly emphasized in the comments of the "noble man" (probably the author/compiler of *Zuozhuan*) attached to the story of Xi's annihilation.[35]

Aside from the moralizing summary by the "noble man," the *Zuozhuan* version of the events contains another segment that is absent from the *Xinian* version. It tells of the tragic life of Xi Gui as a Chu captive: despite winning King Wen's favor, she refused to speak, as a self-imposed punishment for serving two husbands. The story, later embellished in the *Springs and Autumns of Sire Lü* (*Lüshi chunqiu* 呂氏春秋) and *Biographies of Exemplary Women* (*Lienü zhuan* 列女傳), became a celebrated topic for admirers of female chastity.[36] In *Xinian* it is not mentioned at all. Neither Xi Gui's morality nor the self-destructive machinations of the rulers of Xi and Cai merit praise or blame; the focus of the narration clearly lies elsewhere. This focus is fully revealed in the last phrase of the story (which does not exist in *Zuozhuan* and evidently reflects a distinctive Chu perspective): the Cai-Xi intrigue served as a springboard for Chu's expansion beyond the Fangcheng 方城 defensive line into the Ru 汝 River valley.[37] It is this aspect—and only this aspect—that matters to *Xinian*'s authors.

One final point merits our attention. Both *Xinian* 5 and the *Zuozhuan* story of the elimination of Xi contain a phrase that identifies Xi Gui as the mother of two kings of Chu, Du'ao 堵敖 (r. 675–672 BCE) and King Cheng 楚成王 (r. 672–626 BCE). This phrase suggests that the anecdote as we have it in both texts was finalized no earlier than 626 BCE (by which time King Cheng's posthumous name would have been known). It enhances the possibility that it was incorporated into *Xinian* and *Zuozhuan* not from a stand-alone version but from a lengthier Chu history. I return to this point in this and the next chapters.

Xinian 6: Lord Wen of Jin

The preceding comparison between the *Xinian* 5 and *Zuozhuan* accounts strongly suggests the existence of a common third source for both texts. To check this supposition, let us turn now to longer *Xinian* sections. These normally do not parallel *Zuozhuan* but rather compress its (or, more accurately, its sources') materials into a very condensed narrative. Section 6 is the first in a series of narratives focusing on the rise of Jin, its rivalry with Chu, and its relations with other major polities of the age, Qin and Qi. The section tells the story of the most illustrious Jin leader, Ducal Son Chong'er 公子重耳, posthumously known as Lord Wen 晉文公 (r. 636–628 BCE). It starts with the succession struggles in Jin instigated by Chong'er's stepmother, Li Ji 驪姬. Then the text turns to the rule of Chong'er's half-brother, Lord Hui 晉惠公 (r. 650–637 BCE), who was installed by Lord Mu of Qin 秦穆公 (r. 659–621 BCE) but then betrayed and alienated his erstwhile patron. *Xinian* briefly narrates the story of Chong'er's lengthy exile, during which he wandered through the courts of powerful states, seeking support, until finally finding a receptive patron, Lord Mu of Qin, who installed Chong'er in Jin. The section ends with a brief depiction of the nascent Jin-Qin alliance.

The events covered in *Xinian* 6 span twenty years (656–635 BCE). These years are thickly covered in *Zuozhuan* (and the parallel *Discourses of the States*). The depiction of these events, full of folly and wisdom, of treachery and loyalty, of machinations and self-sacrifice, forms one of the major literary masterpieces in *Zuozhuan*. Moralizing speeches of major protagonists provide evaluations of the events and highlight the complexity of the individuals' moral choices; a series of predictions help us to follow the story as it unfolds; and the occasional comments of the narrator (the "noble man") assist us in judging the personages' behavior.[38] In contrast, the *Xinian* narrative is marked by its brevity. Let us focus on the opening sentences of *Xinian* 6, which narrate the unfolding crisis:

> The favorite concubine of Lord Xian of Jin was called Li Ji. She wanted to make her son, Xiqi, ruler. Thereupon she slandered the crown prince, Lord Gong, and caused him to be killed.[39] She also slandered Lord Hui and Lord Wen. Lord Wen fled to the Di, Lord Hui fled to Liang. Lord Xian died, and thereupon Xiqi was established. Its [Jin's] grandee, Ke of Li (Li Ke), thereupon killed Xiqi, and [Li Ji] established Xiqi's younger brother, Daozi (Zhuozi). Ke of Li killed Daozi as well.

This account leaves us with the skeleton of the events, eliminating all their entertaining and moralizing aspects. Gone are the stories of Li Ji's machinations, of the filial self-sacrifice by Crown Prince Shensheng (Lord Gong), and of the moral dilemmas facing the Jin ministers, who time and again had to consider to what they owed loyalty: the will of Lord Xian 晉獻公 (r. 676–651 BCE), who wanted his younger son from Li Ji to be enthroned, or the best interests of their state, which meant that an elder scion (either future Lord Hui or future Lord Wen) should be installed.[40] At times, the abridgement comes at a price. Take, for instance, the sentence "Ke of Li (Li Ke) thereupon killed Xiqi, and [Li Ji] established Xiqi's younger brother, Daozi" (里之克乃殺奚齊，而立其弟悼子). The omission of the second subject (Li Ji) may create a gross misunderstanding: the sentence can easily be read as if Li Ke were the one to establish Daozi (aka Zhuozi 卓子). This, however, is surely wrong: as the next sentence shows, and as is narrated in *Zuozhuan* and elsewhere, it was Li Ji who tried to install her sister's son, Daozi, and it was Li Ke who murdered the young prince. Maybe a Chu scribe considered the story too well known to bother himself with grammatical accuracy in producing its abridged version.

So if neither entertainment nor moral lessons mattered to the *Xinian* compilers, what did? The answer, as is common in *Xinian*, appears in the last sentences of the section. They tell, "Thenceforth, Qin and Jin became friendly, uniting in concerted efforts. The two countries invaded Ruo, relocating it to the Central Area. They laid siege to Shangmi, and captured Ziyi, Duke of Shen, returning with him." Putting details aside (for which see the glosses to the translation of that section in part 2 of this book), the story focuses on the formation of the Jin-Qin alliance, directed against Chu (which was the victim of the allies' attack). The rise and fall of this alliance and its impact on Chu occupy much of sections 7–10 of *Xinian*. All the rest is simply a background story.

Xinian 15: *Chu and Wu*

Stylistic differences aside, the factual skeleton of the events presented in *Xinian* 6 is fundamentally identical to *Zuozhuan*. Whenever factual differences occur (such as in the potential reading of the mentioned sentence as referring to Li Ke as installer rather than murderer of Daozi), they come invariably from flaws in the events' abridgment by *Xinian* authors.[41] Does this mean that the *Xinian* authors abridged the *Zuozhuan* account directly? Before attempting an answer to this question, let us analyze a longer section of *Xinian*, 15, which narrates Chu's evolving conflict with the rising eastern power, the state of Wu. The narrative comprises two parts. The first (spanning 613–584 BCE, segments 1–6 in table 2.6) focuses on a Chu minister, Qu Wuchen 屈巫臣 (or Qu Wu), the Duke (i.e., governor) of Shen County 申公, whom a series of complex intrigues brought from Chu to Jin and then to Wu, where he fostered the Jin-Wu anti-Chu alliance. The second part (segments 7–12) traces the escalation of the Chu-Wu

TABLE 2.6
Xinian 15 and *Zuo zhuan* compared

	Xinian 15	**Zuo zhuan**
1	When King Zhuang of Chu ascended the throne (613 BCE), **Wu was submissive to Chu**.	No mention of Wu's erstwhile submission. In 600 BCE, Chu made the first covenant with Wu and Yue (Xuan 8.3).
2	**Ducal Son Zhengshu** of Chen **took as wife** a daughter of Lord Mu of Zheng named Shao Kong.	Xuan 9.6 and 10.4. Zhengshu was not a ducal son but either great-grandson or grandson. Whether he was Shao Kong's husband or her son is debatable.
3	In the **fifteenth** year of King Zhuang (599 BCE), Ducal Son Zhengshu of Chen killed his ruler, Lord Ling. King Zhuang led an army and laid siege to Chen.	Xuan 10.4 and 11.5. *Xinian* does not tell that Lord Ling of Chen was one of Shao Kong's paramours. The siege of Chen occurred in the sixteenth (not fifteenth) year of King Zhuang.
4	**The King ordered the Duke of Shen, Qu Wu, to go to Qin and ask for troops, and getting the troops, [Qu Wu] returned**.	No traces of this information elsewhere.
5	The King entered the Chen [capital], killed Zhengshu, took his wife and gave her to the Duke of Shen. *Lianyin* Xiang the Elder contended with [the Duke of Shen] and seized Shao Kong. When *lianyin* Xiang the Elder was captured at Heyong, his son, Heiyao, also married Shao Kong.	Xuan 11.5 and Cheng 2.6: minor discrepancies but fundamentally the same narrative.

(continued)

TABLE 2.6 (continued)

	Xinian 15	Zuo zhuan
6	When King Zhuang passed away and King Gong ascended the throne (590 BCE), Heiyao **died**, and Marshal Zifan contended with the Duke of Shen for Shao Kong. The Duke of Shen said: "This is the wife I was given [by King Zhuang]," and married her. The Marshal considered the Duke of Shen incompliant. When the King ordered the Duke of Shen to go on a visit to Qi, the Duke of Shen secretly carried Shao Kong off and left. From Qi thereupon he escaped to Jin, from Jin he went to Wu, thereby facilitating routes of communication between Wu and Jin, and teaching the men of Wu to oppose Chu.	Cheng 2.6 and 7.5 with minor discrepancies in details (most notably: **Heiyao was killed** by Marshal Zifan in 584 BCE and did not merely "die"). Xinian account is also paralleled in Guoyu 17.4 ("Chu yu 楚語 1"). The major omission in Xinian is that **Marshal Zifan massacred the family of Qu Wu** after the latter moved to Jin; this triggered Qu's vengeance and his subsequent commitment to strengthening Jin-Wu ties.
7	Coming to the time of King Ling [of Chu, r. 540-529 BCE], King Ling invaded Wu. He undertook the Nanhuai expedition, seized the Royal Son Jueyou of Wu, and **thereafter the people of Wu again submitted to Chu**.	The Nanhuai expedition and the capturing of Jueyou are narrated in Zhao 5.8; but from Zuo zhuan it is clear that this campaign did not put an end to Chu-Wu hostilities.
8	When King Ling passed away, King Jingping [aka King Ping] ascended the throne (528 BCE). Junior Preceptor [Fei] Wuji slandered lianyin [Wu 伍] She and had him killed. She's sons, Wu Yun, and **Ji of Wu [Wu Ji]** fled and submitted to [the state of] Wu 吳.	Fei Wuji's plot and the killing of Wu She are narrated in Zhao 19.2 and 20.2. There is no mention of Wu Ji who allegedly accompanied Wu Yun (Wu Zixu) to exile in Wu.

TABLE 2.6 (continued)

	Xinian 15	Zuo zhuan
9	**Wu Ji** 伍雞 **led the men of Wu** 吳 **to lay siege on Zhoulai, digging a lengthy moat and filling it with water so as to defeat the Chu army; this is the Moat of Ji's Father.**	The campaign is recorded in Zhao 23.5 (and *Chunqiu*, Zhao 23.7); but Wu Ji is not mentioned there.
10	When King Jingping passed away, King Zhao ascended the throne (516 BCE). Wu Yun became **the grand steward** of Wu; he taught Wu how to cause uprisings among the regional lords [allied with] Chu. Thus he defeated the Chu army at Boju and thereupon entered [the Chu capital,] Ying.	Zhao 30.4 for Wu Zixu's (Wu Yun's) plotting against Chu; Ding 4.3 for Wu's major invasion, the Boju campaign, and capture of Ying. Wu Zixu's position as Wu's grand steward (*taizai* 太宰) is disputed.[1]
11	King Zhao escaped to Sui; and **he fought** the Wu forces at Yi.	Ding 4.3 and 5.5. The battle at Yi was led not by King Zhao but by the **alliance of Chu and Qin** forces.
12	Royal Son Chen of Wu was about to rebel and make trouble for Wu: King Helu of Wu then had to return, and King Zhao thus recovered his state.	Ding 5.5. *Zuo zhuan* emphasizes that the major reason for Wu's withdrawal was its defeat by the **allied forces of Chu and Qin**.

[1] *Zuozhuan* clearly says that Wu Zixu acted as a diplomat, whereas the grand steward position was occupied by Bo Pi. For the attempt to reconcile both texts, see Liu Guang 2017b.

conflict from 537 to 505 BCE, culminating with the brief occupation of the Chu capital, Ying, by Wu invaders. The chief protagonist of this part is Wu Yun 伍員 (better known as Wu Zixu 伍子胥, d. 484 BCE), a son of a senior Chu official, Wu She 伍奢. After Wu She fell victim to a court intrigue in Chu, Wu Zixu fled to the state of Wu, where he eventually masterminded the defeat of Chu.[42] To facilitate the comparison with

Zuozhuan, I subdivided *Xinian* 15 into smaller narrative segments. In table 2.6, I present these twelve narrative segments of *Xinian* 15; for each I provide the *Zuozhuan* parallel and indicate in boldface major discrepancies between the *Xinian* and *Zuozhuan* narratives.

Table 2.6 (pp. 55–57) highlights once again the considerable overlap between the *Zuozhuan* and *Xinian* accounts; yet there are several notable discrepancies between the two. Some of these are minor. For example, *Xinian* identifies Shao Kong, better known under the name Xia Ji 夏姬, as Xia Zhengshu's wife and not his mother (segment 2). The latter identification, which has been the common one, is based not on direct evidence but on the juxtaposition of narratives in *Zuozhuan* and in *Discourses of the States*. If Xia Ji were Zhengshu's mother, this would make her the ultimate age-defying femme fatale, which, indeed, is her image in later texts.[43] *Xinian*, in contrast, "normalizes" her. Interesting as it is, this discrepancy is of minor importance for *Xinian*'s narrative focus on Chu-Wu relations. Other minor discrepancies may derive from *Xinian*'s inaccuracy with regard to such details as Xia Zhengshu's identification as a ducal son (segment 2), or details of plots in Chu that accompanied the contest for Xia Ji's favors (segments 5–6). Once again, the importance of these details in the given context is minuscule. *Xinian* also contains some disputable statements (in segments 1 and 7) that postulate Wu's erstwhile submission to Chu. These statements deviate from the *Zuozhuan* accounts, but the difference relates to the interpretation of "submissiveness" and is not consequential. Whenever major details are concerned, both texts clearly present a similar picture.

Xinian's abridgment of a series of lengthy narratives into slightly more than four hundred characters results in the inevitable omission of certain details that could have shed more light on the actions of major protagonists. For instance, Xia Ji's adultery in the state of Chen, which caused her husband (or son) Xia Zhengshu to murder Lord Ling, is not mentioned. Nor does the text refer to the massacre of Qu Wu's family in Chu, which reportedly was the major reason for turning him into Chu's bitterest enemy. Also, certain details of Wu Zixu's story that could have explained his extraordinary resentment of Chu are absent from *Xinian*. In literary terms these details are surely important, but as has been noted, *Xinian* is concerned neither with entertaining its readers nor with providing moral lessons. Its focus is purely political, and from this point of view the omissions are acceptable.

Of more interest for us may be two cases of information provided in *Xinian* 15 that have no parallels in *Zuozhuan* or elsewhere. These are the story of Qu Wu's mission to Qin to seek support against Chen in 598 BCE, and the exploits of Wu Zixu's brother, Wu Ji (or, as he is named in the text, Ji of Wu 伍之雞).⁴⁴ In both cases I believe, pace Li Xueqin's editorial team, this information is wrong, stemming from the *Xinian* authors' carelessness. In the first case, it is highly improbable that Chu would seek Qin's assistance against Chen, not only because Chen was located far from Qin but mostly because Chu's invasion of Chen was ultimately unopposed and did not require significant coalition building. In my opinion, it is likely that the authors of *Xinian* conflated Qu Wu, the Duke of Shen 申, with the Chu messenger, Shen Baoxu 申包胥, who was indeed dispatched to Qin to seek assistance against Wu in 506 BCE.⁴⁵ As for Ji of Wu, I fully accept Ziju's assertion that this figure is based on the popular etymology of the name of the battlefield where Chu armies were defeated by their Wu adversaries in 519 BCE, Rooster's (or Ji's) Father (雞父).⁴⁶ The place-name, recorded in the *Spring and Autumn Annals* (Zhao 23.7), doubtless existed before the Wu battle against Chu, but later it might have become associated with Wu Zixu's revenge for his father's death in Chu custody. Since the place-name could not be meaningfully associated with Zixu himself, his new brother was invented. It is highly unlikely that such an important personage, if he ever existed, would have evaded the attention of the countless historians and literati who retold Wu Zixu's story, turning it into one of the best-known narratives from the late Spring and Autumn period.⁴⁷

Let us leave aside the issue of *Xinian*'s historical accuracy and try to clarify first its relation to *Zuozhuan* and, second, its authors' utilization of their primary sources. With regard to the first question it is very tempting to assume that the *Xinian* authors utilized the *Zuozhuan* narrative, compressing it to present an account focused on the events that interested them. Should this observation be correct, it would help in dating *Zuozhuan*, but I doubt its veracity. First, not all the discrepancies between the two texts can be attributed merely to the carelessness of the *Xinian* abridgers (which may be the case, e.g., in section 6). In some cases (e.g., in section 5) it is likely that the *Xinian* authors possessed an alternative source for the depicted events. A few other instances in which *Xinian* provides what appears to be accurate information that does not exist in *Zuozhuan* strengthen this point.⁴⁸ Second, the fact that *Xinian* never uses the Lu chronology applied by *Zuozhuan* but rather chronologies of Jin and Chu suggests that direct borrowing from *Zuozhuan* is unlikely. It is much more plausible that the *Xinian* authors used local histories prepared by Jin, Chu, and possibly Zhou scribes, which were also utilized by *Zuozhuan* compilers. Thus, both texts may share common primary sources instead of being directly related.

What did *Xinian*'s (and, by inference, *Zuozhuan*'s) sources look like? Some, like that in section 5, could be short didactic anecdotes, which have been identified by David Schaberg as the building blocks of early Chinese historical texts.[49] Nevertheless, even in the case of *Xinian* 5, I believe that the anecdote was incorporated not from a stand-alone story but from a larger narrative history. In other cases, the borrowing from longer narratives is self-evident. These narratives (a Jin one for section 6, a Chu one for section 15) appear as systematic introductions to the polity's history. In *Zuozhuan* these individual histories of different polities became intertwined, blurring their original form; but from comparison between *Xinian* 6 and 15 and *Zuozhuan*, their nature can be understood with greater clarity. It seems that the Jin and Chu histories, which were utilized for both texts, were quite detailed with regard to both domestic and foreign affairs. *Zuozhuan* preserved many of these details, or perhaps added more from other sources or from the authors' imagination, whereas the *Xinian* authors abridged them and preserved the factual skeleton with a focus on foreign relations. Yet the fact that this skeleton is almost identical to one we could create by abridging relevant narratives from *Zuozhuan* indicates that both texts worked with the same source material. This observation strengthens my assertion from chapter 1 that the *Zuozhuan* compiler(s) operated primarily with lengthy narrative histories from the Spring and Autumn polities; I return to this point below (pp. 64–65). But before drawing conclusions, can we learn more about the nature of *Xinian*'s primary sources? To answer this question, let us jump to the last sections of *Xinian*.

Xinian Sources

The last two sections of *Xinian* (22–23) are more detailed than the earlier ones. They dedicate, quite uncharacteristically, three to four bamboo slips to the events of each year and provide less evidence of radical abridgment than observed in sections 6 and 15. Perhaps insofar as these sections were prepared not long after the occurrence of the reported events, the authors remained reluctant to decide which details were less relevant than others and preferred to retain larger chunks of the original narrative. This allows us to get a better glimpse of *Xinian*'s original sources than is possible in earlier sections.

One of the notable features of the last two sections is the appearance of several phrases that differ stylistically from the rest of the narrative in these sections. I provide two examples:

晉公獻齊俘馘於周王，遂以齊侯貸、魯侯羴（顯）、宋公田、衛侯虔、鄭伯駘朝周王于周。

The Duke of Jin presented the Qi captives and the severed ears [of slain Qi soldiers] to the King of Zhou and then attended the Zhou royal court, bringing with him the Marquis of Qi, Dai; the Marquis of Lu, Xian; the Duke of Song, Tian; the Marquis of Wei [衛], Qian; and the Earl of Zheng, Tai. (*Xinian* 22, slips 124–25)

楚聲桓王立四年，宋公田、鄭伯駘皆朝于楚。

In the fourth year of King Shenghuan (King Sheng) of Chu (401 BCE), the Duke of Song, Tian, and the Earl of Zheng, Tai, attended the Chu court. (*Xinian* 23, slip 126)

Two peculiarities distinguish these sentences from the rest of the narrative in sections 22–23. First is their usage of the "solemn" particle *yu* 于 rather than 於, which is used throughout the rest of both sections. This is not accidental: all five instances of the appearance of 于 in sections 21–23 come exclusively from reports on court visits or covenants.[50] Second, these sentences deviate from the common *Xinian* pattern of naming foreign rulers as lord (or, rarely, marquis) in addition to their posthumous names.[51] The sentences cited here, however, refer to the rulers according to their precise rank in the Zhou aristocratic hierarchy (duke, marquis, or earl) and their personal name. This highly unusual pattern has only one clear parallel in either received or unearthed texts, and that is the canonical *Spring and Autumn Annals* of the state of Lu (in addition to a few related sentences in *Zuozhuan*). It is highly likely that these designations in *Xinian* derive from the materials related to the court annals of the state of Chu, the existence of which is hinted in *Mengzi*.⁵² This observation is valuable by itself, as it provides us with an additional indication to the effect that annalistic tradition was a common feature of early Chinese historiography. Yet we can go a step further to get a deeper clue from the cited sentences regarding Chu historical texts (and by inference other local histories of the Eastern Zhou period).

This step requires a technical digression. The pattern of providing a ruler's official rank and his personal name does recur in the Lu *Annals*, but never in the context of routine reports about court visits and interstate covenants. Rather, the name appears only in extraordinary circumstances, such as the ruler's death, assassination, detention, and the like.⁵³ In routine records, the Lu *Annals* provide only the ruler's state affiliation and rank, whereas *Zuozhuan* normally replaces these with the posthumous designation of the given sovereign. If the Chu annalists followed the same rules of recording that their Lu colleagues did, then why do *Xinian*'s quasi-annalistic records refer to the foreign rulers by their personal names?

The most plausible scenario would be that these records did not come directly from the Chu court annals but rather from the draft materials prepared by the Chu scribes. Conceivably, the draft records had to identify foreign rulers by their individual names. In the official Chu annals, these personal names (the usage of which could be interpreted as a gross breach of decorum) would be omitted; in later historical records they would be substituted with the rulers' posthumous designations. However, when the *Xinian* authors collected source materials for their composition, the substitution of personal by posthumous names had not yet been done, possibly because some of the rulers mentioned in the records were still alive.⁵⁴ If my inferences are correct, this suggests that the draft records for the court annals were the primary raw material utilized by the Chu scribes in drafting the history of their state. Recall that in chapter 1 (pp. 27–29) the same pattern was observed with regard to some of the primary sources of *Zuozhuan*. It would not be far-fetched to conclude that the court scribes in charge of preparing the annals of their states routinely utilized their draft records to prepare detailed histories of their respective polities.

Elsewhere, another careless abridgment of the primary sources by *Xinian* compilers offers us one more glimpse into Chu's historical records. This happens in the last sentences of section 23. The narrative in section 23 focuses on the ups and downs of the Chu struggle with Jin and ends with the devastating defeat of the Chu armies near the fortress of

Wuyang 武陽. Yet having concluded the narrative, the authors add the following passage:

楚師將救武陽,【136】王命平夜悼武君李(使)人於齊陳淏求師。陳疾目率車千乘,以從楚師於武陽。甲戌,晉楚以【137】戰。丙子,齊師至嵒,遂還。【138】

When the Chu army was planning to go to rescue Wuyang, the king ordered Lord Daowu of Pingye to dispatch somebody to Chen Hao of Qi to request military help. Chen Jimu [of Qi] led one thousand chariots and followed the Chu army to Wuyang. On the day *jiaxu* (the eleventh day of the sexagenary cycle), Jin fought with Chu; on *bingzi* (the thirteenth day), the Qi army arrived at Nie and then turned back.

Putting details aside, let us focus on the peculiarity of these sentences. Uncharacteristically for *Xinian*, this appendix breaks the chronological framework of the narrative and goes back to the events that directly preceded the crushing defeat of the Chu armies at Wuyang. The addition might have been made to avoid the pessimistic ending of the text with a defeat that caused Chu soldiers to flee "like dogs" from the battlefield and that resulted in the "loss of many walled cities" by the Chu side (discussed further in chapter 5). Yet the appendix was not properly edited; hence it contains two dates of the sexagenary *ganzhi* 干支 cycle, which appear to be transmitted from a lengthier Chu history without being revised. Normally, as is seen from *Zuozhuan*, *ganzhi* dates are meaningful only when the month is provided, otherwise they do not allow an event to be dated.[55] It is technically possible, of course, that the two dates in the final slip were meant to show that the Qi army missed the battle by two days, but this goal could easily have been achieved without adding the *ganzhi* dating. It is more likely that the editors just transposed the dating from a Chu historical source without modifying it (in that case, the month could have been mentioned in one of the earlier phrases, abridged by *Xinian*'s author[s]). This carelessness is a blessing for us: it shows that meticulous dating of events, characteristic of *Zuozhuan* and its sources, was the rule in the Chu court histories as well.

With these observations in mind, we can now tentatively summarize what the source materials of *Xinian* looked like. These materials were likely to have been produced by the same court scribes who composed the official annals of the canonical Lu type but were incomparably more informative than the latter. These scribal records (*shiji* 史記), possibly akin to those destroyed following the Qin biblioclasm of 213 BCE,[56] may have been prepared for two reasons. First, as I argue in chapter 1, the scribes had to train their replacers to master the "rules of recording" (*shufa* 書法); that is, teach them to produce ritually correct records of events as related to their broader context. Second, and more important for the current discussion, the records could serve as the basis of longer historical narratives that provided members of the educated elite with knowledge of the history of their country and of their lineages. The resultant local histories of Chu and Jin served the compilers of both *Zuozhuan* and *Xinian*, which explains numerous parallels between the two texts. In the case of *Zuozhuan*, Jin and Chu histories were supplemented with similar local histories from Lu, Qi, Zheng, Song, and Wei 衛. *Xinian*, alternatively, added a few Western Zhou records.

What did the original local histories look like? First, they seem to have contained a wealth of details, such as personal and place-names, official titles, precise dates of narrated events, and the like; these details are preserved in many parts of *Zuozhuan* and are also found in *Xinian*—for example, in the appendix to section 23 discussed in the preceding. Second, local histories incorporated many other materials, such as anecdotes, real or imagined speeches by historical personalities, and similar. Some of these materials came from written sources, but others (such as, e.g., the story of Wu Ji, an imagined brother of Wu Zixu's) surely came from oral lore. Local histories were perhaps periodically updated, which allowed their compilers to add more narrative details, such as correct predictions of future events put into the mouths of worthy ministers and eminent scribes. And, of course, many colorful events, such as the exploits of Xia Ji/Shao Kong could be added or modified to entertain readers and to edify them.

The similarities between *Zuozhuan* and *Xinian* demonstrated in the previous section cannot be explained otherwise but by the fact that the authors of both texts operated with identical (or very similar) sets of local histories. Yet the differences between the two texts are no less instructive. *Xinian* is incomparably more laconic than *Zuozhuan*. Gone are minute details; gone are the speeches; gone are predictions; gone are entertaining aspects of history. All is subordinated to the political focus: narrating the evolution of Chu's foreign relations from the rise of this state in the early years of Eastern Zhou and to the first years of King Dao.

If my analysis is correct, then it lends considerable credibility to both the *Xinian* and the *Zuozhuan* accounts. That two distinct texts extracted from their original sources very similar presentations of both individual events (e.g., *Xinian* 5) and lengthy historical narratives (e.g., *Xinian* 6 and *Xinian* 15) suggests that neither introduced radical modifications to their source materials. Differences of emphases do exist, as are analyzed in chapter 5, but overall the existence of a common factual skeleton in both texts proves that both the spirit and often even the wording of the original source were faithfully preserved. This observation alone is highly valuable for those who are interested in the history—and not only the historiography—of preimperial China. But in the context of the current chapter, I prefer to conclude with a few observations about the nature of *Xinian* and its potential audience.

The Nature and Audience of *Xinian*

My selected comparison between the *Xinian* and *Zuozhuan* narratives may serve as a good starting point for analyzing *Xinian* in general. That this text lacks *Zuozhuan*'s abundance of minute details is not surprising; after all, the size of *Xinian* is just about 3 percent of that of *Zuozhuan*. Yet what matters more is that the abridgement of *Zuozhuan* sources performed by *Xinian* authors differs markedly from similar abridgments in, for instance, *Discourses of the States* or later anecdotal collections. If my analysis of these sources as repositories of both detailed information and a variety of interpretative devices is correct, then the conclusion would be that *Discourses of the States* and its like were less interested in the former, whereas *Xinian* abridged the latter. Gone are moralizing speeches; absent are predictions; lacking are stories of ghosts and deities; omitted is preoccupation with ritual correctness. Heaven and the Lord on High (Shangdi 上帝) do appear in the first section of *Xinian*, which duly narrates the Zhou seizure of the Shang mandate, but disappear completely thereafter. In general, drawing lessons from history does not seem to be the priority of *Xinian* authors.

Nor do the authors strive to entertain their readers. We do encounter from time to time dramatic personages and events that occupy pride of place in *Zuozhuan* and elsewhere, but these personages' exploits are deemphasized. The adulteries of Li Ji or Xia Ji, the thorny exile experience of Lord Wen of Jin, the treachery and self-sacrifice of Jin and Chu ministers—all these are outlined with such brevity and lack of interest in details that most if not all their dramatic effects are missing.

Nor does *Xinian* appear as a piece of Chu propaganda disguised as a historical text. Although its pro-Chu bias can be deduced from the consistent avoidance of reporting about Chu's domestic troubles, insofar as Chu's relations with Jin and other polities are concerned, the narrative sounds very much neutral and devoid of any pro-Chu partiality. There is one instance in which *Xinian* 16 seems to adopt a markedly more pro-Chu stance than *Zuozhuan* (as discussed in chapter 5, pp. 139–41), but this is an exception, and even in that case the pro-Chu bias is minor. Overall, the text is much more concerned with narrating facts than with their interpretation.

Xinian is clearly closer to the genre of informative rather than interpretative history. Notwithstanding its omission of minute details, cases of careless abridgement of earlier sources,[57] and minor factual inaccuracies, overall the text excels in presenting a concise and readable version of the history of the Zhou world. Take as an example *Xinian* 15. Its brief and energetic narrative tells in a nutshell the story of Chu's conflict with Wu. This story is told not for its moral or entertaining qualities but in order to provide working knowledge for a reader who wanted to be quickly informed about historical changes in Chu's geostrategic situation. This account is highly informative and, insofar as we can judge from other sources, fairly reliable.

What was, then, the goal of *Xinian*'s compilation, and who were its readers? I would suggest a relatively small group of high officials who needed to know the historical background for the current balance of power. This knowledge would benefit them particularly during diplomatic encounters with representatives of other states. In a recent study David Schaberg explored the speeches of the messengers (*shi* 使) in *Zuozhuan* and analyzed the messengers' common ground with the scribes (*shi* 史) with whom they shared similar training, which "encompassed both ritual formulas and more substantial knowledge of history and official practice."[58] How was "substantial knowledge of history" attained? Some might have studied history in earnest; but many others would prefer a brief résumé of major past geopolitical shifts. Such résumés were perhaps akin to modern briefings for a traveling head of state: not an extensive narrative with plenty of dates, names, and events but a summary presenting the most essential information, which could be utilized during the diplomatic encounter. I suppose that such a summary prepared nowadays would be similar to *Xinian*. Actually, some of the messengers' speeches cited in *Zuozhuan* disclose a very similar degree of historical knowledge to what would be expected of a reader of *Xinian*. The most vivid example is the Jin messenger Lü Xiang's 呂相 memorandum about the breaking of relations with Qin in 578 BCE; but other examples abound.[59]

If my supposition is correct, then *Xinian* represents a heretofore unknown historical genre: a text written for its practical value for policy makers rather than for the moral education or entertainment of a broader elite.[60] This peculiarity of the text may also explain its eventual disappearance. Unlike moralizing anecdotes, the educational or entertainment value of which could transcend their initial historical setting, an informative history had a much shorter life span. As time passed, details of struggles and intrigues among bygone polities and lineages became increasingly irrelevant for the educated audience. *Xinian* would surely be considered anachronistic by about 300 BCE, when the state of Jin had become a distant memory akin to the Austro-Hungarian Empire in our day, while Chu became engaged in a bitter struggle with its onetime ally, the state of Qin. Perhaps long before the Qin biblioclasm of 213 BCE—especially the destruction of historical records—delivered a coup de grâce to the historical narratives of the vanquished Warring States, such documents as *Xinian* were already out of circulation. Having outlived their usefulness, they would have perished from memory, or, what is more likely, been replaced by newer, updated texts, which also probably disappeared in due time. Had not the tomb looters brought them to light in the twenty-first century we would have no idea of their existence whatsoever.

CHAPTER 3

Zhou Historiography in Other Newly Discovered Sources

Aside from *Xinian*, recent paleographic discoveries have yielded many other texts that shed light on aspects of early Chinese historiography. Some of these texts (such as a Chu historical manuscript from the Anhui University collection and another historical or quasi-historical manuscript unearthed from the Longhui River 龍會河 cemetery) still await publication (as of 2019).[1] Among those that have been published, the most notable are another text from the Tsinghua University collection, named *Chu ju* 楚居 (Chu dwellings), manifold historical anecdotes, and a few important bronze inscriptions. In addition, references to past events in other unearthed texts (such as a variety of ideological products of the Warring States era) shed additional light on the uses of history in that age. In what follows I introduce these new discoveries and highlight the new understandings about the production and dissemination of historical knowledge in the Spring and Autumn to the early Warring States periods that they enable, as well as their import for reassessing the reliability of some of the received texts, most notably *Zuozhuan*. I furthermore address an apparent change in attitudes toward historical accuracy in the Warring States–period ideological writings. I conclude with some general observations about the cumulative impact of recent discoveries on the emerging new picture of Eastern Zhou historiography.

Chu ju

Chu ju is a relatively short text. It is written on sixteen slips of approximately 47.5 cm length each; most of the slips are preserved intact. The manuscript's name was given by the editorial team of Tsinghua University on the basis of the text's perceived parallels with the chapter "Residences" (Ju 居) from the now lost late Warring States–period text *Shi ben* 世本 (Roots of generations).² *Chu ju* is the first known example of a pure local history: from the beginning to the end it focuses on a single state, Chu. The text records Chu's history from the semilegendary progenitor of the Chu royal lineage, Jilian 季連, down to King Dao (r. ca. 400–381 BCE). It is likely that, much like *Xinian*, *Chu ju* was composed shortly after the reign of King Dao.³

For the convenience of discussion, we can divide the *Chu ju* manuscript into three sections.⁴ The first, comprising the first four and a half slips, deals with legendary and semilegendary progenitors of the state of Chu. This section narrates among other things a variant of the Chu dynastic legend (discussed in chapter 5), explains the name Chu (literally, "Thorn," related to the thorns used by a shaman midwife to mend the body of the Chu ancestress whose last son, Liji 麗季, was split from her side), introduces the ancestors of some of Chu's major aristocratic lineages, and elucidates the origins of Chu's peculiar custom of night sacrifice called *xi* (宵 = 夕).⁵ Twice this section uses the formula "until now" (*zhi jin* 至今) to emphasize that it speaks of the origins of contemporaneous names and practices.⁶ This section is rich in novel information about Chu's prehistory, and it is the focus of most of the several dozen articles dealing with *Chu ju*.⁷

The second section of *Chu ju* is the shortest one. It starts on slip 5 and continues into slip 8; it moves from legend to history. This section introduces early rulers of the Chu polity and their dwellings. It ends with King Wu of Chu 楚武王 (r. 740–690 BCE), under whose aegis the state of Chu started its territorial expansion, or, following Taniguchi Mitsuru, witnessed its "second birth."⁸ Facing demographic pressure on his early capital, Mian 免, King Wu drained the Jiang Swamps (Jiang Ying 疆浧) and let the people reside in this place. The authors conclude, "Until now, this place is called Ying" (至今曰郢; slip 8).

The establishment of Ying starts the third section of *Chu ju* (slips 8–16). The narrative, even if sketchy, becomes more systematic. It surveys the rule of each of Chu's kings, but with a single focus: the location of the king's dwellings. To demonstrate the narrative style of *Chu ju*, I translate below slips 10–13, which cover the events from the late seventh to early fifth centuries BCE (roughly paralleling the time span of *Xinian* 15 translated in chapter 2):[9]

至穆王自睽郢徙襲爲郢。至莊王徙襲樊郢,樊郢徙居同宮之北。若敖起禍,焉徙居烝之野,烝之野[□□,□□徙]【10】襲爲郢。至恭王、康王、嗣子王皆居爲郢。至靈王自爲郢徙居乾溪之上,以爲處於章[華之臺]。【11】景平王卽位,猶居乾溪之上。至昭王自乾溪之上徙媺郢,媺郢徙居鄂郢,鄂郢徙襲爲郢。闔廬入郢,焉復【12】徙乾溪之上,乾溪之上復徙襲媺郢。【13】

At the time of King Mu (r. 625–614 BCE), he relocated back from Kui Ying to Wei Ying.[10] At the time of King Zhuang (r. 613–591 BCE), he relocated back to Fan Ying.[11] From there he relocated to the north of Tong Palace.[12] When Ruo'ao rose in making troubles, he thereupon relocated to Zheng Wilderness;[13] from Zheng Wilderness . . . [four characters are missing] back to Wei Ying. At the time of King Gong (r. 590–560 BCE), King Kang (r. 559–545 BCE), and the Heir Child King (r. 544–541 BCE),[14] all dwelled in Wei Ying. At the time of King Ling (r. 540–529 BCE), he relocated from Wei Ying to the banks of the Qian Stream, making a residence at Zhang[hua Terrace].[15] When King Jingping (King Ping, r. 528–516 BCE) was established, he still resided at the banks of the Qian Stream. At the time of King Zhao (r. 515–489 BCE), he relocated from the banks of the Qian Stream to Mei Ying, from Mei Ying he relocated to E Ying, from E Ying he relocated back to Wei Ying.[16] When [King] Helu [of Wu] invaded Ying, [King Zhao] thereupon relocated again to the banks of the Qian Stream, and from the banks of the Qian Stream he relocated back to Mei Ying.[17]

This extract is representative of the *Chu ju* narrative as a whole, especially of its third section, which deals with the historical (rather than legendary or semilegendary) past. The text focuses exclusively on identifying the kings' dwellings. Almost no additional information is provided: battles, domestic struggles, victories and defeats are mentioned only when they directly influenced the ruler's location (e.g., the Ruo'ao lineage's revolt of 605 BCE, the Wu occupation of Chu's capital in 506 BCE, or, in a latter part of the text, the revolt of the Duke of Bai 白公 in 479 BCE). Some unpleasant events (such as several instances of regicide) are glossed over, but there is no attempt to systematically avoid the discussion of domestic troubles as evident in *Xinian*. Rather, the authors are simply not interested in anything beyond the location of the royal residence.

Chu ju is a puzzling text. Let us start with its main focus: does it speak about constant relocations of Chu's capitals? If this is the case, then why are these major events in the life of Chu not mentioned in any other received or unearthed text, including, for example, *Zuozhuan* or *Xinian*? Second, why, in contrast, is the shift of the capital from its original location at Ying (commonly, even if controversially, identified with the Ji'nan City 紀南城 remnants near current Jingzhou, Hubei) to the new location at Ruo 鄀, near current Yicheng 宜城 (Hubei), which is reported in *Zuozhuan* under the year 504 BCE, *not* mentioned in *Chu ju*?[18] Third, how can these two dozen relocations to "X + Ying" sites mentioned in *Chu ju* be correlated with the text's insistence (in slip 8) that a single capital established by King Wu of Chu is "until now" called Ying?

The answer to these questions appears to be relatively simple once we avoid the erroneous assumption that every relocation mentioned in *Chu ju* refers to the relocation of the capital city.[19] Actually, such frequent relocations of the capital would simply not be feasible. Think of three relocations just during the first seven years of King Zhuang as mentioned in the extract: these involved shifts from the Han River basin in Hubei to the banks of the Yellow River in Henan and then back to another location in Hubei. Clearly, it would be impossible to relocate the entire capital population, including artisans and their workshops, military and civilian installations, and the like, so frequently. An alternative interpretation would be in line with the one proposed by Shou Bin: *Chu ju* does not speak of shifts of capitals but just of moves of the Chu kings. The locations identified by X + Ying refer then simply to the kings' palaces. It is only the king and his immediate entourage who were on the move, whereas the primary capital, Ying, remained in the same place where it was established by King Wu of Chu, the only "Ying" that does not require additional qualification.[20]

Chu ju's exclusive focus on the king's residence would also explain its silence about the relocation of the capital Ying to Upper Ruo (Yicheng) in 504 BCE: this relocation (initiated, according to *Zuozhuan*, by Chu's prime minister, Ziqi 子期) was not related to the moves of King Zhao himself (who was then at his residence of Wei Ying 為郢, in close proximity to the new capital's location).[21] Moreover, the relocation itself appears to have been a temporary measure: from *Chu ju*'s statement (slip 8) it is clear that the same Ying established by King Wu of Chu remained known as such at the time of the text's composition. In all likelihood, the capital returned to its original location of Ying (Ji'nan City?) at a certain point in the fifth century BCE, a period that is very inadequately covered in the extant sources.[22]

Having resolved (so I hope) the questions concerning the text's content, we are left with a much greater puzzle about the purpose of its creation and its audience. Zhao Ping'an, in a somewhat pathetic attempt to bolster the prestige of the manuscript (and perhaps of the Tsinghua University collection as a whole) claimed the text to "undoubtedly" reflect "the principal content" of Chu historical writing.[23] As I have demonstrated in the previous chapter, this statement is patently wrong: Chu historians produced much more sophisticated texts than a brief list of kings' dwellings, devoid of precise chronology and of major details of Chu's history. Yet I do concur with Zhao on one point: undoubtedly *Chu ju* was produced by Chu's court scribes or at least by somebody closely related to a scribal office. I doubt that anywhere else would information about centuries-old kings' relocations be preserved. The question to be asked is, why did the scribes produce this type of history and for what audience?

Chu ju resembles *Xinian* as a text that is devoid of edifying or entertaining qualities, but in the case of *Chu ju* this feature is even more pronounced than in *Xinian*. The text is purely informative; but the very narrow focus of this information does not allow reading it as an introduction to Chu history as such. Rather, this sketchy, even if informative, text resembles an early version of *gaokao* 高考 examinations material: a draft reply for an exam on Chu's historical geography. Speaking more seriously, I speculate that this short survey of Chu's royal residences could have been prepared specifically for foreigners in the service of Chu kings. Perhaps dwellings of former rulers possessed a certain ritual or cultic importance that needed to be clarified to a newcomer to the state of Chu. Maybe this was a kind of sensitive domestic information, akin to local taboos and prohibitions, which the foreigner should learn upon arrival?[24] This would also explain why the text introduces the etymology of the country's self-appellation (Chu) and some of the peculiarities of its sacrificial culture.

Needless to say, my assertion about the *Chu ju*'s audience is impossible to verify. Yet what is important for the sake of the present discussion is that *Chu ju* demonstrates the existence of yet another previously unknown genre of history writing: histories apparently composed for ritual education rather than for moralizing or entertainment purposes. It also implies that the scribal offices at the courts of major states may have collected a great variety of information, not all of which was deemed appropriate for local histories but that was nevertheless preserved for the sake of ritual or other needs. *Chu ju* is an important testimony to the diversity of historical production in the Eastern Zhou.

Anecdotes

My previous discussion has dealt with two examples of informative histories that lacked pronounced didactic or entertaining qualities. As such, both *Xinian* and *Chu ju* differ markedly from what is usually perceived as the dominant feature of early Chinese historiography; namely, its edifying orientation. By way of contrast, the third sample of unearthed historical texts, which I now discuss, is focused precisely on teaching historical lessons. Didactic anecdotes—vignettes valued for their moralizing messages or amusing features—are ubiquitous in preimperial writings. They permeate most texts later classified as either "histories" (like *Discourses of the States* and *Stratagems of the Warring States*) or "philosophies" (e.g., *Han Feizi*, or *Lüshi chunqiu*), and even some of the "classics" (e.g., *Zuozhuan*). In an excellent study, David Schaberg has summarized some of the essentials of the anecdotal genre. Anecdotes are normally short and easily detachable textual units of several hundred characters' length. Most anecdotes contain an exchange of speech and either a confirmation of one of the speakers' prescience or judgment by a later commentator. Schaberg concludes, "The early Chinese historical anecdote is a fundamentally didactic form, as valuable for instructing rulers and peers as for training young students."[25]

Schaberg's observations can serve as a convenient departing point for the current discussion. There is only one aspect of his analysis with which I disagree; namely, the assertion that the anecdotes were "the basic form of historical narrative" in early China and that they constituted "all" of early Chinese historical production.[26] The examples of *Xinian* and *Chu ju*, as well as my reading of significant segments of *Zuozhuan*[27]—all suggest that the anecdotes were not the building blocks of early Chinese historiography but rather a secondary phenomenon. In my opinion, anecdotes were one segment of larger local histories produced by the scribes of the Spring and Autumn period. It is their didactic (or, in some cases, also entertaining) value that caused later historians and thinkers to detach the anecdotes from larger historical texts. This detachment ensured the anecdotes' relative longevity. Long after the policy makers lost interest in the detailed historical information provided in such texts as *Xinian*, anecdotes retained their relevance as a pool of easily understandable examples of proper and improper political behavior and also as training materials in political rhetoric. In the process of independent circulation, though, the anecdotes became progressively dissociated from their original historical context. This eventually resulted in such features as the same speech attributed to different personalities from different periods, the proliferation of purely fabricated speeches, and an abundance of blatant anachronisms. This cavalier attitude to historical accuracy is particularly notable in the Western Han–period anecdote collections, which, incidentally or not, mark the end of the appeal of the anecdotal genre as a whole.[28]

This detachment of anecdotes from their initial historical context raises the question, what is the value of the individual anecdotes scattered among recently unearthed manuscripts for the current discussion, with its narrow historiographic focus? The answer is not simple. On the one hand, the overwhelming majority of the anecdotes from the Shanghai Museum and Tsinghua University collections belong to didactic literature rather than to the historical genre per se. In contrast to *Xinian* or *Chu ju*, their primary goal is not to inform the reader about the events of the past but rather to edify or entertain him. In some of these anecdotes, the historical setting is of minimal importance: the same speech could be attributed to any pair of a ruler and his courtier.[29] On the other hand, a second look at some of the anecdotes reveals a closer historical focus. These anecdotes are valuable not necessarily in terms of their new information about the past but in terms of the new insights they provide about the circulation of historical knowledge in the Eastern Zhou period.

To demonstrate these insights I have opted to focus on two anecdotes from the Shanghai Museum collection, named *Zhuang Wang ji cheng* 莊王

既成 and *Shen gong chen Ling wang* 申公臣靈王. Both anecdotes are parts of the same manuscript comprising nine bamboo slips of 33.1 to 33.8 cm length with 25 to 26 characters per slip. Each anecdote's end is marked by a black hook √. The first of the titles (*Zhuang Wang ji cheng*) is written on the verso of slip 1, whereas the second title was provided by the editorial team of the Shanghai Museum.[30] That latter title is unfortunate, because it is based on what has been shown to be an inaccurate reading of the opening phrase of the anecdote under discussion.[31] My reading of both anecdotes closely follows that by Yuasa Kunihiro, to whose astute observations my discussion in what follows is greatly indebted.[32] I start with the first of the two anecdotes, which features an exchange between King Zhuang of Chu, the singularly successful Chu ruler, and his adviser, Zijing, the governor of Shěn 沈尹子桱.[33]

莊王既成無射，以問沈尹子桱，曰：「吾既果成無射，以供春秋之嘗，以【1】待四鄰之賓客，吾後之人，幾何保之？」沈尹固辭，王固問之。沈尹子桱答【2】曰：「四與五之間乎？」王曰：「如四與五之間，載之傳車以上乎，抑四舸以【3】逾乎？」沈尹子桱曰：「四舸以逾。」【4】

When King Zhuang had finalized the Wuyi bells,[34] he asked the Governor of Shěn, Zijing, "I have already finalized the Wuyi bells to prepare for the *chang* sacrifices in spring and autumn, and to wait for the guests from the four neighbors.[35] As for my posterity: will they succeed in preserving them?"

The Governor of Shěn stubbornly refused to answer, and the king stubbornly asked him. The Governor of Shěn, Zijing, replied, "Maybe for four to five generations?" The king said, "If for four to five generations, then, will they be carried away upstream by the chariots, or carried away downstream by the four large boats?" The Governor of Shěn, Zijing replied, "Carried away downstream by the four large boats."

The text sounds like a riddle. Its opening phrases are clear enough: having attained a series of great successes in the interstate arena, including the defeat of Jin armies at Bi 邲 in 597 BCE, King Zhuang seems to be anxious regarding his posterity's ability to preserve this momentum. The subsequent exchange with the king's prescient adviser, Zijing, is, in contrast, not easy to follow. What does "four to five" refer to? What does "carrying away upstream or downstream" mean? A reader without a working knowledge of Chu history would be perplexed.

Luckily, thanks to *Zuozhuan*, we can solve the riddle. Zijing hints at the occupation of the Chu capital, Ying, by the invading Wu forces in 506 BCE. This occupation occurred four or five generations after King Zhuang. The discrepancy results from the unclear position of King Jia'ao, who reigned 544 to 541 BCE but was denied a posthumous position in the Chu ancestral temple after being assassinated by his uncle, Prince Wei 王子圍, the future King Ling. As for going upstream or downstream, it refers to the possibility that the bells would be plundered either by Jin invaders from the north (who would carry them upstream of the Han River, using on-land transportation, i.e., chariots), or by Wu invaders from the east (who would transport the bells on boats downstream of the Yangzi [or Huai] River). Zijing correctly predicts that the major trouble to King Zhuang's descendants will come from Wu rather than from Jin.

The exchange between King Zhuang and Zijing would not be comprehensible without a working knowledge of Chu's history. In all likelihood, the source of such knowledge was a Chu local history, the one that served the compilers of *Zuozhuan*, *Xinian*, and other texts. The anecdote itself was surely fabricated after the sack of Ying by the Wu invaders. Whether or not its goal was to absolve King Zhao of Chu (during whose reign the disastrous Wu invasion happened) by shifting the blame from him to his predecessors, possibly even to the faults of King Zhuang himself, is not important for the present discussion.[36] What is important is that the anecdote does not contain any verification of Zijing's prescience. Such verification could be omitted only if the anecdote's authors assumed that the audience possessed a good knowledge of Chu history. We can infer that elite members of Chu were supposed to know the past of their country relatively well.

This expectation of knowing details of Chu's past is implicitly present also in the second anecdote of the same manuscript, *Shen gong chen Ling wang* (hereafter *Shen gong*). The anecdote speaks of an encounter between King Ling of Chu (formerly Prince Wei) and his erstwhile rival and current appointee, the Duke of Chen, Zihuang 子皇. In translating this piece I purposely do not add notes, to allow the reader to assess the anecdote in its pristine form.

禦於棘遂，陳公子皇止皇子。王子圍奪之，陳公爭之。王子圍立爲王，陳公子皇見王。王曰：「陳公忘夫棘遂乎？」陳公曰：「臣不知君王之將爲君。如臣知君王之爲君，臣將有致焉。」王曰：「不穀以笑，陳公是言弃之。今日陳公事不穀，必以是心。」陳公跪拜，起答：「臣爲君王臣，君王免之死，不以振斧質。何敢心之有？」

Having been repelled at Jisui, Zihuang, the Duke of Chen, captured Huangzi. Prince Wei wrested the prisoner from him, and the Duke of Chen contested Prince Wei. When Prince Wei was established as a king, Zihuang, the Duke of Chen, had an audience with the king. The king said, "Duke of Chen, did you forget Jisui?" The Duke of Chen answered, "Your subject was not aware that you, my king, would become the ruler. Had I known that my king would become the ruler, I, your subject, would have handed you [the prisoner]."

The king said, "I was joking. Duke of Chen, discard my words. From now on, you, the Duke of Chen, are to serve me with this [pure] heart."

The Duke of Chen kneeled and made obeisance. He rose up and replied, "I, your subject, am the subject of Your Majesty. Your Majesty the king spared me execution, relieving me of the executioner's block and cleaver. How would I dare to have a different heart!"

Once again, the anecdote (or, more precisely, its opening sentence) appears to be only partly comprehensible. Little wonder that Chen Fengfen, working for the Shanghai Museum team, misread it and misinterpreted several characters. It is only thanks to the studies of Chen Wei, Ebine Ryōsuke, Yuasa Kunihiro and other scholars that this text became readable again.[37] The narrative (albeit not the content of the speeches) parallels two related anecdotes from *Zuozhuan*, recorded under the years 547 and 534 BCE. The first of these tells of the rivalry between two commanders of the Chu army, Chuanfeng Xu 穿封戌 and Prince Wei, in the aftermath of their successful assault on Chengjun 城麇, a town in the state of Zheng. The head of the local Zheng garrison, Huang Jie 皇頡, who tried to repel Chu's attack, was defeated and taken prisoner by Chuanfeng Xu. Prince Wei fought with Chuanfeng over the credit, and their rivalry was adjudicated by another senior Chu commander, Bo Zhouli 伯州梨. The latter manipulated the prisoner's evidence so as to grant the credit to Prince

Wei. "Infuriated, Chuanfeng Xu pulled out his dagger axe and pursued Prince Wei but could not overtake him."[38]

The second encounter between Chuanfeng Xu and Prince Wei is recorded in 534 BCE, after the prince had successfully usurped the throne from his nephew, Jia'ao, and became one of the most powerful (but also ruthless and controversial) rulers of the entire Spring and Autumn period, posthumously known as King Ling of Chu. In 534, the Chu armies annexed the state of Chen and Chuanfeng Xu was appointed the duke (i.e., governor) of Chen.[39] Then the following exchange between him and King Ling is recorded in *Zuozhuan*:

侍飲酒於王，王曰：「城麇之役，汝知寡人之及此，汝其辟寡人乎！」
對曰：「若知君之及此，臣必致死禮以息楚國。」

[Chuanfeng] attended upon the king as he drank, and the king said, "If you had known that I would attain this [status], during the battle of Chengjun you would have yielded to me!" Chuanfeng replied, "If I had known my lord would attain this, I would have died for ritual propriety in order to bring peace to the state of Chu."[40]

There is no doubt that *Shen gong* is dealing with the same story as *Zuozhuan*, despite differences in such details as personal names and place-names.[41] The content of the exchange between the Duke of Chen and King Ling differs in both cases, and I return to this point later. But first, let us start with the anecdote's opening phrases. "Having been repelled at Jisui, Zihuang, the Duke of Chen, captured Huangzi. Prince Wei wrested the prisoner from him, and the Duke of Chen contested Prince Wei." The reader has no hints as to which battle is being referred to, who the protagonists are, and what their relationship is. Moreover, the most dramatic part of the *Zuozhuan* story—namely, that Chuanfeng Xu chased Prince Wei with his dagger axe—is omitted. This is the crucial part of the narrative: it is because of this gross breach of decorum that Chuanfeng should have merited major punishment after Prince Wei's establishment as King Ling. Instead, however, it was King Ling who approved Chuanfeng's promotion to the high position of the Duke of Chen. The omission of this background makes the subsequent exchange much less tense than it is in *Zuozhuan*.

There are two possible explanations for the discrepancy between the *Zuozhuan* and *Shen gong* versions. One is that *Shen gong* presents an earlier version of the anecdote that was subsequently modified in *Zuozhuan* (or in one of its source materials). The second is that *Shen gong* abridges the earlier version. I think the latter explanation is much more plausible. The *Zuozhuan* account of two exchanges between Chuanfeng Xu and Prince Wei/King Ling comes as a part of a lengthy and detailed narrative focusing primarily on Chu's military exploits and secondarily on the very complex figure of King Ling. It is highly likely that this detailed information derived from the Chu local history and was not invented post-factum. Doubtless some details were inevitably added or embellished in the process of the stories' formation and circulation, but it is still more plausible that the detailed version of the events that we encounter in *Zuozhuan* was formed before the *Shen gong* anecdote than vice versa. The *Shen gong* authors abridged the historical background so as to focus the reader's attention on the final dialog between the Duke of Chen and King Ling. From our point of view, this abridgment was awkwardly performed, but any awkwardness probably did not much matter to a reader of the anecdote who was supposed to possess sufficient knowledge of the events surrounding King Ling's career and his tumultuous reign.

The goal of the *Shen gong* anecdote is probably to provide an alternative to the ambiguous exchange between King Ling and Chuanfeng Xu as recorded in *Zuozhuan*. There, the final word remains Chuanfeng Xu's, whose statement allows multiple interpretations, including a veiled regret that he, Chuanfeng Xu, failed to prevent the future King Ling from performing the regicidal coup d'état.[42] In contrast, in the *Shen gong* version King Ling is given the chance to display full magnanimity, and the Duke of Chen reciprocates with full and unequivocal submission.[43] Needless to say, we have no way of ascertaining which of the versions is more trustworthy: probably a few different narratives about the tense exchange between the king and his rival-turned-appointee circulated simultaneously in the state of Chu.

My goal here is not to analyze the specific content of *Shen gong* and other anecdotes but to highlight the intrinsic link between these individual anecdotes and larger historical works (in this context not *Zuozhuan* but rather a Chu local history). The anecdotes were not just derivative of these histories but, at least in the early stage of their circulation, could be composed in a way that presupposed the reader's working knowledge of local histories, without which the anecdote could not be properly understood. If my supposition is correct, it suggests that local histories enjoyed considerably broader circulation among the educated elite than could otherwise be assumed. History mattered for policy makers, and it had to be learned. Quasi-historical works, such as anecdotes, were originally built on this preexisting historical knowledge. It was only later in the process of their circulation that they acquired the features of entirely independent narrative units as described by Schaberg.

Bronze Inscriptions

Bronze inscriptions—short texts inscribed primarily on sacrificial vessels that were put into tombs and ancestral temples of high-ranking nobles—were identified long ago as one of the most important sources for early Zhou history. As several studies have demonstrated, these inscriptions are essential for understanding the geography, administration, and aspects of the cultural history of the Western Zhou.[44] The richness of their information notwithstanding, however, it should be remembered that the inscriptions are not straightforward historical sources. In particular, we should consider their religious nature before utilizing them for historiographic studies.

The major peculiarity of the vast majority of bronze inscriptions is the identity of their addressees. As was demonstrated in a seminal study by Lothar von Falkenhausen, the very placement of the inscriptions on the inner side of the bronze vessels (which meant that they were covered by sacrificial food) or on the verso side of the suspended bells made them unreadable by humans, at least when the inscribed objects were in use. Rather than humans, the inscriptions targeted the ancestral spirits themselves. Actually, many inscriptions serve as a medium of complex interaction between the donors and the recipients of the sacrifices: the final part of these inscriptions consisted of "auspicious words" (guci 嘏辭), which were literally put in the mouths of the ancestral spirits (being consumed with the sacrificial offerings). These words contained the spirits' blessings to the descendants.[45]

Historians are most interested in longer inscriptions, which contain what Falkenhausen calls the "announcements of merit." These usually explain the reasons for which the vessel was produced. The announcements of merit could be copied from an original investiture document (in case the donor merited promotion), but more often they were written in what Falkenhausen identifies as the "subjective mode," in which the donor enumerated his (and his ancestors') achievements. Some of these "subjective mode" reports—such as the Jin Hou Su-*bianzhong* 晉侯穌編鐘 inscription, mentioned in chapter 1—contain precious historical information derived from the lineage's or the state's archives. Yet detailed as some of them appear to be, the inscriptions are highly selective in the information they provide. Falkenhausen observes, "These documents do not convey the full range of human experience; the spirits were not supposed to know everything—there were to be no surprises, no irregularities in ritual exchange."[46] Indeed, the inscriptions never record military defeats or other unpleasant events in the donor's life. Even major and well-known events from the past—such as an inglorious defeat of the Zhou royal armies by the state of Chu around 957 BCE—could be conveniently concealed behind euphemistic formulae.[47]

This intrinsic selectiveness of the bronze inscriptions' records may explain why the historians of Eastern Zhou are less attracted by this medium and prefer to rely instead on transmitted texts—such as *Zuozhuan*, *Discourses of the States*, or *Records of the Historian*. An additional reason for the general lack of interest in the Eastern Zhou inscriptions is their overall brevity. Only a tiny number of Eastern Zhou inscriptions contain announcements of merit, and most of these are written in what may be called the most radical manifestation of the subjective mode: enumerating the donor's positive qualities without bothering the ancestors with depicting actual achievements. These inscriptions are invaluable for understanding the self-image of the donors, be they the rulers of the state of Qin or some of the leading Chu aristocrats, but they are of limited value for those eager to reproduce events from these countries' past.[48]

Nonetheless, a few of the Eastern Zhou bronze inscriptions contain precious historical information. For instance, certain inscriptions highlight the history of political entities not adequately covered in the transmitted texts, such as the state of Qin during the first four centuries of its existence (ca. 800–400 BCE), the state of Wu, which prospered in the sixth to fifth century BCE but was extinguished in 473 BCE, or the state of Zhongshan 中山, which yielded a few exceptionally long and informative inscriptions from the late fourth century BCE.[49] For the purposes of the present discussion with its narrower historiographic concern, however, I want to focus on the inscriptions that do have parallels in the transmitted texts, most notably *Zuozhuan*. These parallels may provide further information about the nature of *Zuozhuan* sources and more broadly about the nature of the Eastern Zhou historiographic tradition.

Comparisons between some of the Spring and Autumn–period inscriptions and *Zuozhuan*'s narrative have already been undertaken by others, and it is not my intention to discuss all the evidence systematically.[50] For the purposes of the current discussion I have chosen two recently unearthed inscriptions on ritual bells—one on the Zifan-*bianzhong* 子犯編鐘 and another on the Zeng Hou Yu-*bianzhong* 曾侯與編鐘. Both inscriptions are important not only because they corroborate aspects of the *Zuozhuan* narrative but also because they shed an indirect light on the content of *Zuozhuan* sources—that is, on local histories from the Spring and Autumn period.

Zifan Bells

The inscription on the Zifan bells is 132 characters long. It is inscribed on two sets of eight bells looted from a Jin tomb in Shanxi and purchased in Hong Kong by the National Palace Museum in Taipei (several bells ended up in a private collection; one bell is missing). The inscription is perfectly readable aside from a single disputed character. Putting aside a series of interesting questions regarding the stylistic characteristics of the bells and their musical qualities, I focus on the first part of the inscription, which narrates the exploits of the bells' donor, Zifan 子犯.[51]

唯王五月初吉丁未。子犯佑晉公左右，來復其邦。諸楚荊不聽命于王所。子犯及晉公率西之六師，搏伐楚荊，孔休。大上楚荊、喪厥師、滅厥□。子犯佑晉公左右、燮諸侯俾朝王，克奠王位。王賜子犯輅車、四馬、衣裳、黼黻、珮。諸侯羞元金于子犯之所、用為和鐘九堵。

It was in the fifth month of the king's [calendar], during the initial auspiciousness, on *dingwei* day.

Zifan assisted the Duke of Jin from the left and the right, helping to restore him to his state. When Chu did not come to court to heed the king's orders, Zifan and the Duke of Jin led the Six Armies of the West, extensively attacked Chu, and achieved great merit.

The Jin armies massively struck Chu, causing the loss of their armies and destroying their [commander?]. Zifan assisted the Duke of Jin in harmonizing the regional lords and causing them to attend the king's court, thereby being able to stabilize the king's position. Therefore, the king presented Zifan with a carriage, four stallions, ceremonial robes, embroidered cloth, and belt ornaments. The regional lords brought auspicious metal to Zifan's place, with which he made the nine sets of harmonious bells.

The author of the inscription, Hu Yan 狐偃 (appellative Zifan 子犯), was the maternal uncle of Ducal Son Chong'er, the future Lord Wen of Jin. The *Zuozhuan* narrative of Lord Wen's wanderings in exile (paralleled and embellished in the *Discourses of the States* and echoed in many later texts) presents a highly positive portrait of Hu Yan, who is depicted as the wisest among Lord Wen's advisers. Hu Yan is credited more than anybody else with Chong'er's successful seizure of power in Jin and with his subsequent successes, such as restoring the power of King Xiang of Zhou 周襄王 in 635 BCE and later defeating the Chu army in the fateful Chengpu 城濮 battle of 632 BCE. These two acts turned Lord Wen (Chong'er) into the hegemon, the single most powerful leader of the Zhou world.

There are many interesting points in the inscription. For instance, it is the earliest Jin inscription that refers to the reigning lord of Jin as "duke" (*gong* 公) rather than "marquis" (*hou* 侯), as is common in earlier Jin inscriptions.[52] This may reflect the elevation of Lord Wen to ducal status following his successful restoration of King Xiang of Zhou, although possibly it is just a polite mention of a ruler by his subject.[53] The inscription is also remarkable for its deferential language toward Lord Wen's nominal superior and de facto protégé, the Zhou king. Notably, Hu Yan uses the Zhou royal calendar rather than the native Jin one (the so-called Xia 夏 calendar, in which the year started two months later than in Zhou). This may be considered a strong expression of deference to the Zhou house in the wake of the recognition of Lord Wen's position as a new hegemon. Another interesting—and to the best of my knowledge entirely neglected—aspect of the inscription is the fact that the donor, Hu Yan, was not a member of the Huaxia 華夏 (Chinese) community but rather a

Rong 戎 noble. His ethnic affiliation notwithstanding, Hu Yan presents himself as a pure member of the Zhou nobility, much as he is presented in contemporaneous texts. Actually, both the Western Zhou style of the bells and some of the expressions in the inscription (e.g., referring to the Jin armies by the archaizing term "Six Armies of the West") put Hu Yan among Zhou cultural conservatives.[54] That this stance—and the explicit support of the Zhou king's legitimacy—is adopted by a member of the non-Zhou nobility is remarkable.

The inscription refers, even if briefly, to three of Hu Yan's achievements. First, he is lauded for "helping to restore [Lord Wen] to his state." Second, he is said to lead together with Lord Wen the "Six Armies of the West" (i.e., the Jin armies) in their successful assault on Chu. Third, Hu Yan is credited with "assisting the Duke of Jin in harmonizing the regional lords and causing them to attend the king's court." This last was properly identified as a reference to the Jiantu 踐土 covenant assembled by Lord Wen in the fifth lunar month of 632 BCE. Most remarkable, the date of the inscription, the *dingwei* day (tenth day) of the fifth month according to the Zhou royal calendar, is precisely the date of the major ceremony of "presenting the Chu prisoners and booty to the Zhou king" as recorded in *Zuozhuan*.[55] This match between the inscription and *Zuozhuan* is surely not accidental. It proves beyond doubt that *Zuozhuan*'s narrative of the Jiantu covenant and, more broadly, of related exploits of Lord Wen and his aides was based on earlier records, most likely the Jin local history.

This understanding is particularly important. Long ago, the saga of Chong'er's wanderings and his subsequent exploits were singled out as representative of early Chinese historical "romance," which was assumed to have little historical value.[56] That the narrative about Chong'er contains plenty of literary embellishments is undeniable. However, this should not obscure the fact—now confirmed by the inscription on the Zifan-bells—that this narrative derives from earlier and fundamentally reliable sources. These sources (i.e., Jin's local history) may well have contained fictional details from the very moment of their composition (and other embellishments could have been added later, during the process of *Zuozhuan*'s compilation and early transmission). What is clear is that the bulk of the narrative is grounded in historical events. This reliability (and even the accuracy of such minor details as the date of the award ceremony to Lord Wen and his aides) is now confirmed by the close parallels between *Zuozhuan* and the Zifan inscription.

Bells of Marquis Yu of Zeng

The inscription on the bells of Marquis Yu of Zeng, unearthed in 2009 from Tomb No. 1, Wenfengta 文峰塔 cemetery, Suizhou Municipality 隨州 (Hubei), is one of the most fascinating paleographic discoveries of recent years. Zeng 曾, a tiny polity near present-day Suizhou, was ruled by a branch of the Zhou royal clan (the Ji 姬). It attracted considerable attention after the spectacular discovery of the tomb of Marquis Yi 曾侯乙 (d. 433 BCE) in 1978, renowned in particular for its magnificent chime bells.[57] Subsequent excavations in several cemetery sites around Suizhou brought to light an unusually large number of Zeng elite tombs. From the inscriptions on some of the unearthed bronze vessels, scholars could trace the history of the state of Zeng from its establishment early in the Western Zhou period and well into the early Warring States era. Puzzlingly, however, Zeng, which appears to be one of the major Zhou strongholds in the eastern part of the Han River valley, is not mentioned in any of the transmitted texts. Instead, *Zuozhuan* and other texts identify the Zhou stronghold in the Suizhou area as Sui 隨. Whether or not Sui and Zeng are two names of the same polity became one of the focal point of decades of scholarly debate. The controversy was finally and unequivocally settled only in 2019, with the discovery of several inscriptions associated with the wife of Marquis Bao of Zeng 曾侯寶, a Chu princess, Mi Jia 嬭加. Since Mi Jia is identified in her betrothal vessels as the spouse of the Sui ruler, it is clear that Zeng and Sui are two names of the same country.[58] The discovery of Marquis Yu's bells ten years earlier has also contributed, even if less unequivocally, to the resolution of the Zeng-Sui controversy. More important for our discussion, it provided further clues as to the nature of Chu historical texts incorporated into *Zuozhuan*.

The 169-character inscription on Marquis Yu's bells is exceptional in its content. It starts with a reference to Zeng's early history but then shifts to more recent events (once again, I translate only the historical part):[59]

惟王正月，吉日甲午，曾侯與曰：「伯括上 嚳（=庸），左右文武，達殷之命，撫定天下。王遣命南公，營宅汭土，君庀[60]淮夷，臨有江夏。周室之既卑，吾用燮 譖（=戚）楚。吳恃有眾庶行亂，西征南伐，乃加於楚，荊邦既削，而天命將誤（=虞）。有嚴曾侯，業業厥聖，親敷武功，楚命是靖。復定楚王，曾侯之靈。」

It was in the first month of the [Zhou] king's calendar, on the auspicious day *jiawu*. Yu, the Marquis of Zeng, said, "The Elder Kuo[61] was enrolled[62] to support from the left and the right Kings Wen and Wu. [He helped them to] attain the Mandate of Yin [i.e., Shang] and console and pacify All Under Heaven. The king [King Wu?] then ordered Nangong[63] to establish his residence at the confluence of the rivers, to rule and govern the Yi of the Huai River and to overlook the Yangzi and Xia Rivers.[64]

The Zhou house had already declined. I am harmonious and amicable[65] with Chu. Wu relied on its multitudes to behave calamitously. They invaded westward, attacked southward, and thereupon added [turmoil] to Chu.[66] The Jing [i.e., Chu] country had been decimated already and Heaven's Mandate was on the verge of being worried about [it].[67] Stern is the Marquis of Zeng, magnificent in his sagacity, he personally promulgated military achievements. Therefore Chu's mandate has been secured. The restoration of the King of Chu is thanks to the numinous power of the Marquis of Zeng.

This is a fascinating text. It starts with the reconfirmation of Zeng's strong connection to the Zhou house: not only did the country's progenitor, Nangong Kuo, play an important role in Zhou's attainment of the Heavenly Mandate from the Shang dynasty but also the very founding of the state of Zeng was a strategic mission on behalf of the Zhou kings. Then, however, the narrative shifts abruptly from Zhou to Chu.[68] Having declared unequivocally that the Zhou house had declined already, the ruler of Zeng proclaims his allegiance to Chu. He commends himself with saving Chu from the Wu incursion and restoring its mandate. The final line in the translated extract reflects Marquis Yu's immense pride: "The restoration of the King of Chu is thanks to the numinous power of the Marquis of Zeng."

Scholars were quick to notice the close relation of Marquis Yu's inscription to the events depicted in *Zuozhuan* under the years 506–505 BCE—namely, the Wu invasion, which almost toppled the state of Chu. After his capital, Ying, fell to the Wu invaders, King Zhao fled his state, eventually finding shelter in Chu's protectorate, Sui. Then *Zuozhuan* depicts the following exchange between Wu and Sui leaders:

The Wu forces . . . said to the Sui leaders, "Of the Zhou descendants located along the Han River, Chu has in fact taken every last one.

Heaven's sentiments have been swayed, and it has inflicted a punishment on Chu (i.e., Wu's invasion). Yet you, lord, give him refuge. What crime has the Zhou house committed? If you should think to avenge the Zhou house and to be kind also to me in bringing Heaven's sentiments to fruition, it would be an act of generosity. The lands to the east of the Han River would then be yours."⁶⁹

Wu's attempt to lure Sui to its camp was based on common descent: both states were said to belong to the Zhou royal clan (even though in the case of Wu this ancestry may well be fictitious). Sui is identified in *Zuozhuan* as the leader of the Ji clan states in the Han River area. It was also one of the earliest targets of Chu's expansion.⁷⁰ Now, the Wu spokesman offered Sui an excellent chance both to avenge the Ji polities and to gain territories to the east of the Han River. King Zhao's brother, Ziqi 子期, was fearful that the Marquis of Sui would yield to Wu's pressure and offered himself to be handed to the Wu army as the king's substitute; yet the Sui leaders had different plans:

> The Sui leaders divined about handing him over, but it was not auspicious, so they declined Wu's offer, saying, "Because Sui is small and remote, and yet close to Chu, it has in fact been Chu that has preserved us. For generations we have made covenants and pledges to Chu, which to this day have not been altered. If in a time of difficulty we should abandon them, then, how should we serve you, my lord? The concern of men in charge should not be for this one man. If you bring peace within the borders of Chu, will we presume not to heed your commands?"⁷¹ The Wu forces therefore retreated.⁷²

This dramatic story could easily be read as a mere literary embellishment. It is part of a larger set of stories about King Zhao's miserable flight from his capital, which highlight the king's vulnerability.⁷³ It is possible that these stories originated in the participants' reminiscences, but one may well suspect them of being pure invention. Nonetheless, the inscription on Marquis Yu's bells calls this latter supposition into question. Actually, the inscription (which was in all likelihood cast very soon after the depicted events took place)⁷⁴ can be understood as a direct explanation of Sui's (i.e., Zeng's) position in reply to Wu's demands. Namely, despite considering themselves proud descendants of the Zhou house, the Sui/Zeng leaders unequivocally decided that Heaven's Mandate favored the state of Chu rather than Zhou, and it is Chu that should be served. Wu's invasion was endangering the mandate, and it is out of their commitment to Heaven's will that Sui continued to support Chu and allowed the eventual restoration of Chu's fortunes.

The inscription on the bells of Marquis Yu is triply precious. First, it serves as a very strong indicator to the effect that Sui and Zeng are the names of the same polity. Even before the discovery of the new evidence to this effect,[75] it was clear that the story told in *Zuozhuan* about Sui and the one told in the Marquis Yu inscription could not refer to two different events. The solution to the long-standing debate about the relation between Sui and Zeng may allow us now to better evaluate this country's political trajectory by further juxtaposing inscriptional and textual evidence. Second, the inscription is invaluable in providing a hint of how the Zeng rulers at the end of the Spring and Autumn period navigated their course between their belonging to the Zhou house and their position as Chu's protectorate.[76] And third, and most important for the current discussion: the inscription indicates that something akin to the scene depicted in *Zuozhuan* must have happened at the Sui court. The story—either embellished or not—was incorporated into a Chu history and later reproduced in *Zuozhuan*. This suggests that at least some of the speeches and other literarily significant segments of the *Zuozhuan* narrative were incorporated from the text's primary sources rather than fabricated by its author/compiler. Even if not entirely accurate, these literary embellishments are sufficiently close to the depicted events to serve as a reliable indicator of the mind-set of Spring and Autumn–period historians, if not of the actual protagonists.

Historical Arguments and Political Rhetoric: The Question of Accuracy

Aside from historical and quasi-historical (anecdotes, bronze inscriptions) texts, another possible source of information about Zhou (and earlier) history comes from frequent references to the past in political and philosophical essays of the competing thinkers of the Warring States period. The thinkers' frequent resort to historical argumentation, including but not confined to the broad usage of historical anecdotes mentioned in the preceding, is well known. The questions that arise are, what is the reliability of their invocations of the past? Did Warring States–period polemicists concern themselves at all with historical accuracy?[77]

The answer to these questions is not simple. On the one hand, it is clear that competing thinkers were prone to twist historical narratives so as to suit their ideological needs. This is particularly noteworthy when events of the remote past were invoked. In stories of legendary paragons down to the early Zhou rulers, it was all too easy to embellish earlier narratives, to add new details, or even to invent new personages.[78] On the other hand, such a cavalier attitude toward historical veracity could backfire once a thinker invoked the events of recent centuries, which were more fully covered in historical sources. Here we can expect a biased presentation of history, but the general framework of events is assumed to be more or less reliable. Clearly the outright invention of recent events would not be prudent. But how much knowledge of these events can we expect from competing thinkers and from their audiences?

Once again, the answer is equivocal. Take, for example, *Han Feizi*, one of the richest philosophical texts in terms of its historical information. On the one hand, there is no doubt that Han Fei 韓非 (d. 233 BCE) (or other contributors to the text that bears his name) was an avid reader of historical texts. Some of his statements appear to be either verbatim citations from *Zuozhuan* or close reproductions of *Zuozhuan* or its source materials.[79] Actually, Han Fei appears more prone than most contemporaneous thinkers to resort to written records in referring to recent events. On the other hand, *Han Feizi* also contains gross historical inaccuracies, owing not only to the author's ideological agenda but also to mere carelessness and inadequate knowledge of the past. For instance, the text mixes the attributes of different historical personages or conflates two personages into one.[80] At times the inaccuracies are more blatant, reflecting complete neglect of even a semblance of historical veracity.[81] That these inaccuracies remained in the text demonstrates perhaps that by the time of this text's composition and early circulation (the very end of the Warring States period), its readers were not expected either to know details of the past or to care about the accuracy of historical statements. If my supposition is correct, it can be contrasted with my earlier assertion that at the early stage of the circulation of historical anecdotes, their authors expected their audience to know enough about the history of their state to understand the anecdote's subtleties. Why and when did the shift away from informative history toward ideologically oriented narration of the past occur?

One clue to this shift can be provided by yet another manuscript from the Tsinghua University collection, named by the editors *Liang chen* 良臣 (Good ministers). This is a short text written on eleven slips of 32.8 cm length. It is divided into twenty sections separated by a thick line on the slips; each section lists a famous former ruler and his model ministers. The text starts with the Yellow Thearch, Yao and Shun, and ends with Lord Ai of Lu 魯哀公 (r. 494–468 BCE).[82] The list is devoid of any details: it provides neither a narrative nor even a short explanation of the reasons for its choice of personages. I concur with Han Yujiao that this text was in all likelihood used as training material for traveling persuaders who required a brief and easily memorized list of model ministers of the past. As such, *Liang chen* may represent what was a fairly common genre of quasi-historical texts that may have enjoyed relatively broad circulation throughout the Warring States period and beyond.[83]

Liang chen is a dull text, but it becomes worth reading once we notice the amazing number of historical inaccuracies in this very short manuscript. Take for instance the statement, "Lord Ai of Lu had Jisun and had Kong Qiu [Confucius]" (魯哀公有季孫、有孔丘; slip 8). The very inclusion of Lord Ai of Lu—a weakling who was ultimately ousted from his state by a coalition of powerful ministerial families—in the list of paragon rulers is an odd choice. Adding Confucius to the list of Lord Ai's outstanding ministers is even odder: after all, Confucius spent most of Lord Ai's reign outside the state of Lu. But the oddest thing is adding Jisun 季孫, the head of the Ji 季 family in Lu, to the list of model ministers who served Lord Ai. Lord Ai's contemporary as head of the Ji family was Ji Kangzi 季康子 (d. 468 BCE), the lord's nominal aide and bitter rival, who ultimately contributed to Lord Ai's inglorious flight from his state. The authors might have thought of a more positive head of the Ji/Jisun family, such as Ji Wenzi 季文子 (d. 568 BCE), who is indeed often hailed in *Zuozhuan* as a paragon of loyalty, but they seem to have had no clear idea of the many heads of the Jisun family. Certainly their knowledge of Lu history was perfunctory.[84]

Yet *Liang chen* provides examples of even more ridiculous inaccuracies. The authors seem to be unaware of the naming patterns in the early Zhou to the Spring and Autumn period. At that time, a single person could be referred to by his name (*ming* 名), appellative (*zi* 字), posthumous name (*shi* 諡), seniority name (*hangci* 行辭), and combinations of these. In *Zuozhuan*, confusingly, a single person may appear in a passage under two or three different appellations.[85] Scribes who produced historical texts of the Spring and Autumn period presumably mastered these complexities, but the *Liang chen* authors did not. Hence, among the model ministers of King Wu of Zhou 周武王 (d. ca. 1042 BCE) one encounters both Lord Shi 君奭 and the Duke of Shao 召公, who are actually the same person! Later, among the ministers of Lord Wen of Jin, we encounter not just Zifan but also Jiufan 咎犯, which is another designation of the same famous minister, Hu Yan.[86] There are more examples of similar inaccuracies,[87] but even the brief mention here shows that the *Liang chen* authors were ignorant of many aspects of both remote and recent history.

Facing these obvious mistakes, scholars have adopted different approaches to *Liang chen*—from ignoring its fallacies and treating it as a normal historical text to explaining its perfunctory nature by its mortuary setting: perhaps a text prepared for entombing did not need to be as accurate as one that was meant to serve living elite members.[88] This is an interesting idea, but it does not appear convincing to me: we are not, after all, speaking of miswritten or missing characters but of obvious mistakes that display the authors' historical ignorance. That such a text was prepared at all and deemed worthy of entombing means that there was a market for such a flawed production.

This brings me to the final point of this discussion. It seems that a change in attitudes toward history occurred in the Warring States period. Earlier historical works, the traits of which are recoverable in *Zuozhuan*, *Xinian*, *Chu ju*, and some bronze inscriptions, were designed to strike a balance between presenting reliable information (based on the records made by court scribes) and a variety of other goals, such as edifying and entertaining. In the Warring States period, history appears to have been hijacked by competing thinkers and traveling persuaders, who did not seek exact information but rather an ideologically convincing bottom line. For them, accuracy mattered less than for court scribes. *Liang chen* is a valuable demonstration of this new tendency precisely because its fallacies are so obvious. Yet it is a part of a much broader shift away from informative histories toward ideologically loaded ones. It is time to assess this shift and summarize our understanding of Eastern Zhou historiography.

Eastern Zhou Historiography Revisited

My discussion of major transmitted and unearthed historical and quasi-historical texts in these first three chapters allows us to draw some preliminary conclusions about the nature of Eastern Zhou historiography. It seems that at least prior to around 400 BCE, the major building blocks of historical knowledge were local histories, which were prepared in all likelihood by court scribes. The factual skeleton of these histories came from meticulous recordings of major events in the life of a polity. The recording itself appears to have been closely related to the court annals (of which the *Spring and Autumn Annals* of the state of Lu are singularly representative). These annals were prepared in all major polities, and they seem to have been an important means of ritual interaction with the ancestral spirits above and among the states of the Zhou *oikouménē* below. Whether the recording of major events was done as part of the ritual tasks of the court scribes or developed independently of preparing the court annals is still unclear. What is beyond doubt is that the tradition of recording events make historical texts of the Spring and Autumn period highly informative insofar as the who, what, when, and where questions are concerned.

Meticulous records of major events aside, local histories prepared by court scribes contained a variety of other information that derived from oral tradition or from the scribes' imagination. Omens and portents, stories of ghosts and deities, moralizing speeches and omniscient predictions—all appear to have been part of the scribes' tool kit when preparing their histories. These devices helped their audience understand why things happened and which lessons should be gleaned from past events. Other devices—a variety of literary embellishments, amusing details, and juicy stories—were added by scribes to captivate an audience. And, since local histories were conceivably updated from time to time, it may be surmised that precise details about long-bygone events were diminished or elided, whereas a variety of literary embellishments proliferated. The invention of Wu Zixu's brother, Wu Ji, in *Xinian* 15 (discussed in chapter 2, p. 59) is just one of many manifestations of this tendency.

In addition to local histories and court annals, scribes would prepare a variety of other materials, such as short résumés of major political developments or texts aimed at ritual education, as exemplified by *Xinian* and *Chu ju*. Yet in the long term, it seems that the most important by-product of their work were didactic anecdotes. Whether these anecdotes predate local histories (as assumed by Schaberg) or are derivative of these histories (as suggested by myself) remains to be seen. What is beyond doubt is that at a certain point between the Spring and Autumn and Warring States periods, their attractiveness seems to have eclipsed that of more informative local histories. The anecdotes were esteemed for their edifying and entertaining value; in addition, they were brief, easily memorized, adaptable to different circumstances, and engaging for a much broader audience than readers interested to learn the detailed history of their country and its neighbors. Unlike other products of the court's scribes—of which we knew next to nothing prior to the recent spate of discoveries—the anecdotes proliferated rapidly throughout the world of the Warring States. Their importance is buttressed by the appearance of major collections of anecdotes such as *Discourses of the States* or *Springs and Autumns of Master Yan* (*Yanzi chunqiu* 晏子春秋), by the broad circulation of individual anecdotes as confirmed by the paleographic discoveries, and by the very massive incorporation of the anecdotes into the Masters' (*zi* 子; i.e., philosophers') texts. In the process, the circulation and creation of the anecdotes was dissociated from the scribes and appropriated by the competing thinkers and their disciples. This in turn resulted in increasing dissociation of the anecdotes from their original historical setting.

The proliferation of the anecdotes and their appropriation by participants in ideological debates reflects a new turn in usages of history. This may be called the edifying turn and it more or less coincides with the age of the Hundred Schools of Thought. Although the court scribes continued to produce local histories and other materials, their impact on the dissemination of historical knowledge in the Warring States period appears to have been smaller than prior to circa 400 BCE. Appeals to history—primarily to the distant past, but sometimes to recent events as well—permeate the texts of the Hundred Schools, but they are uniformly devoid of what was the norm in earlier historical texts, such as emphasis on accuracy, minute details, and the like. The disappearance of the precise dating of events from anecdotes and other quasi-historical texts of the Warring States period (discussed in chapter 1, p. 35) exemplifies this trend. The cavalier attitude toward historical accuracy in both transmitted and unearthed materials discussed in the previous section of this chapter shows a peculiar development: the question of why mattered more than ever, but the questions of who, what, when, and where seem to have lost their appeal.

It is tempting to connect the decline of informative history writing in the early Warring States period with the major social change of that age; namely, the withering of the hereditary aristocracy and proliferation of a new society in which a lineage's past achievements mattered little in determining one's career. In the aristocratic Bronze Age, various aspects of history writing—from genealogy compilations to recording major achievements of meritorious ancestors—were related to the lineage-oriented mentality of the elite. Ancestors' deeds mattered then for determining their descendants' position and social prestige.[89] Even the history of the state as a whole was to a certain extent coequal to the history of its major ruling lineages (see the discussion on pp. 29–30). In the new society, in contrast, one's position was determined primarily by one's individual abilities and was less related to ancestors' merits. In this new situation, an interest in preserving detailed knowledge of ancestors' deeds may have declined as well.

I should caution readers that the preceding analysis may very well be biased because of the fact that no middle to late Warring States–period historical texts have survived the vicissitudes of history. We know from at least one discovery—the *Bamboo Annals* in approximately 280 CE—that the tradition of preparing court annals and certain derivative texts, which were primarily informative rather than didactic, remained intact well into the middle Warring States period.[90] We also know that local histories were produced by the scribal offices of the vanquished Warring States: these histories were eliminated in the Qin biblioclasm of 213 BCE. However, it may be plausibly assumed that the appeal of these histories to the members of the educated elite of the Warring States era was less than in the preceding Spring and-Autumn period. As Sima Qian noted, it was precisely because of the lack of circulation of these histories that their destruction was complete and irreversible.[91] (I provide more on this in the next chapter.) It took the grand project of the Sima family (Sima Qian and his father, Tan 司馬談 [d. 110 BCE], who began the composition of what would become *Records of the Historian*) to revive intellectual interest in informative history. Their success, like the earlier success of *Zuozhuan*, derived in no small measure from the authors' ability to use historical narrative simultaneously for ideological, entertainment, and informative purposes. In the Warring States period, in contrast, this integration seems to not have been achieved.

CHAPTER 4

Beyond Sima Qian

Zhou History Revisited

The discussion in the previous two chapters focused primarily on the parallels between *Xinian* (and other paleographic sources) and *Zuozhuan*, because by comparing these texts it was possible to highlight previously unnoticed aspects of the early Chinese historiographic tradition. In this chapter I shift to those sections of *Xinian* whose narratives predate or postdate *Zuozhuan*. These sections are not only rich in new historical information, which allows us to fill in lacunae in our knowledge, but also historiographically important, because they shed new light on the reliability of another major source for preimperial history, Sima Qian's *Records of the Historian*.

Sima Qian famously lamented the dearth of adequate sources for the history of the Warring States period as a result of the Qin biblioclasm. This dearth inevitably resulted in many inaccuracies and lacunae in Sima Qian's coverage of that period, as was noticed immediately upon the discovery of the *Bamboo Annals* in the late third century CE.[1] The *Bamboo Annals* also provided important correctives to Sima Qian's narrative of Western Zhou history, especially the events related to the crisis and the fall of the Western Zhou. These correctives, however, were less consequential: the mainstream perception of Western Zhou history remained overwhelmingly based on *Records of the Historian*. The publication of *Xinian*, which corroborates certain disputed points from the *Bamboo Annals* and challenges substantial parts of the narrative of *Records of the Historian*,

[95]

thrilled scholars. The new information generated heated controversy between those eager to accept it as a reliable alternative to *Records of the Historian* and those who fear that dramatic changes to Sima Qian's narrative will result in more confusion, rather than clarity, in our understanding of the Western Zhou demise. Not a few scholars preferred therefore to interpret *Xinian* in a way less contradictory of Sima Qian than a plain reading suggests.

My discussion in this chapter focuses on three aspects of *Xinian*'s information that require rethinking of past narratives. The first is related to the crisis and demise of the Western Zhou dynasty, the second deals with Qin's dynastic legend, and the third concerns interstate dynamics at the dawn of the Warring States period. These case studies allow us not only to evaluate more fully the importance of *Xinian* for scholars of Zhou history but also to highlight the challenges faced by those scholars willing to incorporate the unearthed manuscripts' information into the new narrative of China's past.

The Western Zhou Crisis

The major sources for our knowledge of the events that led to the collapse of the Western Zhou are the "Basic Annals of Zhou" (周本紀) in *Records of the Historian*, with additional pieces of information scattered in other chapters, such as the "Basic Annals of Qin" (秦本紀) and "Hereditary House of Wei" (衛世家). A few anecdotes from *Discourses of the States*, which evidently served as the major source material for Sima Qian's account, are of equal importance. Additional pieces of information come from the *Bamboo Annals*, from contemporaneous bronze inscriptions, and from some of the late Western Zhou odes from the *Canon of Poems*. Taken together these sources can provide a coherent view of the Zhou decline, as was demonstrated in the masterful work of Li Feng.[2] Now, the new evidence from *Xinian* allows not just fine-tuning earlier studies but even a more radical revision of parts of the commonly accepted narrative.

The "Basic Annals of Zhou" presents three stages of the Zhou dynastic crisis. First, King Li of Zhou 周厲王 (r. ca. 877–842 BCE) was overthrown by the rebellious "capital dwellers" (*guo ren* 國人) and was replaced by what Sima Qian calls the duumvirate of two chancellors, the Duke of Zhou 周公 and Duke of Shao 召公 (the descendants of two major power holders from the early years of the Zhou dynasty). These two, according to Sima Qian, reigned under the name of "Joint Harmony" (*gonghe* 共和, 841–828 BCE). Second, after the dynasty had been resurrected under King Li's son, King Xuan 周宣王 (r. 827–782 BCE), the latter failed on an external front, having been defeated in 788 BCE by the Rong 戎 ("Belligerent") attackers. The third crisis started under King You 周幽王 (r. 781–771 BCE). The king's general dysfunction was aggravated by his infatuation with the femme fatale Bao Si 褒姒, who is portrayed by Sima Qian as a malevolent spirit aimed at destroying the Zhou house. The king's decision to favor Bao Si's son over the erstwhile crown prince triggered a succession struggle, the rebellion of some of the subordinate regional lords, a renewed incursion of the Rong, and the final collapse of the Western Zhou in 771 BCE. The former crown prince was reinstalled but had to relocate the capital eastward to the Luoyang 洛陽 area. This was the beginning of the Eastern Zhou period.[3]

Xinian provides corroboration for many parts of Sima Qian's account (such as the Zhou defeat by the Rong in 788 BCE and the succession crisis triggered by Bao Si) but also departs from it on two major points: the identity of King Li's replacer and the trajectory of the Zhou crisis after 771 BCE. In what follows I focus on these controversial points because they are valuable not only for refining our knowledge of Zhou history but also and more fundamentally for improving our understanding of flaws in Sima Qian's narrative. Integrating *Xinian* evidence with the *Bamboo Annals* and with a few previously insufficiently understood statements in *Zuozhuan* provides a good antidote to the excessive reliance on *Records of the Historian*, which is observable now in not a few scholarly publications.

The Gonghe Reign

The overthrow of King Li of Zhou owing to popular discontent and the king's expulsion to Zhi 彘 (a settlement in Shanxi, far removed from the royal domain) are mentioned in a great variety of preimperial and early imperial texts. However, no text—not even *Discourses of the States*, which dedicates three anecdotes to King Li[4]—explains who replaced the ousted king and reigned during the fourteen years prior to the enthronement of King Xuan. None of the transmitted texts either questioned or corroborated Sima Qian's story of the "joint harmony" duumvirate by the two chancellors, the Duke of Zhou and the Duke of Shao.⁵

This narrative was challenged with the discovery of the *Bamboo Annals* in around 280 CE. The earliest readers and editors of this text were quick to notice a few instances of major discrepancies between the *Bamboo Annals*' content and that of *Records of the Historian*. Among other matters, the editors noted, "When King You [this should be King Li] had lost [his power], there was Gong Bo He who acted as the replacer of the Son of Heaven; it is not that two chancellors [i.e., the Duke of Zhou and the Duke of Shao] were 'jointly harmonious.'"⁶ That is to say, Sima Qian got the story wrong. The words *gong he* do not mean "joint harmony" but rather refer to a personal name, Gong He, or, more precisely, Gong Bo He. The latter name can be interpreted either as earl of the state of Gong, named He, or (more accurately in my view) as the elder of the Gong lineage, named He. Whatever Gong He's identity is, this person clearly has nothing to do with the alleged duumvirate of the Duke of Zhou and the Duke of Shao.⁷

Gong Bo He, or Gong He (as I prefer to call him henceforth), is an enigmatic figure. He is mentioned in a few transmitted texts. For instance, *Lüshi chunqiu* relates that during the troubles of King Li's time, when "the Son of Heaven's position was discontinued, All Under Heaven came to [Gong He]."⁸ In the same text, as well as in *Zhuangzi* and in the now-lost Warring States–period text *Lu Lianzi* 鲁連子 (cited in a commentary to *Zhuangzi*), Gong He is praised for retiring to the top of Mount Gong after performing an unspecified important mission.⁹ This sketchy information does not allow even an identification of who Gong He was. Later commentators tended to consider him as either a ruler of a tiny polity of Gong, which was eventually annexed by the state of Wei 衛, or as the ruler of Wei itself. Sima Qian might have inadvertently added to this confusion by his tentative (and obviously mistaken) identification of Gong He with Lord Wu of Wei 衛武公 (r. 812–758 BCE).¹⁰

Putting aside the irresolvable question of Gong He's identity, it is important to note that no early text specifies what exactly Gong He's role was in the aftermath of King Li's expulsion. The only unequivocal statement that directly corroborates the *Bamboo Annals* and allegedly comes from an early text (another extract from *Lu Lianzi* cited in Zhang Shoujie's 張守節 [fl. 725–735] commentary on *Records of the Historian*) is actually from a seventh-century gloss on *Lu Lianzi* rather than from the Warring States–period original.¹¹ The many other references to Gong He acting as

King Li's replacer all come from a variety of commentaries on early texts that were written after the discovery of the *Bamboo Annals*.[12] This means that in the final account, the readers of the "Basic Annals of Zhou" were left with the choice of either endorsing Sima Qian's version of the duumvirate or dismissing it and instead accepting the accuracy of the *Bamboo Annals*. Not surprisingly, opinions remained divided. Some scholars, such as the commentator on the *History of the Former Han Dynasty* (*Hanshu* 漢書), Yan Shigu 顏師古 (581–645), unequivocally postulated that Sima Qian's statements about "joint harmony" are "groundless."[13] Others, such as Zhang Shoujie or, much later, the eminent historian Cui Shu 崔述 (1739–1816), gave credit exclusively to Sima Qian's version.[14] The debates continue well into our time.[15] It is against this backdrop that *Xinian*'s information becomes particularly valuable.

The first section of *Xinian* narrates the history of the rise and fall of the Western Zhou. For the present discussion, I focus on its single segment that tells King Li's story:

> At the time of King Li, King Li was greatly oppressive toward Zhou. The chief ministers, all the officials, and the myriad people could not bear this in their hearts. Then they placed King Li at Zhi. Gong Bo He was established [as the king's replacer] for fourteen years. King Li fathered King Xuan. When King Xuan was established (728 BCE), Gong Bo He returned to Song.[16]

The narrative is unequivocal. *Gonghe* is not the name of a period but rather of a man, Gong Bo He, who acted as the king's replacer during the fourteen years of interregnum between the expulsion of King Li and the enthronement of King Xuan. There is no mention of the ministerial duumvirate. The similarity to the *Bamboo Annals* is unmistakable. And the fact that two unrelated texts present a unified version of the event makes it undoubtedly the correct version. The text does not shed light on the identity of Gong He, but it does not appear to support his identification with a Wei ruler.

This understanding has one problematic implication, though. How should we now read Sima Qian's story of the duumvirate? One can easily reach the conclusion that, facing an inexplicable reign-era name, *gonghe*, Sima Qian simply invented the story of the duumvirate to explain the nicely sounding ruling period. Yet plausible as this is, such a conclusion may have negative implications for the reliability of *Records of the Historian* as a whole. This understanding explains why many scholars adopt a somewhat equivocal stance about the implications of the *Xinian* 1 story. For instance, Li Ling suggests that insofar as we do not know the sources of Sima Qian's version, it is better to leave the decision to future contemplation.[17] Others, like Tao Xinghua, perform considerable intellectual acrobatics to make the two alternative views of the Gonghe reign fit. Tao turns the duumvirate into a triumvirate: it was under Gong He's aegis that the Duke of Zhou and the Duke of Shao shared power.[18] Other scholars do arrive at the obvious conclusion that Sima Qian's narrative is wrong[19] but prefer to avoid far-reaching inferences about the reliability of the Western Zhou sections of *Records of the Historian*.

It is appropriate to end this discussion with an ironic observation. When Japanese philologists searched for appropriate Chinese characters for translating the word "republic," they opted for the term *gongheguo* 共和國, as referring to the only nonmonarchical period in the history of Chinese polities.[20] The discovery of *Xinian* makes clear that this interpretation of *gonghe* is wrong. The "republic" is no more than the state of Mr. Gong He. . . .

King Ping and the Zhou Relocation to the East

The fall of the Western Zhou capital in 771 BCE and the subsequent relocation of the Zhou dynastic center eastward, to the vicinity of Luoyang, was one of the most dramatic events in early Chinese history. It was a point of no return from the period of relative stability under the dominance of the Zhou ruling house to the age of prolonged warfare and aggravating interstate conflicts that lasted for more than five centuries. However, despite their momentous impact, the demise of the Western Zhou and the establishment of the Eastern Zhou are among the least understood events in the dynasty's history. The narrative in *Records of the Historian* is extremely sketchy, and its inaccuracies were spotted long ago. Many attempts were made to revise Sima Qian's version of events and present a more convincing scenario of the Zhou relocation to the east. These efforts culminated in a detailed study by Li Feng in his seminal *Landscape and Power in Early China*.[21] However, the discovery of *Xinian* not only reopened the questions concerning the conflicting interpretations of this event but also presented an entirely new version of what happened following the fall of the Western Zhou.

Sima Qian's account of this crisis in the "Basic Annals of Zhou" comprises approximately nine hundred characters, most of which focus on Bao Si's machinations. Only a few dozen characters deal with the political and military aspects of the conflict that caused the dynasty's relocation. From this very brief account we learn that the establishment of Bao Si's son, Bopan 伯盤 (or Bofu 伯服), was the major trigger of the crisis. The erstwhile crown prince Yijiu 宜臼, the future King Ping, received support from his maternal grandfather, the Marquis of Shen 申侯. The coalition of Shen, Zeng 繒, and the Quanrong 犬戎 ("Canine Belligerents") tribesmen attacked King You, killing him and Bopan. In the aftermath of this turmoil, regional lords established Yijiu at Shen, and the latter then relocated his capital to Luo Settlement 洛邑 (Luoyang) to avoid the Quanrong. From the "Hereditary Houses" chapters, we learn that King Ping was supported in his relocation by Lord Xiang of Qin 秦襄公 (r. 777–766 BCE) and by Lord Wu of Wei 衛武公 (r. 812–758 BCE), both of whom were lavishly rewarded thereafter. Oddly, however, Sima Qian glosses over the role of other regional lords—such as Lord Wu of Zheng 鄭武公 (r. 770–744 BCE) and Marquis Wen of Jin 晉文侯 (r. 780–746 or 770–736 BCE)—whose contribution to King Ping's relocation is mentioned in several received texts.[22]

Sima Qian's account integrates the anecdotes scattered throughout the *Discourses of the States* and a few other sources, such as *Lüshi chunqiu*.[23] However, it omits an important story about the dynastic struggle that followed the death of King You. This struggle is hinted at in a letter sent in 516 BCE by the defeated contender for the Zhou throne, Prince Zhao 王子朝, to regional lords. The letter, which hails previous interventions of regional lords in Zhou dynastic struggles, says,

至于幽王，天不弔周，王昏不若，用愆厥位。攜王奸命，諸侯替之，而建王嗣，用遷郟鄏——則是兄弟之能用力於王室也。

When it came to the reign of King You, Heaven was ruthless to Zhou: the king was benighted and incompetent and therefore lost his place. King Xie (or King from Xie) usurped the mandate, but the regional lords put him aside, setting up a successor to the king and moving him to Jiaru (i.e., Luoyang). This, then, is how brothers can exert themselves on behalf of the royal house.[24]

Who was the "King Xie" who usurped the mandate? His name never appears in *Records of the Historian*. Du Yu, the great commentator of *Zuozhuan,* opined that this was the title of Crown Prince Bopan (Bao Si's son, who replaced the future King Ping as the new crown prince).[25] Yet the subcommentary of Kong Yingda 孔穎達 (574–648) corrected this misunderstanding. Kong cited the *Bamboo Annals*:

汲冢書《紀年》云：平王奔西申，而立伯盤以爲太子，與幽王俱死於戲。先是，申侯、魯（鄫?）侯及許文公立平王於申，以本大子，故稱天王。幽王既死，而虢公翰又立王子余臣於攜。周二王並立。二十一年，攜王爲晉文公所殺。以本非適。故稱攜王。

The *Annals*, a book from the Ji Tomb, says, King Ping fled to Western Shen, and [King You] established Bopan as crown prince. [Bopan] together with King You died at Xi. Before that, the Marquis of Shen, the Marquis of Lu [this should be Zeng], and Lord Wen of Xu established King Ping at Shen. Since he was originally the crown prince, he is named Heavenly King. When King You died, Han, the Lord of Guo, established Royal Son Yuchen at Xie, so that two kings of Zhou were established simultaneously. In the twenty-first year, King Xie was killed by Marquis Wen of Jin. Because originally he was not the proper successor, he is named King Xie [King of Discord].[26]

This story was not noted by Du Yu (who, it will be recalled, reviewed the *Bamboo Annals* soon after their discovery). It provides an entirely new understanding of the dynamics of the early years of the Eastern Zhou: not a smooth transition to the east but a prolonged struggle between two candidates to the throne, two Sons of Heaven. That this story is not attested in the transmitted texts (aside from a single phrase in *Zuozhuan*) is revealing. It shows, at the very least, that some substantial aspects of the Zhou transition to the east were not known to those Warring States–period authors whose narratives served Sima Qian in reconstructing early Zhou history. It was the accidental discovery of the *Bamboo Annals* that provided the first major blow to the traditional narrative. Now, more than seventeen centuries since the *Bamboo Annals* came to light, a second accidental discovery has dealt this narrative a new blow.

The fall of the Western Zhou is narrated in the second section of *Xinian*. The narrative there is divided into three parts. The first tells of the succession crisis in the Zhou house instigated by Bao Si, the subsequent conflict between the supporters of the ousted heir (the future King Ping) and King You, and the defeat of King You and his newly appointed heir, Bopan. This segment parallels the accounts in other texts, such as the *Bamboo Annals* and the "Zheng yu" 鄭語 section of *Discourses of the States*.[27] The third part, which narrates power configurations following the Zhou transfer to the east, is not discussed here (for its details, see the introduction to the translation of *Xinian 2*). Of interest here is the second part of *Xinian 2*, which presents a new story of the struggle in the Zhou house following the death of King You:

> The rulers of the states and various officials thereupon established the younger brother of King You, Yuchen, at Guo: this was King Hui from Xie. Twenty-one years after his establishment (750 BCE), Marquis Wen of Jin named Qiu (or Chou) killed King Hui at Guo. For nine years (749–741 BCE) Zhou was without a king, and the rulers of the states and regional lords then for the first time ceased attending the Zhou court. Thereupon, Marquis Wen of Jin greeted King Ping at Shao'e and established him at the royal capital. After three years (738 BCE) he relocated eastward, stopping at Chengzhou (i.e., Luoyang).

This narrative departs dramatically from other accounts of the Zhou downfall. It shows that the restoration of the Zhou dynasty under King Ping was a lengthy and bumpy process. Rather than being endorsed by a broad coalition of regional lords, as is hinted in *Discourses of the States* and *Records of the Historian*, King Ping seems to have been abandoned by the "rulers of the states and various officials," who instead supported his uncle, Yuchen. The latter reigned for a full twenty-one years as King Hui from Xie (hereafter King Xie or the King from Xie),[28] during which time the future King Ping was presumably in exile in the otherwise unknown location of Shao'e.[29] In 750 BCE, Marquis Wen of Jin killed the King from Xie, but this did not bring an immediate enthronement of the new incumbent. The text plainly states that "for nine years (749–741 BCE) Zhou was without a king, and the rulers of the states and regional lords then for the first time ceased attending the Zhou court." It is perhaps out of concern for this void of legitimate power that Marquis Wen acted again, first reinstating the king at the royal capital and then relocating him to Luoyang in 738 BCE.

The narrative itself is plain enough, is written in easily understandable characters, contains no signs of textual corruption, and, because of its strict chronological structuring, appears quite unequivocal. Nonetheless, this reading of the text was rejected outright by the text's editors and by a significant number of other scholars. The reasons for this rejection are not difficult to discover. First, the *Xinian* 2 version is at odds with *Records of the Historian* and, more broadly, with the entire textual tradition, which contains no hints about a kingless situation after the fall of the Western Zhou. Second, the sequence of the events depicted in *Xinian* contradicts some of the chronological information in *Records of the Historian*. Recall that according to Sima Qian, King Ping's relocation was assisted by Lord Xiang of Qin, who died in 766 BCE, and Lord Wu of Wei, who died in 758 BCE. However, if the eastward relocation occurred only in 738 BCE, then surely these leaders could not have assisted King Ping. Furthermore, Marquis Wen of Jin is presumed to have died in 746 BCE, which means that he could neither have enthroned King Ping in 741 BCE nor relocated him eastward three years later. Third, the *Xinian* narrative, which denies King Ping's rule before 741 BCE, contradicts the *Bamboo Annals*' claim that "two kings" coexisted until around 750 BCE. How to reconcile the new information and that in the received and previously unearthed (*Bamboo Annals*) texts?

Facing the ostensible contradiction between our traditional understanding and the newly unearthed text, many scholars tried to resolve it by reinterpreting the content of the latter. The editorial team led by Li Xueqin set the tone by arguing that the phrase 周亡王九年 does not mean "for nine years Zhou was without a king" but "nine years after Zhou lost the king"; that is, in 762 BCE.[30] Other scholars read the sentence as "the ninth year of the king who lost [the Zhou; alternatively, 'the demised king']"; that is, the ninth year of King You (i.e., 772 BCE). In that case, the relocation to the east should have occurred exactly in the year 770 BCE, favored by Sima Qian.[31] Another possible rearrangement is putting a period after *wang* 亡 and reading the sentence as, "Zhou had been lost. In the king's ninth year . . ." (周亡。王九年 . . .), in which case the relocation again would occur in 762 or 761 BCE.[32] Yet another possibility is to read the disputed sentence as in my translation but to argue that the twenty-first year since assassinating King Hui from Xie refers to the twenty-first year of Marquis Wen of Jin; that is, 760 BCE, in which case the events would match Marquis Wen's chronology.[33] On the other hand, not a few scholars did accept the reading of *Xinian* proposed in the preceding.[34] The debates peaked with a series of new articles on the topic published in 2016;[35] the question of interpretation has not yet been settled.

The formidable opposition to the proposed interpretation of *Xinian* 2 notwithstanding, I believe that it is easily defensible insofar as *Xinian*'s text itself is concerned. First, the Zhou story in *Xinian* 2 follows a rigid chronological sequence; to assume that the narrative jumps back from 750 BCE (the year that King Hui from Xie was assassinated by Marquis Wen of Jin) to the events of the 770s or 760s BCE is odd. Nor does the reading of *wang wang* 亡王 as a reference to King You make sense; while in other contexts this epithet ("a demised" or "a losing" king) could be applicable to him, this would not be the case when a king is referred to purely for the sake of counting years. In this latter case the king should be referred to either by his posthumous title (*shi* 謚) or as a "current king," but surely not as a "demised king."

Nor do the chronological problems pointed out by our colleagues appear to be irresolvable. Since I have addressed these issues in a joint study with Chen Minzhen, I will spare readers the largely technical discussion and instead briefly summarize our findings. First, the participation of Lord Wu of Wei in the rescue of King Ping is doubtful: Sima Qian's account about Lord Wu in general is filled with fancy and contradictory details that make its reliability questionable.[36] As for the major hero, Marquis Wen of Jin, it seems that his reign years were miscalculated by Sima Qian because of a scribal error in *Zuozhuan*; actually it is more likely that Marquis Wen died in 736 BCE—that is, after the Zhou relocation.[37] As for the merits of Lords Xiang of Qin and Wu of Zheng to King Ping, these may be less related to the king's final enthronement in 741 BCE and more to do with protecting him during the lengthy years of his uncle's rule. Overall, chronology does not seem to pose a problem to the interpretation in the preceding of the *Xinian* 2 account.[38]

In weighing the evidence pro and contra *Xinian*'s version of the Zhou downfall, three additional observations are due. First, the relative veracity of *Xinian*'s version of the events is supported by the nature of its account. The precise chronology employed in the textual segment discussed in the preceding (what can be called the 770–738 BCE segment) strongly suggests utilization of a relatively detailed primary source. We do not know the nature of this source, but its reliability is corroborated at the very least by the date of the assassination of the King from Xie, which is identical to the date provided in the *Bamboo Annals*. Moreover, the account in *Xinian* 2 appears ideologically neutral. It neither endorses King Ping nor rejects his legitimacy outright. It is not concerned with moral lessons that could be drawn from the depicted events, nor is it interested in blaming villains or hailing heroes. Actually, the narrative's goal is to provide the backdrop for the ascendancy of Jin, Zheng, and, most significantly, Chu (which is done in the last segment of *Xinian* 2). As such, the narrative seems to be free of ideological tampering, which increases its reliability.

Second, in contrast to *Xinian*'s authors, Sima Qian seems to have lacked adequate records for late Western Zhou history. This is exemplified, among others, by his misunderstanding of the nature of the *gonghe* reign, as earlier discussed. Or let us take, for instance, the "Chronological Tables of Twelve Regional Lords" (chapter 14 of *Records of the Historian* that covers events from 841 to 477 BCE). For the first century covered in the tables, the text provides scanty information aside from the ascendancy of regional lords and their reign years. This stands in strong contrast to the much more informative accounts in the same chapter once we enter the period covered by *Zuozhuan*.[39] The same sketchiness is reflected in other sections of *Records of the Historian* that deal with the events of roughly 900 to 722 BCE. The only exception is the coverage of Qin history, in discussing which Sima Qian relied on Qin records (whose problems are taken up in the next section). Yet Qin history aside, Sima Qian's information about the late Western Zhou period seems to come either from the now-lost genealogical compilation *Roots of Generations* (*Shi ben* 世本) or from Warring States–period anecdotes.

What happened to the sources utilized by the *Xinian* authors and unknown to Sima Qian? A possible—even if speculative—explanation may be provided by a short entry in *Zuozhuan*, according to which Prince Zhao, having been defeated in 516 BCE, "fled to Chu carrying with him Zhou canonical documents."[40] The nature of these documents is not known, but they may well have included historical writings. Indeed, a few commentators opined that this plunder of the Zhou archives explains the subsequent dearth of reliable materials concerning early Zhou history.[41] If this supposition is correct and the materials plundered by Prince Zhao ended up in the state of Chu, this might explain why a Chu historical work preserved traces of the Zhou past more accurately than any other text.[42]

The third and final point in support of the *Xinian* 2 chronology, which was noted by several scholars soon after the text's publication, is a previously ignored piece of information in *Zuozhuan*. It says of the year 638 BCE,

初，平王之東遷也，辛有適伊川，見被髮而祭於野者，曰：「不及百年，此其戎乎，其禮先亡矣。」秋，秦晉遷陸渾之戎于伊川。

Earlier, when King Ping had moved the capital to the east, Xin You had gone to Yichuan[43] and, upon seeing someone with unbound hair offering a sacrifice in the countryside, had said, "Within one hundred years this likely will be the Rong's! Ritual propriety had been lost already!" In autumn, Qin and Jin moved the Rong of Luhun to Yichuan.[44]

Xin You's prophecy that the Rong would occupy Yichuan "within one hundred years" was fulfilled in 638 BCE, which means that it was made in 738 BCE. This date greatly puzzled *Zuozhuan*'s commentators. Recall that in *Zuozhuan* prophecies play an important part in the narrative, and they are never made randomly. Normally, they are very precise. In the exceptional cases where they are not, this is explained by discrepancies among the calendars used by different countries (e.g., a Jin prediction made about an event happening within a certain year may be wrong from the point of view of a Lu calendar, according to which a year began two months earlier than in Jin). Alternatively, wrong predictions refer to events that postdate *Zuozhuan*'s composition.[45] Neither applies to Xin You's prediction, and the commentators could not grasp why it presupposes the Zhou relocation in 738 BCE rather than in the commonly accepted 770 BCE. With the publication of *Xinian* the puzzle was finally resolved. As pointed out by several colleagues,[46] Xin You's prediction implies that, by the time of *Zuozhuan*'s compilation, Zhou's relocation date was still thought to be in 738 BCE. This is the strongest external support for the *Xinian* chronology.

The Qin Dynastic Legend

As noted, the only local history that Sima Qian had at his disposal was that of the state of Qin. This was not an ideal source: Sima Qian famously complained about its low quality (sketchiness and imprecise chronology). Besides, according to Sima Qian's testimony, Qin instituted the scribal office only around 753 BCE, meaning that its earlier history was probably based on oral transmission.[47] Add to this the possibility that Qin records were tampered with by the Warring States–period Qin rulers.[48] That there is much confusion in the early sections of the "Basic Annals of Qin" comes therefore as no surprise.

The Qin dynastic legend as presented in *Records of the Historian* indeed appears somewhat perplexing. On the one hand, we are told of the glory of the Qin ancestors: descendants of the legendary thearch Zhuanxu 顓頊, they gained merit in serving almost every important leader in China's mythical and semimythical past, such as thearchs Shun 舜 and Yu 禹, and the kings of the Shang and Western Zhou dynasties. On the other hand, the Ying 嬴 clan, or, more precisely, its segment to which the Qin ruling lineage belonged, appears as a relatively marginal player on the fringes of the Zhou world. Even more confusingly, the narrative provides two conflicting perspectives on the origins of the Qin ruling lineage: some statements strongly connect it to the Shang polity in the east, whereas others emphasize its proximity to the Western Rong, the major tribal group in the west. The confusion may be a result of the conflation of several early legends, or possibly of Qin leaders' search for transregional legitimacy.

In the twentieth century, these contradictory accounts generated a heated controversy about the ethnic origins of Qin. This was the age during which ethnicity became a singularly important analytical tool for historians worldwide and in China itself,[49] and Qin was an important case study. Meng Wentong (1894–1968) was among the first to utilize scattered textual data to argue that Qin belonged to the Rong ethnicity.[50] In contrast, Fu Sinian (1896–1950) argued that Qin originated among the Eastern Yi 東夷, Shang's eastern subjects who were resettled by the Shang to the West.[51] The controversy resurfaced in the 1980s with the flow of archaeological data from Qin. Supporters of the "western origins" paradigm emphasized aspects of Qin burial practices (such as the east-west orientation of tombs and the flexed posture of the corpses within them) that could be linked to the early cultures of Gansu and areas further to the west. The proponents of the "eastern origins" approach pointed to such habits as the use of pottery vessels with Shang characteristics (e.g., *lì* 鬲 vessels with pouch-shaped feet and square lips, and pottery *guǐ* 簋 tureens with triangular patterns), the burial custom of using waist pits with dog sacrifices, the shape and size of the Qin rulers' burials, and the massive use of human sacrifices there as reflective of Qin's early relations to the Shang culture. Recently, scholarly opinion has gradually shifted to support the "eastern origins" approach, particularly because of recent archaeological discoveries (discussed in the following), yet controversies continue.[52]

It is against this backdrop that the third section of *Xinian* appears highly interesting. It reads as follows:

> After King Wu of Zhou had overcome Yin (Shang), he established three supervisors in Yin. When King Wu ascended [to Heaven], the Shang settlement rose in revolt, killing the three supervisors and establishing Luzi Geng (Sheng). King Cheng [of Zhou] invaded and exterminated the Shang settlement and killed Luzi Geng. Feilian fled eastward to the [settlement of] the Shanghe (Shangyan?) lineage; King Cheng attacked Shanghe, killed Feilian, and transferred the Shanghe people westward to Zhuyu, in order to repel the Nucuo(?) Rong: these were the Qin ancestors who for generations acted as protectors of Zhou. When the house of Zhou declined and King Ping relocated to the east, stopping at Chengzhou, Qin Zhong thereupon [moved] eastward, occupying the Zhou lands, in order to preserve the Zhou cemeteries. This was how Qin began to be great.

This text differs notably from other Western Zhou sections of *Xinian*. It is one of the only two sections in the entire *Xinian* that lacks a clear chronological outline.[53] This may indicate that the information here is likely to have originated in orally transmitted materials before it was recorded. This is not surprising: in light of Sima Qian's evidence, it is difficult to believe that Qin had accurate records of its history prior to the eighth century BCE. Therefore, it is plausible to suggest that *Xinian* 3, much like the "Basic Annals of Qin," presents just one of the different versions of Qin's dynastic legend.

If this scenario is correct (and I marshal additional evidence in support of it subsequently), then we should not expect exactitude in minor details.

Hence, a few discrepancies between *Xinian* 3 and the received texts, primarily *Records of the Historian*, come as no surprise. Take, for example, the fate of the "three supervisors" (*san jian* 三監), whom the Zhou conquerors imposed on the recently subjugated population of Yin, the Shang capital. Normally, the three are identified as the brothers of King Wu of Zhou and of the Duke of Zhou—namely, Guanshu Xian 管叔鮮 and Caishu Du 蔡叔度, in addition to either the scion of the Shang royal house, Wugeng 武庚, who is identified in *Xinian* as Luzi Geng 祿子耿 (or Sheng 聖),[54] or (since from *Xinian* it is clear that Wugeng was not a member of the trio) another brother, Huoshu Chu 霍叔處.[55] All the traditional accounts insist that the brothers joined the rebellious Wugeng and were executed or banished after the rebellion's suppression. *Xinian*, however, suggests that they were killed by the rebels. If this information presents a different version of the singularly famous rebellion at the beginning of Zhou rule, this would be fascinating.[56] However, it is equally possible that the authors of the Qin dynastic legend were less concerned with the fate of the "three supervisors," which was after all marginal to the legend's focus. For them it did not matter much whether the supervisors were killed at the beginning of the rebellion or after, and the statement may be just one of the examples of their carelessness. In this case, the novelty of *Xinian* 3 information matters little.

Putting lack of exactitude aside, the real value of *Xinian* 3 is in providing a radically novel account of the origins of the state of Qin. *Xinian* 3 identifies Qin's ancestors with the rebellious subjects of the defeated Shang dynasty, led by Feilian 飛廉. In *Records of the Historian*, Feilian (transcribed as 蜚廉) is identified as one of Qin's ancestors and a Shang loyalist, who died (or committed suicide) for the sake of the defeated Shang king, Zhouxin 紂辛. In the *Xinian* version (which is partly supported in *Mengzi*),[57] Feilian was a more active opponent of the Zhou. After the suppression of the pro-Shang rebellion, he fled to the territory of Shanghe 商蓋, which was identified by the Tsinghua University editorial team as Shangyan 商奄 (alternatively transcribed 商閹), a major Shang stronghold in Shandong, near which the future Lu capital, Qufu 曲阜, was constructed.[58] There he was defeated and killed, after which the Shangyan people were transferred westward, becoming henceforth loyal subjects and supporters of the Zhou. These were the progenitors of the Qin people.

This version of Qin's ancestry attracted the immediate attention of scholars. It has the advantage of neatly solving the riddle of identifiable similarities between Qin's material culture as reflected in early Qin burials (including those observed in recent excavations; e.g., from the Liya 李崖 site in Qingshui 清水 County, Gansu) and Shang culture.[59] There are further hints that support the plausibility of *Xinian*'s version. For instance, Zhuyu 朱圉, to which, according to *Xinian*, the Qin ancestors were relocated, has been identified by traditional geographers as a mountain in Gangu 甘谷 County (Gansu). Gangu County is one of the major locations of early Qin excavated sites. Most intriguingly, as noted by Li Xueqin, modern Zhuyu Township 朱圉鄉 is located close to Maojiaping 毛家坪, one of the best excavated early Qin settlements.[60] This coincidence becomes meaningful once we consider that the archaeological excavations at Maojiaping indicate the coexistence of two distinct cultural (ethnic?) groups in the same settlement.[61] This would be precisely the scenario if one segment of the Maojiaping residents were migrants from elsewhere. Nonetheless, it should be recalled that the earliest layers of Maojiaping settlement are from a later period than the alleged resettlement of Shangyan's people to the west, and that the Maojiaping site has not yielded Shang-related burial objects such as appear in other early Qin sites. The coincidence between *Xinian* 3 and the archaeological record is interesting but not as neat as some scholars assume.[62]

Other indirect pieces of evidence provide further support for the *Xinian* 3 scenario. For example, Sima Qian notes (certainly on the basis of Qin records) that Lord Xiang of Qin established sacrifices to Shaohao 少皞, one of the primordial thearchs.[63] The establishment of sacrifices to this thearch may be related to the fact that Shangyan, from which the Qin ancestors supposedly relocated westward, was located in the vicinity of "Shaohao ruins," possibly one of the earliest sites related to this figure.[64] Besides, that Shangyan was identified in the Warring States period as one of Qin's ancestral settlements is supported by a statement in another Warring States–period manuscript unearthed from Tomb 3, Mawangdui 馬王堆 (Changsha, Hunan). The fifth anecdote of the *Zhanguo zonghengjia shu* 戰國縱橫家書 (Letters of the Warring States[–period supporters of] the vertical and horizontal alliances) cites the famous diplomat Su Qin 蘇秦 (d. ca. 284 BCE) telling the king of Yan 燕王, "Should one be satisfied with what one has ... Qin would not depart from Shangyan" (自復不足 ... 秦將不出商閹). This sentence, which perplexed the editors, now becomes fully understandable, as it fits the *Xinian* narrative perfectly.[65] Clearly, then, the *Xinian* version cannot be dismissed as pure invention.

Those who reject it just because it departs from Sima Qian's narrative hold an untenable position.⁶⁶

Nevertheless, we should not err in the opposite direction of accepting *Xinian* 3 as a wholly reliable historical source. Take its last sentence, for example, which identifies the Qin ruler under whom Qin expanded into the former Western Zhou heartland as Qin Zhong 秦仲. Qin Zhong (d. 822 BCE) is identified in *Records of the Historian* as the first Qin ancestor who was enfeoffed as a ranked noble, but not as a founder of the Qin polity. Qin occupation of the Western Zhou heartlands and its rulers' elevation to the position of regional lords is associated by Sima Qian with Lord Xiang of Qin. The Tsinghua University editors opined that Qin Zhong (literally, "second born from Qin") should stand for Lord Xiang (who was second born), but this would be very odd: deceased rulers are invariably identified by their posthumous titles and not by seniority of birth.⁶⁷ Rather than interpreting Qin Zhong as standing for Lord Xiang or any other Qin ruler, it is simpler to conclude that this inaccuracy is due to the oral transmission of the Qin legend. For a Chu historian who incorporated a Qin dynastic legend, what mattered was not exactly who ruled the state of Qin during the period of its initial expansion but what is expressed in the final line: "This was how Qin began to be great."

Xinian's value for historians of the Qin dynasty is undeniable, but it would be advisable not to follow Wu Wenwen and others who argue that *Xinian* is the final proof of the "eastern origin" of Qin.⁶⁸ The story of Feilian's struggle against the Zhou house and subsequent relocation of his supporters westward should be read not as a "fact" but as yet another variant of the Qin dynastic legend, previously unknown. It is highly probable that this legend contains more than a kernel of historical truth, but even in that case the migrants from the east may have formed just one segment of the future Qin elite. Qin cannot simply be equated with "eastern" culture. The *Xinian* text may fill in an important lacuna of early Qin history, but it is not sufficient for providing definitive answers to questions related to ongoing scholarly research about early Qin's cultural trajectory.

The Dawn of the Warring States Period

The decades starting from the end of *Zuozhuan*'s narrative (468 BCE)⁶⁹ and continuing into the early years of the fourth century BCE remain somewhat of a terra incognita in China's history. Their coverage in *Records of the Historian* is much less detailed (and more confused) than that for the preceding or later years. A few dozen anecdotes scattered throughout the Warring States–period texts provide a number of interesting (albeit not always accurate) details of the events of this age, most notably the domestic strife in the state of Jin and the subsequent downfall of the strongman Zhi Bo 知伯 in 453 BCE. Overall, however, many basic parameters of the contemporaneous interstate dynamics were until recently barely understood. First, the discovery of the *Bamboo Annals*, and now the publication of *Xinian*, in addition to a few other paleographic materials, such as the inscription of the Piao Qiang (or Biao Qiang) 麃羌 bells, have dramatically expanded our knowledge.

In what follows I direct attention to two major points on which the information is particularly rich and illuminating: the role of the state of Yue in the interstate dynamics of the late fifth century BCE, and the background for the official recognition of the heads of the Wei, Zhao, and Han lineages in Jin as regional lords in 403 BCE. The third important addition to our knowledge concerns the construction of the earliest long protective walls, in particular the Long Wall of Qi. Since I address this last point in a separate study, I do not deal with it systematically here.[70]

The Yue Factor

The history of the state of Yue during the early Warring States period is shrouded in mystery. The "Hereditary House of King Goujian of Yue" (越王句踐世家) chapter in *Records of the Historian* is arguably the least accurate and least informative in the entire "Hereditary Houses" section. It provides a detailed account only of King Goujian (r. 496–464 BCE), whose epic struggle with the state of Wu inspired great interest from the end of the Spring and Autumn period onward. It is Goujian, and almost only Goujian and his aides, whom we encounter in multiple narratives about Yue, starting with *Zuozhuan* and *Discourses of the States* and ending with the Han-dynasty compilations *The Springs and Autumns of Wu and Yue* (*Wu Yue chunqiu* 吳越春秋) and *The Glory of Yue* (*Yuejue shu* 越絕書).[71] Post-Goujian history, in contrast, is not narrated in any of the received texts, aside from sketchy references in *Mozi* 墨子, *Stratagems of the Warring States*, *Han Feizi*, and *Records of the Historian*. Of these, the evidence in

Mozi appears most interesting. Mozi (ca. 460–390 BCE) mentions Yue, along with Qi, Jin, and Chu, as the major superpower of his age: the four "had divided All Under Heaven into four parts and possess it."[72] However, no other transmitted text provided any additional clue as to Yue's position after Goujian's death.

The first reliable information about the post-Goujian history of Yue came from the *Bamboo Annals*, many entries from which were incorporated into the *Suoyin* 索引 glosses on *Records of the Historian*. These entries not only provide an exact chronology of the post-Goujian kings but also inform of Yue's expansion into southern Shandong, which peaked with the annexations of the statelets of Teng 滕 and Tan 郯 in 415 and 414 BCE—that is, in the final years of King Zhuju 越王朱句 (r. ca. 447–411 BCE).[73] This Shandong expansion apparently followed the transfer of Yue's capital to the city of Langye 琅琊 (or Langya) in southern Shandong, which took place at the end of Goujian's rule or slightly later.[74] Chen Minzhen refers to the years following this capital transfer as the "Shandong period" in Yue history.[75] This period ended in 379 BCE, when King Yi of Yue (越王翳, r. ca. 410–375 BCE) opted to retreat southward, relocating to the former Wu capital near modern Suzhou.[76]

To these scanty records, *Xinian* adds several pieces of valuable information about Yue's place in the Chinese world during its "Shandong period." Let us start with section 20. The first part of this section narrates the history of the Jin-Wu axis directed against Chu. After Wu was defeated by Yue, the latter inherited its position as Jin's strategic partner in the southeast:

> King Goujian of Yue overpowered Wu. Thereafter, the Yue leaders inherited Wu's friendly relations with Jin. In the eleventh year of Lord Jing of Jin (441 BCE), [a Jin leader] Zhao Huanzi assembled the grandees of the regional lords, making a covenant with *lingyin* Song of Yue at Gong. Thereupon they invaded Qi. The people of Qi then for the first time erected the Long Wall at the Ji [River]; [the wall] stretched from the Southern Mountain to the Northern Sea. In the fourth year of Lord You of Jin (430 BCE), Zhao Gou led an army, and, together with Lord Zhuju of Yue, invaded Qi. The Jin army stormed the Long Wall at the Gu Gate. The Duke of Yue and Duke

of Song defeated the Qi army at Xiangping. Until now Jin and Yue maintain amicable relations.

Putting aside details of personal and place-names mentioned in this section (for which see the discussion in part 2 of this book), the narrative is quite straightforward. The state of Yue had inherited Wu's erstwhile position as Jin's major ally in the southeast. This alliance (which, according to the last sentence of the cited section, continued well into the time of *Xinian*'s composition) was directed primarily against the state of Qi, which faced a temporary setback in its fortunes during the long period of the Tian lineage's consolidation of its power (481–386 BCE). The allies' assault on Qi in 441 BCE caused the Qi rulers to erect the long protective wall, which was meant primarily to fend off Yue's potential pressure. I refrain from discussing here a series of very interesting questions concerning this wall's precise route, its political and economic (aside from purely military) functions, and the like, since this task has been undertaken elsewhere.[77] What is important in the context of our discussion is that the wall did not save Qi from renewed attacks. One was launched shortly after the wall's erection in 430 BCE. Another followed twenty-five years later, as depicted in *Xinian* 22:

> Han Qian, Zhao Ji, and Wei Ji led the armies and, together with Lord Yi from Yue, assaulted Qi.[78] Qi made peace with Yue, submitting to it and [giving it] the fields of Jianyang and Juling, as well as male and female (servants). The Duke of Yue made a covenant with Marquis of Qi, Dai, and the Marquis of Lu, Yan, outside the Ji Gate of Lu.[79] The Duke of Yue entered the Lu [capital] for the banquet: upon his entrance, the Marquis of Lu drove his carriage, and the Marquis of Qi accompanied him in the carriage.

This story depicts Yue's power reaching its apex. Having launched a joint attack on Qi together with Jin and with minor allies, such as Lu, Yue had achieved a major symbolic success: Qi had to not only sue for peace and bribe the king of Yue with fields and other presents but also allow King Yi of Yue to perform a triumphal procession in the Lu capital: "the Marquis of Lu drove his carriage, and the Marquis of Qi accompanied him in the carriage." As shown in the following, this separate peace with Yue did not save Qi from renewed assault by the Jin forces. What matters for the present discussion, however, is the text's unequivocal indication that by the end of the fifth century BCE (i.e., roughly during Mozi's lifetime) Yue indeed was one of the major powers on Chinese soil. That this important period in Yue history was not noted by Sima Qian is indicative of the inadequacy of his sources for the early history of the Warring States period.

The Rise of Wei, Zhao, and Han

Sima Guang 司馬光 (1019–1086), arguably the most eminent historian and political thinker of China's imperial period, began the account in his *Comprehensive Mirror to Aid the Government* (*Zizhi tongjian* 資治通鑒) with what he considered a momentous change in Zhou history. In 403 BCE, King Weilie of Zhou 周威烈王 (r. 425–402 BCE) decided to elevate the heads of the Wei, Zhao, and Han ministerial lineages in the state of Jin to the position of regional lords. For Sima Guang, this meant that the king discarded the ritual norms of the Zhou age, according to which no matter how powerful a minister was, he would never be recognized as a regional lord. The historian considered this the point of no return in Zhou's lengthy decline, and his subsequent discussion of the political implications of this step is one of the most intellectually engaging parts of the *Comprehensive Mirror*.[80] Yet this lengthy discussion conceals the embarrassing brevity of the factual account in Sima Guang's magnum opus. Why did King Weilie decide to abandon the old norms? What was the background for this decision? Sima Guang is silent. This silence is not surprising. It reflects the lack of relevant information in Sima Qian's *Records of the Historian*. There, the elevation of the heads of the Wei, Han, and Zhao lineages is mentioned repeatedly, but no additional information is provided, and some of the dates are confused as well.[81]

Once again, the *Bamboo Annals* provides some clues about the background of King Weilie's decision. It records two instances of Jin clashes with the state of Qi. The first record, dated to the eleventh year of Lord Lie of Jin 晉烈公 (r. 415–389 BCE), 405 BCE, tells of internal turmoil in the state of Qi (the rebellion of Ducal Grandson Hui 公孫會 in his stronghold of Linqiu 廩丘). Ducal Grandson Hui requested assistance from the neighboring Zhao domain. The armies of the Wei, Zhao, and Han lineages indeed helped him to defeat the Qi army.⁸² Another, even more interesting, instance is the record from the next year (404 BCE):

晉烈公十二年，王命韓景子、趙烈子、翟員（角）伐齊，入長城。

In the twelfth year of Lord Lie [of Jin], the king commanded Han Jingzi, Zhao Liezi, and Di Yuan [this should be Di Jiao] to invade Qi. They penetrated the Long Wall.⁸³

The *Bamboo Annals* derives from the Wei 魏 chronicle and probably reflects a Wei perspective of the event. If the invasion of Qi in 404 BCE was performed jointly by the forces of three Jin ministerial lineages turning into independent polities (often called the Three Jin) in response to the Zhou king's command, then it is reasonable to infer that the elevation of these lineages' heads to the position of regional lords in the next year was directly related to this invasion. An additional relevant piece of evidence comes from *Lüshi chunqiu*. The text extols the wisdom of the founder of the independent Wei polity, Marquis Wen of Wei 魏文侯 (r. 445–396 BCE), who excelled in attracting gifted men of service:

文侯可謂好禮士矣。好禮士故南勝荊於連隄；東勝齊於長城，虜齊侯，獻諸天子，天子賞文侯以上卿。

Marquis Wen [of Wei] can be called the one who was fond of being courteous to men of service. He was fond of being courteous to men of service: hence in the south he overcame Jing (i.e., Chu) at Lianti; in the east he overcame Qi at the Long Wall. He captured the Marquis of Qi and presented him to the Son of Heaven. The Son of Heaven rewarded Marquis Wen of Wei with the position of supreme minister (or with supreme renown?).⁸⁴

This brief summary of Marquis Wen's deeds should not be read as an accurate factual account; yet it is tempting to connect it to the *Bamboo Annals* story about the Three Jin attack on Qi and their penetration of Qi's Long Wall. If we combine the two stories, adding to it another reference to the Lord of Qi's capture by the Jin armies (narrated in *Masters of Huainan* [*Huainanzi* 淮南子]),⁸⁵ then it becomes possible to re-create the sequence of events leading to the enfeoffment of the heads of the Wei, Zhao, and

Han lineages. This reconstruction has been undertaken by Yang Kuan. According to his narrative, the Three Jin armies invaded Qi twice, in 405 BCE following Ducal Grandson Hui's rebellion and again in 404 BCE, allegedly on behalf of the Son of Heaven. The second invasion resulted in the capture of the nominal ruler of Qi, Lord Kang 齊康公 (r. 404–386 BCE), the last ruler of the Jiang 姜 clan in Qi. This extraordinary success brought about the subsequent enfeoffment of the Three Jin leaders, as is hinted in *Lüshi chunqiu*.[86]

Two new pieces of evidence support Yang Kuan's reconstruction and add more details to it. The first is section 22 in *Xinian*. In the preceding I have cited its first part, narrating the joint assault of the Three Jin and Yue armies on Qi, following which Qi had to sign a humiliating separate peace with Yue and its ally, Lu. The second part of *Xinian* 22 narrates the events after the Qi-Yue peace accord:

> Si, Marquis Wen of Wei (r. 445–396 BCE) of Jin, followed the Jin army; the Jin army greatly defeated the Qi army.... Qi asked Jin for peace. The Marquis of Qi made a covenant at the [location of the] Jin army. The grandees of the Three Masters of Jin entered the Qi capital and made a covenant with Chen He and Chen Hao[87] outside the Yong Gate, saying, "Do not repair the Long Wall, do not invade Linqiu."[88] The Duke of Jin presented the Qi captives and the severed ears [of slain Qi soldiers] to the King of Zhou and then attended the Zhou royal court, bringing with him the Marquis of Qi, Dai; the Marquis of Lu, Xian; the Duke of Song, Tian; the Marquis of Wei [衛], Qian; and the Earl of Zheng, Tai.

This narrative fully supports Yang Kuan's reconstruction of the events that led to the enfeoffment of the heads of the Wei, Zhao, and Han lineages. Despite the loss of their Yue allies, the Three Jin armies continued their assault on Qi, causing first the nominal ruler of Qi, Lord Kang, to make a covenant in Jin's military camp and then the de facto ruler of Qi, Tian He (Chen He), to make another, more humiliating covenant with the subordinates of Jin's ministers in the precincts of Qi's capital. To celebrate this achievement (which dwarfed even the previous Jin triumph of the An 鞌 battle, 589 BCE),[89] the Jin ministers orchestrated a major event at the court of the Zhou king in the next year (403 BCE). It is perhaps out of gratitude for this rare display of respect to the ailing Zhou house that King Weilie rewarded the Jin ministers by officially elevating them to the rank of marquis and the status of regional lords.

Xinian 22 is corroborated by another piece of paleographic evidence related to the Jin-Qi campaign of 404 BCE, the inscription on the Piao Qiang bells. These bells were unearthed in 1928–1931 near Luoyang and dispersed among museums in Japan and Canada; their inscription provoked heated controversy with regard to both its precise content and its relation to the events depicted in transmitted textual sources. With the publication of *Xinian*, most of these controversies can be settled, as several studies demonstrate.[90] The inscription cast by one of the subordinates of Han Qian, the future Marquis Jing of Han, states,

隹（唯）廿又再祀，屬羌乍（作）戎（介）厶（厥）辟韓宗譱（獻=虔）率（帥），征秦迲齊，入張（長）城，先會于平陰（陰），武侄（至？）寺（郜？），力寡（襲）敓（奪）楚京。賞于韓宗，命于晉公，卲（昭）于天子，用明則之于銘，武文咸刺（烈），永枼（世）母（毋）忘。

In the twenty-second year, Piao Qiang became a deputy.[91] His leader, the head of the Han lineage, Qian, led [an army]: we invaded Qin[92] and pressed Qi. We penetrated the Long Wall, assembling first near Pingyin, martially reaching Shi and forcefully assaulting and seizing Chujing. [I] was rewarded by the head of the Han lineage, received the command of the Duke of Jin, and was illuminated by the Son of Heaven. I have inscribed this to make this pattern illustrious. Let my blazing martiality and refinement forever remain unforgotten.

The twenty-second year in the inscription refers to the reigning year of the Zhou King Weilie, which is 404 BCE; that is, exactly the date of the Jin-Qi war narrated in *Xinian* 22. Judging from the place-names mentioned on the bell, Piao Qiang took part in the first assault on Qi; that is, prior to the Qi-Yue truce.[93] That Piao Qiang's merits were rewarded not only by his immediate superiors, Han Qian and Lord Lie of Jin 盡烈公 (r. 415–389 BCE), but also by the Son of Heaven is yet another indicator to the effect that the Three Jin's victory was rewarded by the Zhou king.

The combined evidence of *Xinian* 22, the *Bamboo Annals*, the inscription on the Piao Qiang bells, and the scattered references in *Lüshi chunqiu* and *Huainanzi* allows us to reconstruct the background for the elevation of the Jin ministers to the position of regional lord. It was the combination of their military prowess and skillful diplomacy (bolstering the prestige of the long-defunct Zhou dynasty) that allowed them to attain a status that was never granted to new families throughout Eastern Zhou history. That the background for such a significant event appears to have been unknown to Sima Qian is yet another indication of the problems we face when relying on *Records of the Historian* as the major source for early Warring States history.

Afterthought: Sima Qian's Sources

In the preceding I have focused on the discrepancies between *Xinian* and *Records of the Historian*. In most (albeit by no means all) of the surveyed cases the evidence tends to support *Xinian*, demonstrating time and again the problems of Sima Qian's narrative. It is important to stress here that by emphasizing these problems I do not mean to diminish the value of *Records of the Historian* and its overall credibility. Recall that much of Sima Qian's information is corroborated rather than refuted by *Xinian* and other sources. And yet the inaccuracies and lacunae are of such magnitude that ignoring them would be highly imprudent.

What do these inaccuracies and lacunae mean? I think they cannot be explained by Sima Qian's (and his father's) laxity or carelessness. We know that whenever Sima Qian could make use of a reliable early work, such as *Zuozhuan*, he did a remarkable job of preserving much of the relevant information.[94] That the events of the ninth to eighth and fifth centuries BCE are not covered with sufficient accuracy reflects the sad state of Sima Qian's sources. What happened to the Western Zhou historical sources is not clear: whether or not they indeed disappeared after being smuggled to Chu by Prince Zhao is impossible to verify. The fate of the Warring States–period histories is narrated by Sima Qian himself, and there is no doubt that Qin's biblioclasm was indeed the major reason for their disappearance.

However, it is useful to pause here and return to Sima Qian's testimony. The historian says that in contrast to the *Canon of Poems* and

Canon of Documents, which were stored privately and hence survived into the Han, "the historical records were stored only in the Zhou archives, and hence were all destroyed. How regrettable! How regrettable!"[95] This reminds us once again of the surprising lack of interest in informative histories during much of the Warring States period. Sima Qian's lamentations are fully justified. As the discussion in this chapter demonstrates, we still depend on incidental discoveries to comprehend even some of the basic events in the history of the Warring States period. Reconstructing the nature of these events from beyond the inaccuracies that accrued in *Records of the Historian* and in later texts remains an arduous task.

CHAPTER 5

Chu Historiography and Chu Cultural Identity

The previous chapters have dealt with various aspects of early Chinese historiography. Here I want to consider the impact of history writing on actual history, or, more precisely, on one of its aspects: formation of cultural identities in the Zhou world. Recall that in China, as elsewhere, historians did not only preserve memories of the past. They also shaped these memories in ways so as to influence readers' values, perceptions, and, at least sometimes, readers' sense of cultural identity. This last point is of particular interest to modern historians. It is widely accepted, for instance, that Sima Qian's integrative history of the Chinese world contributed toward a sense of cultural cohesiveness among educated dwellers of the Han empire and also contributed to the legitimacy of the imperial enterprise as a whole.[1] The immediate questions are, what was the sense of cultural identity among elite members prior to the imperial unification? Did the elites of Qin, Chu, Qi, and the Jin successor states conceive of themselves as members of a shared cultural community or instead primarily as men of Qin, Chu, and so forth? How strong were the local identities among the elite, subelite, and nonelite members of the competing Warring States?

These questions are particularly relevant to the state of Chu. Its cultural identity is one of the most contested issues in studies of early Chinese history. Both textual and material evidence can be interpreted in different ways; hence, whereas some scholars insist that Chu was the cultural Other of the Zhou world, others consider it an intrinsic part of Zhou civilization. To complicate matters, most of the Chu-related narratives in the transmitted texts were created in the northern part of the Zhou world and are suspected to reflect "northern biases,"[2] which means that their reliability with regard to the self-image of Chu elites is doubtful. It is in this context that we can appreciate the importance of the historical and quasi-historical manuscripts recently excavated (or looted) from Chu tombs. By offering a Chu perspective of its history, they allow us to think anew about Chu's cultural trajectory. In what follows, after a brief outline of the debates over Chu's cultural belonging, I attempt to evaluate the impact of these newly discovered manuscripts—the nature of most of which have been discussed in the previous chapters—on ongoing research related to Chu identity. This evaluation will, I hope, be useful not only for the case of Chu but also for some broader conclusions about historiography and identity building in preimperial China.[3]

The Question of Chu's Otherness

Traditional scholars were overwhelmingly inclined to view Chu as the cultural Other of the Zhou world. The reasons for this verdict are not difficult to find. Already some of the Western Zhou sources indicate considerable enmity between the Zhou realm and the state of Chu. The most notable manifestation of this enmity were campaigns of King Zhao of Zhou 周昭王 (r. ca. 975–957 BCE) against Chu in approximately 960–957 BCE. The last of these campaigns ended in the disastrous loss of royal armies, and the king himself perished. The memory of this humiliation lived for centuries.[4]

Tensions between Zhou and Chu continued into the reign of King Xuan of Zhou 周宣王 (r. ca. 827–782 BCE). The ode "Plucking White Millet" (Cai qi 采芑) in the *Canon of Poems* hails a minister of King Xuan's who allegedly invaded and overawed the "savage Jing" (蠻荊). Whether or not this term refers to the state of Chu (which often appears under the name Jing or Jing-Chu in early sources) or to other ethnic groups of the Han and middle Yangzi basin is debatable,[5] but elsewhere the *Canon of Poems* seems to unmistakably signify the state of Chu as a major enemy. Two of the Lu and the Shang (probably Song) hymns contain references to battles with the Jing-Chu, which, in a Lu hymn, is placed unequivocally aside the alien ethnic groups Rong and Di.[6] These hymns probably date from the Spring and Autumn period, but they do indicate that the tradition of political and cultural enmity toward Chu that started in the Western Zhou period continued and perhaps strengthened thereafter. As mentioned in chapter 4, this enmity is visible in some of the Spring and Autumn–period inscriptions from the state of Sui (Zeng), which postulate, "Chu behaved excessively; we came to counterbalance it" (楚既爲忒，吾徠匹之).[7]

Zuozhuan records in great detail the rise of Chu and its epic struggle for supremacy in the Zhou world against the northern coalitions, led first by Qi and then by Jin. A superficial reading of *Zuozhuan* lends support to identification of Chu as a culturally distinct entity. A Lu minister's saying, "They are not of our kin, their heart must be different" (非我族類，其心必異) is commonly—albeit erroneously—interpreted as pertaining to Chu's "racial" otherness.[8] This interpretation is wrong, but *Zuozhuan* does contain many other negative comments about Chu, which is perceived as a rival of the Xia 夏 entity centered on the Zhou royal clan. Thus, a Jin commander accuses Chu of eliminating many polities established by Zhou royal clansmen (the Ji 姬 clan),[9] and many of Chu leaders—from its prime minister (*lingyin* 令尹), Ziyu 子玉 (d. 632 BCE), to infamous King Ling (r. 540–529 BCE)—are singled out as arrogant and aggressive statesmen eager to violate rules of ritual and propriety. All this often leaves an impression of the text's overall enmity toward Chu.

A careful reading of *Zuozhuan*, however, shows that the picture is more complex. Chu is never treated in the text as the cultural Other; in contrast to other southern powers, such as Wu and Yue, Chu is never referred to in terms such as *manyi* 蠻夷 (savages). Certainly some Chu leaders are denigrated, but others—most notably King Zhuang (r. 613–591 BCE)—are shown great respect. Moreover, some of the pejorative remarks about Chu in *Zuozhuan* should be read *cum grano salis*. After all, the very state of Lu, whose statesmen opposed relying on Chu, who "are not of our kin," was at times closely allied with Chu, seeking its military assistance against the neighboring power of Qi. And the elimination of Zhou clansmen polities was performed not just by Chu but also by the self-proclaimed defender of the Zhou, the state of Jin.[10] In fact, some imperial readers considered *Zuozhuan* too biased in favor of Chu, and some of the exegetes—most notably Zhu Xi 朱熹 (1130–1200)—opined that *Zuozhuan* itself was a product of Chu historiography.[11]

In many texts of the Warring States period we encounter ever more pronounced enmity toward Chu. In particular, its association with "barbarians" becomes a commonplace. This association is reiterated throughout *Discourses of the States*,[12] even though the overall view of Chu in this text is far from negative, and parts of it, as we shall see, contain laudatory comments about Chu. A pejorative view of Chu is more explicit in the *Gongyang Commentary* on the *Spring and Autumn Annals*. Chu is consistently identified in the text as a "barbarian" (*yi* 夷 or *yidi* 夷狄) state; it is oddly claimed to have no ranked nobles (which is patently wrong, judging from the *Annals*' text itself), and it is frequently treated with undisguised enmity.[13] One of the *Gongyang Commentary* statements is particularly important because of its lasting influence on subsequent views of Chu:

楚有王者則後服，無王者則先叛。夷狄也，而亟病中國，南夷與北狄交。中國不絕若線。

Chu is the last to submit when there is a True Monarch, and the first to rebel when there is none. They are barbarians (*yidi*) and intensely hate the Central States. When southern savages and northern barbarians established ties, the Central States were like a thread due to be cut.[14]

Statements like this—coming from amid one of the most famous passages in the entire *Gongyang Commentary*—set the framework for discussions of the Chu political and cultural position within the Zhou world for millennia to come. It marked Chu as the epitome of the cultural Other, the malevolent polity that can be subjugated only under the reign of the True Monarch, and even then will forever remain prone to rebel. Coupled with a few other pejorative statements toward Chu in, for example, *Mengzi* and *Records of the Historian*,[15] the *Gongyang Commentary* denigration of Chu attained the position of an orthodox view in traditional Chinese scholarship.

The traditional view of Chu as a distinct cultural entity was reinforced in the last quarter of the twentieth century as many discoveries from Chu tombs brought to light the peculiar, "flamboyant"[16] style of its mortuary objects. Lothar von Falkenhausen observed, "Dazzled by these unique archaeological treasures, many scholars and impressionable laypersons have been clinging to the romantic notion that Chu was a separate southern civilization, an elegant and exuberant Other to the dour, disciplined Zhou in the north."[17] Yet this view of Chu as an "alternative civilization" was questioned later as the result of subsequent archaeological discoveries. The new understanding, summarized by Xu Shaohua in the seminal volume edited by Constance A. Cook and John S. Major is that "there is little archeological evidence of a distinctive Chu culture during the Western Zhou times."[18] It was only from the Spring and Autumn period on that a divergent cultural pattern associated with Chu began emerging, and even then Chu's elite culture remained in conformance with Zhou ritual practices.[19] This suggests an entirely different cultural trajectory: Chu was not a "barbarian entity" attracted by the glory of Zhou culture, as hinted in the *Mengzi*,[20] but a normative Zhou polity that developed cultural assertiveness in tandem with the increase in its political power.[21]

The difficulty of analyzing Chu's identity derives not only from the complexity of its cultural trajectory but also from the nature of our textual sources. The overwhelming majority of Chu-related accounts in transmitted texts come from the histories produced outside the state of Chu. The *Spring and Autumn Annals* and their commentaries were composed in the states of Lu and Qi; most of *Discourses of the States* comes from the Zhou royal domain, Lu, and Jin; and such is the case for most historical anecdotes scattered throughout Warring States–period texts. Although the Chu sections of *Discourses of the States* and of *Stratagems of the Warring States*, as well as segments of *Zuozhuan*, may well have incorporated original Chu materials, we have no idea of the degree of editorial intervention by non-Chu compilers in these materials. Look, for instance, at *Records of the Historian*, our major source for preimperial history. Even those who do not subscribe to the accusation of Sima Qian as one who "describes Chu in the imperialist terms of a northerner,"[22] would not deny the obvious northern bias in his—and other historical—writings. This consideration should dictate utmost caution in reading these texts. To accept, for example, the self-identification of Chu as a "barbarian" polity on the basis of citations in *Discourses of the States* and *Records of the Historian*[23] strikes me as a haphazard conclusion.

It is against this background that we can appreciate the import of the newly unearthed historical and quasi-historical manuscripts from the state of Chu. These materials, most of which were surveyed in chapters 2 and 3, were either products of Chu scribes or at the very least unearthed (supposedly, in the case of looted manuscripts) from Chu tombs. An integrative view of these materials and of the ways they present Chu's identity may yield a novel perspective on Chu's self-image.

That history writing was—and is—commonly utilized to articulate, strengthen, or shape the collective identity of a cultural, ethnic, or political entity is almost a truism. To be sure, this is just one means of strengthening or constructing a separate cultural or political identity, and not necessarily the major one. Yet the importance of history writing in this regard, especially concerning the educated segments of the population, is undeniable.[24] Paul R. Goldin has noted that the emergence of local histories in the Eastern Zhou period may be related to a nascent sense of regional identity.[25] In what follows I test whether or not this observation is valid for the state of Chu. How much do Chu historical texts reflect its separate cultural identity or contribute toward its formation? Do they oppose the denigration of Chu's culture in northern texts? Do they bolster the Chu kings' legitimacy as potential leaders of All Under Heaven? Do they present a different picture of Chu's relations with the Zhou polities from the one we have in the received texts? Do they use such common means of strengthening collective identity as focusing on Chu's wars with its rivals, glorifying its victories, and lamenting its defeats? In answering these questions I hope to advance toward a better understanding both of the issues related to the formation of Chu's separate cultural outlook and of the role of history writing in the cultural processes during the Zhou era.

Chu Historical Anecdotes

Let us start with didactic anecdotes discovered at (or looted from) Chu tombs. These anecdotes figure prominently in the Shanghai Museum collection of Chu manuscripts, of which they constitute more than half of the heretofore published titles and are present, albeit less prominently, among the Chu manuscripts possessed by Tsinghua University, the publication of which is still (2020) ongoing. In addition, a few anecdotes appear in other collections of Chu materials.[26] Since the lion's share of the anecdotes comes from the Shanghai Museum collection, I focus in what follows primarily on this collection.[27]

One striking feature of the anecdotes from the Shanghai Museum collection is what Sarah Allan calls their "cosmopolitan" content.[28] According to Allan's count, of twenty-four vignettes, thirteen come from Chu, while the rest are spread throughout most of the Zhou world, coming from Lu (four), Qi (four), and one each from Jin, Zheng, and Wu. My own count differs slightly from Allan's, primarily because I count two anecdotes embedded in the same manuscript separately, and also because I follow rearrangements of slips into a different sequence of manuscripts as proposed by a few later redactors.[29] Yet the differences are minuscule. Putting aside multiple anecdotes related to Confucius and his disciples, we can summarize that Chu vignettes constitute just slightly more than 60 percent of the anecdotes in the Shanghai Museum collection, and the percentage will further decrease should we add anecdotes from other sites and collections, which are overwhelmingly non-Chu in their focus.[30] This allows an immediate observation: members of the Chu educated elite who took anecdotes with them on their final journey to the netherworld appear to have been interested in the affairs of the entire Zhou realm rather than being narrowly focused on their own country. The next question concerns to what extent the Chu-related anecdotes from the Shanghai Museum collection represent aspects of Chu political or cultural identity. To facilitate discussion of this question, I have summarized the content of these anecdotes in table 5.1.

TABLE 5.1
Chu anecdotes from the Shanghai Museum collection

#	Name	Location[1]	Focus	Comment
1	*Zhao wang hui shi* 昭王毀室	Vol 4: 179-186	King Zhao decides to destroy a new palatial chamber that infringed on his subject's graveyard	Part of the same manuscript as #2
2	*Zhao wang yu Gong zhi Shui* 昭王與龏之脽	Vol 4: 186-190	King Zhao displays humility and self-criticism after his defeat by the Wu invaders	Part of the same manuscript as #1

(continued)

TABLE 5.1 (continued)

#	Name	Location[1]	Focus	Comment
3	Jian da wang po han 柬大王泊旱	Vol 4: 191–215	King Jian discusses proper sacrificial ceremonies to avert drought and to end personal illness	Similar discussion of the importance of ritually appropriate sacrifices to avert troubles recur in many texts starting with Zuo zhuan[2]
4	Zhuang wang ji cheng 莊王既成	Vol. 6: 239–246	King Zhuang hears prediction of Chu's future decline	Part of the same manuscript as #5 (see chapter 3 above)
5	Shen gong chen Ling wang 申公臣靈王	Vol. 6: 246–252	King Ling appoints his erstwhile rival	Part of the same manuscript as #4 (see chapter 3 above)
6	Ping wang wen Zheng Shou 平王問鄭壽	Vol. 6: 255–263	A clever remonstrance causes King Ping to improve his ways	
7	Ping wang yu Wangzi Mu 平王與王子木	Vol. 6: 263–272	Predicts that King Ping's son, Mu (Prince Jian 王子建) will not become a king because he does not grasp the essentials of agriculture	The prince eventually was dismissed by King Ping and ended his life in exile
8	Zheng Zijia sang 鄭子家喪	Vol. 7: 169–188	King Zhuang's actions before and during the Bi battle	Two copies of the text coexist; many parallels with Zuo zhuan (but also considerable differences)[3]
9	Jun ren zhe he bi an zai 君人者何必安哉	Vol. 7: 189–218	Remonstrance to King Zhao of Chu	Two copies of the text coexist in the Shanghai Museum collection

(continued)

TABLE 5.1 (continued)

#	Name	Location[1]	Focus	Comment
10	Wang ju 王居 + slips 4–5 of Ming 命 + most of Zhishu nai yan 志書乃言	Vol. 8: 189–226	The ruler (perhaps King Hui) is cautioned not to listen to slanderers	Merge of three manuscripts into one following Asano Yūichi[4]
11	Ming 命 (except slips 4–5)	Vol. 8: 189–202	Son of Zigao 子高, Duke of She 葉公, remonstrates to prime minister (lingyin) Zichun 子春	Following the reconstruction by Asano Yūichi[5]
12	Cheng wang wei Chengpu zhi xing 成王為城濮之行	Vol. 9: 141–154	Lingyin Ziyu 子玉 displays his incompetence on the eve of the fateful Chengpu battle	Parallels Zuo zhuan (Xi 27.4)
13	Ling wang sui Shen 靈王遂申	Vol. 9: 155–164	A short story about King Ling's oppressiveness and opposition to it	
14	Chen gong zhi bing 陳公治兵	Vol. 9: 165–188	An explanation of military training and rituals	Interlocutors' identity is unknown
15	Bang ren bu cheng 邦人不稱	Vol. 9: 237–268	Praise of Zigao 子高, Duke of She 葉公	Based on the reconstruction by Kudō Takushi[6]

[1] All locations are in Ma Chengyuan 2001–2012.
[2] Chen Jian (2005) 2013.
[3] Wei Cide 2013, 17–22.
[4] Asano 2011.
[5] Asano 2011.
[6] Kudō 2014.

Fifteen Chu anecdotes from the Shanghai Museum collection cover almost two centuries of Chu history: the earliest (12) is related to the events of 633 BCE (on the eve of the Chengpu 城濮 battle), while the latest (3) dates from the time of King Jian of Chu 楚簡王 (r. ca. 431–405 BCE). These eventful centuries witnessed the rise of Chu hegemony and a few severe setbacks, glorious victories and disastrous defeats, periods of domestic stability and of woeful turmoil. One might expect that these events would be the focus of Chu historians' interest, but this is not the case. Of major battles, for instance, only two are mentioned in the anecdotes, and even they are given a marginal place in the narrative. The Chengpu battle of 632 BCE, in which Chu lost its hegemony to the newly rising power of Jin, is the backdrop of anecdote 12; yet rather than focusing on the battle, the anecdote just tells the story of the military incompetence of Chu's prime minster, Ziyu. The story closely parallels the *Zuozhuan* narrative, and the picture of Ziyu's inadequacy presented in it mirrors that in *Zuozhuan*.[31]

That the Chengpu setback is all but glossed over is understandable, but Chu's successes also generally do not attract the authors' attention. An exception is the Bi 邲 battle of 597 BCE, in which King Zhuang of Chu defeated the Jin armies and solidified his hegemony over the Zhou world. This battle, or, more precisely, the events leading to it, are at the center of anecdote 8. The narrative partly parallels *Zuozhuan* but also departs from it in a few important details. Most notably, Chu's assault on Zheng, which led to the Bi battle, is presented as a punitive expedition against Ducal Son Guisheng 公子歸生 (aka Zijia 子家) of Zheng, who assassinated his ruler, Lord Ling 鄭靈公, in 605 BCE. This presentation is obviously biased in favor of Chu. As is clear from the detailed depiction of these events in *Zuozhuan* and elsewhere, King Zhuang's assault on Zheng in 597 BCE had nothing to do with penalizing Zijia, who was already dead by then and who in any case was posthumously chastened by Zheng leaders. The real reason for King Zhuang's assault on Zheng was to punish the perfidy of Zheng's rulers, who repeatedly switched allegiance from Chu to Jin and back to Chu. By replacing power considerations with the noble goal of punishing Zijia, the authors of the anecdote legitimate King Zhuang's assault on Zheng. The anecdote further implies that it is because of the king's morality and ritual correctness that he had subjugated Zheng and defeated the Jin army. So is it purely pro-Chu propaganda? Possibly yes, but not necessarily so. As Wei Cide has noted, the anecdote is less concerned with defending King Zhuang's actions and more with the didactic conclusion: only morally justified military campaigns will meet with success.[32] Hence this anecdote cannot be considered a decisive manifestation of pro-Chu sentiments.

Among the other anecdotes, only one (14) mentions the military affairs of Chu, but this is done very briefly in the context of discussing correct military training; the list of successful campaigns of the past is not invoked to enhance the country's prestige. At times Chu's military successes are hinted at—in anecdote 4, for example—but only as a backdrop for discussing the imminent danger of Chu's decline (see discussion on pp. 75–76). In general, the anecdotes' authors are not much interested in Chu's past attainments and display no pride in the country's successes. When another expansionist ruler, King Ling, is mentioned, it is to reiterate his negative image as an arrogant and intemperate leader rather than to hail his achievements (anecdote 13; for a more amicable portrait of King Ling, see anecdote 5, discussed in chapter 3, pp. 76–79).

The major goal of the Chu-related anecdotes from the Shanghai Museum collection is not to glorify the militarily prominent Chu kings but rather to hail those monarchs who were able to heed remonstrance and mend their ways. Most of the remonstrance-focused anecdotes revolve around two of the least-powerful Chu kings, King Ping (r. 528–516 BCE) and his son, King Zhao (r. 515–489 BCE). The first rose to power in a fratricidal struggle that not only put an end to the reign of King Ling but also caused a considerable decrease in Chu's international prestige and the country's territorial contraction. King Zhao encountered an even greater disaster: an assault by Wu armies in 506 BCE caused him to flee the capital and put the entire country on the verge of collapse. As the weakest ruler on the throne of Chu during the period under discussion, King Zhao appears to have been more prone than his predecessors or successors to heed remonstrance, mend his behavior, and tolerate criticism. These qualities are hailed in several anecdotes (1, 2, and 9). One's impression is that the authors of the anecdotes prefer weak and compliant kings to those who display extraordinary martial prowess but are also less tolerant of critical-minded aides.

To summarize, Chu vignettes from the Shanghai Museum collection—with a possible exception of anecdote 8—appear to be unconcerned with the country's separate identity, its pride, its glorious past, and the like. Most of these anecdotes lack an identifiable Chu flavor: they could be placed in a different setting and with a different list of protagonists without altering their meaning.³³ In some cases—most notably the two anecdotes discussed in chapter 3 (4 and 5), the Chu context is much clearer: as I have tried to demonstrate, these anecdotes were definitely written for a Chu audience and presupposed a working knowledge of Chu history. A knowledgeable reader may discover contained in these anecdotes references to major events in Chu's life—the country's peak of power under King Zhuang, the disasters of the King Zhao years, or the rise and fall of King Ling. Yet even these very "local" anecdotes designed for local consumers contain no traits of glorification of Chu's successes or lamentations of its failures. We are justified to speak of them as identity-neutral texts.

This identity-neutral impression strengthens when taking into account non-Chu-related anecdotes from the Shanghai Museum collection and from other materials discovered in Chu tombs. Consider, for example, a manuscript called *Wu ming* 吳命, which revolves around a speech apparently delivered by the messenger of King Fuchai of Wu 吳王夫差 (r. 495–473 BCE) to the Zhou Son of Heaven.³⁴ The speech justifies Wu's ongoing war with Chu as a defense of the Zhou house; the Chu are accused of "acting not in accordance with the Way" (荊 [or 楚人] 為不道; slips 4 and 9). That this accusation appears in a speech attributed to one of Chu's staunchest foes is to be expected, but that it is not qualified at all in an anecdote that circulated in the state of Chu, was transcribed into a Chu script, and was buried in a Chu tomb is surprising.

The surprise becomes even greater when we note the Chu manuscripts' attitudes to the figure of Wu Zixu 伍子胥 (d. 484 BCE). Recall that Wu Zixu's father was a high-ranking Chu official who fell victim to slanderers and was executed by King Ping. Wu Zixu vowed to avenge his father's death: he fled to the state of Wu and led its assault against Chu, bringing about Wu's occupation of Chu's capital, Ying, in 506 BCE. The occupation was a deeply humiliating and traumatic event; according to the *Guliang Commentary* (*Guliang zhuan* 穀梁傳) on the *Spring and Autumn Annals*, it involved among other things the desecration of King Ping's tomb and flogging of his corpse.³⁵ Wu Zixu made a brilliant career in Wu, but later King Fuchai rejected his advice and ordered him to commit suicide. In due time, Wu Zixu became a paragon of loyalty, entering the pantheon of righteous ministers who met an inglorious end.³⁶ This perspective, however, is decidedly non-Chu: after all, from the Chu point of view, Wu Zixu should be considered a major enemy, a murderous turncoat. Yet in two of the Chu manuscripts—*Poverty and Success Are a Matter of Timing* (*Qiong da yi shi* 窮達以時), from the Guodian collection, and *Good Ministers* (*Liang chen* 良臣), from the Tsinghua collection (discussed in chapter 3)—Wu Zixu is hailed as a model minister without any mention of his anti-Chu deeds.[37]

This example further strengthens my tentative conclusion: Chu historical anecdotes, as well as other historical and philosophical texts, lack any visible interest in Chu identity. Their Chu affiliation is often marginal to their content, and even when it is not their ideological agenda has little if any to do with strengthening the sense of belonging of Chu elites. These anecdotes' focus is decisively supraregional: they concern the affairs of All Under Heaven and could have been produced in any of the competing states.

Chu ju

Let us turn now to *Chu ju* 楚居 (*Chu dwellings*). As a reminder, it is the earliest known example of a historical (or in my view historical-ritualistic) work focused on a single state—Chu. In chapter 3, I discussed primarily the historical part of this manuscript; here I want to focus on its first part, which narrates the Chu dynastic legends. My goal is not to discuss these legends in full (that task has already been undertaken)[38] but instead to focus only on the opening lines of *Chu ju*, which narrate the story of the primeval ancestor of Chu, Jilian. The story relates:

季連初降于騩山，抵于穴窮。前出于騙山，宅處爰波（坡）。逆上洲水，見盤庚之子，處於方山。女曰比隹，秉茲（慈）率【1】相（藏），䜭 甹（甹）四方。季連聞其有聘，從，及之盤，爰生 緸 伯、遠仲。【2】

Jilian first descended onto Mount Gui, then arrived at Qiong Cave. He first emerged from Mount Qiao, making his dwelling on Yuan Slope. He moved upstream of the Chuan River, where he met the son of Pangeng, who lived at Mount Fang. His (Pangeng's son's) daughter was named Ancestress Zhui. She persisted in kindness and was the utmost beauty, outshining everybody among the four quarters.[39] Jilian heard that she sought marriage and pursued her, reaching her at Pan. There she gave birth to the elder son Cheng and the second born, Yuan.

Limitations of space prevent me from adequately dealing with the rich geographical and mythological information in this section; I therefore focus on its political aspects.[40] Jilian—whose "descending" (*jiang* 降) apparently implies divine birth[41]—is considered the forefather of the Mi 芈 clan—that is, the royal clan of Chu. Normally he is not identified as the earliest of the Chu ancestors. According to the "Hereditary House of Chu" chapter in *Records of the Historian,* Jilian was preceded by several primordial ancestors, most notably the primeval Thearch Zhuanxu 顓頊 and the Rectifier of Fire (*huozheng* 火正) Zhurong 祝融.[42] Chu sacrificial materials from Tomb 2, Baoshan, Jingmen 荊門包山 (Hubei), from Tomb 1, Wangshan, Jiangling 江陵望山 (Hubei), and from Tomb 1 at Geling, Xincai 新蔡葛陵 (Henan), all record sacrifices to Zhurong and to his ancestor Laotong 老僮, who were apparently considered more worthy of sacrifice than Jilian.[43] Yet these primeval ancestors are not mentioned at all in *Chu ju*. Instead the focus is on Jilian and on his relations with the son of the Shang 商 king, Pangeng 盤庚, whose daughter Jilian married.[44] Whereas the Anhui University Chu historical manuscript identifies Jilian as one of Zhurong's sons, in *Chu ju* there are no traces of this information.[45] The emphasis is on Jilian only and specifically on his relations with the Shang ruling lineage. It seems that the Shang connection was highly important for the narrators. Evidently, marrying Pangeng's granddaughter was a source of pride for the ancestor of the Chu ruling house, possibly an important asset for bolstering the house's legitimacy and prestige.[46]

The emphasis on Jilian at the expense of his illustrious ancestors and some of his meritorious descendants is significant in the context of my discussion. It shows a surprising modesty of the Chu historians who composed *Chu ju*. To demonstrate the degree of this modesty it may be useful to compare *Chu ju* with a rarely noticed piece of pro-Chu propaganda in a transmitted text; namely, the Zheng section of the *Discourses of the States*. The "Zheng yu" 鄭語 narrates advice given by Zhou Scribe Bo 史伯 to Lord Huan of Zheng 鄭桓公 (r. 806–770 BCE) on the eve of the collapse of the Western Zhou. The dating of the text is debatable, but it is likely that it is anterior to *Chu ju*, or at least cannot postdate it by much.[47] One of the most interesting parts of this text is the section in which Scribe Bo predicts the unstoppable rise of Chu. According to his analysis, Chu's good fortunes derive from the merits of its leaders, past and present.

夫荊子熊嚴生子四人：伯霜、仲雪、叔熊、季紃。叔熊逃難于濮而蠻，季紃是立，薳氏將起之，禍又不克。是天啓之{心}[48]也。又甚聰明和協，蓋其先王。臣聞之，天之所啓，十世不替。夫其子孫必光啓土，不可偪也。且重、黎之後也，夫黎爲高辛氏火正，以淳耀敦大，天明地德，光照四海，故命之曰「祝融」，其功大矣。. . . 融之興者，其在羋姓乎？羋姓夔越不足命也。闡羋蠻矣，唯荊實有昭德，若周衰，其必興矣。[49]

Viscount Xiong Yan of Jing [i.e., Chu] had four sons: [the eldest] Boshuang, [the second] Zhongxue, [the third] Shuxiong, and [the youngest] Jixun.[50] Shuxiong avoided troubles fleeing to Pu, where he became a savage; hence Jixun was established.[51] The Wei lineage planned to establish [Shuxiong] but failed to overcome troubles. This means that Heaven opened the path for him [Jixun].[52] Moreover, he is perspicacious and clear minded, harmonious and amicable; [his merits] exceed those of the former kings. I have heard: one for whom Heaven opens the path cannot be replaced for ten generations. His descendants will surely greatly expand their territory: they cannot be pressed.

Besides, he is the descendant of Chong and Li. Li was the Rectifier of Fire under Gaoxin.[53] He was brilliant and resplendent; bright like Heaven and virtuous like Earth; he broadly illuminated all within the four seas, hence he was named Zhurong. His merits were great. . . . The resurrection of [Zhu] Rong's descendants: will it start with the Mi clan?[54] Among the Mi, Kui and Yue do not deserve the mandate; Mi of the Min are savages; only Jing [Chu] really possesses brilliant virtue.[55] If Zhou declines, [Chu] will surely prosper.

This passage—which is exceptional in its pro-Chu attitudes among all the texts of the Warring States period—provides two justifications for the anticipated rise of Chu: the good qualities of its contemporaneous ruler, Jixun 季紃 (fl. ca.770 BCE), and the merits of Chu's mythical ancestor, Zhurong. Surely this line of argumentation in bolstering Chu's prestige was known to Chu statesmen and historians of the early Warring States period (which is the approximate time of the *Chu ju* compilation). That they opted to ignore it and to emphasize instead relations of the Mi clan to the Shang king Pangeng cannot be accidental. For whatever reasons, the composers of *Chu ju* may have considered intermarriage with the Shang royal clan as a more significant factor in supporting Chu royalty than deeds of meritorious ancestors. Once again, a Chu historical text appears much less concerned with pro-Chu propaganda than could have been expected.

Xinian

Let us turn now to *Xinian*. As noted in chapter 2, this is a composite text that incorporates materials from several Zhou polities, but there are indicators that it was edited by Chu scribes. Among these, the concealment of instances of domestic turmoil in Chu, which reminds one of the canonical *Spring and Autumn Annals*, is one of the clearest indicators of the text's Chu origin. In contrast, *Xinian* does not conceal cases of Chu's military defeats, nor does it attempt to soften their impact. Let us look at section 21, which deals with the struggle between Jin and Chu of the late fifth century BCE. I focus on its second part, which concerns the campaigns of around 421 BCE:

> In the next year (421 BCE?), the king ordered *moao* Yang Wei to lead an army to invade Jin. He seized Yiyang and laid siege to Chiyan in retaliation for the Huangchi campaign.[56] The Jin [leaders] Wei Si, Zhao Huan, and Han Qizhang led an army to assist Chiyan. The Chu army gave up the siege and retreated, and it fought the Jin army near the Long Wall.[57] The Chu army achieved nothing. They threw away their banners and tents and fled by night. Therefore Chu harbored strong resentment against Jin.

The story of a continuous tit-for-tat struggle between Jin and Chu is depicted in such a neutral fashion that except for the Chu chronology (employed at the beginning of this section) nothing indicates its Chu origin. The text narrates in detail the humiliating defeat of the Chu armies: first, they abandoned the siege of Jin's Chiyan, retreating to Chu's Long Wall at Fangcheng; then they were battered there, throwing away "banners and tents" and fleeing by night. *Xinian* authors, who do their best to conceal Chu domestic troubles, narrate quite candidly how ingloriously Chu's armies fought. This candor becomes even more pronounced in the last section, which depicts a series of Chu-Jin campaigns about 400–396 BCE. That section ends with the following passage:

After two years (395 BCE?), Han Qu and Wei Ji led an army and laid siege to Wuyang, to avenge the incursion into Gao.[58] The Duke of Luyang led an army to help Wuyang and fought the Jin army below the walls of Wuyang.[59] The Chu army was greatly defeated. Three lord possessors of the *gui* tablet, the Duke of Luyang, Lord Daowu of Pingye, and Lord Huanding of Yangcheng, as well as *youyin* Si of Zhao (Zhao Si), died in that battle.[60] The Chu forces threw away their banners, tents, chariots, and weapons and returned, running like fleeing dogs. The Chen people thereupon rebelled and let Royal Son Ding back to Chen.[61] Thus the state of Chu lost a lot of walled cities.

Putting the precise details of these campaigns aside, we can immediately notice the highly unflattering depiction of Chu military performance in the text. The author not only frankly admits the magnitude of Chu's defeat but even buttresses it through a humiliating comparison of Chu's escaping armies to fleeing dogs. Clearly, the idea of strengthening the Chu identity and its pride was not the concern of the *Xinian* composers.

These two examples suffice to show how candid the *Xinian* authors are in depicting Chu's military defeats. Nor do they hail the victories too much. The beginning of Chu's territorial expansion is briefly mentioned in sections 2 and 5, but it is neither eulogized nor connected to any merits of Chu kings. Rather, it is presented as coincidental: favorable interstate circumstances allowed Chu to advance first into the Han and then into the Huai River valleys. The great victories of Chu under King Zhuang, the singularly successful Chu leader, are noted but do not merit detailed discussion. Oddly, King Zhuang's exploits are highlighted in *Xinian* much less than in *Zuozhuan*. Nor does the text single out any other Chu leader for exceptional praise.

That *Xinian* is not concerned with Chu's local pride requires no further illustrations. Yet its discovery may allow us to pose another question, how does its presentation of Chu history differ from that in the transmitted sources, especially *Zuozhuan*? Scholars who have addressed this problem point out the overall similarity between the two texts amid minor discrepancies that may or may not reflect a pro-Chu stance of *Xinian* authors.[62] I focus on each case of these discrepancies in part 2 of this book; here I focus on a single section of *Xinian* that adopts a distinctive pro-Chu stance in contrast with *Zuozhuan*. Section 16 of *Xinian* reads as follows:

In the seventh year of King Gong of Chu (584 BCE), Prime Minister Zichong invaded Zheng, initiating the Fan campaign. Lord Jing of Jin assembled the regional lords to rescue Zheng. The people of Zheng captured [a Chu officer] Yi, the Duke of Yun, and presented him to Lord Jing. Lord Jing returned [to Jin] taking [Yi] with him. [After?] one year (582 BCE?), Lord Jing wanted to establish amicable relations with Chu; hence, he released the Duke of Yun and let him go back and seek peace. King Gong of Chu dispatched the Duke of Yun for an official visit to Jin and approved the peace. Lord Jing dispatched Pei of Di (Di Pei) on an official visit to Chu, renewing peace. Before [Di Pei] returned, [Lord Jing] died, and Lord Li was established (580 BCE).

King Gong dispatched Royal Son Chen on an official visit to Jin and also renewed peace. The king also sent the Song commander of the right, Huasun Yuan (Hua Yuan), to arrange peaceful relations between Jin and Chu. In the next year (579 BCE), Royal Son Pi of Chu met Wenzi Xie (i.e., Shi Xie 士燮, aka Shi Wenzi 士文子) of Jin and grandees of the regional lords and made a covenant at Song, saying, "Put to rest the armor and weapons of All Under Heaven." The next year (578 BCE), Lord Li [of Jin] was the first to raise an army and lead the regional lords to invade Qin, reaching the Jing River. King Gong also led an army, laying siege to Zheng. Lord Li came to rescue Zheng and defeated the Chu army at Yan. Lord Li also encountered misfortune and died leaving no posterity.

This narrative focuses on the first attempt to establish a lasting peace between Chu and Jin—the peace conference in the state of Song in 579 BCE—and the rapid breakup of amicable relations between the two parties thereafter. I do not address here a few very minor discrepancies between the *Xinian* and *Zuozhuan* narratives (for which see the section's translation in part 2). What matters for me is the core of the story: who was responsible for the breakup of the first attempt to reconcile the two rival powers?

The events depicted in *Xinian* are narrated in great detail in *Zuozhuan*, and the two sources agree on the basic facts. What differs, though, is the nature of the peace conference in 579 BCE and the reasons for its failure. In *Zuozhuan*, the conference was attended by just two parties, Jin and Chu, and the covenant (the content of which is cited) focused on establishing amicable relations between the two parties only.[63] In *Xinian*, however, the meeting was also attended by the "grandees of the regional lords" (i.e., was multilateral), and the covenant's goal was attaining peace in "All Under Heaven," similar to the later multilateral peace conferences of 546 BCE and 541 BCE.[64] On this point, *Zuozhuan* appears more reliable: were a 579 BCE peace conference attended by more parties, it is likely that this would be reflected in the *Spring and Autumn Annals* as well, which is not the case. It is more plausible that *Xinian*'s authors conflated the agreements of 546 and 541 BCE with the accord of 579 BCE.

What happened after the agreement? *Zuozhuan* insists that Chu was perfidious: soon after the covenant was sealed, the Chu prime minister warned a visiting Jin colleague that the two rulers, if they ever met, would only exchange arrows and not ceremonial greetings.[65] The subsequent Jin assault on Qin in 578 BCE is presented as unrelated to the Jin-Chu peace agreement and as fully justifiable in light of Qin's anti-Jin machinations. It is Chu's attack on Zheng in 576 BCE that breaches the covenant with Jin; *Zuozhuan* repeatedly cites pronouncements by Chu and Jin dignitaries, who blame the Chu leadership for violating the peace and leading to the disastrous (for Chu) battle of Yan (Yanling 鄢陵) in 575 BCE. Only at the depiction of the battle itself does the *Zuozhuan* narration shift to a more critical stance toward Jin: its success is presented as a Pyrrhic victory, soon leading to domestic turmoil.

Xinian's interpretation of these events differs radically. The Jin assault against Qin is viewed as a violation of an agreement to establish "universal" peace; Chu's assault on Zheng appears as a retaliatory measure. Moreover, the *Xinian* authors are manipulative in their account: by dispensing with precise chronology after 578 BCE, they present all the events that spanned five years (Chu's attack on Zheng, Jin's retaliation, the Yanling battle, and the coup against Lord Li of Jin) as happening immediately one after another in the direct aftermath of Jin's anti-Qin aggression. The compression results in factual inaccuracies: for instance, on the eve of the Yanling battle, the state of Zheng was not Chu's victim but its ally.[66] The blame for the collapse of peace is placed squarely on Lord Li of Jin, whose violent death a year after the Yanling battle may be seen as divine retaliation for his perfidy. Chu was the victim; and although it was defeated militarily, the perpetrator, Lord Li, was punished by a humiliating death. The similarities and discrepancies between the two narratives are summarized in table 5.2.

TABLE 5.2
Zuo zhuan and *Xinian* accounts of Chu-Jin relations, 582–575 BCE compared

Zuo zhuan	Xinian
Chu and Jin seek peace after 582	Chu and Jin seek peace after 582
579 peace conference: both states vow not to attack each other	579 peace conference: **all the regional states vow to stop war**
Chu displays perfidy and prepares for renewed conflict	—
578: Jin attacks Qin (unrelated to Chu)	578: Jin's attack on Qin **violates its obligations** to preserve peace
576: Chu attacks Jin's ally, Zheng	Chu attacks Zheng **to relieve Jin's attack on Qin**
575: Zheng allies with Chu; Jin attacks Zheng and Chu; defeats them in Yanling	Jin helps Zheng; defeats Chu in Yanling
574/3 domestic troubles in Jin	Domestic troubles in Jin: **Heaven's punishment?**

There is no doubt that we have here two radically different interpretations of the same chain of events: the predominantly pro-Jin narrative of *Zuozhuan* versus the unequivocally pro-Chu version of *Xinian*. Yet we should notice immediately that in terms of facts both narratives do not differ substantially (except for the precise content of the 579 covenant and Zheng's role in the 575 BCE battle). And whereas each of the accounts is manipulative, neither appears to abandon the basic factual framework. Furthermore, this is the only instance in which we can tentatively identify clear biases in both *Zuozhuan* (which favors Jin in this case) and *Xinian*, which strongly defends Chu. Elsewhere, *Xinian* authors frankly acknowledge that it was the Chu leaders, such as King Ling, who violated the interstate peace accords.[67] We can say in summary that despite certain traits of pro-Chu sentiments in *Xinian*, in general this text does not present a radically novel picture of Chu's foreign relations in comparison with that obtained from *Zuozhuan*. More generally, *Xinian* contributes little—if at all—to strengthening the Chu identity. Much like the anecdotes and *Chu ju*, *Xinian* remains overwhelmingly neutral in its depiction of Chu's past.

Rongchengshi

The final text that I want to consider here is *Rongchengshi* 容成氏 from the collection of the Shanghai Museum. This relatively lengthy text of slightly more than two thousand characters presents the history of the Chinese world from the time of legendary thearchs down to the founding of the Zhou dynasty. The goal of this presentation is not purely historical: the narrative is built so as to convince the reader of the advantages of nonhereditary power transfer (ideally through the ruler's abdication in favor of a worthier candidate). Since the text has been translated and discussed twice elsewhere,[68] I do not address its complexity here but consider only its Chu-related aspects.

The Chu affiliation of *Rongchengshi* is not self-evident. Although the manuscript was produced by a Chu scribe using Chu orthography and was in all likelihood interned in a tomb of a Chu elite member, almost nothing in its content relates it to Chu. The only possible Chu trait is in the final phrase of the narrative about the creation of the Nine Provinces by Thearch Yu 禹 in the aftermath of the great flood. The narrative itself has no observable Chu connection, and the map of the Nine Provinces in *Rongchengshi* is markedly shifted to the north in comparison with its variants scattered through other texts, leaving Chu on the southern margins of the habitable world.[69] Yet the ending lines say, "Yu then created five hundred famous valleys to the south of the Han River and five hundred famous valleys to the north of the Han River."[70] This centrality of the Han River strongly suggests a Chu affiliation of the text's authors. However, as noted by Vera Dorofeeva-Lichtmann it is also possible that the line was added by a Chu transmitter who wanted to make the text—originally produced elsewhere—more relevant to Chu.[71] Aside from this single line, no other aspect of *Rongchengshi* connects it with the state of Chu.

I remain reluctant regarding the origin of *Rongchengshi*: perhaps we should not at all consider it as a product of Chu historiography. However, insofar as the manuscript was looted from a Chu tomb and insofar as it can be assumed that the text circulated in the state of Chu (and might have enjoyed sufficient prestige to merit internment in a tomb) it is justifiable to consider it in the framework of the present discussion. Two points should be raised here. First is the marked absence of identifiable Chu royal ancestors—such as Zhuanxu, Zhurong, and the like—from the lengthy list of legendary heroes discussed in the text. Second, the *Rongchengshi* narrative is markedly "center oriented," as it focuses exclusively on the monarchs who ruled the entire subcelestial realm. Regional lords, be they the kings of Chu or leaders of other polities, are simply ignored. The norm, as the authors repeatedly emphasize, is universal rule, whose attainment represents the apex of the monarch's achievements. Thus, the text hails a primordial thearch whose reign preceded that of Thearch Yao 堯:

上下貴賤，各得其世。四海之外賓，四海之內貞。禽獸朝，魚鱉獻，有無通。

Superiors and inferiors, noble and mean—each attained their [predestined] years. [The people] from beyond the four seas arrived as guests, and those from within the four seas were corrected. Birds and beasts came to court; fish and turtles submitted [tribute]; there was [smooth] communication between [localities with] abundant and deficient [resources].[72]

Elsewhere, the text hails the rule of Thearch Yu:

乃因迩以知遠，去苛而行簡，因民之欲，會天地之利，夫是以近者悅治，而遠者自至。四海之內及，四海之外皆請貢。

He understood the distant from [inspecting] the near, eradicated quibbling and pursued simplicity; he relied on the people's desires, brought together the beneficent [matters of] Heaven and Earth, so that the near rejoiced the orderly rule while the distant came on their own initiative. Everybody within and outside the four seas requested to submit tribute.[73]

Both passages emphasize the universality of the thearch's rule. In the first case the encompassing power of an unnamed thearch transcends the boundaries of humankind, reaching down to birds, beasts, fish, and turtle: all those strive to become the thearch's subjects.[74] In the second case unity remains confined to the realm of humans, but it is still comprehensive: all those from "within and outside the four seas" duly request to submit tribute. In both cases the entire subcelestial realm—"near" and "distant" alike—remains under unified control. Regional polities transpire in the text only when we enter the calamitous age of the last Shang tyrant, Zhouxin 紂辛 (d. ca. 1046 BCE). Then, rebellions by regional lords and the danger of political disintegration appear as important symptoms of the political deterioration that eventually justified the overthrow of the Shang.

The *Rongchengshi* insistence that a politically unified world is the only normative situation may explain why Chu remains outside the narrative. In the unified universal realm independent or semi-independent regional lords (such as the king of Chu) are an aberration. Accordingly, the multi-state system, which stands at the center of *Xinian* and which was the norm for centuries prior to the composition of *Rongchengshi*, is glossed over altogether. Under the rule of sage kings regional states have no role, nor is there any meaning for regional identities. In the political vision of *Rongchengshi* there is simply no place for the state of Chu.

Where Is Chu Identity?

We can summarize our findings to this point. Four different types of texts discussed in the preceding share certain commonalities insofar as their views of Chu are concerned. First, none of them (with the minor exceptions of anecdote 8 and section 16 of *Xinian*) provide an alternative pro-Chu narration of the country's history. Second, none—with the partial exception of *Chu ju*—displays any interest in primeval deified ancestors of the Chu ruling house.[75] Third, none appears attentive to the Chu kings' claims for supreme authority in All Under Heaven. Fourth, none seems to be interested in eulogizing Chu's military achievements or lamenting its failures so as to bolster readers' identification with their country. Fifth, all the surveyed texts refrain in their narrations from overt identification with Chu. They refer to their country neutrally as "Chu" rather than employing the first-person pronouns "we, us" (*wo* 我), which is used from time to time in sections of *Zuozhuan* that deal with Lu. In addition to all these, texts unearthed from Chu tombs pay little attention to Chu's local sensitivities (as is seen, for instance, from their eulogizing of Wu Zixu). When we compare these texts with identity-focused historical writings elsewhere (just think of Greek or Jewish historiography, for example), we can conclude that Chu historians were simply not interested in articulating or strengthening a separate cultural or political identity for their country.

How should we understand this almost counterintuitive conclusion? Does it mean that the otherness of Chu is just a myth, a by-product of our uncritical acceptance of anti-Chu propaganda in some of the received texts? Not necessarily. There is ample evidence to show that Chu identity did matter at least to some of its elite members. Look, for instance, at the divination slips from the tombs at Baoshan, Wangshan, and Geling (all tombs of top-ranking Chu nobles): these routinely mention divinized ancestors of the Chu royal clan as objects of sacrifice, and also incidentally refer to Chu as "our" (*wo* 我) state. Although these texts do not belong to historical accounts *strictu senso*, they do appear much more Chu oriented than the historical texts surveyed in the preceding. Or take the famous *Chu Songs* (*Chuci* 楚辭). Without entering into discussions about their authorship and dating, we can state that at the very least some of them— such as "Lamenting Ying" (Ai Ying 哀郢) or "Fallen to the State" (Guo shang 國殤)—display a strongly pronounced Chu identity.[76] Why, then, is this identity absent from the historical texts surveyed?

I think there are two complementary explanations for this phenomenon. First, let us consider certain peculiarities of the early Chinese historiographic tradition. Recall that history writing in China did not start in individual polities of the Spring and-Autumn period but was instead part of the common Zhou legacy. This common legacy is most vivid in the annalistic tradition represented by the *Spring and Autumn Annals*. As discussed in chapters 1 and 2, the *Annals* were not peculiar to the state of Lu but belonged to what appears as a common Zhou tradition of ritualized historical records; among other courts these records were prepared also at the court of Chu. In chapter 2, I demonstrated that the Chu court chronicle may have followed the same sophisticated "rules of recording" (*shu fa* 書法) that we encounter in the Lu *Annals*. It is through this common knowledge of their "subtle language" (*wei yan* 微言) that the *Annals* could become a useful means of censuring political misconduct (chapter 1). As such, despite their localized nature the court chronicles (i.e., court annals) were a means of perpetuating cultural cohesiveness among the Zhou elites rather than a vehicle of estrangement.[77]

I believe that the similarities among the annalistic traditions of different courts were reflected in other products of court historians; namely, the narrative histories of individual states. These similarities in terms of structure, narration style, didactic messages, and the like in the local histories created throughout the Zhou realm may explain the seamless incorporation of some of these local historical accounts into *Zuozhuan*. Although our evidence is still very limited, it suggests that narrative histories produced in regional states did not exclusively target members of a single polity but rather addressed common concerns of the educated elite throughout the Zhou realm. Once again, history writing was a unifying rather than dividing exercise.

The pan-Zhou similarities in historical production might reflect commonalities in the education and training of court scribes, who were the major (or exclusive) producers of historical texts throughout the Spring and Autumn period. By the Warring States period, as noted in chapters 1 and 3, these scribes appear to have lost their erstwhile monopoly on preparing historical texts. New historical products—be they didactic anecdotes or quasi-historical texts, such as *Rongchengshi*—were composed and read by members of the *shi* 士 stratum, who rose from the margins of nobility to become the new ruling elite throughout the Zhou realm. What matters for our discussion is that the *shi* were much less attached to individual polities than the hereditary nobles of the Spring and Autumn period. Rather, they traversed the realm in search of better employment, serving "Qin in the morning and Chu in the evening" (*zhao Qin mu Chu* 朝秦暮楚). The focus of their concerns was the entire subcelestial realm and not a single state, and this is duly reflected in their philosophical and historical production.[78] Therefore, even under these new circumstances newly prepared historical texts continued to perpetuate rather than weaken pan-Zhou ties.

This brings me to the second point relevant to our discussion. When we speak of "Chu identity," we should distinguish among cultural identities of distinct social strata in the state of Chu. The highest segment of the Chu hereditary aristocracy, represented among others by the occupants of the Baoshan, Wangshan, and Geling tombs, were members of the royal clan, whose ancestors for generations had served the Chu kings. These men were strongly attached to the state of Chu, and it is natural that their identity was Chu focused. It is furthermore likely (albeit it cannot be proven beyond doubt) that local identity was strong among the commoners, whose destiny was also intrinsically linked to their ancestral state.[79] But the intermediate group—namely, the *shi*, who were the producers and major consumers of philosophical and historical texts discovered in Chu tombs—remained less Chu oriented than either top aristocrats above or commoners below. Their very career pattern, which led many (most?) of them to seek employment outside their native state, was conducive to the formation of an outlook prioritizing the whole over its parts, All Under Heaven over an individual state, common culture over local customs.[80] That we discern in the Chu historical anecdotes (and in other Chu historical texts) what Sarah Allan dubs a cosmopolitan outlook comes, therefore, as no surprise.[81]

If my second point—based as it is on Chu materials only—is correct, then it may explain why local and regional identities, which became increasingly articulated during the Warring States period,[82] never developed into a true "national" identity akin to what happened in early modern Europe. Insofar as intellectuals—the stratum that contributed decisively toward formation of national identities in Europe—remained overwhelmingly focused on the interests of the *oikoumēnē* as a whole rather than on an individual state, regional identities could not coalesce into a politically meaningful factor. The discussion here demonstrates that history writing—a potent means of identity creation elsewhere—remained in the Zhou world a means of cultural integration rather than separation.

PART II
Xinian Translation and Commentary

Xinian 1

The first section occupies a somewhat exceptional place in *Xinian*. First, it is the only section that deals exclusively with Western Zhou history. Second, it the only section that does not mention anything directly or indirectly related to Chu history. Third, it also the only section to address the divine powers: the Lord on High (Shangdi 上帝) and Heaven. It hints, though does not state explicitly, that by forsaking proper sacrifices the last king of Shang (i.e., Zhouxin 紂辛) lost his mandate. Zhouxin's replacement, King Wu of Zhou 周武王 (r. ca. 1046–1042 BCE), had learned the lesson: his success is associated with the revival of the sacrificial system. Later, renewed disregard of sacrifices is directly related to the decline in Zhou fortunes, specifically the defeat of King Xuan 周宣王 (r. 827–782 BCE) by the Rong 戎 belligerents.

Aside from providing a brief introduction to Western Zhou history, *Xinian* 1 serves a subtler, ideological function. Its narrative reminds the reader of the importance of maintaining proper sacrifices as the way to ensure good political fortune. Recall that *Xinian* was a product of scribal activities (section 1 in particular was produced either by Zhou or by Jin scribes and later utilized by their Chu colleagues; see chapter 2). Recall also that among their many tasks, the scribes were in charge of maintaining sacrifices.[1] It would be natural for the scribes in their capacity as historians to bolster their position as ritual specialists as well. This may explain their interpretation of Zhou's destiny as closely related to the proper maintaining of sacrifices.

In terms of its historical information there are two notable points in *Xinian* 1. First, as discussed in chapter 4, it resolves a centuries-old controversy about the identity of the replacer of the ousted King Li of Zhou 周厲王 (r. ca. 877–842 BCE). Exactly as told in the *Bamboo Annals*, this replacer is Gong Bo He 共伯和 (certainly a high-ranking Zhou noble but one whose precise identity remains unknown; see note 7). That two unrelated texts have exactly the same version of events can serve as ironclad proof of their accuracy and puts an end to Sima Qian's erroneous interpretation of the term *gonghe* 共和 as referring to the duumvirate of the Duke of Zhou and Duke Shao. Second, the story of King Xuan's discarding the One-Thousand-*mu* sacrificial fields, the revenue of which served for sacrificing to the Lord on High, and his subsequent defeat by the Rong in 789 BCE precisely at the location of the One-Thousand-*mu* fields is echoed in *Discourses of the States* (where it is accompanied by a lengthy admonition to King Xuan by Lord Wen of Guo 虢文公).[2] Once again, the identity between two unrelated texts may serve as proof of the story's historicity (albeit not necessarily the historicity of Lord Wen's admonition).

★ ★ ★

昔周武王監觀商王之不恭上帝，禋祀不寅，乃作帝籍，以登祀上帝天神，名之曰【1】千畝，以克反商邑，敷政天下。至于厲王，厲王大虐于周，卿士、諸正、萬民弗忍于厥心，【2】乃歸厲王于彘。共伯和立十又四年。厲王生宣王，宣王即位，共伯和歸于宋。宣【3】王是始棄帝籍弗田。立卅又九年，戎乃大敗周師于千畝。【4】

Formerly, King Wu observed[3] that the king of Shang was irreverent toward the Lord on High, and his sacrifices were disrespectful. Then he created a revenue [field] for the Lord, so as to submit the sacrifices upward to the Lord on High and Heavenly deities.[4] It was named the One-Thousand-*mu* [field].[5] Therewith he successfully overthrew the Shang, spreading his government through All Under Heaven.

At the time of King Li, King Li was greatly oppressive toward Zhou. The chief ministers, all the officials, and the myriad people could not bear this in their hearts. Then they placed King Li at Zhi.[6] Gong Bo He was established [as the king's replacer] for fourteen years.[7] King Li fathered King Xuan. When King Xuan was established (827 BCE), Gong Bo He returned to Song.[8]

King Xuan for the first time abandoned the revenue [field] to the Lord and did not cultivate it. He ruled for thirty-nine years, and then (789 BCE) the Rong greatly defeated the Zhou army at the One-Thousand-*mu* [field].[9]

Notes

1. See, e.g., Schaberg 2013, 27–28.
2. *Guoyu* 1.6 ("Zhou yu shang").
3. The term used for "observing" here (*jianguan* 監觀) is highly unusual; in the "Huang yi" 皇矣 ode in the *Canon of Poems* it is associated with the Lord on High. That the term is used here to depict King Wu (who, after all, was still subordinate to the king of Shang) reflects extraordinary respect for King Wu.
4. The character for "Lord on High" (*shangdi* 上帝 combined into a single graph, 帝) appears twice on the first slip of *Xinian*, but, as has been noted by several scholars, the two appearances are not entirely identical (the upper line in the first appearance is abridged). Several scholars have proposed alternative readings for the first appearance. For instance, Guo Yongbing (2018, 227–30) proposes reading the two characters as 帝帝 = 禘帝, where 禘 refers to sacrifices to the ancestors and superior deities. This interpretation is plausible, but Guo then adopts a highly speculative argument according to which the second appearance of *shangdi* 上帝 should be read as *tu di* 土帝, Thearch of Earth, referring to the mythical Yellow Thearch 皇帝 (see also Chen Weiwu 2016 for a similar inference). The latter view is surely far-fetched: neither does the Yellow Thearch play a significant role in the heretofore published manuscripts in the Tsinghua corpus, nor is *tu di* used as his designation anywhere. Nor does Guo's discussion fit the well-known usage of the "revenue field" as being directed exclusively at the Lord on High or Heaven. From *Xinian* 1 as well it is clear that the objects of King Wu's sacrifices were the Lord on High and *tian shen* 天神. The latter term can stand for either a singular heavenly deity or multiple heavenly deities. As noted in Luo Xinhui 2016, 94–95, the compound *tianshen* is not attested in the texts preceding the Warring States period.
5. The locus classicus for the tradition of allocating a field of one thousand *mu*, the revenue of which was directed to sacrifices to supreme deities, is *Lüshi*

chunqiu. According to this text, at the beginning of the year the Son of Heaven, accompanied by high officials, had personally to plow this field (*Lüshi chunqiu* 1.1 ["Mengchun ji" 孟春紀]).

6. This expulsion of King Li from the royal domain is narrated in *Guoyu* 1.3–1.4:10–14 ("Zhou yu shang"). Zhi 彘 is located in present-day Huozhou 霍州, southern Shanxi.

7. As explained in chapter 4 (p. 98), Gong Bo He 共伯和 can be translated either as "He, the Earl of [the state of] Gong" or "He, the Elder of the Gong [lineage]." Since the evidence is inconclusive, I prefer to transliterate. See more in Satō 2017.

8. The text quite unequivocally indicates that Gong Bo He "returned to Song." The editors refuse to accept this reading because it contradicts a widespread (although not necessarily correct) assertion that He was a man of Wei 衛 and returned there (this assertion is based in turn on the alleged extract from the lost text *Lu Lianzi* 魯連子 cited in Zhang Shoujie's 張守節 [fl. 725–735] gloss on *Records of the Historian* [*Shiji* 4:144]; for its problems, see chapter 4, note 11). They then read Song 宋 as Zong 宗, following Sima Biao's 司馬彪 (d. 306) gloss on *Zhuangzi*, according to which He "returned to Zong," which in turn is glossed as "returning to his ancestral home." As I have argued in chapter 4, the association of Gong Bo He with the place-name Gong in the state of Wei is dubious at best, and there are no reasons to revise the text of *Xinian*. See Yoshimoto 2013, 7–8, for cautioning against reading Song as Zong.

9. As noted in the introduction to this section, the abandonment of the divine revenue field by King Xuan and his subsequent defeat by the Jiang Rong 姜戎 tribesmen is mentioned in *Guoyu* 1.6. The defeat, presumably inflicted on the Zhou near their heartland, is indicative of the diminishing ability of the late Western Zhou kings to withstand alien invasions, as discussed in Li Feng 2006, 141–92.

Xinian 2

The second section of *Xinian* is one of the most fascinating in terms of the novelty of its information: it presents a radically new version of the events that unfolded after the collapse of the Western Zhou in 771 BCE. Its narrative starkly contradicts that in *Records of the Historian*, which, for more than two millennia, was unanimously accepted as the singularly correct version of these events. As discussed in chapter 4, the precise interpretation of *Xinian*'s text became the focal point of several heated controversies in China (and more recently in Japan as well), with many colleagues proposing alternative interpretations of the phrase that I translate as "for nine years (749–741 BCE) Zhou was without a king." For details of these controversies and for the defense of my interpretation, see chapter 4; here I briefly summarize major points of *Xinian* 2.

The following narrative can be divided into three subsections, each of which is marked by a new paragraph. The first retells the story of dynastic turmoil during the reign of King You of Zhou 周幽王 (r. 781–771 BCE). King You's replacement of the elder heir, Yijiu 宜臼 (here identified by his posthumous name, King Ping 平王), by Bopan 伯盤, a younger son of his favorite concubine, Bao Si 褒姒, set the king on course to conflict with Yijiu's maternal relatives, the rulers of the domain of Western Shen 西申. King You's assault on Shen backfired: Shen was joined by another neighboring polity, Zeng 繒, and by the Western Rong 西戎 ("Belligerent") attackers. The result was disastrous: "King You and Bopan both were killed, and Zhou was destroyed."

The narrative in this paragraph fundamentally conforms to that in the "Basic Annals of Zhou" chapter of *Records of the Historian*, which, in turn, incorporates much of the scattered references to these events in preimperial sources, such as *Discourses of the States*.[1] In the second paragraph, however, the story departs dramatically from the accepted narratives. Whereas Sima Qian asserts that in the aftermath of the collapse of Western Zhou the regional lords immediately acclaimed Yijiu (King Ping), who then transferred the capital eastward, to Luoyang, *Xinian* presents a very different sequence of events. First, King Ping's uncle, Yuchen, was established as king at Xie,[2] where he ruled for twenty-one years; then he was murdered by Marquis Wen of Jin 晉文侯 (r. 780–746 or 770–736 BCE), and for nine years there was no recognized king on the Zhou throne. Only then, in 741 BCE, did Marquis Wen establish King Ping, and only in 738 BCE did the relocation of the capital to Luoyang take place. Of these events, the received texts contain a single hint: in *Zuozhuan*, where the reign of the King from Xie is briefly mentioned (Zhao 26.9). The existence of this king was confirmed also by the *Bamboo Annals*, as cited by Kong Yingda 孔穎達 (574–648) in his gloss on the *Correct Meaning of the Spring and Autumn Annals and Zuo Commentary*.[3] Yet the situation of a kingless Zhou and the chronology of the events outlined in *Xinian* are not attested in any of the transmitted texts. For further discussion on how—if at all—this information can be reconciled with the transmitted sources, see chapter 4.

The third subsection of *Xinian* 2 shifts the narrative from the Zhou dynasty to the regional lords, who seized the opportunity to expand their power in this period of upheaval. It shows how the downfall of the Zhou benefited the states of Jin and Zheng, especially the latter, whose Lord Wu 鄭武公 (r. 770–744 BCE) started to "rectify" (*zheng* 正, or "govern" *zheng* 政, or "invade" *zheng* 征) the eastern parts of the Zhou realm. However, as Zheng was weakened by prolonged domestic turmoil during the first quarter of the seventh century BCE, this allowed the state of Chu to start its expansion into the northern and eastern Han River valley. The information in this subsection is fundamentally in accord with *Zuozhuan*, although *Xinian*'s abridgment of Zheng history caused minor inaccuracies in the depiction of the coups and countercoups within Zheng, as is explained in the following notes.

★ ★ ★

周幽王取妻于西申,生平王,王又取褒人之女,是褒姒,生伯盤。褒姒嬖于王,王【5】與伯盤逐平王,平王走西申。幽王起師,圍平王于西申,申人弗畀。曾(繒)人乃降西戎,以【6】攻幽王,幽王及伯盤乃滅,周乃亡。邦君諸正乃立幽王之弟余臣于虢,是攜惠王。【7】立廿又一年,晉文侯仇乃殺惠王于虢。周亡王九年,邦君諸侯焉始不朝于周,【8】晉文侯乃逆平王于少鄂,立之于京師。三年,乃東徙,止于成周。晉人焉始啓【9】于京師,鄭武公亦正東方之諸侯。武公即世,莊公即位;莊公即世,昭公即位。【10】其大夫高之渠彌殺昭公而立其弟子亹(眉)壽。齊襄公會諸侯于首止,殺子【11】亹(眉)壽,車轢高之渠彌,改立厲公,鄭以始政。楚文王以啓于漢陽。【12】

King You of Zhou married a lady from Western Shen,[4] who gave birth to King Ping.[5] He also married a daughter of a Bao leader, who was Bao Si.[6] She gave birth to Bopan. Bao Si was favored by the king; the king and Bopan expelled [the future] King Ping, and King Ping fled to Western Shen. King You mobilized an army and encircled King Ping at Western Shen, but the Shen leaders did not hand him [King Ping] over. The people of Zeng thereupon deferentially requested assistance[7] from the Western Rong, therewith attacking King You. King You and Bopan both were killed, and Zhou was destroyed.[8]

The rulers of the states and various officials thereupon established the younger brother of King You, Yuchen, at Guo:[9] this was King Hui from Xie. Twenty-one years after his establishment (750 BCE), Marquis Wen of Jin, named Qiu (or Chou), killed King Hui at Guo.[10] For nine years (749–741 BCE) Zhou was without a king,[11] and the rulers of the states and regional lords[12] then for the first time ceased attending the Zhou court. Thereupon, Marquis Wen of Jin greeted King Ping at Shao'e and established him at the royal capital.[13] After three years (738 BCE) he relocated eastward, stopping at Chengzhou (i.e., Luoyang).

The people of Jin thereupon opened [lands] in the area of the royal capital.[14] Lord Wu of Zheng also rectified[15] the regional lords in the east. When Lord Wu passed away (744 BCE), Lord Zhuang ascended the throne; when Lord Zhuang passed away (701 BCE), Lord Zhao ascended the throne.[16] Its [Zheng's] noble, Qumi of Gao (Gao Qumi), killed Lord Zhao and established his [Lord Zhao's] younger brother Zi Meishou.¹⁷ Lord Xiang of Qi assembled the regional lords at Shouzhi;¹⁸ he killed Zi Meishou and tore Qumi of Gao apart by chariots. He replaced [Meishou] and established Lord Li.¹⁹ Then Zheng started to be stabilized.²⁰ King Wen of Chu used this to open up lands to the north and east of the Han River.²¹

Notes

1. For the most detailed study of the story of Zhou's downfall published prior to the discovery of *Xinian*, see Li Feng 2006, 193–278; for a brief summary of the information in transmitted texts, see Chen Minzhen and Pines 2018, 3–7.
2. From the *Bamboo Annals* (cited by Kong Yingda; see note 3) it is clear that Xie 攜 is a place-name, which, following the parallel *Xinian* passage, was likely located in the state of Guo 虢. Kong Yingda, somewhat confusingly, interpreted Xie as both a place-name and derogatory designation for Yuchen ("King of Discord").
3. *Chunqiu Zuozhuan zhengyi* 52:2114.
4. For debates over the location of Western Shen, see Li Feng 2006, 221–31.
5. Note that *Xinian* refers to the future King Ping by his royal title from the moment of his birth. King Ping's traditional reign dates are 770–722 BCE, but *Xinian*'s narrative requires reconsidering these to 741–722 BCE.
6. Bao was the name of a polity. Bao Si should be translated more precisely as "Si from Bao."
7. Literally, "submitted" (*xiang* 降). The character *xiang* has caused considerable polemics (summarized in Wang Hui 2016). Following the parallel with *Guoyu* 2.1:46 ("Zhou yu zhong" 周語中), I read it as "behaving deferentially to request military assistance." Note that *Xinian* does not explain why Zeng allied with Shen against King You.
8. The narrative here closely parallels that in *Discourses of the States* (*Guoyu* 16.1:474–75 ["Zheng yu"]), where, however, it is presented as the prediction of a prescient Scribe Bo 史伯 of Zhou.
9. The location of the state of Guo in which Yuchen was enthroned is contested: some scholars consider it as referring to Eastern Guo near present-day Sanmenxia 三門峽 City, while others insist on Western Guo, near current Baoji 寶鷄. For a summary of these debates, see Su, Wu, and Lai 2013, 66–74.
10. Marquis Wen of Jin is one of the regional lords mentioned as a major supporter of King Ping's restoration in *Discourses of the States* (*Guoyu* 10.1 ["Jin yu 4"]) and *Lüshi chunqiu* (22.3 ["Yi si" 疑似]); this role is hinted at also in

Zuozhuan (Xuan 12.2). The "Decree to Marquis Wen" (文侯之命), a chapter of the *Canon of Documents*, is also in all likelihood related to this support. In the *Bamboo Annals*, much like in *Xinian*, he is merited with killing the "usurper," the King from Xie (*Chunqiu Zuozhuan zhengyi* 52:2114). However, the rest of the information about his support of King Ping in *Xinian* (establishing King Ping in 741 BCE and arranging the relocation to the east in 738 BCE) contradicts the accepted dates of his lifetime. For a possibility that Marquis Wen reigned 770–736 BCE and not 780–746 BCE, see Cheng Pingshan's (2015) somewhat speculative—yet in parts convincing—analysis.

11. In Warring States–period Chu manuscripts, and in particular in *Xinian*, the character *wáng* < *maŋ 亡 can appear either in its literal meaning of "to be destroyed," "lose," "perish" (as in the preceding 周乃亡) or, as frequently, in the meaning of "not have/exist" (which in non-Chu texts is usually rendered by the word *wú* < *ma 無). In the sentence 周亡王九年, the latter meaning appears more fitting. I am grateful to Chen Minzhen and to a reviewer of our article in *Asia Major* (Chen and Pines 2018) for clarifying this point. For a systematic discussion of the usage of 亡 as 無 in Chu manuscripts and the possibility that this usage reflects Chu local flavor, see Richter 2013, 73–77.

12. Yoshimoto Michimasa (2017, 23) suggests that "rulers of the states" (*bang jun* 邦君) should refer to the enfeoffed nobles from within the Zhou royal domain, whereas "regional lords" refers to the outsiders. For this interpretation of *bang jun*, see also Chen Yingjie 2007, 119–21.

13. The royal capital (Jingshi 京師) here clearly refers to the original Western Zhou capital, or, more precisely, to the cultic center in which the enthronements of the new kings took place. See Mizuno 2017. For Shao'e as possibly located in the Nanyang 南陽 Basin, see Shim 2017.

14. This sentence implies Jin's expansion into the heart of the Wei River basin, which is not attested elsewhere. Some scholars have proposed interpreting the term Jingshi 京師 here as referring to Jin's capital, but this does not make much sense: surely the Jin leaders did not have to wait until Zhou's downfall to develop their own lands! See a summary of the discussions in Zhu Fenghan 2016, 180–81. A possible—even if odd—solution would be reading Jingshi as a broad designation for the territories of the Zhou royal domain in the Wei River basin to the west of the Yellow River. Jin indeed expanded into these territories, which remained under its control well into the Warring States period.

15. The character *zheng* 正 here can also stand for 征, "to invade," or 政, "to govern." See Li Songru 2015, 70.

16. According to the *Zuozhuan* account, the enthronement of Lord Zhao 鄭昭公 (r. 696–695 BCE) was unsuccessful: he was expelled by his half brother, Lord

Li 鄭厲公 (r. 700–697 and 679–673 BCE). In 697 BCE, Lord Li fled his state because of a quarrel with the powerful minister Zhai Zhong 祭仲, and Lord Zhao returned to power. *Xinian* abridges these events.

17. This assassination occurred in 695 BCE (*Zuozhuan*, Huan 17.8). Zi Meishou 子眉壽 appears in *Zuozhuan* as Ducal Son Wei 公子亹, or simply as Ziwei 子亹. There are two possibilities for reading his name in *Xinian*: treat *zi* 子 as a polite prefix and Meishou as a personal name, or read Zimei as an appellative (*zi* 字) and Shou as a personal name. See details in Yuan 2016. Qumi of Gao 高之渠彌 is Gao Qumi 高渠彌. Using the possessive *zhi* 之 between one's lineage name and personal name is a common feature in *Xinian*.

18. For details of this 694 BCE assembly, see *Zuozhuan*, Huan 18.2. Shouzhi 首止 was located southeast of present-day Sui County 睢縣, Henan, between the states of Zheng and Song (map 3).

19. According to *Zuozhuan*, the replacer of Ziwei/Meishou was Ducal Son Ying 公子嬰 (r. 693–680 BCE); only in 680 BCE did Lord Li return to his state and assassinate Ying. Again, *Xinian* abridges this.

20. The original can be read as follows: "Zheng started to be [properly] governed" (鄭以始政). The editors (Li Xueqin 2011a, 140n18) read *zheng* 政 as a substitute for 正, which is then glossed as *ding* 定 ("to stabilize," or "be stabilized").

21. Oddly, *Xinian* starts the story of Chu expansion with King Wen 楚文王 (r. 689–675 BCE), although from *Zuozhuan* it is clear that the expansion had already begun with King Wen's father, King Wu of Chu 楚武王 (r. 740–690 BCE). For Hanyang 漢陽 as referring to broad territories to the north and east of the Han River, see Wei Dong 2018.

Xinian 3

This section narrates the rise of the state of Qin to the position of a major regional power. Despite its brevity it covers more than three centuries of history. Its most interesting part narrates the course of the anti-Zhou rebellion in the former Shang territories. The uprising of the Shang loyalists, led by Wugeng 武庚 (named in *Xinian* Luzi Geng 祿子耿), the son of the last king of Shang, had brought about the elimination of the Zhou "three supervisors" (三監) established in the occupied Shang territory and threatened to annul the results of the Zhou victory of 1046 BCE. The rebellion was suppressed by King Cheng of Zhou 周成王 (r. ca. 1042–1021 BCE), but the diehard loyalists led by Feilian 飛廉 continued resistance in the east, from the territory of present-day Shandong Province. This required a new campaign by King Cheng, after which the defeated rebels were transferred from their Shandong stronghold of Shanghe 商蓋 (or Shangyan 商奄) westward to the area of Zhuyu 朱圄 (present-day Gangu County 甘谷縣, Gansu). There they established the Qin polity. The Qin acted thenceforth as faithful protectors of the Zhou from the heretofore unheard of Nucuo(?) Rong ethnic group. After the collapse of the Western Zhou (narrated in *Xinian* 2), Qin occupied the territories of the former Zhou domain. The narrative concludes, "This was how Qin began to be great."

The novelty and problematics of *Xinian* 3 have been discussed in great detail in chapter 4, consequently only a brief summary is needed here.

First, it is likely that the narration, lacking as it does an accurate chronological outline, reflects a version of the Qin dynastic legend. Several discrepancies between this narrative and the transmitted texts, as well as inaccuracies in *Xinian* 3 itself, thus come as no surprise. For instance, whether or not the supervisors established by King Wu of Zhou in the occupied Shang capital were killed by the rebels (as in *Xinian*) or actually joined the rebellion (as is narrated in numerous other texts) is impossible to ascertain. On some points *Xinian* 3 is clearly wrong—with regard to, for example, the identity of the lord of Qin, who occupied Zhou lands following the dynasty's relocation eastward. Overall, one should treat the information in this section with the utmost caution. Second, inaccuracies aside, the *Xinian* version of the Qin legend may contain kernels of truth insofar as it hints that at least some segment of the Qin ruling elite were immigrants from the east, possibly affiliated to the Shang dynasty. Third, *Xinian* confirms that Qin indeed was an important ally of the Zhou house. This information is hinted at in *Records of the Historian*, and now its reliability is firmly confirmed.[1]

★ ★ ★

周武王既克殷，乃設三監于殷。武王陟，商邑興反，殺三監而立祿子耿。成【13】王踐伐商邑，殺祿子耿。飛廉東逃于商蓋(奄?)氏，成王伐商蓋，殺飛廉，西遷商【14】蓋之民于朱 虐(圉)，以御奴 虘 之戎，是秦之先，世作周 忽 (衛)。周室既卑，平王東遷，止于成【15】周，秦仲焉東居周地，以守周之墳墓，秦以始大。【16】

After King Wu of Zhou had overcome Yin (Shang), he established three supervisors in Yin. When King Wu ascended [to Heaven], the Shang settlement rose in revolt, killing the three supervisors[2] and establishing Luzi Geng (Sheng?).[3] King Cheng [of Zhou] invaded and exterminated the Shang settlement and killed Luzi Geng. Feilian fled eastward to the [settlement of] the Shanghe (Shangyan?) lineage;[4] King Cheng attacked Shanghe, killed Feilian, and transferred the Shanghe people westward to Zhuyu, in order to repel the Nucuo(?) Rong:[5] these were the Qin ancestors who for generations acted as protectors of Zhou. When the house of Zhou declined and King Ping relocated to the east, stopping at Chengzhou,[6] Qin Zhong thereupon [moved] eastward, occupying the Zhou lands, in order to preserve the Zhou cemeteries.[7] This was how Qin began to be great.

Notes

1. For archaeologically observable evidence of Qin's identification with the Zhou house, see Falkenhausen with Shelach 2014.
2. As discussed in chapter 4 (p. 110), the three supervisors are normally identified as the brothers of King Wu of Zhou, Guanshu Xian 管叔鮮 and Caishu Du 蔡叔度; the third supervisor is either a scion of the Shang royal house, Wugeng, or the third brother, Huoshu Chu 霍叔處. *Xinian* clearly distinguishes Wugeng from the three supervisors, so Huoshu is likely to be the third one (Xing 2013). The problem is that all the transmitted texts agree that the supervisors joined the Shang rebellion and were later punished by their brother, the Duke of Zhou. Nobody has succeeded in solving the puzzle of the contradiction between *Xinian* and other sources. Technically it is possible that the unidentified "three supervisors" of *Xinian* are not the trio of brothers (Lu Yihan 2013c), but this is very odd.
3. For reading Luzi Geng 祿子耿 as Luzi Sheng 祿子聖, and for the connection between this name and Wugeng, the scion of the defunct Shang dynasty, see Li Xueqin 2011b, 72–73; Lu Yihan 2013b.
4. Feilian is identified in *Records of the Historian* as a Shang loyalist who committed suicide for the sake of the slain king of Shang, Zhouxin 紂辛; the *Xinian* version of events is supported by *Mengzi* 6.9. Shanghe 商蓋 is read by the editors of *Xinian* (Li Xueqin 2011a, 142n8) as Shangyan 商奄 (alternatively transcribed 商閹), a major Shang stronghold in Shandong, near which the future Lu capital, Qufu 曲阜, was constructed. See more in Su, Wu, and Lai 2013, 168–72.
5. For attempts to identify the Nucuo(?) Rong, see Li Xueqin 2011c; Su, Wu, and Lai 2013, 180–83; Shen Jianhua 2016.
6. For the possibility that the date of the capital transfer to Chengzhou should be 738 BCE rather than the traditional 770 BCE, see *Xinian* 2 in this book and the discussion there.
7. According to *Records of the Historian*, Qin Zhong (r. 845–822 BCE) was the first Qin leader to be enfeoffed by a Zhou king as a ranked noble. According to that narrative, the occupation of the Western Zhou territories following the Zhou relocation to the east was carried out by Qin Zhong's grandson, Lord Xiang 秦襄公 (r. 777–766 BCE). The editors of the *Xinian* volume (Li Xueqin 2011a, 143n15) opined that Qin Zhong 秦仲 (literally, "the second-born Qin scion") can refer to Lord Xiang, who was indeed second born (*Shiji* 5:178). What they did not notice is that even according to their own reconstruction of the capital transfer to the east, Lord Xiang

was already dead by then, and in any case no single ruler is referred to posthumously by his birth-seniority designation. In my view, there is no doubt that the *Xinian* authors were confused about the identity of the ruler under whom Qin "began to be great." See more in chapter 4 of the present volume (p. 112).

Xinian 4

Xinian 4 focuses on the early history of the state of Wei 衛. It starts as a direct continuation of the first two slips of section 3, which narrate the rebellion of the Shang loyalists and its suppression. *Xinian* 4 tells how in the aftermath of this suppression multiple polities ruled by the Zhou clansmen were established in the east, to control the "Xia and Shang" territories. Of these polities, Wei, located near the ruins of the former Shang capital, was planned to be one of the major Zhou strongholds. This did not happen, though: *Xinian* jumps from the eleventh to the seventh century BCE and shows how badly Wei was battered by the Di 狄 invaders. Wei's misfortunes, and the repeated relocations of its capital further from the marauding Di, are presented perhaps to indicate the failure of the Zhou system of "extensively establishing clansmen to serve as protectors of the Zhou."

Xinian 4 is exceptional in the entire work insofar as its focus remains purely in the eastern parts of the Zhou realm, far from the major foci of Chu's activities.[1] Its information on early Wei history is novel inasmuch as it allows us to resolve the enigma around the appellation of the founder of the Wei polity, Kangshu Feng 康叔封. From *Xinian*, it is clear that "Kang" in his appellation refers to the earliest location of his fief, the Kang Hill 康丘, before the polity was relocated to the nearby Wei on the Qi River 淇衛, where it received its name, Wei (see note 6). The second half of *Xinian* 4, which narrates Wei's history between 660 and 629 BCE, largely parallels the discussion in *Zuozhuan*, with only minor discrepancies, summarized in the notes.

★ ★ ★

周成王、周公既遷殷民于洛邑，乃追念夏商之亡由，旁設出(之)² 宗子，以作周厚【17】屏。乃先建衛叔封于康丘，以侯殷之餘民。衛人自康丘遷于淇衛。周惠王立十【18】又七年，赤狄王峕 䖒 起師伐衛，大敗衛師於瓊，幽侯滅焉。狄遂居衛，衛人乃東涉【19】河，遷于曹，焉立戴公申，公子啓方奔齊。戴公卒，齊桓公會諸侯以城楚丘，囗【20】公子啓方焉，是文公。文公即世，成公即位。狄人又涉河，伐衛于楚丘，衛人自楚丘【21】遷于帝丘。【22】

When King Cheng of Zhou and the Duke of Zhou transferred the Yin people to the Luo Settlement (Luoyi; i.e., Luoyang),[3] they recalled that the Xia and Shang [people] had nobody to lead them[4] and extensively established clansmen to serve as protectors of the Zhou.[5] Then they first established Weishu Feng in Kang Hill to govern the remnants of the Yin people. The people of Wei moved from Kang Hill to Wei on the Qi.[6] In the seventeenth year of King Hui of Zhou (660 BCE), King Maohu[7] of the Red Di raised an army to invade Wei; he greatly defeated the Wei army at Qiong,[8] and Marquis You [of Wei] was annihilated there.[9] Thereupon, the Di occupied Wei, and then the people of Wei moved east of the [Yellow] River, relocating to Cao.[10] There they established Lord Dai, named Shen, whereas Ducal Son Qifang fled to Qi. When Lord Dai died,[11] Lord Huan of Qi assembled the regional lords to fortify Chu Hill (Chuqiu); he X [established?][12] Ducal Son Qifang at that place; this was Lord Wen.[13] When Lord Wen died (635 BCE), Lord Cheng ascended the throne. The Di people again crossed the river and attacked Wei at Chu Hill. The people of Wei moved from Chu Hill to Di Hill (Diqiu).[14]

Notes

1. Infrequently Wei did ally with Chu (e.g., on the eve of the fateful Chengpu battle of 632 BCE), but overall this state remained marginal for Chu, as either ally or rival.
2. Reading 之 instead of 出 following Ziju 2012.
3. The transfer of segments of the Shang population to the newly built Zhou secondary capital at Luoyi (Luoyang) is mentioned in *Shiji* 4.133.

4. Several scholars have suggested reading *you* 由 as 胄, meaning "descendants" (see the debates in Su, Wu, and Lai 2013, 202–4), but I do not think this reading fits the text. The Zhou leaders were not worried that the Xia and Shang peoples would be without descendants but, rather, that they would remain without proper leadership (reading *you* as "to cause" and by extension "to lead"). "Xia and Shang" here refers broadly to the dwellers of the eastern part of the Zhou realm—the people beyond direct Zhou rule.
5. This phrase encapsulates the political rationale for the formation of the Zhou fiefs in the eastern part of their realm: to provide proper leadership to the local population by establishing polities led by Zhou clansmen (see details in Li Feng 2006). For reading *pang* 旁 as "extensively," see Su, Wu, and Lai 2013, 205.
6. According to Lu Yihan 2013a, Kang should be considered the earliest state name of Wei. Feng, the younger brother of the Duke of Zhou, is called in *Xinian* Weishu 衛叔, but he is better known as Kangshu 康叔, according to his earliest enfeoffment (see, e.g., "Kang gao" 康誥 [Declaration to Kang], in the *Canon of Documents*, which was directed precisely to Feng). See more in Li Xueqin 2013 and Škrabal 2014, 23–25. Kang Hill was located near the remnants of Yin 殷, the last Shang capital. Wei on the Qi River 淇衛 was a nearby location to which the polity's capital was relocated; since then the country was no longer called Kang but Wei.
7. The Huadong Normal University Team proposes reading the king's name as Liuyu 留吁, a name of a branch of the Di ethnic group (Su, Wu, and Lai 2013, 234–35).
8. Qiong probably stands for Jiong (泂 or 熒) Marsh, where, according to *Zuozhuan* (Min 2.5a) and the *Bamboo Annals* (cited by Du Yu in *Chunqiu Zuozhuan zhengyi* 60:2188), the Wei army was defeated by the Di invaders (Su, Wu, and Lai 2013, 235–37).
9. See details in *Zuozhuan* (Min 2.5:265–68). The Di are identified as Red Di 赤狄 in the *Bamboo Annals*. *Zuozhuan* names the Wei ruler as Lord Yi 衛懿公 (r. 668–660 BCE). You 幽 (benighted) is probably a more appropriate posthumous name of this ruler, who, according to *Zuozhuan*, was single-handedly responsible for the inglorious defeat. Note that in *Xinian* this ruler is called Marquis You 幽侯, whereas subsequent Wei rulers are all called "dukes" or "lords" (*gong* 公).
10. Cao 曹 is a town within the domain of Wei (not to be confused with the eponymous state located further to the south); see map 3.
11. Lord Dai died in the year of his enthronement (i.e., 660 BCE; *Shiji* 37:1594). *Zuozhuan* reports his ascendancy but not his death, perhaps because the *Spring and Autumn Annals* remain silent on this.
12. The character is not legible.

13. These events are narrated in *Zuozhuan*, Min 2.5, 2.9; Xi 2.1. The narrative differs in minor details: thus, the future Lord Wen (Ducal Son Qifang) seems to have fled to Qi even before Wei's defeat by the Di. Chu Hill was fortified in the spring of 658 BCE (*Zuozhuan*, Xi 2.1). Note that in the Warring States period a tradition evolved around Ducal Son Qifang's problematic behavior at the court of his benefactor, Lord Huan of Qi (for details, see Škrabal 2014, 26; Su, Wu, and Lai 2013, 243–51). *Xinian* is silent on this.
14. The Di pressure on Wei is recorded in *Zuozhuan*: in 648 BCE, the regional lords assembled to erect outward fortifications around Chu Hill (Chuqiu 楚丘; *Zuozhuan*, Xi 12.1); in 629 BCE, Wei was relocated to Di Hill (Diqiu 帝丘, located not far from Chu Hill; map 3), which was done to avoid Di pressure. *Zuozhuan* contains a prediction that Wei rule in Di Hill would last three hundred years (*Zuozhuan*, Xi 31.5). This prediction is perplexing: either it was incorporated from an early source (in which case it is a rare example of a false prediction in *Zuozhuan*) or it refers to an unknown event from Warring States–period Wei history.

Xinian 5

Xinian 5 is the first section that focuses on the state of Chu and the beginning of its territorial expansion northward and eastward, toward the northern banks of the Huai River and its major tributaries, the Ru 汝 and Ying 潁. The expansion started almost accidentally. A conflict between two Ji 姬 clan polities, Cai 蔡 and Xi 息, was caused by adultery on the part of Marquis Ai of Cai 蔡哀侯 (r. 694–675 BCE) with his sister-in-law, the wife of the Xi ruler. The rulers of Xi and then Cai sought the intervention of King Wen of Chu (r. 689–675 BCE) against each other, allowing the latter to capture Marquis Ai and then to swallow up Xi (which became a county of Chu and its major stronghold in the Huai River basin). This set Chu on the course of northward expansion, which would duly overawe Cai and other polities in the Ying River valley and further to the north and northeast (see map 2).

As discussed in detail in chapter 2 (pp. 49–52), the story in *Xinian* 5 closely parallels two entries in *Zuozhuan* (Zhuang 10.3 and 14.3). Factually speaking, the only meaningful discrepancy between the two narratives is the timing of the annihilation of Xi. *Xinian* suggests that it happened just a year after King Wen helped the Marquis of Xi to avenge his grievance and punish Marquis Ai of Cai, whereas in *Zuozhuan* the two events are separated by four years. Here it is possible that *Xinian* is more accurate: *Zuozhuan*'s compiler could have manipulated the dates so as to make the annihilation of Xi (which followed a plot by Marquis Ai of Cai) closely related to Chu's second incursion into Cai, which would highlight the stupidity of Marquis Ai's behavior. *Xinian* authors are indifferent toward the moral aspects of their story. They bother themselves neither with the perfidy of the Xi and Cai rulers nor with the chastity (or its lack) of the widow of Marquis of Xi, who was forced to marry King Wen of Chu (for which see p. 52). What matters to them is the bottom line: the fraternal struggle among the Ji polities in the Huai River basin provided Chu with an opportunity to start its northward expansion.

★ ★ ★

蔡哀侯取妻於陳，息侯亦取妻於陳，是息媯。息媯將歸于息，過蔡，蔡哀侯命止之，【23】曰：「以同姓之故，必入。」息媯乃入于蔡，蔡哀侯妻之。息侯弗順，乃使人于楚文王【24】曰：「君來伐我，我將求救於蔡，君焉敗之。」文王起師伐息，息侯求救於蔡，蔡哀侯率師【25】以救之，文王敗之於莘，獲哀侯以歸。文王爲客於息，蔡侯與從，息侯以文【26】王飲酒，蔡侯知息侯之誘己也，亦告文王曰：「息侯之妻甚美，君必命見之。」文【27】王命見之，息侯辭，王固命見之。既見之，還。明歲，起師伐息，克之，殺息侯，取【28】息媯以歸，是生堵敖及成王。文王以北啓出方城，圾蕆（遂）於汝，治旅於陳，焉【29】取頓以䧟（陷？）陳侯。【30】

Marquis Ai of Cai took a wife in Chen. The Marquis of Xi also took a wife in Chen, who was Xi Gui. When Xi Gui was going to be married, she passed through Cai.[1] Marquis Ai of Cai ordered her to be stopped, saying, "Since she is from the same family [as my wife], she must enter [the city]." Xi Gui then entered into Cai, and Marquis Ai of Cai "wived" her.[2] The Marquis of Xi considered [Marquis Ai] incompliant;[3] then he sent a messenger to King Wen of Chu, saying, "My lord should come and attack us; we shall seek help from Cai, and you can thereupon defeat them." King Wen raised an army and attacked Xi, the Marquis of Xi requested help from Cai, and Marquis Ai of Cai led his army to save Xi. King Wen defeated him at Shen and captured Marquis Ai of Cai, returning with him.[4]

King Wen was a guest at Xi, and the Marquis of Cai accompanied him. The Marquis of Xi was serving ale to King Wen. The Marquis of Cai knew that he had been lured by the Marquis of Xi; hence he told King Wen, "The wife of the Marquis of Xi is extraordinarily beautiful; my lord must demand to see her." King Wen ordered her to be shown to him. The Marquis of Xi refused, but the king insistently ordered her to be shown to him. Having seen her, he went back [to Chu].[5] The next year, he raised an army and invaded Xi. He overpowered it, killed the Marquis of Xi, and took Xi Gui with him to return. She [eventually] gave birth to Du'ao and [the future] King Cheng.⁶

Thanks to this, King Wen opened lands northward beyond Fangcheng,⁷ advanced, and acquired [territories up] to the Ru River,⁸ trained his armies near Chen, and thereupon seized Dun⁹ so as to overawe the Marquis of Chen.¹⁰

Notes

1. Cai was located midway between Chen and Xi.
2. "To wife" 妻 is glossed by Hu Sanxing 胡三省 (1230–1302) as "to commit adultery with a married woman" (私他人婦女), and this gloss fits perfectly here. See Cheng Wei 2012b and Chen Wei 2012a, 118. See also Su, Wu, and Lai 2013, 276–77.
3. I read *shun* 順 in 弗順 as a transitive verb; this usage ("to consider somebody incompliant," or, more precisely, "to bear a grudge against somebody") is peculiar to *Xinian* (see also *Xinian* 15). Shen 莘 was a Cai locality, near present-day Runan County 汝南縣, Henan.
4. This capture of Marquis Ai of Cai is mentioned in the *Spring and Autumn Annals* (*Chunqiu*, Zhuang 10.5). Shen 莘 was a Cai locality, near present-day Runan County 汝南縣, Henan.
5. The *Zuozhuan* version implies that Marquis Ai of Cai lured King Wen to take Xi Gui not immediately after his capture but at some later date, and the annihilation of Xi took place a full four years after the initial events (*Zuozhuan*, Zhuang 14.3).
6. Du'ao is referred to as Zhuang'ao in *Records of the Historian*. Following the narrative there (*Shiji* 40:1696), Du'ao inherited King Wen in 677 BCE (or in 675 BCE if we trust *Zuozhuan*); in 672 BCE he plotted to kill his brother, the future King Cheng, but the latter escaped to the neighboring state of Sui 隨 and overthrew Du'ao (note that in 672 BCE both were still young children of around ten to twelve years old, so surely the plots were conducted by their advisers). "Ao" (perhaps a reference to a burial place) appears in the posthumous titles of the Chu kings who were deposed and denied a legitimate place in the Chu ancestral temple (see more in Su, Wu, and Lai 2013, 291–94). King Cheng ruled the state of Chu from 672 to 626 BCE. Under his aegis Chu became the most powerful polity on Chinese soil, until its rise was checked by the Chengpu defeat at the hands of the Jin in 632 BCE (for which see *Xinian* 7).
7. The precise identification of Fangcheng is disputed, because in different contexts the term can refer to mountain ranges, a single fortification, a town, or a

man-made wall. In the context of *Xinian* 5 (as well as in *Zuozhuan*), it refers to mountain ranges, hills, and fortifications stretching from the Funiu Mountains (伏牛山) eastward and then southward toward the Tongbai Mountains (桐柏山). These crescentlike ranges and hills served as a natural boundary of the Nanyang 南陽 Basin, which was the major gate to Chu's heartland to the east of the Han River (see map 2). For the complex nature of fortifications along this line, see Li Yipi 2014.

8. The Ru River runs parallel to the Fangcheng line to the east; Cai was located on its banks (map 2).

9. Dun 頓 is located further eastward from Cai, on the banks of the Ying River and close to the state of Chen (map 2). *Zuozhuan* (Xi 23.3) reports that King Cheng of Chu fortified Dun as part of his strategy of intimidating Chen.

10. The reading of several characters in this sentence is hotly disputed. I tentatively follow the reconstruction of Ziju 2012. However, putting the precise identification of a few characters aside, the overall meaning (expansion into the Ru River valley) is clear enough. Note that the sentence parallels the summary of the achievements of King Wen of Chu's prime minister cited in *Zuozhuan*: "He made Shen and Xi into Chu counties, caused Chen and Cai to pay court visits, and fixed our borders at the Ru River" (*Zuozhuan*, Ai 17.4; Shen 申 was probably acquired earlier than Xi).

Xinian 6

Xinian 6 shifts the narrative from Chu to Jin, the state that will remain at the center of the next five sections. It starts with a brief depiction of the domestic turmoil in Jin that followed the prolonged fratricidal struggle among the sons of Lord Xian of Jin 晉獻公 (r. 676–651 BCE). The struggle ended in 636 BCE, when Chong'er, the protégé of Lord Mu of Qin 秦穆公 (r. 659–621 BCE), eliminated his nephew and ascended the throne as Lord Wen of Jin 晉文公 (r. 636–628 BCE), one of the most illustrious leaders of the entire Spring and Autumn period. The text ends with the first joint exploits of the Jin-Qin alliance and in particular the beginning of the allies' conflict with the state of Chu.

Fundamentally, the text follows the narration in *Zuozhuan* with only tiny deviations (i.e., the sequence of Chong'er's wanderings is slightly altered to divide the states he visited into those that treated him well and those that did not). The major difference between the two narratives, as discussed in chapter 2, is *Xinian*'s indifference toward the literary or didactic aspects of the story. Politically speaking, two abridgments are significant. First, *Xinian* remains conspicuously silent on how the king of Chu treated Chong'er. Unlike *Zuozhuan*, *Xinian* avoids mentioning either Chu's courtesy or Chong'er's subsequent promise to repay it by retreating from the invading Chu armies for the distance of three days' march.[1] Second, *Xinian* does not tell of one of Lord Wen of Jin's major achievements soon after his seizure of power—namely, restoring power to King Xiang of Zhou 周襄王 (r. 651–619 BCE). Perhaps from the authors' point of view, what mattered more was the evolving conflict between Jin and Chu, the discussion of which begins in the final sentences of section 6 and continues through most of the subsequent sections.

★ ★ ★

晉獻公之嬖妾曰驪姬，欲其子奚齊之爲君也，乃讒太子共君而殺之，又讒【31】惠公及文公，文公奔狄，惠公奔于梁。獻公卒，乃立奚齊。其大夫里之克乃殺奚齊，【32】而立其弟悼子，里之克又殺悼子。秦穆公乃內（納）²惠公于晉，惠公賂秦公曰：「我【33】苟果內（入），使君涉河，至于梁城。」惠公既內（入），乃背秦公弗予。立六年，秦公率師與【34】惠公戰于韓，戡（捷）³惠公以歸。惠公焉以其子懷公爲質于秦，秦穆公以其子妻之。【35】文公十又二年居狄，狄甚善之，而弗能內（納），乃適齊，齊人善之；適宋，宋人善之，亦莫【36】之能內（納）；乃適衛，衛人弗善；適鄭，鄭人弗善；乃適楚。懷公自秦逃歸，秦穆公乃召【37】文公於楚，使襲懷公之室。晉惠公卒，懷公即位。秦人起師以內（納）文公于晉。晉人殺【38】懷公而立文公，秦晉焉始合好，戮力同心。二邦伐鄀，徙之中城，圍商密，戡（捷）【39】申公子儀以歸。【40】

The favorite concubine of Lord Xian of Jin was called Li Ji. She wanted to make her son, Xiqi, ruler.[4] Thereupon she slandered the crown prince, Lord Gong, and caused him to be killed.[5] She also slandered Lord Hui and Lord Wen.[6] Lord Wen fled to the Di, Lord Hui fled to Liang.[7] Lord Xian died, and thereupon Xiqi was established. Its [Jin's] grandee, Ke of Li (Li Ke), thereupon killed Xiqi, and [Li Ji] established Xiqi's younger brother, Daozi (Zhuozi).[8] Ke of Li killed Daozi as well.

Thereupon Lord Mu of Qin installed Lord Hui in Jin. Lord Hui bribed the Duke of Qin, promising, "If I am able to return [to Jin], I will let you, my lord, reach the Yellow River all the way to the city of Liang."[9] Yet as Lord Hui returned [to Jin] he reneged on [his promise] to the Duke of Qin and did not give him [the lands]. Six years after he was established (655 BCE), the Duke of Qin led an army and made a battle with Lord Hui at Han. He captured Lord Hui, returning with him.[10] Lord Hui then made his son, Lord Huai, hostage at Qin.[11] Lord Mu of Qin betrothed him to his daughter.

Lord Wen resided for twelve years among the Di. The Di treated him exceptionally well but could not install him [in Jin]. Thereupon he turned to Qi. The Qi leaders treated him well. He went to Song. The Song leaders treated him well but also could not install him. He thereupon turned to Wei. The Wei leaders did not treat him well. He turned to Zheng. The Zheng leaders did not treat him well. He thereupon turned to Chu.[12] As Lord Huai fled from Qin back [to Jin], Lord Mu of Qin thereupon summoned Lord Wen from Chu and let him to take over the wife of Lord Huai.[13]

When Lord Hui of Jin died, Lord Huai ascended the throne. The Qin leaders then raised an army to install Lord Wen in Jin. The people of Jin killed Lord Huai and established Lord Wen.[14] Thenceforth, Qin and Jin became friendly, uniting in concerted efforts. The two countries invaded Ruo, relocating it to the Central Area.[15] They laid siege to [Ruo's capital], Shangmi, and captured Ziyi, Duke of Shen, returning with him.[16]

Notes

1. See *Zuozhuan*, Xi 23.6e; see also *Guoyu* 10.1:331–33 ("Jin yu 4").
2. For reading the same character 内 intermittently as a transitive verb 納 (to install somebody) or intransitive 入 (to enter), see Su Jianzhou's gloss in Su, Wu, and Lai 2013, 329–30.
3. For reading the character 敨 as *jie* 捷 (to capture), see Chen Jian 2013.
4. For Li Ji and her machinations, see *Zuozhuan*, Zhuang 28.2; Xi 4.6.
5. The crown prince was named Shensheng 申生. Lord Gong ("Respectful," 共) stands as a substitute for 恭) is the posthumous name granted him by his brother, Lord Hui of Jin 晉惠公 (r. 650–637 BCE). Presumably, it was given out of respect to Shensheng's decision to commit suicide after being slandered by Li Ji, rather than whitewash his name and break his father's heart by implicating Lord Xian's beloved concubine.
6. Both Lord Hui (named Yiwu 夷吾) and Lord Wen (named Chong'er 重耳) were Shensheng's half brothers and were the most expected candidates to become crown prince after his death.
7. The Di tribal territories were to the north of Jin. Liang was located on the western banks of the Yellow River, near modern Hancheng 韓城 (map 3). According to *Zuozhuan* 卓子) (Xi 6.1), Yiwu opted for this location because of its proximity to Qin and the chances of obtaining Qin's support.
8. The omission of the subject here may create a gross misunderstanding: the sentence can easily be read as if Li Ke were the one to establish Daozi (who is more often transcribed as Zhuozi 卓子). This, however, is surely wrong: as the

next sentence shows, and as is narrated in *Zuozhuan* (Xi 4.6 and 9.4) and *Discourses of the States* (*Guoyu* 8.8 ["Jin yu 2"]), it was Li Ji who tried to install her sister's son, Daozi, and it was Li Ke who murdered the young prince.

9. That is, the entire territory to the west of the Yellow River (in modern Shaanxi) would be ceded to Qin. Note that at the time, Qin's locus of gravity was near its capital, Yong, in the middle reaches of the Wei 渭 River and quite distant from the promised new territories (map 3). See also *Zuozhuan* (Xi 15.4a).

10. This battle, which caused a major setback to Jin, is narrated in great detail in *Zuozhuan*, Xi 15.4.

11. Lord Huai of Jin 晉懷公 ruled Jin for several months in 637–636 BCE before being deposed and killed by his uncle, Lord Wen. For his stay as a hostage in Qin, see *Zuozhuan*, Xi 17.2; for his escape home, see Xi 22.5.

12. Note that the text is silent on Chu's treatment of Chong'er. According to *Zuozhuan*, Chong'er's relations with his host, King Cheng of Chu, were somewhat ambiguous: King Cheng was polite, but the future clash between him and Jin was already well predictable.

13. The wanderings of Chong'er (future Lord Wen of Jin) during his nineteen years of exile became a celebrated literary piece "and is as close as we come in *Zuozhuan* to a story of a hero's journey" (Durrant, Li, and Schaberg 2016, 251; for the story, see *Zuozhuan*, Xi 23.6, 24.1). For the sake of brevity *Xinian* organizes these visits into those to pro-Chong'er and those to anti-Chong'er countries, sacrificing the chronological and geographical sequence of his wanderings (e.g., his visit to Wei came before coming to Qi, Song, and Zheng; the visit to the state of Cao 曹 is omitted). An important addition of *Xinian* to our knowledge of Chong'er's career is its clear indication that Qin's support to Chong'er was meant to punish Lord Huai of Jin, who had escaped from Qin custody. The daughter of Lord Mu of Qin, who was first given to Lord Huai and then to Lord Huai's uncle, Lord Wen, was due to play an important role in the state of Jin (see *Zuozhuan*, Wen 6.5).

14. See *Zuozhuan*, Xi 24.1a, where it is clarified that the assassination of Lord Huai was ordered by his uncle, Lord Wen.

15. Following Guo Tao 郭濤 and Su Jianzhou (in Su, Wu, and Lai 2013, 350–53), I accept the identification of Ruo with Lower Ruo (the capital of which was Shangmi 商密) (see also Huang Jinqian 2017a). The Central Area is then identical to Xi 析, slightly to the north and closer to the Qin and Jin borders (map 2). The assault on Ruo and the subsequent capture of the Chu governor, Ziyi, the Duke of Shen, by Qin forces took place in 635 BCE (*Zuozhuan*, Xi 25.3). As noted in the introduction to this section, *Xinian* ignores the story that preceded this campaign: Lord Wen's successful restoration to power of King Xiang of Zhou.

16. Ziyi is the appellative of Dou Ke 鬭克 (d. 613 BCE), who acted as the governor of Shen, the major Chu county near the modern city of Nanyang 南陽, Henan (map 3). Many local Chu governors bore the rank of duke (*gong* 公). Note that *Xinian* 6 does not at all explain who Ziyi was (presumably, Chu readers knew that the Duke of Shen would be a Chu executive). Ziyi's release is narrated in *Xinian* 8 (see note 8 there).

Xinian 7

Section 7 focuses on one of the most dramatic military encounters of the entire Spring and Autumn period: the defeat of Chu and its allies by the forces of the northern coalition, led by Lord Wen of Jin. The battle at Chengpu 城濮 in 632 BCE put an end to decades of Chu's robust expansion and divided the Zhou world into two competing alliances: the northern one, led by Jin, and the southern one, led by Chu. The struggle between these alliances occupies much of the subsequent *Xinian* narrative.

Despite the brevity of *Xinian*'s discussion, it captures all the politically significant elements of the battle's background, outcome, and aftermath, as narrated in *Zuozhuan*. The abridgment does come at the expense of clarity in certain details, and some dates are confused (as the notes explain). However, fundamentally the information in *Xinian* 7 is fully compatible with that in *Zuozhuan*. The only potentially meaningful discrepancy is related to the composition of the warring coalitions. *Xinian* adds the Rong forces to the Jin-led northern alliance, and the Man and Yi forces to the Chu-led southern alliance. Whether this information comes from sources unknown to *Zuozhuan* or the addition was made primarily to create an impression of a truly "world war" is currently unverifiable.

★ ★ ★

晉文公立四年，楚成王率諸侯以圍宋、伐齊，戍穀，居緡。晉文公思齊及宋之【41】德，乃及秦師圍曹及五鹿，伐衛以脫齊之戍及宋之圍。楚王舍圍歸，居方城。【42】令尹子玉遂率鄭、衛、陳、蔡及群蠻夷之師以交文公。文公率秦、齊、宋及群戎【43】之師以敗楚師於城濮，遂朝周襄王于衡雍，獻楚俘馘，盟諸侯於踐土。【44】

In the fourth year of Lord Wen of Jin (632 BCE), King Cheng of Chu led the regional lords to lay siege to Song and invade Qi. He garrisoned Gu and stayed at Min.¹ Lord Wen of Jin thought of the virtue of Qi and Song.² Thereupon he, together with the Qin army,³ laid siege to Cao and Wulu and assaulted Wei, so as to relieve Qi of the [Chu] garrison and raise a siege of Song.⁴ The king of Chu abandoned the siege and returned back, residing at Fangcheng.⁵ The prime minister, Ziyu, led the armies of Zheng, Wei, Chen, Cai, and many Man and Yi⁶ to fight⁷ Lord Wen. Lord Wen led the armies of Qin, Qi, Song, and many Rong,⁸ therewith defeating the Chu army at Chengpu. Thereupon he paid a visit to King Xiang of Zhou at Hengyong, presenting Chu prisoners and ears of the dead and [then] made a covenant with the regional lords at Jiantu.⁹

Notes

1. According to *Zuozhuan* (Xi 26.6), the Chu assault on Song, which shifted its alliance from Chu to Jin, started in 634 BCE with laying siege to Min 緡. Min was located near present-day Jinxiang County 金鄉縣, to the north of the Song capital. This means that the Chu invaders moved along the southern bank of the Si River (map 3). *Xinian* says that the king of Chu "resided" at Min, which implies that the siege of 634 BCE was successful. Gu 穀 was an important town between Lu and Qi, on the eastern bank of the Ji River (map 3). During the brief Chu-Lu alliance of 634–632 BCE, the allies occupied this town and placed one of the contenders for the Qi throne, Ducal Son Yong 公子雍, there. Chu garrisoned Gu, assigning this task to Shuhou, the Duke of Shen 申公叔侯 (*Zuozhuan*, Xi 26.6). Yet Chu laid siege to the Song capital a full year later, in the winter of 633/632 BCE (*Zuozhuan*, Xi 27.4). *Xinian* compresses these events into a single sentence.
2. Referring to these states' positive treatment of Lord Wen during his lengthy wanderings in exile (see *Xinian* 6).
3. Qin participation in this assault is not mentioned in *Zuozhuan*.
4. The background for this assault is given in *Zuozhuan*: Hu Yan 狐偃, Lord Wen's major adviser, suggested attacking Cao and Wei 衛 because both were newly allied with Chu, and the latter would have to dispatch troops to save them and abandon therewith its anti-Qi and anti-Song acts (*Zuozhuan*, Xi

27.4). Wulu was a city in Wei, where Lord Wen was allegedly maltreated by a local peasant, who offered him a clod of earth instead of food. Hu Yan then said that the clod symbolized the gift of earth—that is, Wulu's future surrender to Jin (*Zuozhuan*, Xi 23.6)

5. For Fangcheng, see *Xinian* 5, note 7.

6. This account of the Chu coalition forces differs slightly from that in *Zuozhuan*. First, the state of Zheng is said there to have offered military assistance to Chu, but it is hinted that the Zheng forces did not take part in the battle (Xi 28.3). On the other hand, the account in *Records of the Historian* ("Hereditary House of Zheng") suggests that Zheng forces did join the Chu assault on Jin's army (*Shiji* 42:1766). Here the *Xinian* narrative supports Sima Qian's version. Second, no other text mentions the Man and Yi ethnic groups fighting alongside the Chu forces. Their presence alongside the Chu army is surely possible and attested elsewhere (e.g., *Zuozhuan*, Cheng 16.5), but it is equally possible that the "many Man and Yi" fighting on the Chu side and the "many Rong" fighting on the Jin side (see the following note 8) were added to post factum accounts of the epic Chengpu battle, to represent it as an even greater military encounter than it really was. Third, *Xinian* abridges the story according to which King Cheng, who did not like the belligerent stance of his prime minister, Ziyu, allocated only a limited number of troops to the encounter with Jin. This last information could have diminished the magnitude of Chu's defeat, but the authors do not appear to be interested in assuaging Chu's sensitivities.

7. Reading *jiao* 交 as in *jiaobing* 交兵 (to wage war). See Su Jianzhou's gloss in Su, Wu, and Lai 2013, 380–81 (378–80 for alternative readings of *jiao*).

8. The Rong presence among the Jin coalition troops is not attested elsewhere. Note that Lord Wen himself was half Rong, that his major adviser, Hu Yan (aka Zifan 子犯), was of pure Rong stock, and that some of the Rong had an important role in Jin's victory over Qin in Yao in 627 BCE (*Zuozhuan*, Xi 33.3). Hence, Rong assistance to Jin troops is plausible.

9. According to *Zuozhuan*, Hengyong and Jiantu were close to each other. The ceremony of presenting the spoils of war to King Xiang of Zhou was performed on the tenth day of the fifth month (as confirmed also by the inscription on the Zifan bells; see chapter 3, pp. 82–84), and the covenant was sworn on the twenty-sixth day of the same month. Although most commentators identify Hengyong and Jiantu as locations in the state of Zheng, Ziju 2012 (partly cited in Su, Wu, and Lai 2013, 387–88) convincingly argues that both locations were on the northern bank of the Yellow River between present-day Mengzhou City 孟州市 and the Jili District of Luoyang Municipality (洛陽市吉利區). Both locations were conveniently placed between the Zhou and Jin capitals and were very close to the town of Wen 溫, where another covenant between Jin and its allies was sworn five months later (map 3).

Xinian 8

The narrative in *Xinian* 8 continues that in the previous two sections. The Qin-Jin alliance, which allowed Lord Wen's ascendancy, came to an end with the quarrel over the state of Zheng, which had skillfully utilized the competition between the allies and surrendered to Qin only, gaining its temporary protection against Jin. Soon, however, Lord Mu of Qin was enticed by the prospect of using the Qin garrison in Zheng as a fifth column and decided to conquer Zheng, notwithstanding the considerable distance that separated Qin from Zheng. The plan failed miserably, and, more significantly, it served as a casus belli for Lord Xiang of Jin 晉襄公 (r. 627–621 BCE), who assaulted the Qin army on its route back home and inflicted a major defeat upon Qin. This was the starting point of a long-term Qin-Jin rivalry and of Qin's alliance with Chu, which lasted until the final year of *Xinian*'s narrative and beyond.

This section closely parallels the *Zuo zhuan* narrative (Xi 30.3, 32.3, 33.1, 33.3) with no factual discrepancies between the two.

★ ★ ★

晉文公立七年，秦、晉圍鄭，鄭降秦不降晉，晉人以不慭。秦人豫（舍）戍於鄭。鄭人屬北門之管於秦之【45】戍人，秦之戍人使人歸告曰：「我既得鄭之門管矣，來襲之。」秦師將東襲鄭，鄭之賈人弦高將西【46】市，遇之，乃以鄭君之命勞秦三帥。秦師乃復，伐滑，取之。晉文公卒，未葬，襄公親【47】率師禦秦師于

崤，大敗之。秦穆公欲與楚人爲好，焉脫申公儀，使歸求成。秦焉【48】始與晉執亂，與楚爲好。【49】

In the seventh year of Lord Wen of Jin (630 BCE), Qin and Jin laid siege to Zheng. Zheng surrendered to Qin but not to Jin. The Jin leaders were unhappy about this.[1] The men of Qin stayed[2] at Zheng to garrison [it]. The Zheng leaders entrusted the key of the Northern Gate to the Qin garrison men. The Qin garrison men dispatched somebody to return to Qin, saying, "We have obtained the key of Zheng's gate already, come to make a surprise attack."[3] The Qin army headed east to attack Zheng. The Zheng merchant, Xian Gao, headed west to the market and encountered them. Thereupon, he presented gifts to the three armies of Qin on behalf of Zheng's ruler.[4] The Qin army then turned back. It attacked [the statelet of] Hua and seized it.[5]

Lord Wen of Jin died but was not yet buried.[6] [His heir] Lord Xiang personally led an army to block the Qin army at Yao, greatly defeating it.[7] Lord Mu of Qin wanted to improve relations with the Chu leaders. He thereupon released Yi, the Duke of Shen, and dispatched him back home to request peace.[8] Thenceforth, Qin started to have troublesome relations with Jin and friendly relations with Chu.

Notes

1. These events are narrated in *Zuozhuan* (Xi 30.3). According to that narrative, the Zheng diplomat succeeded in convincing Lord Mu of Qin that Qin would gain nothing from the annexation of Zheng by Jin but, rather, would strengthen its potential rival thereby. Hence, Lord Mu decided to make a separate peace with Zheng and even to garrison it with Qin's forces to protect it against Jin.
2. For reading *yu* 豫 as *she* 舍 in the meaning "to stay," see Sun Feiyan's gloss in Su, Wu, and Lai 2013, 394–95.
3. This dispatch is dated in *Zuozhuan* to 628 BCE (*Zuozhuan*, Xi 32.3).
4. These events are depicted in *Zuozhuan* under the year 627 BCE (Xi 33.1). The Zheng merchant was heading to the market in the Zhou royal domain. By making presents to the Qin army on behalf of the Zheng ruler, Xian Gao made it clear that the Qin plot had been discovered.
5. Hua was a tiny polity located to the west of Zheng, near present-day Yanshi County 偃師縣 in Henan (i.e., along the route utilized by the Qin army in its

aborted invasion of Zheng; see map 3). For the elimination of Hua, see *Zuozhuan* (Xi 33.1).

6. Lord Wen died in the twelfth month of the preceding year (according to the Zhou calendar). His burial was conducted in the fourth month, after the defeat of the Qin army at Yao.

7. The Yao ridge battle is convincingly identified by Ziju (Su, Wu, and Lai 2013, 402–3) as having been conducted in a narrow mountain valley near current Xiashi Township 硤石鄉, thirty kilometers to the southeast of Sanmenxia City. For the battle, see *Zuozhuan*, Xi 33.3.

8. The seizure of the Duke of Shen is reported at the end of *Xinian* 6 (see note 16 there). His appellative Ziyi 子儀 is abridged here to Yi. Ziyi's mission is recorded in *Zuozhuan*, Wen 14.10. His release from Qin captivity stands at the center of a short vignette, *Ziyi*, in the sixth volume of the Tsinghua manuscripts (Li Xueqin 2016, 127–35).

Xinian 9

Xinian 9 briefly shifts the narrative from Jin's external affairs to domestic problems. A succession crisis erupted following the death of Lord Xiang in 621 BCE. The crown prince, the future Lord Ling of Jin 晉靈公 (r. 620–607 BCE), was still a toddler, and the Jin grandees were inclined to replace him with his uncle, Yong, who remained in exile in Qin. However, the tearful intervention of Lord Xiang's widow caused the grandees to reconsider and to appoint Lord Ling. The story parallels the *Zuozhuan* narrative (Wen 6.5 and 7.4), with certain abridgments, but its focus clearly differs from the latter. In *Zuozhuan* what matters most is, first, the growing discord among the Jin grandees because of the succession struggle and, second, the future enmity between Lord Ling and the prime minister, Zhao Dun 趙盾 (d. 601 BCE), who had wanted to prevent Lord Ling's ascendance in the first place. In *Xinian*, in contrast, the story told in section 9 serves as a preface to section 10, which narrates how Jin's domestic conflict further aggravated Jin's uneasy relations with Qin.

* * *

晉襄公卒，靈公高幼，大夫聚謀曰：「君幼，未可奉承也，毋乃不能邦？」獸求強君，乃命【50】左行蔑與隨會召襄公之弟雍也于秦。襄夫人聞之，乃抱靈公以號于廷，曰：「死人何罪？【51】生人何辜？舍其君之子弗立，而召人于外，而爲將實此子也？」大夫閔，乃皆背之曰：「我莫命召【52】之。」乃立靈公，爲葬襄公。【53】

When Lord Xiang of Jin died (621 BCE), Lord Ling [of Jin], named Gao, was [still] young.[1] The grandees discussed among themselves: "The ruler is young, he is not ready yet to inherit [the ruler's position]. Can it be that he is unable to rule the state?"[2] They planned to request an adult[3] ruler; hence they ordered the Commander of the Left Column Mie[4] and Sui Hui[5] to summon Lord Xiang's younger brother Yong from Qin. When Lord Xiang's widow heard about it, she carried [the future] Lord Ling and cried out in the court, saying, "What was the crime of our former ruler? And what is the offense of this living [heir]? If you reject the ruler's son and do not establish him [as a ruler] and moreover summon [another] candidate from abroad, then where will you place this son?" The grandees sympathized with her. And all of them said, "We did not order him (Yong) to be summoned." Thereupon they established Lord Ling and then buried Lord Xiang.[6]

Notes

1. In the *Spring and Autumn Annals*, Lord Ling's name is transcribed Yigao 夷皋. As noted by the editors of *Xinian*, the characters 高 and 皋 are interchangeable (Li Xueqin 2011a, 157n2).
2. This sentence summarizes lengthy deliberations presented in *Zuozhuan* (Wen 6.5).
3. For *qiang* 強 as "adult" (literally, "more than forty years old"), see *Liji* I.1:12 ("Quli shang") (following the Tsinghua editorial team's gloss; Li Xueqin 2011a, 158n6).
4. This is Xian Mie 先蔑, who was appointed the commander of the left column (*zuo hang* 左行) in 632 BCE. The official position could become a new lineage name in Jin and elsewhere; the most famous instance is the Zhonghang (中行, Commanders of the Central Column) lineage.
5. Sui Hui is also known by other lineage names: Shi 士 (the original one) and Fan 范, which, like Sui, derives from his allotment.
6. See *Zuozhuan*, Wen 7.4. Although the intervention of Lord Xiang's widow is recorded in *Zuozhuan* under the year 620 BCE, it is certain that it occurred immediately after the decision to forsake her son, the future Lord Ling, in 621 BCE. If so, *Xinian* is likely to be right in placing the Jin grandees' change of mind in that year—that is, prior to the burial of Lord Xiang (for which see *Chunqiu*, Wen 6.6).

Xinian 10

This very short section (only two bamboo slips) continues the narrative from section 9. Lord Kang of Qin 秦康公 (r. 620–609 BCE) escorted his protégé, Ducal Son Yong, back to Jin, only to be assaulted by the Jin army, since Jin had changed its plans about Ducal Son Yong. This aggravated the Jin-Qin rivalry, starting a series of tit-for-tat campaigns. Once again, there are no discrepancies between *Xinian* and *Zuozhuan*, aside from *Xinian*'s possible correction of *Zuozhuan*'s inaccuracy in evaluating the role of one of Jin's ministers (see note 2) and the place-name of one of the campaigns.

★ ★ ★

秦康公率師以送雍子，晉人起師，敗之于堇陰。左行蔑、隨會不敢歸，遂【54】奔秦。靈公高立六年，秦公以戰于堇陰之故，率師爲河曲之戰。【55】

Lord Kang of Qin led an army to accompany Sir Yong (Ducal Son Yong). The Jin leaders raised an army and defeated [Lord Kang] at Jinyin.[1] The Commander of the Left Column Mie and Sui Hui dared not return, so they then fled to Qin.[2] In the sixth year of Lord Ling (615 BCE), named Gao, the Duke of Qin led an army to [repay] the battle of Jinyin and made a battle at Hequ.[3]

Notes

1. *Zuozhuan* tells that the Jin army decided at Jinyin to assault the Qin army, but the battle took place at Linghu 令狐, which was located slightly to the south of Jinyin, on the eastern bank of the Yellow River (see map 3).
2. There is much confusion in *Zuozhuan* about the exact role of Xian Mie in these events. On the one hand, he was dispatched to Qin to escort Ducal Son Yong back; on the other, he is reported to have led one of Jin's armies that defeated Qin (*Zuozhuan*, Wen 7.4). As noted in Yoshimoto 2013, 47, *Xinian*'s "dared not return" implies that Xian Mie and Shi Hui remained with the Qin armies that escorted Ducal Son Yong. If so, *Zuozhuan* may be mistaken.
3. This campaign is reported in *Zuozhuan* (Wen 12.6). Both sides eschewed a decisive encounter and disengaged without getting the upper hand, but since Qin renewed its incursions into Jin shortly thereafter, the Hequ campaign can be considered a success for Qin.

Xinian 11

The narrative in *Xinian* 11 and in the two subsequent sections shifts back to Chu, which was approaching one of the peaks of its power under King Zhuang 楚莊王 (r. 613–591 BCE). Chu's steady northeasterly expansion put immense pressure on the major polities located between the Huai and Yellow Rivers; namely, Chen, Zheng, and Song. *Xinian* 11 focuses on Chu's pressure on the last. Song tried to appease King Zhuang's father, King Mu of Chu 楚穆王 (r. 625–614), but to no avail: the Duke of Song was humiliated by a Chu official, Shen Wuwei 申無畏 (who is misidentified in *Xinian*). The Song leaders got the chance to avenge their humiliation later, when Shen Wuwei passed through Song territory without proper authorization. Shen Wuwei was seized and executed, causing in turn Chu's retaliation. Only through deep self-humiliation, including making Song's leader, Huasun Yuan 華孫元 (i.e., Hua Yuan), a hostage in Chu, could Song appease the southern superpower.

The narrative in *Xinian* 11 closely parallels that in *Zuozhuan* (Wen 10.5 and Xuan 14.3), but there are some notable discrepancies. Most of these clearly derive from the *Xinian* authors' carelessness. Thus, they attribute to Hua Yuan certain actions in 618 BCE that were actually performed by his father, Hua Yushi 華御事. Elsewhere, they misidentify the Chu leader who humiliated the Duke of Song as Shuhou, the Duke (Governor) of Shen 申公叔侯, whereas in *Zuozhuan* it is clear that the culprit was Shen

Zhou 申舟 (aka Shen Wuwei). This confusion makes the motif of Song revenge upon Shen Wuwei (which is implied in *Xinian*'s narrative) much less clear than in the *Zuozhuan* version of the events.

Minor discrepancies aside, there is one point of important difference between *Xinian* and *Zuozhuan*. According to the latter, King Zhuang explicitly forbade Shen Wuwei from asking for a permit to pass through Song territory, which infuriated the Song leaders and caused their outrageous killing of the messenger. *Xinian*, in contrast, emphasizes that Wuwei asked for the right to pass through Song, and his murder should thus be considered a pure act of revenge by the Song leaders for their earlier humiliation. Needless to say, we are not in a position to decide whether it is *Zuozhuan* that blackens the image of King Zhuang of Chu or *Xinian* that whitewashes it.

★ ★ ★

楚穆王立八年，王會諸侯于厥𧏡（貉），將以伐宋。宋右師華孫元欲勞楚師，乃行。【56】穆王使驅孟渚之麋，徙之徒㮚（林）。宋公爲左盂，鄭伯爲右盂。申公叔侯知之，宋【57】公之車暮駕，用抶宋公之御。穆王即世，莊王即位，使申伯無畏聘于齊，假路【58】於宋，宋人是故殺申伯無畏，奪其玉帛。莊王率師圍宋九月，宋人焉爲成，以女子【59】與兵車百乘，以華孫元爲質。【60】

In the eighth year of King Mu of Chu (618 BCE), the king met the regional lords at Juemo. They were going to attack Song.[1] Song's commander of the right, Huasun Yuan, wanted to present gifts to Chu troops.[2] He thereupon set off. King Mu let them hunt the deer at Mengzhu Marsh and then shifted their hunting to Tulin.[3] The Duke of Song led the left curved formation, and the Earl of Zheng led the right curved formation.[4] Shuhou, the Duke of Shen,[5] supervised[6] [the hunt]. The chariot of the Duke of Song was hitched up only in the evening; and [the Duke of Shen] flogged the chariot driver of the Duke of Song.[7]

When King Mu passed away, King Zhuang ascended the throne (613 BCE). He sent the Shen Elder Wuwei[8] to pay a visit to Qi, seeking the right to pass through Song.[9] Therefore, the Song leaders killed the Shen Elder Wuwei and snatched his jade and silk.[10] King Zhuang led an army that besieged Song for nine months.[11] Thereupon, the Song leaders asked for peace. They presented [Chu] with female musicians[12] and one hundred war chariots and made Hua Yuan a hostage [in Chu].[13]

Notes

1. The Juemo assembly between King Mu of Chu and the lords of Chen, Zheng, and Cai took place in the winter of 617 BCE (*Zuozhuan*, Wen 10.5). As noted by Sun Feiyan (2012), this meeting took place during the ninth year of King Mu of Chu and not the eighth. For the location of Juemo, I follow Ziju (2012), who rejects common glosses and proposes to locate it near Zhecheng 柘城, some fifty kilometers to the southwest of the Song capital, Shangqiu 商丘 (Shang Hill) (map 2).
2. *Xinian* is mistaken here. According to the very detailed *Zuozhuan* narrative (Wen 10.5), the initiative to appease the Chu army by presenting gifts honoring the exertions of the troops was of Hua Yuan's father, Hua Yushi 華御事. Hua Yuan was appointed commander of the right only in 611 BCE (*Zuozhuan*, Wen 16.5). Probably in light of his later prominence, the *Xinian* compilers attributed to him the plan proposed by his father. Note that the Hua lineage is repeatedly called Huasun 華孫 in *Xinian*, which reflects a common practice of that age of adding "sun" 孫 (Descendants) to the lineage's name.
3. Mengzhu Marsh is identified by the Tsinghua editorial team as located to the northwest of the Song capital, Shangqiu (Li Xueqin 2011, 161n6). Tulin is often identified as a location in Yunmeng Marsh, near the Chu heartland in Hubei (see, e.g., Yuan Jinping's gloss in Su, Wu, and Lai 2013, 454–55). I concur with Ziju (2012) that such a shift would not be feasible; probably Tulin was located to the southwest of Shangqiu, closer to the state of Chen. The shift of the hunting expedition from Mengzhu Marsh to Tulin is not reported in *Zuozhuan*.
4. This phrase appears verbatim in *Zuozhuan* (Wen 10.5), except that there the Duke of Song leads the right and the Earl of Zheng leads the left.
5. *Xinian* again seems to be confused here. Judging from the rest of the narrative (and from the parallels with *Zuozhuan*, Wen 10.5 and Xuan 14.3), the personage here should be not the Duke (Governor) of Shen named Shuhou but an unrelated person named Shen Zhou 申舟 (aka Shen Wuwei 申無畏). Note that Shen was ruled by appointees of the Chu central government and not by hereditary lords (Xu Shaohua 2011); hence the dukes of Shen were unrelated to the Shen lineage. Scholars continue to debate the origin of the Shen lineage in Chu: some opine that it could have been established by one of the governors of Shen, such as Shuhou; others consider it related to King Wen of Chu; and still others consider it related to the former state of Shen, which was conquered by Chu but not extinguished entirely but relocated and allowed to retain the position of Chu's dependency (Xu Shaohua 2005). Whatever the answer is (see more in Su, Wu, and Lai 2013, 457–62), I believe that the *Xinian* 11 authors confused here a duke of Shen with a member of the Shen lineage.

For a similar confusion in *Xinian* 15 (between the Duke of Shen, Qu Wu, and Shen Baoxu), see the discussion in chapter 2.

6. Reading *zhi* 知 in the meaning of "to supervise" following the Tsinghua editorial team (Li Xueqin 2011a, 161n9).
7. According to *Zuozhuan*'s version (Wen 10.5), Shen Wuwei commanded the chariots be hitched up in the morning; the Duke of Song was thus obviously late. The duke himself could not be punished, but flogging his charioteer was nonetheless deeply humiliating.
8. This Shen Bo Wuwei 申伯無畏 is Shen Zhou (see note 5). Su Jianzhou considers Bo 伯 as standing for "earl," citing many examples of this usage in Chu bronze inscriptions with regard to Chu district governors and their progeny (Su, Wu, and Lai 2013, 460–61). I am not convinced by his examples; in my view, Bo is more likely to refer to Wuwei's position as the elder son in his family.
9. It is noteworthy that *Zuozhuan* explicitly says that King Zhuang, who dispatched Shen Zhou to Qi in 595 BCE, *forbade* him to seek passage through Song. This humiliated the Song leaders and prompted them to kill Shen Zhou (*Zuozhuan*, Xuan 14.3). *Xinian*'s version seems to obscure this provocation.
10. According to *Zuozhuan* (Xuan 14.3), this killing was directly masterminded by the Song strongman Hua Yuan. In *Xinian*, Shen Zhou's killing is presented as pure revenge for his humiliation of the Song ruler twenty-two years earlier. In *Zuozhuan*, the motive of revenge is also present but is sidelined by the problem of Chu's violation of Song sovereignty.
11. This siege lasted from the ninth lunar month of 595 BCE until the fifth month of 594 BCE. It caused awful devastation to Song capital dwellers, who reportedly were reduced to "exchanging children and eating them and splitting up their bones to kindle the fires" (易子以食，析骸以爨) (*Zuozhuan*, Xuan 15.2).
12. Reading *nüzi* 女子 as female musicians (*nüyue* 女樂), following Yoshimoto 2013, 49.
13. The *Zuozhuan* (Xuan 15.2) narrative tells of Hua Yuan becoming a hostage but not about the Song gifts to Chu.

Xinian 12

Xinian 12 is among the shortest sections in the text: it comprises two slips only and deals with the events of a single year (600 BCE). Despite this brevity, Xinian 12 is important insofar as it supplements information missing from *Zuozhuan*. The latter mentions en passant that "during the Li campaign, the Earl of Zheng escaped and returned."[1] For millennia, commentators were perplexed by the reference to the "Li campaign" (厲之役). Now, from *Xinian* 12 we know that this was an assembly of regional lords called upon by King Zhuang of Chu; hence, escape from the assembly became a casus belli justifying Chu's incursion into Zheng.

Xinian disagrees with *Zuozhuan* about the outcome of this incursion, too. According to its narrative, Lord Cheng of Jin 晉成公 (r. 606–600 BCE) assembled Jin's allies to rescue Zheng but died during the assembly. *Zuozhuan* presents a different version of the story. There it is told that in the ninth month Lord Cheng of Jin assembled the regional lords at Hu 扈; however, the goal was evidently not to rescue Zheng but to punish the state of Chen, which had shifted its allegiance to Chu. Lord Cheng of Jin died after the campaign against Chen was completed. Chu's invasion of Zheng is reported in *Zuozhuan* under the tenth month (or later); the Jin army assisted Zheng, and the Chu troops were defeated. *Xinian*, in contrast, implies that Jin and its allies did not come to Zheng's aid. Whether or not *Xinian*'s version of events is meant to obscure the fact of Chu's defeat by the armies of the Jin-Zheng alliance remains to be seen.[2]

★ ★ ★

楚莊王立十又四年，王會諸侯于厲，鄭成公自厲逃歸，莊王遂加鄭亂。晉成【61】公會諸侯以救鄭，楚師未還，晉成公卒于扈。【62】

In the fourteenth year of King Zhuang of Chu (600 BCE), the king assembled the regional lords at Li.[3] Lord Cheng (Xiang) of Zheng fled home from Li.[4] King Zhuang subsequently added to the turmoil in Zheng.[5] Lord Cheng of Jin assembled the regional lords to rescue Zheng. Before the Chu army came back, Lord Cheng of Jin died at Hu.[6]

Notes

1. *Zuozhuan*, Xuan 11.6; see also Xuan 9.7.
2. For the Hu assembly, the death of Lord Cheng of Jin, and the subsequent campaign against Chu to rescue Zheng, see *Zuozhuan*, Xuan 9.4 and 9.8. For the possibility that *Xinian*'s version of events is meant to cover up the eventual defeat of Chu, see Cai 2016, 67–69.
3. As mentioned in the introduction to this section, the Li 厲 assembly was not known heretofore except through indirect references in *Zuozhuan* about the "Li campaign." The location of Li 厲 is disputed: the two options are near Suizhou 隨州, northern Hubei, or Li Township 厲鄉, Luyi County 鹿邑縣, Henan. Ziju (2012) opts for the second option as more fitting to the general pattern of Chu's northward expansion.
4. "Lord Cheng" is a scribal error. Zheng was then ruled by Lord Xiang 鄭襄公 (r. 604–587 BCE).
5. Commentators debate the precise meaning of *jia* 加 (to add) in this sentence (Su, Wu, and Lai 2013, 476–77). Following Wei Dong 2016b, 62, I read "adding turmoil" as standing for a military incursion.
6. As mentioned in the introduction to this section, the narration here differs from that in *Zuozhuan*. Note that the *Spring and Autumn Annals* also imply that the Hu meeting and the death of Lord Cheng of Jin occurred *before* Chu's invasion of Zheng and before Jin's troops came to support Zheng (*Chunqiu*, Xuan 9.7, 9.8, 9.9, 9.12, 9.13).

Xinian 13

Xinian 13 is the only damaged section in the entire text. It tells—with the utmost brevity—about the epic Bi 邲 battle (597 BCE), the apex of Chu's military successes. The crushing defeat of Jin's armies there (following the surrender of the Lord of Zheng a few weeks earlier) is narrated at length in *Zuozhuan* (Xuan 12.2). There are no factual disagreements between *Xinian* and *Zuozhuan*, but the brevity of *Xinian* is perplexing. Clearly, glorification of Chu's victories is not a matter of concern for *Xinian*'s authors (discussed at greater length in chapter 5).

* * *

... [(楚)莊]王圍鄭三月，鄭人爲成。晉中行林父率師救鄭，莊王遂北【63】... [楚]人盟。趙旃不欲成，弗召，㳄（射？席？）于楚軍之門，楚人【64】被駕以追之，遂敗晉師于河[上] ... 【65】

... King [Zhuang of Chu] besieged Zheng for three months, and the Zheng leaders sued for accord.[1] Zhonghang Linfu from Jin led an army to assist Zheng.[2] Then, King Zhuang turned northward.[3] ... [to make a] covenant [with the] leaders [of Chu].[4] Zhao Zhan did not want an accord, and he did not invite them [the Chu leaders to make a covenant].[5] He stayed at the gates of Chu's military camp.[6] The people of Chu put on armor and harnessed the horses, pursuing him. Then they defeated the Jin army at the [banks of the Yellow] River ...

Notes

1. The missing characters at the beginning of the broken slip should perhaps stand for "In the seventh year of King Zhuang of Chu" (suggestion in Ziju 2012). Zheng was besieged because of the repeated breach of its alliance with Chu in previous years. After three months it did not just "sue for an accord" but actually surrendered.
2. The Jin commander is better known as Xun Linfu 荀林父. He assumed command over the Central Column (*zhonghang* 中行) of the Jin army in 632 BCE, and this office became the lineage name of him and his descendants, the Zhonghang lineage.
3. According to *Zuozhuan*, the move of the Chu army northward was planned as a symbolic one: "They intended to water the horses at the [Yellow] River and then turn back" (*Zuozhuan*, Xuan 12.2d). During this move, however, they learned that the Jin army had crossed the river and started preparing for battle. Notice that without the *Zuozhuan* narrative, it is not possible to make much sense of *Xinian*'s sentence.
4. Following *Zuozhuan*'s account, Su Jianzhou (Su, Wu, and Lai 2013, 485) proposes as characters missing from the broken slips the following (boldface indicates the characters present on the broken slip): 楚求成于晉，晉人許之，遂與楚人盟 (Chu asked for accord from Jin, and the Jin leaders approved it. Then they **made a covenant** with the **leaders of** Chu). Note that because of belligerent Jin commanders the covenant was not made.
5. *Zuozhuan* relates that Zhao Zhan begrudged his insufficiently high position in Jin and sought to provoke battle, perhaps in order to win merit. He was appointed a messenger in charge of fixing the timing of the covenant but forsook the mission and provoked battle instead.
6. There is considerable debate about the correct meaning of the character 狀, but most commentators agree that it refers to the same event told in *Zuozhuan*: instead of inviting the Chu people to the covenant, Zhao Zhan spread his mat near the gates of the Chu camp, as an obviously insulting and provocative action. For debates about the precise meaning of 狀, see Su, Wu, and Lai 2013, 487–92.

Xinian 14

Xinian 14 shifts the narrative from Chu back northward, toward Jin and its struggle with the major eastern power, the state of Qi. Since the start of Lord Wen of Jin's hegemony, Qi had been a half-hearted Jin ally, but its territorial disputes with Jin's allies, Lu and Wei, brought about Qi's alienation from Jin. *Xinian* starts its account with Jin's attempt in 592 BCE to press Qi into renewed recognition of its authority. This attempt backfired, though: Jin's envoy Xi Ke, who allegedly suffered from physical deformity, was laughed at by the ladies at the court of Qi (among whom, according to other texts, was the mother of Lord Qing of Qi 齊頃公 [r. 598–582 BCE]). This infuriated Xi Ke, who vowed revenge. Three years later, the Lu plea for help against Qi's aggression gave Xi Ke the chance to avenge his humiliation. He led an army, which inflicted a major defeat on Qi, causing its renewed submission to Jin. This battle is known in *Zuozhuan* as the battle of An 鞌; *Xinian* identifies it as the battle of Miji 靡笄 (see note 11). In the short term, the battle was a triumph for Jin, allowing it to reassert its authority in northern China, shattered after the defeat in the Bi battle (*Xinian* 13). Strategically speaking, though, Jin's success was short-lived, as Qi subsequently drifted away from Jin and entered into a loose alliance with Chu (see *Xinian* 17, 18, 20, 22, 23).

The discussion in *Xinian* 14 closely parallels that in *Zuozhuan* (Xuan 17.1, Cheng 2.3 and 3.9). There are minor differences, summarized in the notes to this section, but none of them appears to be consequential. Overall, as in most sections concerning Jin's history, *Xinian* and *Zuozhuan* seem to be in full agreement about basic facts.

★ ★ ★

晉景公立八年,隨會率師,會諸侯于斷道,公命駒之克先聘于齊,且召高之固曰:【66】「今春其會諸侯,子其與臨之。」齊頃公使其女子自房中觀駒之克,駒之克將受齊侯【67】幣,女子笑于房中,駒之克降堂而誓曰:「所不復詢於齊,毋能涉白水。」乃先【68】歸,須諸侯于斷道。高之固至莆池,乃逃歸。齊三嬖大夫南郭子、蔡子、晏子率師以【69】會于斷道。既會諸侯,駒之克乃執南郭子、蔡子、晏子以歸。

齊頃公圍魯,魯臧孫許適【70】晉求援。駒之克率師救魯,敗齊師于靡笄。齊人爲成,以甗(甑?)、骼(輅)、玉磬(磬)與淳于之【71】田。明歲, 齊頃公朝于晉景公,駒之克走援齊侯之帶,獻之景公,曰:「齊侯之來也,【72】 老夫之力也。」【73】

In the eighth year of Lord Jing of Jin (592 BCE), Sui Hui led an army and assembled the regional lords at Duandao.[1] Lord [Jing] ordered Ke of Ju (Ju Ke; i.e., Xi Ke)[2] first to pay an official visit to Qi and to summon Gu of Gao (i.e., Gao Gu),[3] saying, "This spring we are assembling the regional lords and hope that you will join us [in the assembly]." Lord Qing of Qi allowed his womenfolk to observe Ke of Ju from their chamber.[4] When Ke of Ju delivered gifts to the Marquis of Qi, the ladies laughed in their chamber.[5] Ke of Ju descended from the hall and vowed, "If I do not repay Qi for this humiliation, let me not be able to cross these bright waters!"[6] Thereupon, he returned first [to Jin] and waited for the regional lords at Duandao. Gu of Gao reached the Pu Pond and fled back [to Qi].[7] Three favorite grandees of Qi—Sir Nanguo, Sir Cai, and Sir Yan, led an army to assemble at Duandao.[8] After they met the regional lords, Ke of Ju thereupon detained Sir Nanguo, Sir Cai, and Sir Yan and returned with them [to Jin].[9]

When Lord Qing of Qi besieged Lu, Zangsun Xu of Lu turned to Jin to request help.[10] Ke of Ju led an army to rescue Lu and defeated the Qi army at Miji.[11] The men of Qi sought accord, [presenting Jin] with a *yǎn* vessel, a grand chariot, jade chime stones,[12] and the fields at Chunyu.[13] In the next year, Lord Qing of Qi attended the court of Lord Jing of Jin. Ke of Ju approached the Marquis of Qi, seized his belt, and presented it to Lord Jing, saying, "The arrival of the Marquis of Qi is due to the efforts of myself, this old fellow."[14]

Notes

1. The Duandao meeting was summoned by Jin in 592 as part of its ongoing attempt to restore the anti-Chu coalition of northern states. According to the *Spring and Autumn Annals*, it was attended by the leaders of Jin, Lu, Wei, Cao, and Zhu 邾 (*Chunqiu*, Xuan 17.6). Sui Hui (Shi Hui) was at that time the supreme commander of Jin's central army—that is, the acting prime minister of Jin. He retired later that year and handed the government over to his deputy, Xi Ke. *Zuozhuan* does not report that he commanded an army to attend the meeting but notes that after the meeting "the Jin army returned" (*Zuozhuan*, Xuan 17.1). The *Xinian* and *Zuozhuan* records are complementary here (see also Fang Tao 2017).
2. Xi Ke 郤克 (d. 587 BCE) was at that time the deputy commander of Jin's central army and a rising star in Jin politics. He was enfeoffed at Ju 郇 (transcribed in *Zuozhuan* as 駒); Ju thus serves as his alternative linage name.
3. Gao Gu 高固 was at the time the leading Qi minister. That a minister rather than the ruler was invited to the assembly (which was otherwise attended by the regional lords) reflects the situation in which high ministers became increasingly important politically. *Zuozhuan* does not mention a personal invitation to Gao Gu.
4. These "womenfolk" (*nüzi*, which can also refer to singular "woman") are not identified either here or in *Zuozhuan* (where they are called *furen* 婦人). The *Gongyang* and *Guliang* commentaries both suggest the inference that the term refers to Lord Qing's mother, Xiao Tongshu Zi 蕭同叔子 (or Xiao Tongzhi Zi 蕭同侄子). Her identity is hinted at in *Zuozhuan*, Cheng 2.3 (see also Durrant, Li, and Schaberg 2016, 720n63).
5. Xi Ke was presumably ridiculed because of his physical impairment (see Durrant, Li, and Schaberg 2016, 689n325).
6. "Bright waters" (*bai shui* 白水) stands for the Yellow River (see *Zuozhuan*, Xi 24.1). That this term was applied to the Yellow River (which was not called "Yellow" before the Han dynasty) implies that prior to the massive deforestation of the Loess Plateau the river's water was still bright. See Elvin 2004, 24–25.
7. The Pu Pond is tentatively identifiable as a location near the Yellow River to the north of the Wei 衛 city of Puyang 濮陽. It was halfway between Qi and Jin (where Duandao was located).
8. These three ministers are named in *Zuozhuan* as Nanguo Yan 南郭偃, Cai Zhao 蔡朝, and Yan Ruo 晏弱 (d. 556 BCE, the father of the famous Qi wise counselor Yan Ying 晏嬰). Their position as the lord's favorites is not mentioned in *Zuozhuan*.

9. According to *Zuozhuan* (Xuan 17.1), after the arrest of the Qi ministers, the Jin leaders repented their harshness and allowed one of them (Yan Ruo) to flee home.
10. The narrative here jumps three years to 589 BCE. Meanwhile, the state of Lu, which suffered repeated incursions of Qi troops, sought help intermittently from Jin or Chu. By 590 BCE, the Qi-Chu anti-Jin axis had been formed, allowing Qi to increase its pressure on its two weaker neighbors, Lu and Wei. Desperate, the Lu and Wei envoys turned to Jin, applying directly to Xi Ke, who was known to hate Qi. Xi Ke was glad to seize an opportunity to exact revenge on Qi and led an invading force of eight hundred chariots against Qi. Note that in *Zuozhuan* Lu was not besieged but just attacked from the north.
11. Mount Miji is identified as present-day Mountain of One Thousand Buddhas (Qianfoshan 千佛山) near the city of Ji'nan. A more precise location of the battle would be nearby An 鞌. According to *Zuozhuan*, the Jin army arrived at Miji on the sixteenth day of the sixth lunar month and fought near An on the seventeenth day (*Zuo*, Cheng 2.3; see also *Chunqiu*, Cheng 2.3). During the battle, Xi Ke displayed great personal courage (he led the army on an offensive despite being wounded), and the battle ended with the crushing defeat of Qi forces.
12. There is considerable confusion about the nature of the Qi gifts (Su, Wu, and Lai 2013, 519–26; see also Fan 2018). The first, *yǎn* 甗, usually refers to a ceramic or bronze double boiler. *Zuozhuan* (Cheng 2.3) mentions that this vessel came from the state of Ji 紀, extinguished by Qi. The second character is even more controversial; I tentatively accept its reading as *lu* 輅, a ceremonial grand chariot. It is also possible that both characters should be read as *xianlu* 獻賂 (to bribe). The details of the gifts cannot be ascertained, but surely they were lavish.
13. The Chunyu fields were in the area of Anqiu County 安丘縣, Shandong, to the southeast of the Qi capital, Linzi. It is not clear how, if at all, these lands might have been used by either Jin or its allies, Lu and Wei, located far to the west of the fields. According to *Zuozhuan* (Cheng 2.3h), the Lu people demanded—and received—the fields to the north of the Wen 汶 River, in the area traditionally contested between Qi and Lu.
14. This encounter between Xi Ke and the visiting Lord Qing of Qi is depicted in *Zuozhuan* (Cheng 3.9). There is no mention of an offensive seizing of Lord Qing's belt by Xi Ke, but it seems nonetheless that Xi behaved in a ritually improper manner. This lack of ritual propriety is emphasized in *Discourses of the States*, where Xi Ke is said to perform a ritual due to those who escaped death for the visiting Qi lord, thus hinting that the ruler of Qi was lucky to escape death on the battlefield. Xi is duly criticized there as "being valorous but not understanding ritual" (*Guoyu* 11.12 ["Jin yu 5"]). *Xinian* is much more blatant in depicting Xi Ke's lack of ritual propriety. As for "old fellow," Fang Tao (2017, 146–47) assumes that it suggests having reached the age of fifty at least. Note that Xi Ke died a year after the depicted events.

Xinian 15

Section 15, the second longest in *Xinian*, narrates Chu's deteriorating relations with its major eastern rival, the state of Wu 吳. The narrative is divided into two parts. The first subsection (spanning 613–584 BCE) focuses on a Chu minister, Qu Wuchen 屈巫臣 (or Qu Wu), the Duke of Shen 申公, whom a series of complex intrigues brought from Chu to Jin and then to Wu, where he fostered the Jin-Wu alliance directed against Chu. The second part traces the escalation of the Chu-Wu conflict from 537 to 505 BCE, culminating in the brief occupation of the Chu capital, Ying, by Wu invaders. The major hero of this part is Wu Zixu 伍子胥 (d. 484 BCE), whose father was slandered and executed in Chu and who subsequently defected to Wu, leading the Wu armies to their astounding success: the capture of Chu's capital, Ying, in 506 BCE. The reader may well conclude that the folly of Chu leaders brought the Wu disaster upon them: two brilliant Chu statesmen were pushed out of their country and turned into its bitter enemies, facilitating the rise of Wu. Yet *Xinian* does not seem too interested in the personal stories of Qu Wuchen and Wu Zixu; major elements of these stories that appear in *Zuozhuan* (e.g., the story of how all Qu Wuchen's kin were massacred in Chu after he left for Jin, or an offer made by the king of Chu to Wu Zixu to spare his father if he were to turn himself in) are not mentioned in *Xinian*. Stories of love and hate, of machinations and countermachinations, of loyalty and vengeance are presented only in a nutshell and do not develop fully, in contrast to *Zuozhuan*, or (in the case of Wu Zixu) to later literature.[1]

Xinian's cursory interest in the individual's role in history also characterizes its treatment of the third major protagonist of section 15, Shao Kong (who is known elsewhere as Xia Ji 夏姬 and is henceforth referred to by this name). Xia Ji is depicted in *Zuozhuan* and elsewhere as the ultimate femme fatale, who "killed three husbands, one ruler, and one son, and brought one state and two high ministers to their destruction."[2] Her seductiveness caused major domestic turmoil in the state of Chen; later she became an apple of discord in Chu, fought over by Wuchen and other leading nobles. It was the ongoing rivalry for Xia Ji's favors that caused Wuchen to abandon his home state and eventually become Chu's bitterest enemy. *Xinian* does tell the story, but again with major omissions. For instance, Xia Ji's brazen adultery in the state of Chen that caused her son (or, in the *Xinian* version, her husband) to assassinate her paramour, Lord Ling of Chen 陳靈公 (r. 613–599 BCE), which in turn brought about the subsequent Chu invasion (*Zuozhuan*, Xuan 9.6), is not reported at all.

One notable difference between *Xinian* and the received sources is the former's insistence that Xia Zhengshu was Xia Ji's husband and not her son. *Discourses of the States* is the earliest text to insist explicitly that Xia Zhengshu was Xia Ji's son (*Guoyu* 17.4 ["Chu yu shang"]), and this is probably implied in *Zuozhuan* as well (Cheng 2.6 and Zhao 28.2), although never stated explicitly. Were the latter in fact the case, Xia Ji's ability to remain devilishly seductive a full twenty years after the assassination of Lord Ling of Chen, when she was in her late forties or early fifties, would turn her into the ultimate age-defying femme fatale.[3] In contrast, *Xinian* turns her into Xia Zhengshu's wife rather than his mother, which somewhat normalizes her. The chances are good that on this point *Xinian* is right, and this allows us to correct a millennia-old misunderstanding.[4]

The precise nature of Xia Zhengshu and Xia Ji's relations is one of a few details in *Xinian* 15 that diverge from *Zuozhuan*'s narrative. On a few points (i.e., the precise configuration of the struggle over Xia Ji's favors among the Chu ministers) the differences do exist, but they are minuscule and negligible. Elsewhere, *Xinian* appears to be less accurate than *Zuozhuan*. The three major inaccuracies are the identification of Xia Zhengshu as a ducal son (he was actually a ducal great-grandson, or possibly grandson); the story of Qu Wuchen's mission to attain Qin's support for an assault on Chen; and the story of Wu Zixu's elder brother, Wu Ji, who allegedly joined him to serve Wu. Since the two latter inaccuracies have been analyzed in chapter 2 (p. 59), I omit that discussion here. What is important to note is that, overall, the lengthy narrative, which spans a whole century (613–505 BCE), is remarkably close to that of *Zuozhuan*. It seems highly likely that both texts derived their information from a common third source (as discussed in chapter 2).

★ ★ ★

楚莊王立,吳人服于楚。陳公子徵舒取妻于鄭穆公,是少𡱥。莊王立十又五年,【74】陳公子徵舒殺其君靈公,莊王率師圍陳。王命申公屈巫適秦求師,得師以【75】來。王入陳,殺徵舒,取其室以予申公。連尹襄老與之爭,抈(奪)之少𡱥。連尹散(捷)⁵於河【76】灉,其子黑要也或(又)室少𡱥。莊王即世,共王即位。黑要也死,司馬子反與申【77】公爭少𡱥,申公曰:「是余受妻也。」取以爲妻。司馬不順申公。王命申公聘於齊,申【78】公竊載少𡱥以行,自齊遂逃適晉,自晉適吳,焉始通吳晉之路,教吳人反楚。【79】

以至靈王,靈王伐吳,爲南懷(淮?)之行,執吳王子蹶由,吳人焉又服於楚。靈王即世,【80】景平王即位。少師無極讒連尹奢而殺之,其子伍員與伍之雞逃歸吳。伍雞將【81】吳人以圍州來,爲長壑而洍之,以敗楚師,是雞父之洍。景平王即世,昭王即【82】位。伍員爲吳太宰,是教吳人反楚邦之諸侯,以敗楚師于柏舉,遂入郢。昭王歸【83】隨,與吳人戰于析(沂)。吳王子晨將起禍於吳,吳王闔廬乃歸,昭王焉復邦。【84】

When King Zhuang of Chu ascended the throne (613 BCE), Wu was submissive to Chu. Ducal Son Zhengshu of Chen took as wife a daughter of Lord Mu of Zheng named Shao Kong.[6] In the fifteenth year of King Zhuang (599 BCE), Ducal Son Zhengshu of Chen killed his ruler, Lord Ling.[7] King Zhuang led an army and laid siege to Chen. The king ordered the Duke of Shen, Qu Wu, to go to Qin and ask for troops, and, getting the troops, [Qu Wu] returned.[8] The king entered the Chen [capital], killed Zhengshu, took his wife, and gave her to the Duke of Shen. *Lianyin* Xiang the Elder contended with [the Duke of Shen] and seized Shao Kong. When *lianyin* Xiang the Elder was captured at Heyong,[9] his son, Heiyao, also married Shao Kong.[10] When King Zhuang passed away (591 BCE) and King Gong ascended the throne, Heiyao died, and Marshal Zifan contended with the Duke of Shen for Shao Kong.[11] The Duke of Shen said, "This is the wife I was given [by King Zhuang]," and married her. The marshal considered the Duke of Shen incompliant.[12] When the king ordered the Duke of Shen to go on a visit to Qi, the Duke of Shen secretly carried Shao Kong off and fled.[13] From Qi he thereupon escaped to Jin, from Jin he went to Wu, thereby facilitating routes of communication between Wu and Jin and teaching the men of Wu to oppose Chu.[14]

Coming to the time of King Ling (r. 540–529 BCE), King Ling invaded Wu. He undertook the Nanhuai expedition, seized the Royal Son Jueyou of Wu, and thereafter the people of Wu again submitted to Chu.[15] When King Ling passed away (529 BCE), King Jingping (King Ping) ascended the throne. Junior Preceptor [Fei] Wuji slandered *lianyin* [Wu 伍] She and had him killed.[16] She's sons, Wu Yun and Ji of Wu [Wu Ji], fled and submitted to [the state of] Wu (吳).[17] Wu Ji led the men of Wu to lay siege to Zhoulai, digging a lengthy moat and filling it with water so as to defeat the Chu army; this is the Moat of Ji's Father.[18] When King Jingping passed away (517 BCE), King Zhao ascended the throne. Wu Yun became the grand steward of Wu;[19] he taught Wu leaders how to cause uprisings among the regional lords [allied with] Chu. Thus he defeated the Chu army at Boju and thereupon entered [the Chu capital,] Ying.[20] King Zhao escaped to Sui, and he fought the Wu forces at Yi.[21] Royal Son Chen of Wu was about to rebel and make trouble for Wu:[22] King Helu of Wu[23] then had to return, and King Zhao thus recovered his state.

Notes

1. For the evolution of Wu Zixu's story, see Johnson 1981.
2. *Zuozhuan*, Zhao 28.2.
3. This indestructible seductiveness of Xia Ji was noted long ago. The tradition starting with Liu Xiang's 劉向 *Biographies of Exemplary Women* (*Lienü zhuan* 列女傳) and culminating with a Ming novel attributes to Xia Ji the ability to rejuvenate herself through mastery of the art of sexual intercourse (see Durrant, Li, and Schaberg 2016, 726n84).
4. See more in Wei Cide 2013, 25; Zhang Chongyi 2017.
5. For reading the character 戠 here as *jie* 捷 (to capture), see Chen Jian 2013.
6. From *Zuozhuan* and *Guoyu* it is clear that Zhengshu was not a ducal son (his grandfather was); here *Xinian* is obviously mistaken. Shao Kong is known in other texts as Xia Ji 夏姬; Shao is an abridgment of Shaoxi 少西, the lineage name of her husband (or son?), Zhengshu. (Zhengshu's lineage was founded by a Chen prince named Shaoxi, who had Xia 夏 as an appellative; both the personal name and the appellative could be employed to create a lineage name for his descendants; see *Zuozhuan*, Xuan 11.5, and Yang Bojun's gloss on p. 714); Kong is her

personal name (Li Xueqin 2011a, 171n2). For the possibility that she was Xia Zhengshu's mother and not his wife, see the introduction to this section.

7. *Zuozhuan* (Xuan 9.6 and 10.4) and *Discourses of the States* (*Guoyu* 2.21 ["Zhou yu zhong"]) narrate in great detail how the brazen behavior of Xia Ji—who liberally bestowed her favors on Lord Ling of Chen and two other high nobles—was the cause for Xia Zhengshu's assassination of his lord. By omitting this major detail, *Xinian* minimizes the role of Xia Ji in this event.

8. As discussed in chapter 2 (p. 59), the entire story of Qu Wu's mission to Qin appears to be a mistake (possibly conflated with the mission of Shen Baoxu, who, on behalf of Chu, requested Qin's help against Wu in 506 BCE).

9. *Lianyin* 連尹 is an official title in the Chu hierarchy—Durrant, Li, and Schaberg 2016, 658n239, translate it as "court deputy." Being "captured at Heyong" refers to capturing Xiang's body after he died in action during the Bi 邲 battle between Chu and Jin in 597 BCE (*Zuozhuan*, Xuan 12.2); for Heyong's proximity to Bi, see Wu Wenwen's gloss in Su, Wu, and Lai 2013, 555–56.

10. In *Zuozhuan* (Cheng 2.6) Heiyao is said to have "consorted" (*zheng* 烝) rather than "married" Xia Ji, implying illicit relations.

11. In *Zuozhuan* (Cheng 2.6 and 7.5), the sequence of events differs: Heiyao was murdered by Marshal Zifan and his accomplices at the same time that Qu Wu's family was massacred; these events occurred after Qu Wu had smuggled Xia Ji (or Shao Kong) out of Chu (between 589 and 584 BCE).

12. As in section 5, I read *shun* 順 in this context as a putative verb: "to consider somebody incompliant"; that is, to bear a grudge against him.

13. According to *Zuozhuan* (Cheng 2.6), this happened in 589 BCE.

14. Note that *Xinian* does not mention Qu Wu's resentment against the Chu leaders, who had massacred his kinsmen left behind in Chu. In *Zuozhuan* (Cheng 7.5) this serves as the major reason for Qu Wu's becoming the matchmaker between Wu and Jin.

15. For the invasion of Wu in 537 BCE and the capture of Royal Son Jueyou, see *Zuozhuan*, Zhao 5.8. From *Zuozhuan* it is clear that the Nanhuai campaign (fought to the south of the Huai River) was not successful and that Wu did not submit to Chu in the campaign's aftermath (for a different view, see Liu Guang 2018).

16. *Zuozhuan* presents an extremely negative view of Fei Wuji as a malicious conspirator who brought down many innocent people. Wu She (Wu Zixu's father) was Fei Wuji's superior: a senior preceptor of Crown Prince Jian 建 (another victim of Fei Wuji's machinations). It is not clear why *Xinian* refers to Wu She as *lianyin*.

17. Wu Yun is the famous Wu Zixu 伍子胥 (see the introduction to this section). There is no evidence for Wu She's other son, Ji of Wu, in any other historical source. *Zuozhuan* describes Wu Yun's other brother, Wu Shang, who submitted to King Ping and was executed together with Wu She.

18. The *Spring and Autumn Annals* records Wu's defeat of Chu and its allies in 519 BCE at the location called Ji's Father (or Rooster's Father? 雞父) (*Chunqiu*, Zhao 23.7). As argued in chapter 2 (p. 59), the figure of Wu Ji was in all likelihood invented to explain the etymology of this place-name. Wu Ji (under the name Uncle Ji 雞父) is mentioned in another manuscript from the Tsinghua University collection, *Yue gong qi shi* 越公其事, where he is identified as the mastermind of Wu's victory over Chu in 506 BCE. See Li Xueqin 2017: 119 and Li Shoukui 2017: 77–78.
19. According to *Zuozhuan*, Wu Zixu acted as Wu's messenger (*xingren* 行人), whereas the position of the grand steward (*taizai* 太宰) was occupied by Bo Pi 伯嚭 (whose grandfather, just like Wu Zixu's father, had been executed in Chu). Liu Guang (2017b) argues that both positions were ad hoc appointments, and it is possible that Wu Zixu did act temporarily as a Wu grand steward.
20. For these dramatic events of 506 BCE, when Chu was on the verge of extinction, see *Zuozhuan*, Ding 4.3; see also *Xinian* 19. There is much uncertainty about the precise location of Boju 柏舉, but it is likely to have been north of Tianmen Municipality 天門市, Hubei (see map 2).
21. Sui was a Chu satellite; it is widely identified with the statelet of Zeng, located in present-day Suizhou 隨州, Hubei (details can be found in chapter 3, pp. 85–88). Regarding the battle's location, I accept Li Xueqin's reading of Xi 析 as Yi 沂. The latter is mentioned in *Zuozhuan* (Ding 5.5) as the location of the battle between the Chu-Qin allied forces and their Wu opponents. Yang Bojun (*Zuozhuan*, p. 1551) identifies Yi as a location on the northern bank of the Huai River, near modern Zhengyang 正陽 County (map 2). Note that *Xinian*, unlike *Zuozhuan*, does not mention the presence of the Qin forces and attributes the battle to King Zhao himself. Qin's assistance to Chu against the Wu invaders is mentioned, however, in *Xinian* 19.
22. Royal Son Chen is normally called in *Zuozhuan* by the title he adopted during his brief reign in 505 BCE, King Fugai 夫槩. He was a younger brother of King Helu of Wu 吳王闔盧 (r. 514–496 BCE) and tried to exploit the opportunity of King Helu's stay in the occupied areas of Chu to establish himself as a king. *Zuozhuan* (Ding 5.5) emphasizes that the major reason for Wu's withdrawal was not Fugai's short-lived rebellion but repeated defeats of Wu forces at the hands of Chu-Qin alliance troops.
23. King Helu of Wu is the one who led the Wu forces occupying the Chu capital in 506 BCE. Note that his name was not mentioned as the invasion's leader: in *Xinian* this achievement is attributed squarely to Wu Zixu.

Xinian 16

Xinian 16 shifts the narrative back to the Jin-Chu conflict. It deals with the first significant attempt to put an end to this conflict through a peace agreement between the belligerents. A peace initiative that started with the release of a captive Chu officer brought about the first détente treaty in 579 BCE. Unfortunately, the agreement was not viable. Just a few years thereafter, in 575 BCE, both countries were engaged in war, which ended with a crushing defeat of Chu.

The factual skeleton of the events presented in *Xinian* 16 is very close to *Zuozhuan*, but a few discrepancies between the two texts convey a radically different message. The issue has been discussed in great detail in chapter 5 (pp. 138–41), so I confine myself here to a few brief observations. First, *Xinian* 16 presents a different content of the Jin-Chu covenant from that reported in *Zuozhuan*: in the latter it was only a bilateral agreement between Chu and Jin regarding the cessation of mutual hostilities, whereas the former speaks of a multilateral agreement aimed at "putting to rest the armor and weapons of All Under Heaven." In my view, the *Xinian* authors are wrong on this point: in all likelihood they confuse the 579 BCE covenant with the multilateral peace conferences of 546 and 541 BCE (for which see *Xinian* 18). Second, *Xinian* 16 presents Jin's assault on Qin in 578 BCE as the violation of a peace accord, whereas in *Zuozhuan* this war was not related to Jin-Chu relations at all. Third, by omitting the dates of subsequent campaigns, the *Xinian* authors suggest that Chu's assault on Zheng and the resultant war with Jin were directly related to Jin's aggression against Qin, which, according to *Zuozhuan*, was patently *not* the case. This chronological mess creates a lot of factual inaccuracies as well, implying, for example, that in 575 BCE Zheng was Jin's ally (actually, it was the target of Jin's attack! See note 8). Finally, whereas the *Xinian* authors admit Chu's defeat in the battle of Yan (Yanling 鄢陵) in 575 BCE, they try nonetheless to allow Chu the moral high ground, implying that the assassination of Lord Li of Jin shortly after the fateful battle may have been a kind of divine retribution for his perfidy.

Xinian 16 is the only section of *Xinian* that has a clearly identifiable pro-Chu bias (note, for instance, that in section 18 the breakdown of the multilateral peace agreement is squarely blamed on King Ling of Chu). Interestingly, *Zuozhuan*'s account of the events following the 579 BCE peace treaty displays an equally strong pro-Jin and anti-Chu bias (as discussed in chapter 5). Perhaps through these biases we can catch a glimpse of elite opinion in both states. Who was to blame for violating the peace accord mattered a great deal at the time. Historical texts composed in Jin and Chu reflect this sensitivity. Attaining the moral high ground signified in the interstate politics of the sixth century BCE no less than it does nowadays.

★ ★ ★

楚共王立七年，令尹子重伐鄭，爲沷（氾？）之師。晉景公會諸侯以救鄭，鄭人敓（捷）鄖公儀，獻【85】諸景公，景公以歸。一年，景公欲與楚人爲好，乃脫鄖公，使歸求成，共王使鄖公聘於【86】晉，且許成。景公使糴之茷聘於楚，且修成，未還，景公卒，厲公即位。共王使王【87】子辰聘於晉，又修成，王又使宋右師華孫元行晉楚之成。明歲，楚王子罷會晉文【88】子燮及諸侯之大夫，盟於宋，曰：「弭天下之甲兵。」明歲，厲公先起兵，率師會諸侯以伐【89】秦，至于涇。共王亦率師圍鄭，厲公救鄭，敗楚師於鄢。厲公亦見禍以死，亡（無）後。【90】

In the seventh year of King Gong of Chu (584 BCE), Prime Minister Zichong invaded Zheng, initiating the Fan campaign.[1] Lord Jing of Jin assembled the regional lords to rescue Zheng. The people of Zheng captured [a Chu officer] Yi, the Duke of Yun, and presented him to Lord Jing.[2] Lord Jing returned [to Jin] taking [Yi] with him. [After?] one year (582 BCE?),[3] Lord Jing wanted to establish amicable relations with Chu; hence, he released the Duke of Yun and let him go back and seek peace. King Gong of Chu dispatched the Duke of Yun for an official visit to Jin and approved the peace. Lord Jing dispatched Pei of Di (Di Pei) on an official visit to Chu, renewing peace. Before [Di Pei] returned, [Lord Jing] died, and Lord Li was established (580 BCE).[4]

King Gong dispatched Royal Son Chen on an official visit to Jin and also renewed peace. The king also sent the Song commander of the right, Huasun Yuan (Hua Yuan), to arrange peaceful relations between Jin and Chu.[5] In the next year (579 BCE), Royal Son Pi of Chu met Wenzi Xie (i.e., Shi Xie 士燮, aka Shi Wenzi 士文子) of Jin and grandees of the regional lords and made a covenant at Song, saying, "Put to rest the armor and weapons of All Under Heaven."[6] The next year (578 BCE), Lord Li [of Jin] was the first to raise an army and lead the regional lords to invade Qin, reaching the Jing River.[7] King Gong also led an army, laying siege to Zheng. Lord Li came to rescue Zheng and defeated the Chu army at Yan.[8] Lord Li also encountered misfortune and died leaving no posterity.[9]

Notes

1. This campaign took place in 584 BCE; the river is identified as Fan 氾, following *Zuozhuan* (Cheng 7.4). For the problems concerning this identification and the confusion between Fan 氾 and Si 汜, see Jin 2016.
2. Yi (or, more precisely, Zhong Yi 鍾儀) was the duke of the Chu county of Yun. Recall that Chu governors frequently bore ducal titles.
3. It is not clear what the reference of "one year" (一年) is; Yoshimoto 2013, 63, notes that this term does not normally occur in historical texts. The dating inserted by me here follows *Zuozhuan*. Su, Wu, and Lai 2013, 646, proposes reading 一 as a mistake for 二 and interprets the phrase as "after two years."
4. The narrative closely parallels that in *Zuozhuan* (Cheng 9.9, 9.14, and 10.1), with only a minor discrepancy: the Chu return visit in 582 BCE was by Royal Son Chen 公子辰 (who is mentioned in *Xinian* 16) and not by the Duke of Yun.
5. The second visit of Royal Son Chen is not recorded in *Zuozhuan* (and it is highly probable that *Xinian* conflated it with the visit in 582 BCE erroneously attributed to the Duke of Yun). *Zuozhuan* (Cheng 11.8) does record Hua Yuan's mission to both Chu and Jin in 581 BCE.
6. The covenant between Chu and Jin was made in the fifth month, but it dealt exclusively with bilateral relations and not with the universal cessation of hostilities (for the latter, see *Xinian* 18). For the text of the covenant, see *Zuozhuan*, Cheng 12.2.

7. In late 580 BCE, Jin and Qin had almost reached accord, but the lack of mutual trust undermined the attempt. In 578, emboldened by the peace with Chu, Jin indeed launched a major assault on Qin (*Zuozhuan*, Cheng 11.9–13.3). Crossing the Jing River meant advancing deep into Qin's heartland (in *Zuozhuan*, Cheng 13.3c, the precise location of the battle is given: Masui 麻隧, in present-day Jingyang County 涇陽縣). Note that *Zuozhuan* specifically blames Qin for instigating war with Jin by trying to ally itself with Chu and with Di 狄 polities (Cheng 13.3c).
8. The narrative here deviates from the chronological precision of the previous years and contains several inaccuracies. Actually, Chu's invasion of Zheng occurred in 576 BCE, a full two years after Jin's attack on Qin. It did not include laying siege to Zheng. Moreover, in 575 BCE Zheng switched its allegiance from Jin to Chu. The ensuing Jin expedition and the battle of Yan (or Yanling) were to punish Zheng rather than to rescue it. See *Zuozhuan*, Cheng 15.3, 16.1, 16.5; see also *Chunqiu*, Cheng 16.6, for Zheng being Chu's ally rather than victim in 575 BCE.
9. Lord Li of Jin attempted in 574 BCE to eliminate powerful ministerial lineages; he succeeded in wiping out a major one—the Xi 郤 lineage—but was overpowered by the Luan 欒 lineage; he was murdered and humiliatingly buried as a lowly noble and succeeded by a scion of another branch of the Jin ruling lineage. See *Zuozhuan*, Cheng 17.10 and 18.1.

Xinian 17

Xinian 17 shifts attention back to the Jin-Qi conflict. Lord Ping of Jin 晉平公 (r. 557–532 BCE), the last of the Jin rulers to hold a semblance of real power in his hands, renewed the campaign against Chu (557 BCE), with limited success, but then shifted his attention to the recalcitrant state of Qi. The ensuing Pingyin campaign (555 BCE) was greatly successful, but the triumph was short-lived. Lord Zhuang of Qi 齊莊公 (r. 553–548 BCE) utilized domestic turmoil in Jin (the rebellion by one of the most powerful ministers, Luan Ying 欒盈) and invaded Jin (552 BCE). Although Jin succeeded in regaining initiative, and Qi sank in its own domestic turmoil following the assassination of Lord Zhuang in 548 BCE, this continuous tit-for-tat struggle further weakened Jin's ability to subjugate Chu. It may have served as the background for Jin's willingness to embrace peaceful relations with Chu, as described in the next section.

The narrative in Xinian 17 closely parallels that of Zuozhuan. Two minor discrepancies (concerning the relocation of Xǔ in 557 BCE and the details of the Pingyin campaign) in all likelihood derive from scribal carelessness (see notes 2 and 6).

★ ★ ★

晉莊平公即位元年，公會諸侯於溴梁，遂以遷許於葉而不果。師造於方城，齊高厚【91】自師逃歸。平公率師會諸侯，爲平陰之師以圍齊，焚其四郭，驅車至于東海。

平公【92】立五年，晉亂，欒盈出奔齊，齊莊公光率師以逐欒盈。欒盈襲巷（絳）而不果，奔內（入）於曲沃。齊【93】莊公涉河襲朝歌，以復平陰之師。晉人既殺欒盈于曲沃，平公率師會諸侯，伐齊，【94】以復朝歌之師。齊崔杼殺其君莊公，以爲成於晉。【95】

In the first year of Lord Zhuangping of Jin (i.e., Lord Ping) (557 BCE), the lord assembled the regional lords at the Ju Dam.[1] Then he utilized [the assembly] to transfer the state of Xǔ to She, but without success.[2] The army was dispatched to Fangcheng.[3] Gao Hou of Qi fled from the army back [to Qi].[4] Lord Ping led the troops and assembled the regional lords. He conducted the Pingyin campaign, laying siege to Qi.[5] They burned the four suburbs of Qi['s capital] and rushed the chariots all the way to the Eastern Sea.[6]

In the fifth year of Lord Ping (552 BCE), there was turmoil in Jin.[7] Luan Ying fled to Qi.[8] Lord Zhuang of Qi, named Guang, led an army to follow Luan Ying.[9] Luan Ying made a surprise attack on [Jin's capital] Jiang, but was not successful. He fled and entered Quwo.[10] Lord Zhuang of Qi crossed the [Yellow] River and made a surprise attack on Zhaoge to retaliate for the Pingyin campaign.[11] After the Jin leaders killed Luan Ying at Quwo, Lord Ping led an army and assembled the regional lords to invade Qi, in retaliation for the Quwo campaign. Cui Zhu of Qi killed his ruler, Lord Zhuang, and made an accord with Jin.[12]

Notes

1. This meeting of 557 BCE is recorded in the *Spring and Autumn Annals* (*Chunqiu*, Xiang 16.2) and *Zuozhuan* (Xiang 16.1). It was attended by the rulers of Jin, Lu, Song, Wei, Zheng, Cao, Ju 莒, Zhu, Xue 薛, Qǐ 杞, and Lesser Zhu 小邾. The state of Qi was represented not by the ruler but by its high officer, Gao Hou.
2. *Xinian* is obviously confused here. *Zuozhuan* (Cheng 15.7) states that in 576 BCE, the ruler of Xǔ 許 asked for Chu's protection against the intimidating power of Xǔ's neighbor, Zheng. The Chu leaders moved Xǔ to the area of She (modern She County 葉縣; map 2). In 557 BCE, the ruler of Xǔ asked for Jin's protection and wanted the state to be transferred back north. However, because of opposition from Xǔ nobles, the program was thwarted (*Zuozhuan*, Xiang 16.2). Surely the transfer was planned *from* and not *to* She.

3. *Zuozhuan* mentions that following the unsuccessful attempt to transfer Xǔ back to Jin's protection, the Jin armies defeated the Chu army slightly to the north of She and then "invaded the area beyond Fangcheng" (Xiang 16.3). For Fangcheng, see *Xinian* 5, note 7.
4. *Zuozhuan* places this flight of Gao Hou from the joint campaign back to Qi at an earlier stage: according to its report, Gao had already ignited the ire of the Jin leaders during the meeting at the Ju Dam and fled in order to escape arrest (Xiang 16.1).
5. This campaign was fought in 555 BCE. Jin and its allies broke up Qi's defense near Pingyin (a narrow pathway into Qi from the south) and advanced northward to the Qi capital, plundering its suburbs and performing acts of bravado near its gates. See *Zuozhuan*, Xiang 18.3.
6. The editors initially suggested that the allies advanced toward "Eastern *mu*" 東畝, but the reading of the second character was rejected in favor of *hai* 海, as proposed by Chen Wei (2012a). The problem is that, geographically speaking, this interpretation is inaccurate. *Zuozhuan* (Xiang 18.3d) mentions the allies' advancement east to the Wei 濰 River, which flows into the Bohai Gulf (the Northern Sea). The advancement toward the shores of the Eastern Sea is highly unlikely. I am unable to resolve the puzzle except to assume it is a scribal error. Note a similar puzzling reference to "Northern Sea" instead of "Eastern Sea" in *Xinian* 20, slip 112, and the introduction to section 20.
7. In 552 BCE, the conflicts among ministerial lineages in Jin resulted in an open rebellion by the second most powerful minister, Luan Ying. For the outburst of the rebellion, see *Zuozhuan*, Xiang 21.5.
8. Luan Ying initially fled to Chu but in 551 BCE moved to Qi, finding support there from Lord Zhuang (*Zuozhuan*, Xiang 22.3).
9. For reading *zhu* 逐 as "to follow," see the glosses in Su, Wu, and Lai 2013, 675–78. For Lord Zhuang's support of Luan Ying's attempt to regain power in Jin, see *Zuozhuan*, Xiang 23.3a.
10. This Jiang was Jin's new capital, Xintian 新田, near the city of Houma 侯馬 (it bore the name of the previous capital, Jiang, located slightly to the east; map 3). Quwo was Jin's secondary capital and Luan Ying's stronghold. For Luan Ying's assault on Jiang, see *Zuozhuan*, Xiang 23.3.
11. In 550 BCE, following Luan Ying's attempt to seize power in Jin and the ensuing turmoil there, Lord Zhuang of Qi first attacked Jin's ally, Wei, and then followed up with an attack on Zhaoge, Jin's stronghold on the northern bank of the Yellow River, near modern Qi County 淇縣, Henan (*Zuozhuan*, Xiang 23.4).
12. Jin planned a major retaliation campaign against Qi in 549 BCE, but it was canceled because of floods that prevented crossing the Yellow River

(*Zuozhuan*, Xiang 24.7). In 548 BCE, just as the renewed expedition was preparing again to cross the river, Cui Zhu, Qi's strongman, assassinated Lord Zhuang and blamed him for the troubles between Qi and Jin. Cui Zhu had lavishly bribed the Jin military leaders, and they canceled the retaliation campaign (*Zuozhuan*, Xiang 25.2–3).

Xinian 18

The narrative in *Xinian* 18 refocuses on the dynamics of Jin-Chu relations, which were at the focus of *Xinian* 16. It starts with the famous peace conferences of 546 and 541 BCE, in which the prime ministers of Jin and Chu agreed to "put to rest the armor and weapons of All Under Heaven." *Xinian* 16 had squarely blamed Jin for the cessation of the earlier peace agreement of 579 BCE. *Xinian* 18, by contrast, blames King Ling of Chu 楚靈王 (r. 540–529 BCE) as the one who was "the first to raise an army." King Ling focused his pressure on smaller polities on the one hand and on his archenemy, the state of Wu (see *Xinian* 15), on the other. Although he did not assault Jin directly, the text of *Xinian* unequivocally censures him for undermining interstate détente. That the hostilities between the two powers did not resume was owing only to a series of domestic problems in each of them, such as the "misfortune" (i.e., the overthrow) of King Ling of Chu in 529 BCE and the premature deaths of two lords of Jin, Zhao 晉昭公 (r. 531–526 BCE) and Qing 晉頃公 (r. 525–512 BCE).

Historiographically speaking, the most interesting part of *Xinian* 18 consists of the last four slips, which deal with the reign of King Zhao of Chu 楚昭王 (r. 515–489 BCE). Incidentally, these years coincide with the period during which the *Zuozhuan* narrative becomes much sketchier than before.[1] *Xinian* duly complements manifold lacunae in *Zuozhuan*. In particular, it discloses the degree of Jin military activity in the last years of the sixth century BCE. Chu was then under severe pressure from Wu (which eventually occupied, albeit briefly, the Chu capital, Ying, in 506 BCE), and Jin seemed to have seized this opportunity in a much more robust way than is reported in *Zuozhuan*. First, it succeeded in intervening in domestic turmoil in a Chu long-term satellite, the statelet of Xŭ 許, providing shelter to its fugitive ruler, Tuo, and then "spreading fortresses along the northern bank of the Ru River and placing the Lord of Xŭ in Rongcheng." If this information is correct (and I have no reason to doubt it), it means that Jin briefly advanced its sphere of influence very close to the Chu defense line of Fangcheng (on which see *Xinian* 5, note 7). Soon enough, Jin allied with Wu to attack Chu from the north, assaulting Fangcheng. This information—which is missing from *Zuozhuan*—provides crucial background for the Shaoling 召陵 assembly of 506 BCE: the last major interstate meeting convened by Jin.

The depiction of the Shaoling assembly in the *Spring and Autumn Annals* and *Zuozhuan* is confusing. The *Annals* plainly state that the allies "invaded Chu." *Zuozhuan*, however, explains that the Jin leaders refused to invade Chu on behalf of smaller polities, and those turned to Wu instead.[2] Perplexingly, Wu, the archenemy of Chu, did not take part in the Shaoling assembly. Now, in light of *Xinian* 18, we can surmise that a joint Jin-Wu assault against Chu did take place on the eve of the Shaoling assembly, but it was not particularly successful. After that, the allies parted ways: Wu continued its pressure on Chu, which resulted after a few months in its astounding occupation of Ying. Jin, in contrast, turned its attention northward, toward the state of Zhongshan 中山. This attack—about which, again, we knew very little from the sketchy records in the *Spring and Autumn Annals* and *Zuozhuan*—ended in disaster: "The Jin troops suffered from pestilence and starvation and had to consume humans."

The last lines of *Xinian* 18 confirm, even if indirectly, the information that can be deduced from *Zuozhuan*. Following its unsuccessful campaigns against Zhongshan (and, if *Zuozhuan* is to be trusted, its leaders' arrogant behavior during the Shaoling assembly),[3] Jin started rapidly losing support among the northern polities, which began organizing themselves into defensive anti-Jin alliances, such as the one between Qi and Zheng beginning in 503 BCE. Domestic troubles in Jin accelerated its problems. The text concludes with the point that "until now the people of Qi ... had not submitted to Jin. Thus, the dukes of Jin were weakened." Although the last sections of *Xinian* will show how Jin resurrected its power, the persistent rivalry with Qi remained a major impediment in its plans to renew southward expansion.

★ ★ ★

晉莊平公立十又二年，楚康王立十又四年，令尹子木會趙文子武及諸侯之大夫，盟【96】于宋，曰：「弭天下之甲兵。」康王即世，孺子王即位。靈王爲令尹，令尹會趙文子及諸侯之大夫，盟于【97】虢。孺子王即世，靈王即位。靈王先起兵，會諸侯于申，執徐公，遂以伐徐，克賴、朱邡(=朱方)，伐吳，【98】爲南懷之行，縣陳、蔡，殺蔡靈侯。靈王見禍，景平王即位。晉莊平公即世，昭公、頃公皆【99】早世，簡公即位。景平王即世，昭王即位。許人亂，許公(佗)出奔晉，晉人羅城汝陽，居【100】許公於容城。晉與吳合爲一，以伐楚，閔(門?)方城。 遂盟諸侯於召陵，伐中山。晉師大疫【101】且飢，食人。楚昭王侵伊洛以復方城之師。晉人且有范氏與中行氏之禍，七歲不解甲。【102】諸侯同盟于鹹泉以反晉，至今齊人以不服于晉，晉公以弱。【103】

In the twelfth year of Lord Zhuangping (Lord Ping) of Jin and the fourteenth year of King Kang of Chu (546 BCE), [Chu's] prime minister, Zimu, met Zhao Wenzi of Jin, named Wu, and the grandees of the regional lords and made a covenant in Song, which said, "Put to rest the armor and weapons of All Under Heaven."[4] When King Kang passed away (545 BCE), the Child King ascended the throne.[5] [Future] King Ling was prime minister. The prime minister met Zhao Wenzi and the grandees of the regional lords and made a covenant in Guo.[6] When the Child King passed away (541 BCE), King Ling ascended the throne.[7] King Ling was the first to raise an army and gather the regional lords in Shen. He detained the Duke of Xú and then with [the regional lords' troops] invaded Xú, overcame Lai and Zhufang, invaded Wu, and conducted the Nanhuai campaign.[8] He turned Chen and Cai into counties and killed Marquis Ling of Cai.[9]

When King Ling encountered disaster (529 BCE), King Jingping (King Ping) was established.[10] When Lord Zhuangping of Jin passed away (532 BCE), Lords Zhao and Qing all passed away early, and [then] Lord Jian (Lord Ding)[11] was established (511 BCE). When King Jingping passed away (516 BCE), King Zhao was established. There was turmoil in Xǔ. Tuo, the Lord of Xǔ, fled to Jin.[12] The Jin leaders spread fortresses along the northern bank of the Ru River and placed the Lord of Xǔ in Rongcheng.[13]

Jin allied with Wu to attack Chu, assaulting Fangcheng.[14] Thereafter it made a covenant at Shaoling[15] and assaulted Zhongshan. The Jin troops suffered from pestilence and starvation and had to consume humans.[16]

King Zhao of Chu invaded the areas of the Yi and Luo Rivers to retaliate for the Fangcheng campaign.[17] Moreover, Jin had the trouble of the Fan and Zhonghang lineages, and for seven years could not take off their armor.[18] The regional lords made a treaty at Xian Spring to oppose Jin.[19] Until now the people of Qi for this reason had not submitted to Jin.[20] Thus, the dukes of Jin were weakened.

Notes

1. A sudden decrease in the density of narration in *Zuozhuan* after the years of Lord Zhao of Lu (541–510 BCE) is one of the interesting topics that await future discussion.
2. *Chunqiu*, Ding 4.2, and *Zuozhuan*, Ding 4.2.
3. *Zuozhuan*, Ding 4.2.
4. This is the first of the two famous disarmament conferences during which the participants tried to merge two competing coalitions into one universal mega-alliance. See details in *Zuozhuan* (Xiang 27.4) and discussion in Kōno 1978. Zimu is Qu Jian 屈建 (d. 545 BCE).
5. The Child King is known by the posthumous designation Jia'ao 郟敖 (r. 544–541 BCE).
6. This covenant was made in 541 BCE. See *Zuozhuan*, Zhao 1.1.
7. King Ling actually murdered his nephew, Jia'ao (*Zuozhuan*, Zhao 1.13a). As usual, *Xinian* conceals this.
8. This account conflates several events. The Duke of Xú 徐 was arrested both in 538 BCE, when he attended the Shen 申 assembly (*Zuozhuan*, Zhao 4.2), and two years later, in 536 BCE, when he arrived in Chu for an official visit. In the second case, the Duke of Xú escaped, and Chu retaliated with a punitive expedition, which was thwarted thanks to Wu's intervention (*Zuozhuan*, Zhao 6.9). The attack on Wu did take place in 538 BCE following the Shen assembly, during which the allies occupied the town of Zhufang (near modern Zhenjiang 鎮江, Jiangsu, very close to Wu's heartland; see map 2), which Wu granted as an allotment to the fugitive Qi minister Qing Feng 慶封. Lai was exterminated during the same campaign, albeit there are ongoing debates about its location and whether it was extinguished before or after the assault on Wu (*Zuozhuan*, Zhao 4.4). For the Nanhuai campaign, see *Xinian* 15, note 15.
9. Chu annexed Chen in 534 BCE and Cai in 531 BCE, after it had killed Cai's ruler, Lord Ling 蔡靈公 (r. 542–531 BCE) (*Zuozhuan*, Zhao 8.6, 11.2, and 11.10).

10. In 529 BCE, King Ling was overthrown and replaced by his brother, Qiji (King Ping). It is the only instance in *Xinian* in which domestic turmoil in Chu is hinted at.
11. The Jin ruler referred to here as Lord Jian 簡公 is better known as Lord Ding 晉定公 (r. 511–475 BCE).
12. Nothing is known about these events, but their historicity is beyond doubt. *Xinian* is the only text to refer to Xǔ's leader by his personal name Tuo 鴕 (= 佗). In the *Spring and Autumn Annals* (*Chunqiu*, Ding 6.1), this ruler is identified as Si 斯. However, a Xǔ Zi Tuo-*zhǎn* 許子佗盞 vessel unearthed in 2003 at Nanyang 南陽, Henan, in the vicinity of Tuo's new capital, Rongcheng 榮成, identifies this ruler by the same name (鴕 = 佗) as recorded in the *Xinian*. See more in Huang Jinqian 2012.
13. This sentence is challenging for the commentators. I tentatively accept Ziju's (2012) reading of 羅 as standing for *lie* 列 (to arrange, to spread along). Following Ziju's logic, in around 510–506 BCE, the Jin leaders spread fortresses along the northern bank of the Ru River, but then they placed Xǔ in a location much closer to the Chu defense line of Fangcheng, as a possible springboard for future expansion. Note that no other text relates Xǔ's transfer to Rongcheng to Jin's activities. Rongcheng was located slightly to the northwest of She 葉, which twice served as Xǔ's capital (map 2). In 524 BCE, the Chu leaders, fearful of a potential clash between Xǔ and Zheng, relocated Xǔ westward, to the town of Xi 析 (map 2). That it was Jin that could now determine Xǔ's location means that Chu was no longer in control of its northern periphery. For more about Xǔ's relocations, see Wei Dong 2016a.
14. 閦 is usually glossed as the verb 門, "to assault." Normally it implies an assault on the gate of a fortress. It is possible that the use of this verb hints at the existence of a protective wall in Fangcheng, but more likely the attack was directed against one of the fortifications of the Fangcheng line (see *Xinian* 5, note 7). There is no other evidence of the joint Wu-Jin assault on Fangcheng. The major Wu assault on Chu in the winter of 506 BCE (narrated in sections 15 and 19 of *Xinian* and in *Zuozhuan*, Ding 4.3) was not related to the Jin attempt to build an anti-Chu coalition earlier in that same year. From the *Xinian* chronology we can assume that a nonsequential common Wu-Jin operation against Chu could have taken place in the winter of 507 BCE or early spring of 506 BCE. See also *Xinian* 20.
15. The Shaoling assembly of the third lunar month of 506 BCE was the last serious attempt by Jin leaders to restore their position as hegemons. The assembly, attended by the representative of the Zhou royal house and no fewer than eighteen other leaders (but *not* those from Wu), did not result in a decisive action against Chu (although an invasion of Chu is mentioned in the *Spring and Autumn Annals*, Ding 4.2). Following the *Annals* (Ding 4.4), the covenant

was made not during the Shaoling assembly itself but two months later, in nearby Gaoyou 皋鼬. Shaoling is located between the upper reaches of the Ying and Ru rivers, close to the outer perimeter of Chu defenses (see map 3).

16. *Zuozhuan* and the *Spring and Autumn Annals* record three campaigns of Jin against the Xianyu 鮮虞 state of Zhongshan: in the autumn of 507 BCE (*Zuozhuan*, Ding 3.2), autumn of 506 BCE (*Chunqiu*, Ding 4.12), and the winter of 505 BCE (*Chunqiu*, Ding 5.6; *Zuozhuan*, Ding 5.8). None of the records is particularly informative, but note a statement by a Jin leader in early 506 BCE: "The rainwater floods have just receded, pestilence arises throughout, and Zhongshan has not submitted" (*Zuozhuan*, Ding 4.1). This statement may be related to the depiction of the Jin army's difficulties as narrated in *Xinian*, although, chronologically speaking, the two texts contradict each other. In *Zuozhuan*, the pessimistic estimate of the campaign against Zhongshan was made during the Shaoling assembly, whereas *Xinian* places this campaign after the assembly. It is likely that the campaign against Zhongshan included several dispatches of troops. See more in Cheng Wei 2012a.

17. The details of this retaliation campaign are not clear, but there is no doubt that having restored his power, King Zhao resumed expansion northward (for a rare instance of Chu's northward campaign against the Man 蠻 polities, which was actually assisted—rather than opposed—by Jin, see *Zuozhuan* Ai 4.2). For some interesting conjectures, see also Ziju's (2012) analysis. The Yi River joins the Luo River to the east of Luoyang, before the latter reaches the Yellow River (map 2). Note a similar retaliation attack by Chu on the Jin strongholds in the Yi-Luo confluence area as reported in *Xinian* 21.

18. This domestic struggle lasted from 497 to 490 BCE; it ended with the elimination of both lineages. Note that *Xinian* does not follow strict chronology here.

19. This agreement between Qi and Zheng was made in the autumn of 503 BCE; Wei joined the anti-Jin alliance shortly after (*Zuozhuan*, Ding 7.4).

20. This is the first instance of "until now" in *Xinian*, which indicates the immediate relevance for the authors of the narrated information.

Xinian 19

Xinian 19 takes a break from depicting major powers and focuses instead on Chu's tiny neighbors and multiple dependencies. These states and statelets, most of which were scattered through the Huai River basin, were victims of Chu's rivalry first with Jin and then with Wu. The pressure on them increased dramatically during the reign of ruthless King Ling of Chu, who annexed two major states in the Huai basin, Chen and Cai, and relocated many smaller polities to new locations (as we know from *Zuozhuan*, but not from *Xinian*). King Ling's overthrow brought to Chu's tiny neighbors a temporary respite, but soon enough the pressure resumed. It was the support of these polities—such as Chen, Cai, Hu 胡, and Tang 唐—that allowed Wu to inflict a dramatic defeat on Chu in 506 BCE. However, with Wu's power receding subsequent to its successful anti-Chu campaign, the tiny polities once again became victims of Chu's intimidation. This time, most of them ended as Chu's counties (*xian* 縣).[1] The information in *Xinian* 19 is fully paralleled in *Zuozhuan* except for the final phrases, which confuse the annihilation of Chen (in 478 BCE) and that of Cai (in 447 BCE) (see note 9).

★ ★ ★

楚靈王立，既縣陳、蔡。景平王即位，改封陳、蔡之君，使各復其邦。景平王即世，昭【104】[王]即位，陳、蔡、胡反楚，與吳人伐楚。秦異公命子蒲、子虎率師救楚，與楚師會伐唐，縣之。【105】昭王既復邦，焉克胡、圍蔡。昭王即世，獻惠

王立十又一年，蔡昭侯申懼，自歸於吳，吳緐（洩）庸【106】以師逆蔡昭侯，居于州來，是下蔡。楚人焉縣蔡。【107】

When King Ling ascended the throne (540 BCE), he turned Chen and Cai into counties.[2] After King Jingping (King Ping) ascended the throne (528 BCE), he enfeoffed anew the rulers of Chen and Cai, allowing each to restore his country.[3] When King Jingping passed away, King Zhao ascended the throne, and Chen, Cai, and Hu[4] rebelled against Chu and allied with the Wu leaders to invade Chu.[5] Lord Yi of Qin ordered Zipu and Zihu to lead troops to rescue Chu.[6] Together with the Chu troops, they invaded Tang and turned it into a county.[7] After King Zhao recovered his state, they thereupon overpowered Hu and besieged Cai.[8] After King Zhao passed away, in the eleventh year of King Xianhui (King Hui) (478 BCE), Marquis Zhao of Cai, named Shen, became fearful and on his own initiative submitted to Wu. Xieyong of Wu, leading troops, welcomed Marquis Zhao of Cai and let him reside at Zhoulai, which became the Lower Cai.[9] Thereupon, the Chu leaders turned Cai into a county.[10]

Notes

1. Chu was one of the first polities (perhaps with Qin) to establish the *xian* 縣 as a unit of regional administration. Not every *xian* of that period merits translation as a "county" (which in the Chinese context implies centralized administration), but in the case of Chu (where *xian* were ruled on a strictly nonhereditary basis), this translation is permissible. See Masubuchi 1993; see also Creel 1964.
2. See *Xinian* 18, note 9.
3. From *Zuozhuan* (Zhao 13.2) we know that the nobles of Chen and Cai had a pivotal role in the uprising that toppled King Ling; actually the future King Ping acted then as the governor (duke) of Cai. The restoration of the two polities was in repayment of King Ping's debt for their support.
4. Hu was a minor polity near present-day Fuyang (Anhui) (map 2); it was a Chu satellite and bore the brunt of Chu's wars with Wu. The *Spring and Autumn Annals* report on Hu's taking part in the 506 BCE Shaoling assembly organized by Jin to oppose Chu (*Chunqiu*, Ding 4.2).
5. This refers to the major invasion of Chu by Wu in 506 BCE (narrated also in *Xinian* 15).

6. This vital assistance of Qin to Chu was thanks to the heroic pledge of a Chu minister, Shen Baoxu 申包胥 (*Zuozhuan*, Ding 4.3 and 5.5). Lord Yi of Qin is also known as Lord Ai 秦哀公 (r. 536–500 BCE).
7. Tang was one of the minor polities that tried to liberate itself from Chu's dominance by turning to Wu and actively participating in Wu's invasion of 506 BCE. This is the first appearance of this polity in *Xinian*. Presumably, the reader was supposed to know the background. The annihilation of Tang by the Chu-Qin coalition forces is narrated in *Zuozhuan* (Ding 5.5).
8. Both events are reported in *Zuozhuan* (Ding 15.2, Ai 1.1). Hu was annihilated in 495 BCE, and the next year Cai was besieged and then relocated closer to Chu's borders. Nonetheless, as *Zuozhuan* clarifies, Cai continued its reliance on Wu. The complex maneuvering of Cai rulers among their nominal sovereigns, the Zhou kings and the two nearby powers of Chu and Wu, is duly reflected in the inscriptions on several bronze vessels cast by Cai rulers from the late sixth to mid-fifth centuries BCE. See Falkenhausen 1988, 1126–47; Wang Zewen 2002, 69–86.
9. There is obvious chronological confusion in the *Xinian* story. According to *Zuozhuan*, the relocation of Cai from its erstwhile capital, present-day Xincai 新蔡, to the new one, located one hundred sixty kilometers to the east, near present-day Fengtai 鳳台, Anhui (on the Huai River; map 2), took place in 493 BCE, which was still during the reign of King Zhao of Chu. Marquis Zhao of Cai was actually murdered in 491 BCE by his disgruntled officials who disliked the close alliance with Chu (*Zuozhuan*, Ai 2.4 and 4.1). The final extermination of Cai in its new location was carried out, according to *Records of the Historian*, by King Hui of Chu in 447 BCE (the forty-second year of his reign) (*Shiji* 15:699). In the eleventh year of King Hui (i.e., 478 BCE), Chu exterminated Chen. In *Xinian*, both events are conflated.
10. It is possible that the text refers here to the original Xincai location that became absorbed into Chu following Marquis Zhao's relocation to Lower Cai. As mentioned in the previous note, the final subjugation of Cai took place only in 447 BCE.

Xinian 20

Section 20 shifts away from Chu and focuses on the major geopolitical achievement of Jin: its alliance with the state of Wu and then with Wu's replacer in the position of the major southeastern power, the state of Yue. Whereas the first part of the story (the Jin-Wu alliance) is well known from *Zuozhuan*, the second part, which starts with the Yue annihilation of Wu in 473 BCE, tells us of previously unknown events. Three points merit our attention. First, *Xinian* 20 provides precious evidence of what is sometimes called the Shandong period in the history of the state of Yue.[1] As discussed in chapter 4, heretofore Yue history after the reign of King Goujian 越王句踐 (r. 496–464 BCE) was terra incognita, with just a few scattered pieces of evidence from the *Bamboo Annals* and *Mozi* highlighting this state's ongoing importance. The new information provided by *Xinian* 20 (and 22) clarifies beyond doubt Yue's position as the major power in Shandong during the second half of the fifth century BCE. Second, and related to the first, *Xinian* explicates the importance of the Jin-Yue axis, directed primarily against Qi (but potentially also against Chu), in changing the balance of power in the eastern parts of the Zhou world. From the last sentence of the text we know that the Jin-Yue alliance continued well into the time of *Xinian*'s composition. The allies' two incursions into Qi in 441 and 430 BCE were highly successful. Not incidentally, it was in response to these incursions that the Qi rulers opted to create a long protective wall, which may well be the first Long Wall in China's history.

The story of Qi's Long Wall is the third major contribution of *Xinian* 20 to historical research. Since I have dedicated a separate article to it,[2] I make only a few observations here. First, *Xinian* 20 is the first unequivocal reference to a long wall's erection anywhere in China. Second, its insistence that the wall was built in 441 BCE, following the Jin-Yue assault on Qi, allows speculations about earlier dates of the wall's erection to be dismissed. Third, the fact that *Xinian* and other sources (such as the inscription on the Piao Qiang bells, discussed in chapter 4, pp. 119–20) speak of attempted breaches of the wall or of demands to stop repairing it (*Xinian* 22), it is clear that immediately upon its erection, the Qi wall became a formidable obstacle in the path of invaders. Finally, aside from solving a lot of mysteries regarding the wall's construction, *Xinian* creates a new one—regarding its route. The text clearly says that the wall "stretched from the Southern Mountain to the Northern Sea," implying that it paralleled the course of the Ji 濟 River. This route, however, does not fit either the archaeologically verifiable route of the Qi wall nor the textual evidence about the attempted breaches of the wall, nor military logic. It is likely then that, just as in *Xinian* 17 (see note 6 there), the authors inexplicably confused the Eastern and the Northern Sea.[3]

★ ★ ★

晉景公立十又五年，申公屈巫自晉適吳，焉始通吳晉之路，二邦爲好，以至晉悼公。悼公【108】立十又一年，公會諸侯，以吳王壽夢相見于虢。晉簡公立五年，與吳王闔盧伐【109】楚。闔盧即世，夫秦（差）王即位。晉簡公會諸侯，以與夫秦（差）王相見于黃池。越王句踐克【110】吳，越人因襲吳之與晉爲好。晉敬公立十又一年，趙桓子會[諸]⁴侯之大夫，以與越令尹宋盟于【111】邢（鞏），⁵遂以伐齊。齊人焉始爲長城於濟，自南山屬之北海。晉幽公立四年，趙狗率師與越【112】公朱句伐齊，晉師　関（門?）長城句俞（瀆）（=穀?）之門。越公、宋公敗齊師于襄平。至今晉、越以爲好。【113】

In the fifteenth year of Lord Jing [景] of Jin (585 BCE), Qu Wu, the Duke of Shen, departed from Jin to Wu.[6] Thenceforth, the communications between Wu and Jin were established, and both countries were on good terms until the reign of Lord Dao of Jin. In the eleventh year of Lord Dao (563 BCE), the lord assembled the regional lords to meet King Shoumeng of Wu in Guo.⁷ In the fifth year of Lord Jian of Jin (aka Lord Ding) (506 BCE), he allied with King Helu of Wu and invaded Chu.⁸ After Helu passed away, King Fuchai ascended the throne (495 BCE). Lord Jian of Jin assembled the regional lords and met Fuchai at Huangchi.⁹ King Goujian of Yue overpowered Wu.¹⁰ Thereafter, the Yue leaders inherited Wu's friendly relations with Jin.

In the eleventh year of Lord Jing of Jin (441 BCE), Zhao Huanzi assembled the grandees of the regional lords, making a covenant with *lingyin* (prime minister) Song of Yue at Gong.¹¹ Thereupon they invaded Qi. The people of Qi then for the first time erected the Long Wall at the Ji [River]; [the wall] stretched from the Southern Mountain to the Northern Sea. In the fourth year of Lord You of Jin (430 BCE), Zhao Gou led an army and, together with Lord Zhuju of Yue, invaded Qi.¹² The Jin army stormed the Long Wall at the Gu Gate.¹³ The Duke of Yue and Duke of Song defeated the Qi army at Xiangping.¹⁴ Until now Jin and Yue maintain amicable relations.

Notes

1. Chen Minzhen 2017.
2. Pines 2018b.
3. For archaeological studies of the route of the Qi wall, see Lu Zongyuan 1999 and Ren Xianghong 2005. For debates about the route of the wall in light of *Xinian*'s evidence, see Wang Yongbo and Wang 2013 (which advocates an L-shaped route for the wall, which would include both the Ji River route and the archaeologically verifiable west-east route); Chen Minzhen 2013 (updated in Chen Minzhen 2015a, 85–87); Chen Jie 2016; Pines 2018b, 751–54.
4. The character 諸 is missing.
5. Reading the character as 冀 following Su, Wu, and Lai 2013, 780–81.
6. See details in *Xinian* 15, slip 79.
7. This meeting of 563 BCE, in which no fewer than eleven states aside from Wu were represented, is recorded in the *Spring and Autumn Annals* and *Zuozhuan* (Xiang 10.1). The location of the meeting there is given as Zha 柤, a place in northern Jiangsu, northwest of Pei County 邳縣. It seems that *Xinian* is mistaken here (see Su, Wu, and Lai 2013, 767–69).
8. See *Xinian* 18, note 14. Sun Feiyan (2012) notes that the invasion took place during the sixth rather than fifth year of Lord Jian (i.e., Lord Ding) of Jin.

9. The Huangchi meeting of 482 BCE marked the apex of Wu's power as a new hegemon. There is considerable confusion in the accounts of this meeting in *Zuozhuan* (Ai 13.2–13.4) and *Discourses of the States* (*Guoyu* 19.6:545–48 ["Wu yu" 吳語]), especially concerning the precedence of smearing the sacrificial blood: did Jin yield its traditional leadership to Wu, or were the Wu delegates more deferential after learning of the Yue aggression against their country? What is indisputable is that there was considerable tension between the nominal allies, the leaders of Jin and Wu, during that meeting.
10. The extermination of Wu was accomplished in 473 BCE.
11. Zhao Huanzi 趙桓子 is variously depicted as either brother or son of the de facto founder of the Zhao independent polity, Zhao Xiangzi 趙襄子. According to a convincing correction to the *Shiji* chronology proposed by Wang Zhengdong (2014), Zhao Huanzi headed the state of Zhao in 442–424 BCE (Xiong 2017, 267–76, emends this to 441–424). Alternatively, Liu Guang (2017a) suggests that Zhao Huanzi was a usurper who seized power from his nephew in 441 BCE but died a year later. Zhao Huanzi may be the convener of the covenant among members and supporters of the Zhao lineage, the text of which was discovered in 1965 at the site of Houma 侯馬 (Shanxi) (Williams 2012–2013 and Qiu Xigui 2016). Nothing is known of Yue's prime minister, Song, nor is the location of Gong identifiable.
12. Zhao Gou was a Jin military commander, mentioned under the posthumous name Muzi of Xinzhi 新稚穆子 in *Discourses of the States* (*Guoyu* 15.18 ["Jin yu 9"]). Lord Zhuju of Yue is King Zhuju (r. 447–411 BCE); inexplicably, Yue rulers after King Goujian are invariably referred to in *Xinian* as lords or dukes (*gong* 公) and not as kings (*wang* 王).
13. The text editors proposed reading 句俞 as 句瀆, which, following numerous parallels in the *Spring and Autumn Annals* and *Zuozhuan*, can stand for the single character Gu 穀. See Li Xueqin 2011a, 188n6; see also, for more, Xiaohu 2012; Su, Wu, and Lai 2013, 784–85; Ma Nan 2015, 447–48. See, finally, Chen Jie 2016, 110–12. Gu was a major fortress, contested by Qi and Lu, near the Ji River and to the south of the westernmost point of the Long Wall (map 4); the Gu Gate should be located in the western section of the wall.
14. Xiangping was tentatively identified by Chen Jie (2016, 112–14) as another location in the Taishan range—that is, along the western route of the Long Wall of Qi.

Xinian 21

Xinian 21 focuses on the renewal of the Jin-Chu conflict. It tacitly hints that the renewed hostilities were provoked by Chu. When the newly ascendant Lord Dao of Song asked for Chu's help against domestic rivals, this gave the Chu leaders the needed pretext to advance northeastward in order to entrench their forces in the strategically located towns of Huangchi and Yongqiu (Yong Hill), conveniently located at the intersection of Song, Zheng, and Jin territories. For Jin, this was an unbearable provocation, and it retaliated by assaulting Huangchi and (apparently) expelling the Chu army from there. This was followed by a Chu attack on the southwestern borders of Jin, which in turn induced a major response by the heads of the soon-to-be-formed Three Jin polities (i.e., the Wei, Han, and Zhao lineages, which were soon to gain their de jure independence from Jin). Their counterattack ended with a spectacular defeat of the Chu armies, who retreated to the Long Wall and were defeated there anew. This time, Chu soldiers "threw away their banners and tents and fled by night." Clearly, the authors do not plan to whitewash the magnitude of Chu's defeat.

Two points in *Xinian* 21 are of special interest. One concerns chronology. The text clearly indicates the problems in the chronologies of different rulers applied in *Records of the Historian*, but it creates certain confusions of its own (see notes 2 and 9). The solutions, proposed by Li Rui and followed by Su Jianzhou and his collaborators (note 2), are tentative, but they certainly offer a step toward improving Sima Qian's inaccuracies. Second, the text's mention of the Long Wall of Chu is the first instance in which the existence of this wall is unequivocally stated. None of the early references to the Fangcheng defensive line scattered throughout *Zuo zhuan* and *Xinian* mention a Long Wall, at least not explicitly (see *Xinian* 18, note 14). It is tempting to assume that at a certain point in the fifth century BCE the Chu leaders decided to augment the Fangcheng line of fortifications with a newly erected Long Wall (probably defending the relatively flat terrain in the area of present-day Fangcheng County 方城縣, Henan). If this supposition is correct, then it may suggest that the Chu Long Wall was erected more or less simultaneously with that of Qi (see section 20). This strengthens my assumption that the fifth century BCE, which witnessed a proliferation of infantry armies, should be considered the starting point in China's tradition of building lengthy protective walls.[1]

★ ★ ★

楚簡大王立七年，宋悼公朝于楚，告以宋司城㱿之弱公室。王命莫敖陽爲率【114】師以定公室，城黃池，城雍丘。晉魏斯、趙浣、韓啓章率師圍黃池，遠週而歸之【115】於楚。二年，王命莫敖陽爲率師侵晉，奪宜陽，圍赤岸，以復黃池之師。魏斯、趙浣、韓啓【116】章率師救赤岸，楚人舍圍而還，與晉師戰於長城。楚師無功，多棄旆幕，宵遁。楚以【117】與晉固爲怨。【118】

In the seventh (tenth?) year of King Jianda (King Jian) of Chu (422 BCE?), Lord Dao of Song attended the court audience in Chu,[2] reporting that Pi, the minister of public works, acts to weaken the lord's house.[3] The king ordered *moao* Yang Wei to lead an army to stabilize the lord's house [of Song].[4] [This army] walled Huangchi and walled Yongqiu.[5] The Jin [leaders] Wei Si, Zhao Huan, and Han Qizhang led an army laying siege to Huangchi;[6] they assaulted it and then returned it to Chu.[7] In the next year (421 BCE?), the king ordered *moao* Yang Wei to lead an army to invade Jin. He seized Yiyang and laid siege to Chiyan in retaliation for the Huangchi campaign.[8] The Jin [leaders] Wei Si, Zhao Huan, and Han Qizhang led an army to assist Chiyan. The Chu army gave up the siege and retreated, and it fought the Jin army near the Long Wall.[9] The Chu army achieved nothing. They threw away their banners and tents and fled by night. Thus, Chu harbored strong resentment against Jin.

Notes

1. See more in Pines 2018b. For Fangcheng fortifications, see Li Yipi 2014.
2. There is much confusion about the dates mentioned here: as stated in chapter 4, there is considerable chronological confusion in *Records of the Historian*, and even with the help of the information in the *Bamboo Annals* and *Xinian*, it cannot be fully resolved. Tentatively, I accept the reconstruction proposed by Li Rui (2013) and followed by Su, Wu, and Lai 2013, 831–38. According to this tentative reconstruction, King Jian of Chu 楚簡王 reigned not until 408 BCE (as in *Shiji* 15:708) but 405 BCE; the reign years of the subsequent King Sheng 楚聲王 are 404–401 BCE, and the first year of King Dao of Chu 楚悼王 is 400 BCE. The reign years of Lord Dao of Song should be 421–404 BCE. The seventh year of King Jian should be emended to "tenth" (a scribal confusion between 七 and 十). This puts us in 422 BCE, when Lord Dao of Song had just ascended the throne (his official reign would start only in the first month of the next lunar year, 421 BCE) and sought Chu's assistance against domestic rivals.
3. Nothing is known of the identity of Pi, the Song minister of public works, but it is well known that the ruling house of Song had been under persistent pressure from powerful aristocratic lineages ever since the sixth century BCE and until the usurpation of power by the minister Zihan 子罕 in about 355 BCE (for the latter, see Fang and Wang 2005, 131–32).
4. *Moao* is a high military rank in the state of Chu; for debates about the identity of *moao* Yang Wei, see Li Shoukui 2014a versus Su 2014.
5. Huangchi and Yongqiu were both contested by Zheng and Song, with the former being also an objective of Jin's expansion. Huangchi is located on the southern banks of the Ji River 濟水, to the north of the future Wei 魏 capital of Daliang 大梁. Yongqiu is located to the southeast of Daliang, halfway to the Song capital (map 4). Ma Nan (2015, 449n2) suggests that Chu was using the assistance to Song as a pretext to establish a military presence in the area, which was a focus of potential military expansion by its Jin rivals. Therefore, walling both cities caused Jin's retaliation.
6. Wei Si, Zhao Huan, and Han Qizhang were Jin political-military commanders who were in the process of establishing their independent polities at the expense of Jin. Wei Si is the famous Marquis Wen of Wei 魏文侯 (r. 445–396 BCE); Zhao Huan is Marquis Xian of Zhao 趙獻侯 (r. 423–409 BCE); Han Qizhang is Han Wuzi 韓武子 (d. 409 BCE).
7. The precise meaning of what the Jin armies attained is contested. The text's editors read 逭 迵 as *hengtong* 衡通, referring to Jin's assault on Huangchi; they also opine that *gui zhi yu Chu* 歸之於楚 means causing the Chu armies to

return to their homeland. This latter reading is obviously wrong since *zhi* 之 cannot refer to the Chu armies in this context. Du Xinyu (2015) has proposed reading the two disputed characters as a verb and an object: *chong tong* 潼同, in which *tong* stands for military conscripts. The meaning according to him is that the Jin armies took many Chu prisoners and then returned them to Chu. This explanation seems to me far-fetched and not fitting the text's grammar. An easier solution would be that the Jin armies assaulted the city of Huangchi but were unable to occupy it permanently and returned it to Chu. Another alternative is a scribal error: the city was returned to Zheng and not to Chu.

8. Yiyang was under Han control; it is located to the west of Luoyang (map 4). Chu wanted to shift the campaign westward, closer to its major power bases. The location of Chiyan is unknown.

9. As argued in the introduction to this section, the Long Wall here in all likelihood refers to the newly completed line of Chu fortifications along Fangcheng 方城, the traditional protective perimeter around the Nanyang 南陽 Basin; that is, Chu's heartland. For the nature of these fortifications, see Li Yipi 2014. The battle led by *moao* Yang Wei against the Jin armies near the Chu Long Wall is mentioned in the divination slips from Tomb 1, Geling, Xincai 新蔡 葛陵 (Henan) (e.g., slips *jia* 甲 36 and 296; Chen Wei 2009, 395). However, the date for the Jin incursion provided in *Xinian* (ca. 420 BCE) is considerably earlier than other dates mentioned in the Geling slips; Li Rui (2013, 103–4) thus opined that the Geling slips refer to another battle.

Xinian 22

X*inian* 22 deals with the affairs of a single year (404/403 BCE), but this was one of the most eventful years in the more than half a millennium covered by *Xinian*. It witnessed the culmination of the Jin-Qi conflict that had begun almost two centuries earlier (*Xinian* 14, 16, 20). The successful assault on Qi by the Jin-Yue axis caused the ruler of Qi to sue for a separate peace with Yue, allowing the Yue ruler to hold a triumphal procession in the Lu capital, during which "the Marquis of Lu drove his carriage, and the Marquis of Qi accompanied him in the carriage." This neutralization of Yue, however, did not save Qi from a renewed assault by the forces of the three Jin ministerial lineages, Wei, Han, and Zhao. The Jin armies scored a major victory, which resulted in two covenants: one, with the newly ascended nominal ruler of Qi, Lord Kang 齊康公 (r. 404–386 BCE), the last ruler of the Jiang 姜 clan in Qi, and the second with the would-be replacer of Lord Kang, the Qi strongman Chen He 陳和 (aka Tian He 田和, posthumously known as Lord Tai of Qi 齊太公, d. 384 BCE). The first of the covenants was made at the Jin military camp; the second, even more humiliatingly, in the Qi capital, and to add insult to injury, the heads of the Jin ministerial lineages did not participate in the latter covenant personally but only through their subordinates, thus demonstrating their ritual superiority over Chen He.

Having scored this major victory in 404 BCE, the three Jin leaders utilized it for yet another triumphal event: under the aegis of their nominal leader, Lord Lie of Jin 晉烈公 (r. 415–389 BCE), they presented the Qi captives and the severed ears [of slain Qi soldiers] to King Weilie of Zhou 周威烈王 (r. 425–402 BCE), who, in turn, decided to grant the heads of the Wei, Zhao, and Han lineages the status of regional lords. This was the symbolic start of a new era, the age of the Warring States, in which one's achievements rather than one's pedigree determined one's status. As noted in chapter 4 (pp. 116–18), prior to *Xinian*'s publication, these events were known only through a series of scattered references in the *Bamboo Annals* and a few received texts, such as *Lüshi chunqiu*. The publication of *Xinian* (and the light it sheds on other paleographic sources such as the inscription on the Piao Qiang bells) fills in this major lacuna in our knowledge of the history of the late fifth century BCE.

A few additional points of interest for *Xinian* 22 concern its sources. First, it is notable that the text uncharacteristically employs Chu chronology, even though the narrative focuses on Jin and its enemies and allies. It is likely, then, that the section comes from Chu rather than Jin sources. Second, whereas *Xinian* normally refers to the heads of Wei, Han, and Zhao lineages as Jin ministers rather than regional rulers, once (on slip 121) it refers to Marquis Wen of Wei 魏文侯 (r. 445–396 BCE) by his official title as "Marquis," implying thereby recognition of his newly elevated status. Third, as discussed in chapter 2 (pp. 60–62), *Xinian* 22 contains several sentences that were in all likelihood incorporated either from the Chu court chronicles or from the draft materials of these chronicles. The sentences (e.g., the final one in the section) referring to the rulers of non-Chu polities by their official rank in the Zhou ranking system (roughly equivalent to European duke, marquis, etc.) and by personal name rather than by the usual Lord plus posthumous name are important indirect evidence that Chu court scribes were composing chronicles of the same type as the *Spring and Autumn Annals* of the state of Lu.

★ ★ ★

楚聲桓王即位，元年，晉公止會諸侯於任，宋悼公將會晉公，卒于鼬。韓虔、趙籍、魏【119】擊率師與越公翳伐齊，齊與越成，以建陽、郚陵之田，且男女服。越公與齊侯貸、魯侯衎（衍）【120】盟于魯稷門之外。越公入饗於魯，魯侯御，齊侯參乘以入。晉魏文侯斯從晉師，晉師大敗【121】齊師，齊師北，晉師逐之，入至汧（岍？）水，齊人且有陳瘇子牛之禍，齊與晉成，齊侯【122】盟於晉軍。晉三子之大夫入齊，盟陳和與陳淏於溋（雍？）門之外，曰：「毋修長城，毋伐廩

【123】丘。」晉公獻齊俘馘於周王，遂以齊侯貸、魯侯羴（顯）、宋公田、衛侯虔、鄭伯駘朝【124】周王于周。【125】

King Shenghuan of Chu (King Sheng) ascended the throne. In his first year (404 BCE), Zhi, the Duke of Jin, assembled the regional lords in Ren.[1] Lord Dao of Song intended to meet the Duke of Jin but died at You.[2] Han Qian, Zhao Ji, and Wei Ji led the armies and, together with Lord Yi from Yue, assaulted Qi.[3] Qi made peace with Yue, submitting to it and [giving it] the fields of Jianyang and Juling, as well as male and female (servants).[4] The Duke of Yue made a covenant with the Marquis of Qi, Dai, and the Marquis of Lu, Yan, outside the Ji Gate of Lu.[5] The Duke of Yue entered the Lu [capital] for the banquet: upon his entrance, the Marquis of Lu drove his carriage, and the Marquis of Qi accompanied him in the carriage.

Si, Marquis Wen of Wei (r. 445–396 BCE) of Jin, followed the Jin army;[6] the Jin army greatly defeated the Qi army. The Qi army fled; the Jin army followed it, entering [Qi territory] reaching the Xian River.[7] Moreover, the people of Qi had suffered from the calamity of Chen Jing (?) Ziniu; hence Qi asked Jin for peace.[8] The Marquis of Qi made a covenant at the [location of the] Jin army. The grandees of the Three Masters of Jin entered the Qi capital and made a covenant with Chen He and Chen Hao[9] outside the Yong Gate, saying, "Do not repair the Long Wall, do not invade Linqiu."[10] The Duke of Jin presented the Qi captives and the severed ears [of slain Qi soldiers] to the King of Zhou and then attended the Zhou royal court, bringing with him the Marquis of Qi, Dai; the Marquis of Lu, Xian; the Duke of Song, Tian; the Marquis of Wei [衛], Qian; and the Earl of Zheng, Tai.[11]

Notes

1. For the reign dates of King Sheng of Chu (r. 404–401 BCE), see section 21, note 2. Zhi is Lord Lie of Jin. Ren 任 is identified by Xiaohu 2012 as a location to the southeast of modern Jining City 濟寧市, situated between Song and Lu (map 4).
2. For Lord Dao of Song, see *Xinian* 21, note 2.
3. Han Qian is Marquis Jing of Han 韓景侯 (r. 408–400 BCE); Zhao Ji is Marquis Lie of Zhao 趙烈侯 (r. 408–387 BCE); Wei Ji is Marquis Wu of Wei 魏武侯 (r. 395–370 BCE), who acted at the time on behalf of his father, Marquis Wen of Wei. Lord Yi is King Yi of Yue 越王翳 (r. ca. 410–375 BCE).

4. Jianyang is tentatively identified as a location near modern Zaozhuang City 棗莊市 in southern Shandong province. If this identification is correct, it means Qi's retreat was from the southernmost parts of its territory, much to the south of its Long Wall. See more in Su, Wu, and Lai 2013, 848–50. I read *fu* 服 as "servants" following the text's editors (Li Xueqin 2011a, 193n5).
5. The Marquis of Qi, Dai, is Lord Kang. The Marquis of Lu, Yan 衍, is Lord Mu 魯穆公 (r. ca. 416–383 BCE) (whose name is transcribed as Xian 轟 [顯] on slip 124). The Ji Gate was the southern gate of the Lu capital.
6. Note that an initial assault on Qi was led by Marquis Wen's son, the future Marquis Wu of Wei; Marquis Wen joined the campaign only in its second stage.
7. Xiaohu (2012) identifies Qian 汧 as the Xian 峴 River, a location near the Muling Pass 穆陵關, the major southern gate into Qi, at the eastern section of Qi's Long Wall (map 4).
8. The details of the "calamity" caused by Chen Jing (or Qing) Ziniu are difficult to verify, but it probably refers to internal strife among the scions of the Chen (Tian) lineage, the de facto rulers of Qi. See more in Ma Weidong 2014.
9. The Three Masters of Jin are the heads of the Wei, Han, and Zhao lineages. The covenant was made between their subordinates and the de facto (but still not de jure) leader of Qi, Chen He (Tian He 田和). This arrangement apparently reflected the fact that the Three Masters of Jin were already acting as heads of independent polities, whose ranks were superior to Chen He's rank; by dispatching their subordinates they emphasized the lowly position of Chen He, who still acted on behalf of the puppet lord of Qi (Li Xueqin 2011a, 194n12). Xiong 2017, 148–52, identifies Chen Hao as one of the leaders of the Chen lineage, probably second in command among them. His importance is hinted at in the last sentences of *Xinian* 23 as well.
10. Linqiu 廩丘 was a locus of contention between Qi and Jin; in 405 BCE (one year before the campaign depicted in the preceding) its governor, Ducal Grandson Hui 公孫會, rebelled against the Chen/Tian lineage of Qi and surrendered his territory to the state of Zhao. For details, see Ma Weidong 2014.
11. These leaders are Lord Kang of Qi; Lord Mu of Lu (whose name is transcribed as Yan 衍 on slip 120); Lord Xiu of Song 宋休公 (r. ca. 403–385 BCE); the Lord of Wei, whose rule is not recorded in *Records of the Historian* (he was supposedly the father of Lord Shen of Wei 衛慎公; for attempts to reconstruct the chronology of Wei rulers, see Xiong 2018 versus Liu Zhuoyi 2018); and Lord Xu of Zheng 鄭繻公 (r. ca. 422–396 BCE). For the references to the rulers of non-Chu polities by their official rank in the Zhou ranking system as indicative of the incorporation of Chu court chronicles into *Xinian*, see the introduction to this section.

Xinian 23

The last section of *Xinian* is the longest and most informative about the events at the turn of the fourth century BCE. It depicts an immensely complex web of campaigns centered on the Jin-Chu struggle in the area between the Yellow and Huai River basins. These campaigns, which involved not just Jin and Chu but also their smaller neighbors of Zheng and Song, as well as the other major powers of Qin, Qi, and possibly Yue, left almost no traces in the received texts. We are left with only a few scattered entries in Sima Qian's "Chronological Table of the Six States" (六國年表), which suffer from various inaccuracies and cannot be fully integrated with the *Xinian* narrative.[1] That a series of major military encounters had all but disappeared from the transmitted texts is yet another indication of the inadequacy of our sources for approximately 470 to 370 BCE, as noted in chapter 4.

Judging from *Xinian*, the campaigns started when Chu tried to regain the initiative after Jin's astounding defeat of Qi narrated in *Xinian* 22. In 401 BCE, King Sheng 楚聲王 (r. ca. 404–401 BCE) summoned the leaders of Zheng and Song, who had participated two years earlier in the celebrations of Jin's military triumph over Qi at the Zhou court. Following that visit, Song shifted allegiance to Chu, fortifying the strategic Yu Pass 榆關 at the intersection of Zheng, Jin, and Song territories and establishing a new fortress, Wuyang, which soon became the focus of major campaigns. In addition, Qin attacked Jin from the west, preventing the latter's intervention against Chu.

Soon enough, matters soured for Chu. King Sheng was assassinated in 401 BCE, possibly prompting a domestic crisis in Chu (a rebellion by his son or brother, Royal Son Ding, who sought Jin's assistance). *Xinian* as usual glosses over Chu's domestic problems, but it is clear that attacks on Chu started immediately after the enthronement of King Dao 楚悼王 (r. ca. 400–381 BCE). The first series of tit-for-tat campaigns occurred in 400–399 BCE and were indecisive: neither Zheng's assault on the Yu Pass, nor Chu's attack northward into Guiling, nor the Jin-Zheng attempt to install Royal Son Ding in Chu achieved any results.

In 398 BCE the situation appeared to favor Chu: it had "completely subdued the Zheng army" and captured its four generals. This, in addition to domestic troubles in Zheng, had neutralized this country, prompting Chu to release the Zheng prisoners in 397 BCE. However, the campaigns between Chu and Jin continued as before, without any decisive victory. The change came in around 395 BCE, with a new major attack on Jin led by the heads of the newly established Wei and Han polities. This assault on Wuyang ended in a crushing defeat for Chu, which lost four of its top political-military leaders. Worse, "the Chu forces threw away their banners, tents, chariots, and weapons and returned, running like fleeing dogs." This, in addition to a renewed rebellion by supporters of the fugitive Royal Son Ding, resulted in "the state of Chu losing a lot of walled cities." Notably, Qi tried to save its Chu allies, but the powerful reinforcement of a thousand Qi war chariots missed the battle by two days.

Xinian 23 is a very informative text, but it leaves many questions unanswered. Why did the ruler of Zheng, who attended Chu's court in 401 BCE, decide to side with Jin a year later? Why did the Chu leaders display unusual leniency to the captured Zheng commanders and their "myriad people"? What was the fate of rebellious Royal Son Ding? Who was to blame for Chu's defeat? What lessons if any should be deduced from these events? The text remains silent. And readers, lacking a source like the *Zuo zhuan*, remain perplexed and unable to answer these questions. Once again, the text demonstrates *Xinian*'s peculiarity as informative rather than interpretative history.

★ ★ ★

楚聲桓王立四年，宋公田、鄭伯駘皆朝于楚。王率宋公以城榆關，寘武陽。 秦人【126】敗晉師於洛陰，以爲楚援。聲王即世，悼哲王即位。鄭人侵榆關，陽城桓定君率【127】榆關之師與上國之師以交之，與之戰於桂陵，楚師無功。景之賈與舒子共𢦏（捷）而死。明【128】歲，晉𧶠余率晉師與鄭師以入王子定。魯陽公率師以交晉人，晉人還，不果入王子。

明歲，【129】郎（梁？）莊平君率師侵鄭，鄭皇子、子馬、子池、子封子率師以交楚人，楚人涉氾，將與之戰，鄭師逃【130】入於蔑。楚師圍之於蔑，盡逾（降）鄭師與其四將軍，以歸於郢。鄭太宰欣亦起禍於【131】鄭，鄭子陽用滅，無後於鄭。明歲，楚人歸鄭之四將軍與其萬民於鄭。晉人圍津、長陵，【132】克之。王命平夜悼武君率師侵晉，降郜，𢦏（捷）滕公涉澗以歸，以復長陵之師。

厭（薦？）年，韓【133】取、魏擊率師圍武陽，以復郜之師。魯陽公率師救武陽，與晉師戰於武陽之城【134】下，楚師大敗，魯陽公、平夜悼武君、陽城桓定君、三執珪之君與右尹昭之竢死焉，楚人盡棄其【135】旃幕車兵，犬逸而還。陳人焉反而入王子定於陳。楚邦以多亡城。

楚師將救武陽，【136】王命平夜悼武君使人於齊陳淏求師。陳疾目率車千乘，以從楚師於武陽。甲戌，晉楚以【137】戰。丙子，齊師至喦，遂還。【138】

In the fourth year of King Shenghuan (King Sheng) of Chu (401 BCE),[2] the Duke of Song, Tian, and the Earl of Zheng, Tai, attended the Chu court. The king ordered the Duke of Song to fortify the Yu Pass and establish Wuyang [fortress?].[3] Qin forces defeated the Jin army at Luoyin in order to help Chu.[4] When King Sheng passed away, King Daozhe (King Dao) ascended the throne (400 BCE).[5] The Zheng forces assaulted the Yu Pass, and Lord Huanding of Yangcheng[6] led the forces of the Yu Pass and of the upper parts of the country[7] to repel them. He fought the [invaders] at Guiling, but the Chu armies did not succeed.[8] Jia of Jing (i.e., Jing Jia) and Shuzi Gong were captured and died [there].[9] In the next year (399 BCE), Fu[10] Yu of Jin led the Jin and Zheng armies to install Royal Son Ding.[11] The Duke of Luyang led an army to combat the Jin forces;[12] the Jin forces returned, having failed to install the prince.

In the next year (398 BCE), Lord Zhuangping of Liang led an army to invade Zheng.[13] Four generals of Zheng—Huangzi, Zima, Zichi, and Zifengzi—led an army to combat the Chu forces. The Chu forces crossed the Fan River and prepared to fight, and the Zheng army fled, entering [the city of] Mie.[14] The Chu army laid siege to Mie and completely subdued the Zheng army and its four generals, returning with them to [Chu's capital] Ying. Moreover, Grand Steward Xin of Zheng made trouble in Zheng: Ziyang of Zheng was eliminated, leaving no posterity in Zheng.[15] In the next year (397 BCE), Chu returned the four Zheng generals and their myriad people to Zheng. The Jin forces encircled Jin and Changling and overpowered [these cities].[16] The king [of Chu] ordered Lord Daowu of Pingye to lead an army and invade Jin.[17] He subdued Gao, captured Duke of Teng, Shejian,[18] and returned with [the captured duke] to avenge the invasion of Changling.

After two years (395 BCE?),[19] Han Qu and Wei Ji led an army and laid siege to Wuyang, to avenge the incursion into Gao.[20] The Duke of Luyang led an army to help Wuyang and fought the Jin army below the walls of Wuyang. The Chu army was greatly defeated. Three lord possessors of the *gui* tablet, the Duke of Luyang, Lord Daowu of Pingye, and Lord Huanding of Yangcheng, as well as *youyin* Si of Zhao (Zhao Si), died in that battle.[21] The Chu forces threw away their banners, tents, chariots, and weapons and returned, running like fleeing dogs. The Chen people thereupon rebelled and let Royal Son Ding back to Chen.[22] Thus the state of Chu lost a lot of walled cities.

When the Chu army was planning to go to rescue Wuyang, the king ordered Lord Daowu of Pingye to dispatch somebody to Chen Hao of Qi to request military help.[23] Chen Jimu [of Qi] led one thousand chariots and followed the Chu army to Wuyang. On the day *jiaxu* (the eleventh day of the *ganzhi* cycle), Jin fought with Chu; on *bingzi* (the thirteenth day),[24] the Qi army arrived at Nie[25] and then turned back.

Notes

1. See Chen Yingfei 2018; see also note 11 for an example of Sima Qian's confusion.
2. For the dates of the late fifth century BCE Chu kings, see *Xinian* 21, note 2.
3. The Yu Pass 榆關 was a strategic point halfway between the capital of Zheng and Daliang 大梁 (now Kaifeng), the future capital of the state of Wei 魏 (map 4). The precise location of Wuyang is unverifiable, but if it was located not far from the Yu Pass, this meant a radical expansion of Song westward, toward Zheng's territory. This may explain why Zheng turned against Chu after the court visit of 401 BCE.
4. Luoyin is located to the west of the Yellow River near its confluence with the Wei 渭 River (map 4). In about 408 BCE it was fortified by Wei 魏 troops, becoming the westernmost part of Jin territory (*Shiji* 15:708). Qin's assault on Jin exemplifies the ongoing functioning of a loose Qin-Chu alliance, which persisted from the late seventh century BCE well into the fourth century BCE.

5. According to *Shiji* 40:1720, King Sheng was assassinated. As is common in *Xinian*, dramas from the domestic life of Chu are glossed over. The character "Dao" in King Daozhe's posthumous name is written 刀, which is different from the common Chu transcription of this character 悼, leading Su Jianzhou to opine that *Xinian* was not produced by a Chu scribe (Su, Wu, and Lai 2013, 882–83). This view was refuted by Ōnishi Katsuya, who explained the reason for the odd character: it seems that the scribe had originally forgotten to add the character "Dao," and when he inserted it above the character "zhe" he did not have enough space to add a "heart" radical below, resulting in an odd character (2017, 40–42).
6. Yangcheng County was located near the modern city of Suzhou 宿州 (Anhui), to the south of the state of Song (map 4). For debates about its location, see Zheng 2012, 122–27.
7. *Shang guo* 上國, "upper parts of the country" (i.e., of Chu), refers to western areas of Chu, which were upstream of the rivers that flow through the country. See Du Yu's gloss on this term in *Zuozhuan* cited by Yang Bojun (*Zuozhuan*, Zhao 14.3:1365). That western forces were assigned to the Lord of Yangcheng, whose stronghold was near Chu's eastern frontiers, sounds odd to me.
8. Guiling is located to the north of the Yellow River, in present-day Changyuan 長垣 County, Henan (map 4). That the battle was waged there means that the Chu armies had penetrated deeply into Jin territory.
9. These two persons are tentatively identified by the Tsinghua University editorial team as two Chu nobles (Li Xueqin 2011a, 198n8).
10. For reading the surname of a Jin commander as 賻 Fu, see Su 2012, 73–74.
11. The "Chronological Tables" in *Records of the Historian* mention that in 399 BCE "Royal Son Ding fled to Jin" (*Shiji* 15:710). Confusingly, this item is put in the affairs of the Zhou domain. From *Xinian* it is clear that Royal Son Ding was a Chu person. His fleeing and resort to Jin's support may be related to the murder of King Sheng (his father?).
12. Luyang 魯陽 was located at the upper reaches of the Ru 汝 River, near modern Lushan 魯山 County (map 4). Zheng Wei insists that the Duke of Luyang 魯陽公 was the governor of the county and is not identical to the enfeoffed Lord of Luyang 魯陽君 (who is known as one of Mozi's interlocutors—i.e., in *Mozi* XIII.49:733–34 ["Lu wen" 魯問]). See Zheng 2012, 109–15; 2017, 27–30, but see also note 21.
13. Lang 朗 was identified by Dong Shan (2014, 108–9) as Liang 梁, a city in the Ru River valley, on Chu's northern frontier. See also Ma Nan 2015, 472n4.
14. For the Fan River, see *Xinian* 16, note 1; Mie's location is unverifiable. Dong Shan (2014, 109–10) proposes reading Mie as Kuai 鄶, an important stronghold to the northwest of Zheng's capital, Xinzheng.

15. Ziyang 子陽 was the most powerful Zheng statesman of the time; his elimination by Grand Steward Xin appears to have been a critical step toward Zheng's weakening en route to its elimination at the hands of the state of Han in 375 BCE. For debates about the details of Ziyang's death and its consequences, see Su, Wu, and Lai 2013, 903–7. Note that the plot of Grand Steward Xin is mentioned in *Han Feizi* XVII.44:407 ("Shuo yi" 說疑), which confused generations of commentators. With *Xinian*'s publication the puzzle is solved.
16. The location of both these fortresses is unclear; the identification proposed by the Tsinghua editorial team (Li Xueqin 2011a, 199n19) does not make sense geographically, placing Jin in the westernmost part of Chu and Changling in the Huai 淮 River valley. As Su Jianzhou has correctly noted, it is highly unlikely that the Jin armies would have penetrated so deeply into Chu's hinterland (Su, Wu, and Lai 2013, 908).
17. The lords of Pingye belonged to a collateral branch of the Chu royal lineage, enfeoffed at Pingye in the southern Ru 汝 River valley (map 4). Su, Wu, and Lai 2013, 908–9, identifies Lord Daowu as a son of another lord of Pingye, who was the occupant of Tomb 1, Geling, Xincai, excavated in 1994 (for whom see Song 2010, 113–35). For the lords of Pingye, see Zheng 2012, 115–18.
18. Gao is tentatively identified as a former statelet located between Song and Lu, near modern Chengwu County 成武縣 (Shandong) (Li Xueqin 2011a, 199n21) (map 4). The state of Teng 滕 was conquered by Yue 越 circa 420 BCE (see the *Bamboo Annals* information in the gloss on *Shiji* 41:1747). I suspect that Duke Shejian was a Yue governor of Teng, which may suggest that Yue was actively involved in the Jin-Chu struggle on Jin's side.
19. The precise reading of 厭年 is contested; it may refer to "the next year" or "after two years." See more in Su, Wu, and Lai 2013, 912–16.
20. Han Qu is Marquis Lie of Han 韓烈侯 (r. 399–387 BCE) and Wei Ji is Marquis Wu of Wei 魏武侯 (r. 395–370 BCE). Notably, despite the official elevation of the lords of Han and Wei to the status of regional lords in 403 BCE, *Xinian* treats them here as military leaders of the unified state of Jin. However, this is not a consistent ideological stance: recall that section 22 (slip 121) does recognize the "marquis" (*hou* 侯) title of Marquis Wu's father, Marquis Wen of Wei.
21. Possession of the *gui* 珪 tablet marked the highest degree of authority in Chu: the ducal position of an enfeoffed noble (Chen Yingfei 2012, 106). In this case, the Duke of Luyang may be an enfeoffed noble after all, pace Zheng Wei (note 12). Zhao Si 昭䎸 was another important noble, probably a descendant of King Zhao of Chu 楚昭王 (r. 516–489 BCE).
22. Originally, the text's editors identified Chen in this sentence as a reference to the state of Qi, which was already ruled (de facto if not de jure) by the Chen 陳 (Tian 田) lineage (Li Xueqin 2011a, 200n28). Later, this understanding was challenged: it is likely that Chen here refers to a Chu county—that is, the

former state of Chen that was annexed by Chu in 534 BCE, regained independence in 529 BCE, and was annexed again in 478 BCE (see *Xinian* 19 and the notes there). Little is known of its subsequent management, but it is possible that the former Chen territory, which served as a springboard for the dynastic coup of 529 BCE, had a similar role in the attempts of the ousted Royal Son Ding to regain power in Chu. See Su, Wu, and Lai 2013, 923–24.

23. This sentence shifts the narrative back to the moment before Chu's defeat at Wuyang. For Chen Hao, see *Xinian* 22, note 9.
24. As argued in chapter 2 (pp. 62–63), the *ganzhi* dates that appear here are meaningless, since they are not accompanied by the month's number. It is highly likely that they were mechanically transposed into *Xinian* from its source material (a Chu local history?). Certainly in the latter the month number had appeared on one of the earlier slips.
25. Nie 嵒 is recorded in *Zuozhuan* (Ai 12.6) as a location between Song and Zheng. This is another indication that Wuyang fortress was located near the Yu Pass (which is situated between Song and Zheng but much closer to Zheng).

Notes

Note on Translations, References, and Dates

1. Many alternatives to these European ranks have been proposed by other translators, most notably by Durrant, Li, and Schaberg (2016). None seems to resolve the problems. Note that the European ranks as equivalents of Chinese titles were adopted by Japan following the Meiji Restoration (except that Japan opted to use "prince" instead of "duke" and "count" instead of "earl").

Introduction

1. Liang Qichao (1922) 2000, 16, 24.
2. See, e.g., Twitchett 1992; Kurz 2012.
3. Studies of Sima Qian, his personal agendas, and his revision of his sources are too voluminous to be summarized here. For a sample, see Durrant 1995; Hardy 1999; van Ess 2014; Durrant, Li, Nylan, and van Ess 2016.
4. See, e.g., van Ess 2014 for an excellent example.
5. Another quasi-annalistic text, the *Bamboo Annals* does not belong to transmitted literature *sensu stricto* because it was unearthed in around 280 CE. See also note 9.
6. For the *Spring and Autumn Annals* and *Zuozhuan*, see chapter 1; for the *Canon of Documents* and its complexity, see the articles collected in Kern and Meyer

2017; for the anecdotes, see Schaberg 2011; van Els and Queen 2017; and the discussion in chapters 1 and 3 in this book.

7. For the "noble man" comments in *Zuozhuan*, see chapter 1, note 58. Note that similar comments appear also in a parallel text, *Discourses of the States* (*Guoyu* 國語).

8. For example, the comparison between accounts in *Zuozhuan* and parallel accounts in the major collection of historical anecdotes, *Discourses of the States*, is hindered by the ongoing debates about whether or not one of these texts served as source material for the second (see more in Zhang Yiren 1962).

9. For the *Bamboo Annals*, their nature, transmission, and the relation between the "old" (*guben* 古本) version (which exists only in citations in later texts) and the "current" (*jinben* 今本) version, the authenticity of which remains questionable, see the indispensable Shaughnessy 2006, 131–256; cf. Cheng Pingshan 2013; Nivison 2009. Note that in what follows, whenever I refer to the *Bamboo Annals*, I refer invariably to the old version reconstructed from the citations in different third- to tenth-century texts (Fang and Wang 2005) and not to the "current" version. I agree with Shaughnessy that outright rejection of the current version's historical value is not entirely justified, but I prefer to exercise extra caution here. For the *Bamboo Annals*' impact on the emerging spirit of historical criticism, see Qiu Feng 2013.

10. Among recent discoveries, one can mention short collections of historical anecdotes, such as the *Chunqiu shiyu* 春秋事語 and the *Zhanguo zonghengjia shu* 戰國縱橫家書 silk manuscripts from Tomb 3, Mawangdui 馬王堆, Changsha 長沙 (Hunan). For the historical value of the first of these, see Yoshimoto 1990b; Pines 2003; for the second, Mawangdui Hanmu boshu zhengli xiaozu 1976. See also the badly damaged text from Tomb 36 at Shibancun 石板村, Cili 慈利 County (Hunan), which parallels the "Wu yu" 吳語 section of the *Discourses of the States* (Zhang Chunlong 2004), and the equally badly damaged collection of anecdotes from Tomb 1, Shuanggudui 雙古堆, Fuyang 阜陽 (Anhui) (Hu Pingsheng 2013). The so-called *Annals* (*Biannian ji* 編年記) from Tomb 11, Shuihudi 睡虎地, Yunmeng 雲夢 (Hubei), are also sometimes discussed as a historical text (Mittag 2003; Shaughnessy 2014), although this manuscript may be closer to the genre of personal calendars of tomb occupants (*shiri* 視日) than to historical texts per se (see the summary of debates in *Qin jiandu heji shiwen zhushi xiuding ben* 2016, 1:7–9). Another "Annals" text discovered at Tomb 1, Shuanggudui, was too damaged to allow meaningful reconstruction (see Hu Pingsheng 1989). For a systematic (even if by now outdated) discussion of historical texts among recently unearthed paleographic materials, see Li Ling 2004, 260–80; for additional materials, see Yang Bo 2019, 38–114.

11. There are at least two recently unearthed manuscripts that have been preliminarily identified as Chu historical works, and their publication will surely

require correction of some of my preliminary conclusions presented in this book. One of these manuscripts (or, possibly, two separate manuscripts) is part of yet another cache of looted texts acquired by Anhui University (Huang Dekuan 2017). The second Chu historical book was scientifically excavated in 2019 from a cemetery on the northern bank of the Longhui River 龍會河, Jingzhou (Hubei). According to the preliminary publication, it covers roughly the same period as *Xinian* (Li Huibo and Wu 2019). The nature of the text is still not clear: maybe it has a narrower military focus (Ke 2019).

1. Zhou Historiography as Seen from the Transmitted Texts

1. Du Weiyun 2010, 1:32–49.
2. For the evolution of the meaning of *shi*, see Durrant 2020. For earlier discussions about *shi* and their various functions, see, e.g., Vogelsang 2003/2004 and 2007, 17–91; Yates 2011, 345–360; Schaberg 2013; Selbitschka 2018.
3. Whether or not Chinese legendary heroes, such as the so-called Five Thearchs (*wu di* 五帝), came from early oral lore is a question beyond the scope of the present book.
4. For introductions to the Shang inscriptions, see Keightley 1997 and Eno 2009.
5. The "Duo shi" 多士 (Many officers) chapter of the *Canon of Documents* contains a phrase allegedly pronounced by the Duke of Zhou 周公 (d. 1035 BCE) to the leaders of the subjugated Shang people: "You know that the former Yin (Shang) people had wooden tablets and documents about Yin's replacement of Xia's mandate" (惟爾知，惟殷先人有冊有典，殷革夏命) (*Shangshu jinguwen zhushu* 20:429). If we accept this as a genuine statement by the Duke of Zhou, it may lend credibility to the possibility that some records of the Shang overthrow of their predecessors, the Xia, did exist then. Yet it is highly likely that the text comes from the tenth century BCE or even later, by which time the legend of the Shang overthrow of the Xia became one of the core topoi in the justification of Zhou's own possession of Heaven's Mandate (Gentz 2017). The statement's relation to Shang historical records remains dubious at best.
6. For Sima Qian's relative accuracy in reconstructing a list of the Shang kings (despite his meager understanding of the Shang polity), see, e.g., Keightley 1978, 429–34. For *Shi ben*, see Cang Xiuliang 2006, 1:78–90 (for the attempts to reconstruct the text from different quotations in transmitted texts, see *Shi ben bazhong*). For the possibility that at least one additional genealogy—that of the Ni 兒 lineage—is preserved among the Shang bone inscriptions, see Chen Kuang Yu 2012.

7. See Li Feng 2006 for the scope of the Zhou expansion.
8. I use the appellation Zhouxin, which combines the king's name, Zhòu, and his posthumous designation, Xin, to avoid confusion between the king and the Zhōu 周 dynasty.
9. For the ideology of Heaven's Mandate, see Creel 1970; Luo Xinhui 2012; for the concept of *de*, see Kominami 1992; Kryukov 1995.
10. Kern 2018.
11. For these commemorative practices, see Kern 2009; see also Gentz 2017.
12. For some of the problems in dating the allegedly Western Zhou portion of the *Canon of Documents*, see, e.g., discussions scattered through Gu and Liu 2005; see also Vogelsang 2002. I concur with the suggestions of Kern 2009 and Gentz 2017 for the dating of some of the documents I use in the current study.
13. See "Wen wang" 文王 (Mao 235) in Cheng Junying and Jiang Jianyuan 1991, 745–51 (Waley 1996, 227–28).
14. See *Shangshu* 20:423–32 and 23:459–68; analysis in Gentz 2017.
15. See *Shangshu* 21:433–45; analysis in Pines 2017b (cf. Hunter 2017).
16. For the Shang as the mirror to the Zhou, see the ode "Wen wang"; for the Xia as the "mirror" to the Shang, see the ode "Dang" 蕩 (Mao 255).
17. *Shangshu* 15:361.
18. For different analyses of this text, compare Shaughnessy 1997, 31–68, and Grebnev 2016; see also Gentz 2017, 152–56.
19. For the nature of these inscriptions, see Falkenhausen 1993a; for their utilization as sources for the political and administrative history of the Western Zhou, see Li Feng 2006 and 2008. It is likely that major aristocratic lineages of the Western Zhou period maintained their own scribes who produced the records on the basis of which the inscription was made (Shaughnessy 2007; Škrabal 2019).
20. See Shim 1997; Nivison and Shaughnessy 2000; and Cook and Goldin 2016, 213–18.
21. *Mengzi* 6.9.
22. See more in Puett 2001, 56–57.
23. *Gongyang zhuan*, Ai 14.
24. The *Gongyang Commentary* presumes that there was a preedited copy of the *Annals* with which Confucius allegedly operated. See *Gongyang zhuan*, Zhuang 7; Gentz 2015, 70.
25. The *Annals* start in 722 BCE. In the *Gongyang* and *Guliang* versions they end with the capture of a "unicorn" (*lin* 麟) in 481 BCE. In the *Zuozhuan* version they end two years later, with the death of Confucius.
26. This number of the commentaries is mentioned in *Hanshu* 30:1715. Note that other canonical texts acquired systematic commentaries only in the Han period.

27. My analysis of the *Annals* is based on Pines 2009a, 318–23. For other studies, see, e.g., Karapet'iants 1988; Zhao Shengqun 2000; Van Auken 2007 and 2016a.
28. Pines 2009a: 318–19.
29. Lord Yin of Lu 魯隱公 (r. 722–712 BCE) was not the crown prince; according to the common interpretation he ascended his position to act as a regent for his younger brother, the future Lord Huan 魯桓公 (r. 711–694 BCE).
30. *Zuozhuan*, Yin 1.4.
31. *Xin lun* 9:39.
32. Pines 2009a.
33. My understanding of the *Gongyang* tradition is indebted to studies by Joachim Gentz (2001, 2005, 2015). Admittedly, I have never attempted to analyze the parallel *Guliang* tradition in its own right, nor am I aware of an adequate secondary study on a par with those of Gentz.
34. See an example in *Gongyang zhuan*, Xiang 7, discussed in Pines 2009a, 329–32.
35. For "weighing" as an essential means of dealing with situations that cannot be adequately covered by ritual norms, see *Gongyang zhuan*, Huan 11, analyzed in Gentz 2015, 94–98. See also Vankeerberghen 2005–2006 and Goldin 2005.
36. *Zuozhuan*, Zhao 31.5; see also Cheng 14.4.
37. See examples analyzed in Pines 2009a, 326–27.
38. Liu Fenglu 劉逢祿 (1776–1829), one of the major critics of *Zuozhuan*, averred, "The *Spring and Autumn Annals* is not a historical text. Those who speak from the point of view of Mr. Zuo treat the *Annals* as a historical text and, expectedly, lose its meaning" (《春秋》非史文，言《左氏》者以史文視《春秋》，宜其失義也) (Liu Fenglu 1955, 599). For similar views of Zhu Xi 朱熹 (1130–1200) and Pi Xirui 皮錫瑞 (1850–1908), see *Zhuzi yulei* 93:2151; Pi (1907) 1998, 4:45–47.
39. Van Auken 2016a, 43–52.
40. See details in Guan 1998.
41. *Chunqiu*, Yin 11.4, Huan 18.2, Min 2.3, Wen 18.6.
42. See *Zuozhuan*, Xi 17.4, Wen 2.3, Cheng 10.7, Zhao 16.1. See also Van Auken 2016a, 59–61.
43. *Chunqiu*, Zhao 25.5; when other dignitaries or foreign rulers went into exile, the *Annals* report them as "departing" (*chu* 出) or "fleeing" (*ben* 奔).
44. The rules of concealment could be extended to the Zhou kings. In 632 BCE, when King Xiang 周襄王 (r. 651–619 BCE) was humiliatingly summoned to the interstate meeting at Wen 溫 by Lord Wen of Jin 晉文公 (r. 636–628 BCE), the *Annals* laconically stated, "Heavenly King hunted at Heyang" (天王狩于河陽) (*Zuozhuan*, Xi 28.6). See more in Chao Yuefeng 2000, 10–11.
45. I borrow the term "ritual reality" from Gentz 2005.

46. *Zuozhuan*, Xuan 2.3c. For other cases in which the *Annals*' condemnation of a ruler's murderer hints at a legally responsible person, even if technically he was not the killer, see Zhao Shengqun 2000, 251–57.
47. The existence of the Jin and Qi annals is confirmed by the fact that local historians (such as Dong Hu) were making records in these annals. For the case of Qi, see *Zuozhuan*, Xiang 25.2d.
48. *Chunqiu*, Xuan 2.4. For an insightful discussion of the annals as the perpetuator of joint cultural ties among the Zhou polities, see Karapet'iants 1988.
49. *Zuozhuan*, Zhao 2.1.
50. *Zuozhuan*, Wen 15.2, Xiang 20.7; see also discussion in Pines 2009a, 322.
51. See Schaberg 2001; Pines 2002; Li Wai-yee 2007.
52. Durrant, Li, and Schaberg 2016.
53. *Hanshu* 36:1967–70.
54. Tang scholar Dan Zhu 啖助 (724–770) was the first to opine that *Zuozhuan* was initially a compilation of historical works from different Spring and Autumn–period states, whereas the commentarial layer was added by later transmitters. See *Chunqiu jizhuan zuanli* 1:5–6. By the Song dynasty, several scholars had questioned the dates of *Zuozhuan*'s composition in general, averring that it was composed in the late Warring States period or even later. For a representative criticism, see Zheng Qiao's 鄭樵 (1104–1162) *Liu jing aolun* 4:36–39. For earlier criticisms of *Zuozhuan*, see the brief summary in Pines 2002, 26–28; for a detailed discussion, see the relevant sections of Shen Yucheng and Liu 1992 and Zhao Boxiong 2004.
55. For Kang Youwei's views, see Kang 1955; for criticism of Kang's scholarly weaknesses, see van Ess 1994, 148–50; for the intellectual background of Kang's iconoclastic assault on *Zuozhuan* and certain other classics, see Wong Young-tsu 2010.
56. See Gu 1988b, 16 (this is a summary of Gu's lectures from 1929 to 1930); for similar views, see Qian (1931) 1963. For Western scholarship parallels, see, e.g., Henri Maspero's views of *Zuozhuan* as a "historical romance" ([1927] 1965, chapter 7), or, much later, Jacques Gernet's labeling it "a semi-fictional chronicle" (1982, 86).
57. See Kern 2016; see also Zhang Hanmo 2018. Paul R. Goldin (2020, 4) avers that the oldest surviving single-authored work is probably *New Discourses* (*Xinyu* 新語), by Lu Jia 陸賈 (ca. 228–ca. 140 BCE): a sequence of twelve essays written in response to a request by Emperor Gao of Han 漢高祖 (r. 202–195 BCE) (see also Goldin and Sabattini 2020, 6).
58. For debates over the comments by a "noble man" (and Confucius) in *Zuozhuan*, compare Henry 1999 and Van Auken 2016b.
59. I have no doubt that this consideration was of primary importance for the dismissal of *Zuozhuan* as a commentary by such scholars as Zhu Xi, Liu

Fenglu, and even Kang Youwei. However, a detailed discussion of this question lies beyond the scope of the present study.

60. For a representative sample of these scholars, see Zhao Guangxian 1982; Hu Nianyi 1987; Wang He 2011; for a critical summary of these debates, see Van Auken 2016a, 19–40.
61. This peculiarity was noticed by the great commentator of *Zuozhuan*, Du Yu 杜預 (222–285) (*Chunqiu Zuozhuan zhengyi* 1:1705). See also Zhao Boxiong 1999.
62. See, e.g., Yoshimoto 1991.
63. See the brief summary in Pines 2002, 27–28.
64. These cases (*Zuozhuan*, Xiang 28.1, 30.10; Zhao 8.6, 9.4, 11.2) are summarized in Hu Nianyi 1987, 57–61. Qiao Zhizhong (2016) put forward strong arguments in favor of identifying these passages (and a few parallel passages in *Discourses of the States*) as Liu Xin's interpolation.
65. *Zuozhuan*, Wen 6.3. After a prolonged period of relative weakness in the fifth century BCE (*Shiji* 5:198–202), Qin regained power under lords Xian 秦獻公 (r. 384–362 BCE) and Xiao 秦孝公 (r. 361–338 BCE). It scored its first major victories against its eastern neighbor, Wei 魏, in 364 and 362 BCE.
66. For some examples of these interpolations, see Pines 2002, 221–26 and 233–46.
67. That Liu Xin's intervention may have influenced certain aspects of *Zuozhuan*, such as the dating of certain events, is asserted in Xu Jianwei 2017, 181–246; see also Qiao 2016. Du Yu's major intervention was the interspersing of the *Annals* with *Zuozhuan* (Durrant, Li, and Schaberg 2016, lvii).
68. For major studies that deal with the dating of *Zuozhuan* and its different layers, see, e.g., Gu 1988a (which is a summary of Gu's lectures of the 1940s); Zhang Handong 1988 (penned in the 1960s), Hu Nianyi 1987 (originally published in 1981); Zhao Guangxian 1982; Wang He 1984 and 2011. See also Pines 2002, 221–26 and 233–46, for further exploration of this topic.
69. I accept Yang Bojun's identification of Yi as a tiny polity in Shandong and not as a reference to an ethnic group (*Chunqiu Zuozhuan zhu*, 17; for a different view, see Durrant, Li, and Schaberg 2016, 15n34).
70. Whether or not this exegetical layer is identical to what Van Auken (2016a) identified as an early commentary on the *Spring and Autumn Annals* embedded in *Zuozhuan* is a matter for a separate discussion.
71. For a detailed analysis of annalistic-type records scattered throughout *Zuozhuan*, see the indispensable Durrant 2019.
72. *Zuozhuan*, Zhao 26.5 and 26.7.
73. This degree of detail characterizes several other accounts from Lord Zhao's time—e.g., those about the civil war in Song (522–520 BCE) and about the domestic turmoil in Lu (517–510 BCE). Whether or not their preservation

implies that the initial composition of *Zuozhuan* was designed to end with Lord Zhao of Lu's reign requires further study.

74. For just a few examples, see *Zuozhuan*, Zhuang 8.3, Xi 10.3, Zhao 7.9 (ghosts); Zhuang 32.3 (a deity's apparition); Zhao 8.1 (speaking stone); Zhao 19.10 (dragons' fight).

75. 晉則每一出師具列將佐，宋則每因興廢備舉六卿。 This observation by Dan Zhu is cited from *Chunqiu jizhuan zuanli* 1:5. Note that Dan Zhu viewed this reliance on primary sources by *Zuozhuan* compilers as a weakness from the point of view of its commentarial content.

76. The best studies of didactic aspects of *Zuozhuan* are Schaberg 2001 and Li Wai-yee 2007; see also Durrant, Li, and Schaberg 2016, lx–lxix.

77. For *Zuozhuan*'s contribution to China's literary tradition (and for some of its literary qualities), see Durrant, Li, and Schaberg 2016: lxxvi–lxxxiii.

78. For ideological differences among *Zuozhuan* speeches, see Pines 2002; for the text's multivalence this allowing the drawing of divergent lessons from its narratives, see Li Wai-yee 2007. For proof that at least some of the predictions must have derived from the text's original sources (as they use different calendric systems), see Wang He 1984.

79. Sima Qian attributed the composition of *Discourses of the States* to the same Zuo Qiuming who is considered the composer of *Zuozhuan* (*Shiji* 130:3300). This identification caused some scholars, most notably Kang Youwei, to assert that Liu Xin derived *Zuozhuan* from *Discourses of the States*.

80. For the clearest demonstration of the separate origins of *Discourses of the States* and *Zuozhuan*, see Zhang Yiren 1962 and 1963.

81. There are still no systematic studies of the dating of *Discourses of the States* and of the degree of editorial intervention in its content. For my preliminary observations, see Pines 2002, 39–45, and 2005b, 207–13. For an example of both texts' sharing a common third source, see Boltz 1990.

82. Note that not all scholars consider the two texts to be fundamentally different in their orientations. For an insistence on their proximity rather than difference, see Schaberg 2001.

83. Liu Xiang's preface is cited in most editions of *Stratagems*; see, e.g., *Zhanguo ce zhushi*, 1355–57. Among the component texts of *Stratagems*, Liu Xiang mentions *Affairs of the States* (*Guo shi* 國事) and *Affairs and Speeches* (*Shiyu* 事語). For a detailed study of *Stratagems*, its composition, and its nature, see He Jin 2001.

84. See, e.g., *Zhanguo ce* 7.1:201 (Qin 5), 17.1:567 (Chu 4), 18.17:649 (Zhao 1), 21.1:761 (Zhao 4), 25.1:925 (Wei 4), 25.13:939 (Wei 4) *et saepe*.

85. A classic example of this approach is the earlier partial translation of *Zuozhuan* by Burton Watson. Watson averred that "the aim of the *Zuozhuan* . . . is to edify, and its lessons are overwhelmingly political and moral in nature. . . . [Its

speeches] are generally uniform in style and express the same philosophical outlook.... [Its narratives and speeches] are marked by an attitude of underlying rationalism and humanism" (1989, xx, xxi, xxiv). Watson's selection of translated segments of *Zuozhuan* was designed precisely to prove these points.

2. *Xinian* and Zhou Historiography

1. For details, see Liu Guozhong 2016.
2. There are minor mistakes in the numbering: number 52 appears on both slips 52 and 53; slip 88 is left unnumbered, and so is the last slip (138). See Staack 2015, 166.
3. *Xinian* was published in December 2011 (Li Xueqin 2011a) and was immediately accompanied by fervent commentary and analyses published primarily online. Much of these were incorporated in Su, Wu, and Lai 2013. In 2015, the Tsinghua University team published simultaneously ten monographs on *Xinian* (not all of them of equally high quality); they were followed by a collected volume edited by Li Shoukui (2016). In addition, *Xinian* figures prominently in many other studies, such as Yang Bo (2019). Among major Japanese publications, one should mention the studies by Asano Yūichi (2012b), Fujita Katsuhisa (2013), Yoshimoto Michimasa (2013) and Kotera Atsushi (2016). In the West, the earliest publications include Pines (2014), Škrabal (2014), and Milburn (2016). In addition, several theses and dissertations have been published in China (mainland, Hong Kong, and Taiwan), and more will undoubtedly appear in the coming years.
4. It is possible that the Zhou royal chronology was applied by Jin history writers when referring to early Zhou history. This pattern in the original *Bamboo Annals* was noticed by Du Yu, who surveyed the *Bamboo Annals* shortly after their discovery (see *Chunqiu Zuozhuan zhengyi* 52:2114).
5. For Li Xueqin's arguments, see Li Xueqin 2011b, 70, and 2012b. Li's insistence on *Xinian*'s proximity to the *Bamboo Annals* may explain why the Tsinghua University editorial team, led by Li, adopted the title *Xinian* for this text. Actually, the chronological principle of organizing the materials is much less prominent in *Xinian* than in the *Annals*-like chronicles.
6. The earliest *jishi benmo* compilation was that of the Song historian Yuan Shu 袁樞 (1130–1205), who prepared a topically arranged version of *Zizhi tongjian* 資治通鑒. For a very good analysis of the *jishi benmo* style of *Xinian*, see Xu Zhaochang and Qi 2012 and Luo Yunhuan 2015; see also Liao Mingchun 2012, 51. Other scholars have proposed alternative genres for *Xinian*: Chen Minzhen 2012 affiliated it with the so-called *zhi* 志 histories; Chen Wei (2013, 48) speculated that it may be related to the now lost *Subtleties of Mr. Duo* (鐸氏

微), a text from circa 340 BCE composed by Duo Jiao 鐸椒, whereas Li Xueqin, as noted, related it to the *Bamboo Annals*.

7. The study by Li Shoukui and Xiao Pan (2015) shows that not a few characters in *Xinian* are closer to Jin (and even to earlier Western Zhou) orthography than to that of Chu. Nonetheless, even in these cases there is a clear tendency to adapt these characters to Chu's orthographic norms (285–300). Clearly, the manuscript was composed in the state of Chu.
8. For the coverage of Qin in preimperial texts, see Pines 2013.
9. This observation applies even to the state of Qi. The exploits of Lord Huan of Qi 齊桓公 (r. 685–643 BCE), which occupy pride of place in *Zuozhuan*, are given only marginal attention in *Xinian*. Qi becomes important to the authors only beginning in the sixth century BCE, when a loose Qi-Chu alliance was formed.
10. The only indirect reference to the overthrow of King Ling comes in section 18 (slip 99), where King Ling's death is referred to as his having "encountered misfortune" (*jian huo* 見禍). This caution in reporting domestic turmoil resembles the style of the *Spring and Autumn Annals* with regard to their home state of Lu (discussed in chapter 1).
11. See Chen Wei 2013, 44–45.
12. For the problematic of this dating, see Petersen 2019.
13. Guo Yongbing 2016. The only scholar who dates *Xinian* to the second half of the fourth century BCE is Yoshimoto Michimasa (2013). Yoshimoto's dating is based on his supposition that *Xinian* is based on *Zuozhuan*, which Yoshimoto elsewhere dated to the mid-fourth century BCE.
14. Goldin 2013.
15. Most notably by Martin Kern (2019, 45–49).
16. Certainly, any scholar is free to make her or his decision on whether to engage with a certain type of document or not. Unfortunately, in some cases these individual choices seem to be imposed on other colleagues. My current manuscript was originally (April 2018) submitted for consideration to the Tang Center for Early China, which immediately refused to review the manuscript because of the "complex ethical issues pertaining to professional and scholarly use of looted manuscripts." Notably, this de facto boycott of looted manuscripts is *not* announced (as of April 2020) on the Tang Center's website (http://tangcenter-columbia.org/publications/), perhaps because colleagues there realize the dubious nature of such a boycott. The clandestine nature of this boycott makes the center's avowed ethical stance look hypocritical.
17. Issues related to the forgery and authenticity of bamboo manuscripts are discussed in Hu Pingsheng 2010 and Foster 2017. For a dissenting opinion regarding the Zhejiang University collection's authenticity, see Asano and Ozawa 2013; for a counterargument, see Petersen 2019.

18. For a brief summary of scholarly doubts regarding some of the Tsinghua University manuscripts (but not *Xinian*), see Liu Chengqun 2016, 21–23 (note that Liu himself, as a graduate of Tsinghua University, dismisses all these doubts).
19. See more in Staack 2015; Wei Cide 2016, 329–32.
20. Chen Minzhen 2012.
21. In Chu manuscripts (prior to the publication of the Tsinghua collection) *ji* appears as "with" only in 6 cases while *yu* is used in 99 cases (or 127 cases if Zeng 曾 manuscripts are added). In Qin manuscripts, by contrast, *yu* is used only 4 times, while *ji* appears 313 times. See Zhang Yujin 2011, 251–81.
22. For the *Annals*' usage of *ji* and the problem it created for the *Gongyang* and *Guliang* commentators, who misunderstood it, see Van Auken 2014.
23. I cite these numbers from Wu Xueru 2019, 198 (other scholars' calculations differ, but the picture remains more or less stable; see Zhang Yujin 2011, 648–52). A major exception in the pattern of predominant resort to *yu* among the Warring States–period texts is in the military chapters of *Mozi* 墨子, where *ji* clearly predominates. Note that these chapters were in all likelihood produced in the state of Qin, which may explain this peculiarity (Yates 1979).
24. My calculations are based on Chen Yingdi 2013. For slightly different statistics, see Chen Minzhen 2015b, 50–51; Wu Xueru 2019, 200–201.
25. Lan Bixian 2016.
26. Li Meiyan 2017.
27. From a brief survey of the Chinese Text Project database, I have discovered only two occurrences of *yan shi* (one in *Mozi* and once in *Guoyu*); Li Meiyan reached similar results (2017, 159). Li does not discuss the reasons for *Xinian*'s exceptional preponderance of *yan shi*. Note that the compound *yan shi* appears in another quasi-historical text from the Tsinghua University collection, the *Chu ju*, discussed in chapter 3.
28. This conjecture for *nai* appears in Lan Bixian (2016) and is echoed for *yan* in Li Meiyan (2017).
29. This is based on my personal count. Chen Yingdi (2013) counts 70 于 and 50 於; Chen Minzhen (2015b) counts 74 于 and 54 於. Wu Xueru (2019, 207) counts 69 于 and 47 於.
30. For the usage of *yu* 于/於 particles in *Zuozhuan* and comparison with other preimperial texts, see He Leshi 2004, 81–122; see also Zhao Daming 2007, 34–158; Pines 2002, 217–20; for their usage in paleographic materials from the Warring States period, see Zhang Yujin 2011, 61–106; for the possibility of using these particles as an indicator of the texts' dates, see Zhang Huaitong 2013, 109–18. For a comprehensive discussion of *yu* particles in *Xinian*, see Zhu Qixiang 2014; Chen Minzhen 2015b; Wu Xueru 2019, 202–8. The *yu* particles have merited dozens of additional studies; for a recent comprehensive examination, see Chang 2012.

31. For the observation that Warring States–period copyists were careful in reproducing distinct *yu* particles even when their grammatical usage was identical, see Venture 2007.
32. See Li Shoukui 2014b for the first observation; Li Shoukui and Xiao 2015, 285–300, for the second.
33. In the introductory chapters, I provide only a short translation of relevant passages in *Xinian* with minimal annotations (and, except for this single case, without Chinese characters). For full annotations and the characters, see the translation in part 2 of this book.
34. Judging from *Xinian*, it is possible that the Chu historical text, which probably served as a common source for the *Xinian* and *Zuozhuan* compilers, did not contain an exact chronology of the events. The *Zuozhuan* chronology evidently derives from the *Spring and Autumn Annals*, which report only Chu's assaults on Cai but not the fate of Xi. In this case, tampering with the date of the destruction of Xi would be an easy task.
35. For the "noble man's" comments, see *Zuozhuan*, Zhuang 14.3.
36. *Lüshi chunqiu* 14.5 ("Chang gong" 長攻); *Gu lienü zhuan* 4:6–7 ("Zhen shun zhuan" 貞順傳); Kinney 2014, 49–50. Note that the *Biographies of Exemplary Women* version strengthens the dramatic effect by saying that Xi Gui committed suicide. This is patently wrong: the lady appears to have outlived King Wen, and her story—including her loyalty to the dead King Wen and to the state of Chu—is narrated in *Zuozhuan* (Zhuang 28.3). For the treatment of Xi Gui in later literary tradition, see Li Wai-yee 2014: 28–32.
37. For these locations, see *Xinian* translation in Part II of this book (section 5, notes 7–8).
38. See discussions in Schaberg 2001 *passim*; Li Wai-yee 2007, 254–76; see also Gálik 2010.
39. Lord Gong ("Respectful") is the posthumous name of Crown Prince Shensheng 申生, who opted to commit suicide after being slandered by Li Ji rather than redeeming his name and breaking his father's heart by accusing Lord Xian's beloved concubine (*Zuozhuan*, Xi 4.6).
40. For these dilemmas, see Pines 2002, 150–55.
41. Another discrepancy of section 6 is related to the sequence of Chong'er's wanderings: *Xinian* groups the states visited by Chong'er according to their attitude to the fugitive prince rather than according to the stricter chronological framework followed in *Zuozhuan*; hence the visit to Wei 衛 is placed at a later stage of his wanderings. Also, Chong'er's visit to Cao is omitted from *Xinian*.
42. Wu Zixu's story became immensely popular beginning in the Warring States period. For its evolution and fluctuations, see Johnson 1981.
43. See Wei Cide 2013, 25, and Zhang Chongyi 2017; for details about Xia Ji's image, see the introduction to the translation of *Xinian* 15 in part 2 of this book.

44. *Xinian* often adds the possessive particle *zhi* 之 between an individual's lineage name (surname) and his personal name.
45. For Shen Baoxu's heroic mission to Qin to request assistance against Wu, see *Zuozhuan*, Ding 4.3, Ding 5.5. Qin's assistance (but not Shen's role in ensuring it) is mentioned in section 19 of *Xinian*.
46. See Ziju 2012 and Su, Wu, and Lai, 2013, 601. "Rooster" may be just a river's name (Ji 雞).
47. See Johnson 1981.
48. For example, *Xinian* 12 provides information about the interstate assembly at Li 厲, conducted in 600 BCE. The assembly itself is not recorded in *Zuozhuan* or elsewhere, but *Zuozhuan* does refer to it in passing, which perplexed commentators for centuries. Surely, *Xinian* had to rely on an alternative source of information for this event. More on this is provided in the introductions to *Xinian* sections in part 2 of this book.
49. Schaberg 2011; more discussion can be found in chapter 3.
50. See also section 21, slip 114; section 22, slips 119 and 120–21.
51. For more on the naming patterns in *Xinian*, see "Note on Translations, References, and Dates."
52. Mengzi said, "The *Sheng* of Jin and *Taowu* of Chu are identical with the Lu *Spring and Autumn Annals*" (晉之《乘》、楚之《檮杌》、魯之《春秋》，一也。) (*Mengzi* 8.21 ["Li Lou (離婁) xia"]).
53. The *Zuozhuan* commentary implies that naming the ruler invariably means his condemnation (Xuan 4.2), but the accuracy of this inference is disputed (Durrant, Li, and Schaberg 2016, 608–9n82).
54. Recall that *Xinian* mentions the posthumous designation of King Dao of Chu (d. 381 BCE, referred to as King Daozhe 悼哲 in section 23, slip 127), which means that the final composition of the text took place after 381 BCE. By then, most (but not all) of the foreign rulers mentioned in *Xinian* 22–23 were already dead (see details in Pines 2016, 247–49), but the source materials of *Xinian* had not yet been updated. The *Xinian* compilers did not bother to update the rulers' names, except in the case of King Dao, who, in the original Chu annalistic record, would be mentioned as the "current king."
55. The *ganzhi* sixty-day cycle was unrelated to the month counting, and in any case in every month only a half of the *ganzhi* dates could occur. Without a month, the *ganzhi* date does not provide adequate chronological information.
56. The destruction of the scribal records of the Warring States in the aftermath of the Qin unification is lamented in *Shiji* 15:686.
57. Recall that abridgment of earlier sources was a tough task; even Sima Qian could commit major inaccuracies in the process (Nienhauser 2007).
58. Schaberg 2013, 40. Note that *shi* 史 and *shi* 使 are obvious cognates.

59. For Lü Xiang's memorandum, see *Zuozhuan*, Cheng 13.3; for similar examples, see, e.g., *Zuozhuan*, Xiang 14.1, Xiang 25.10, Zhao 26.9. Only exceptionally could a messenger display real in-depth knowledge of the past; see *Zuozhuan*, Ding 4.1.
60. For a similar view, see Huang Ziyong 2015, 248–49.

3. Zhou Historiography in Other Newly Discovered Sources

1. For a preliminary introduction of the former, see Huang Dekuan 2017; for the latter, see Li Huibo and Wu 2019 and Ke 2019.
2. Extracts from *Shi ben*, including from the "Residences" chapter, were reconstructed by Qing 清 period (1636/44–1912) philologists (see chapter 1, note 6). For the extant collection of extracts from this chapter and their comparison with the *Chu ju* manuscript, see Zhao Ping'an 2011.
3. See Asano 2012a. Zhao Ping'an (2011, 33) proposes a mid-fourth century date, which would better fit the radiocarbon analysis of one of the Tsinghua University slips, which fixed the cache's date as 305±30 BCE. It is a pity that separate radiocarbon tests were not undertaken for *Xinian* and *Chu ju*.
4. For a different division of the text, into six sections, see Fujita 2013, 2–6.
5. Chu's dynastic legend as narrated in *Chu ju* is discussed in Cook and Luo 2017, 75–92; see also Luo Dan 2015. For the stories about the progenitors of Chu's aristocratic lineages, see Lai 2013. For the custom of night sacrifice and its explanation, see Chen Wei 2012b.
6. In the first section of *Chu ju* this formula is used to introduce the name Chu (slips 3–4) and the *xi* sacrifice (slip 5). Note that *Xinian* also employs the "until now" formula to emphasize that it speaks of the origins of the contemporaneous interstate situation.
7. For a brief summary of studies related to *Chu ju*, see Shen Guangming and Yi 2017.
8. Taniguchi 2011, 29–30.
9. My translation is based primarily on Li Xueqin 2011a, 180–94; Ziju 2011; Chen Minzhen 2011, supplemented with specific studies as mentioned in the notes.
10. Kui Ying 睽郢 was the last residence of King Mu's father (and that of the victim of his patricidal plot, King Cheng) in the territory of the former Kui 夔 statelet near the current city of Zigui 秭歸 (Hubei). Wei Ying 鳶郢 was the most often used operational center of Chu kings during the Spring and Autumn period. Zhao Ping'an (2012) identifies it as Yan 鄢, in the vicinity of present-day Yicheng 宜城 (Hubei). The compound *tuxi* 徙襲 in *Chu ju* refers to the relocation of the king's residence back to one of its earlier locations.

11. Fan Ying 樊郢 was located upstream on the Han River, near the modern city of Fancheng 樊城 (part of Xiangfan 襄樊 Municipality). It served previously as a residence of King Wen of Chu.
12. Ziju (2011) and Chen Minzhen (2011) agree that "Tong Palace" is a location close to the Luo 洛 River in Henan, where, according to the legend, the righteous Shang minister Yi Yin 伊尹 detained the second king of the Shang dynasty, Taijia 太甲, for reeducation. If this identification is correct, it may be related to the peak of Chu's territorial expansion northward toward the Yellow River basin, around 606 BCE, as reported in *Zuozhuan* (Xuan 3.3).
13. The rebellion of the Ruo'ao 若敖 lineage led by Dou Jiao 鬬椒 in 605 BCE was a major instance of aristocratic turmoil in Chu history (for details, see *Zuozhuan*, Xuan 4.3). The location of Zheng Wilderness (烝之野, or 烝野 in *Zuozhuan*, Xuan 4.3) is disputed.
14. The Heir Child King is King Kang's son, who was assassinated by his uncle, King Ling. He did not receive an official posthumous name in the Chu ancestral temple and is known posthumously by his burial place as King Jia'ao 郟敖.
15. The Qian Stream (Qianxi or Ganxi 乾溪) is located near Bozhou 亳州, Anhui. This location was close to the territory of Wu, the major enemy of Chu from the time of King Ling onward. The location of Zhanghua Terrace was disputed for a long time, but from *Chu ju* it is clear that it was located near the Qian Stream.
16. Mei Ying is identified by Ziju (2011) as a location near Mount Mei in Jinsai County (Anhui), 金寨縣梅山. This location was the focus of Wu assaults on Chu in 511 BCE, as recorded in *Zuozhuan* (Zhao 31.4). The location of E Ying is disputable; Chen Minzhen (2011) suggests that it should be near the modern city of Wuchang 武昌 (part of Wuhan, Hubei). If this identification is correct, this means a radical retreat by King Zhao to the southwest, away from the Wu armies. Wei Ying, in contrast, would mean a move radically northward up the Han River. For a series of less-convincing identifications of these placenames, see Zhang Shuo and Xiao 2013.
17. Helu's invasion of Chu and the conquest of Ying happened in 506 BCE. The subsequent relocation of King Zhao to locations in the Huai River basin reflects the weakening of Wu and a renewed assertiveness of Chu leaders in the early fifth century BCE (Ziju 2011).
18. See *Zuozhuan* (Ding 6.4). For the location of (Upper) Ruo near the Yicheng area, see Huang Jinqian 2017a. For an attempt to explain *Chu ju*'s silence on this essential move, see Niu 2013.
19. This simple understanding escaped the attention of some scholars, who tried—somewhat pathetically in my view—to reconcile *Chu ju* with the received texts by arguing that they speak more or less of the same events (see, e.g., Zhang Shuo and Xiao 2013).

20. See Shou 2011. The same scenario, with certain modifications, is supported by Taniguchi 2011 and Xin 2017, 1–18. Shou Bin noted that a similar short list of rulers and their dwellings existed in the state of Qin; currently it is preserved as an appendix to the "Basic Annals of the First Emperor" in *Records of the Historian* (*Shiji* 6:285–90). This parallel, however, misleads Shou Bin to assume that most of the X + Ying locations were palaces in the vicinity of the major capital, Ying. This should not be so: the kings of Chu appear to have been much more peripatetic than the lords of Qin, and they were willing to depart from the capital for a considerable time and distance (for tentative locations of various "Yings," see notes 10–16 in the preceding).
21. Recall that Wei Ying was located near Yan 鄢 (Zhao Ping'an 2012), slightly to the north of the Upper Ruo to where the capital Ying was relocated.
22. Whether or not Ji'nan City served as Chu's capital in the Spring and Autumn period, or whether it acquired this function only at the beginning of the Warring States period, is a subject of considerable controversy (see, e.g., Guo Dewei 1999, 20–45; Xin 2017, 1–18). Limitations of space prevent me from fully addressing these debates; suffice it to say that I accept Guo's suggestion that the relocation of Ying to the Upper Ruo was a temporary measure, after which the capital shifted back to the vicinity of the Yangzi (i.e., to Ji'nan City?) (Guo Dewei 1999, 39).
23. Zhao Ping'an 2011, 33.
24. For the latter, see *Liji* IV.1:91 ("Qu li shang" 曲禮上).
25. Schaberg 2011. Many insightful observations about the anecdotes are scattered throughout van Els and Queen 2017.
26. Schaberg 2011, 394–95.
27. For the nonanecdotal layers of *Zuozhuan*, see Pines 2017a, 264–70.
28. For the progressive detachment of anecdotes from their original setting, and for the cessation of the anecdotes' circulation after the Western Han, see van Els 2017. For blatant anachronisms, see Henry 2003. For attributing the same speech to different personages, see, e.g., an important speech that is normally attributed to the Qi courtier Yan Ying 晏嬰 (d. 500 BCE) (*Zuozhuan*, Zhao 20.6; *Yanzi chunqiu* 1.12 and 7.7; and the *Jing Gong nüe* 競公瘧 manuscript from the Shanghai Museum collection [Pu 2007]). Another of the Shanghai Museum manuscripts, *Bao Shuya yu Xi Peng zhi jian* 鮑叔牙與隰朋之諫 (Lin 2008), clearly borrows from Yan Ying's remonstrance but attributes it to the courtiers of Lord Huan of Qi (r. 685–643 BCE). For other examples related to Yan Ying, see Liu Jiao 2018.
29. This is the case, for instance, of the *Jian da wang po han 柬大王泊旱 anecdote from the Shanghai Museum collection: its discussion of the importance of ritually appropriate sacrifices to avert troubles recurs in many texts starting

with *Zuozhuan* and is not necessarily related to the avowed protagonist, King Jian of Chu 楚簡王 (r. ca. 431–405 BCE) (see details in Chen Jian [2005] 2013).
30. Chen Fengfen 2007, 240.
31. Chen Wei 2007. By now it is accepted that the first character should be read as Chen 陳 rather than Shen 申.
32. Yuasa 2017, 89–112. Yuasa in turn utilized earlier studies, especially the rearrangements in Chen Wei 2007. See also the more recent study in Krijgsman and Vogt 2019.
33. Shěn was a Chu County, but its location and the identity of its governor were hotly contested (see Yang Bojun's gloss in *Zuozhuan*, Xuan 12.2d:728–29). The *Zhuang wang ji cheng* anecdote may resolve this controversy: the Governor of Shěn (who led the central army of Chu during the Bi 邲 battle in 597 BCE) is clearly not Sunshu Ao 孫叔敖. Whether or not Shěn County was located in the territory of the statelet of Shěn, near modern Linquan County 臨泉縣, remains to be seen.
34. The term "Wuyi bells" probably refers to an exceptional set of bells, akin to those cast by King Jing of Zhou 周景王 (r. 544–520 BCE) (*Zuozhuan*, Zhao 21.1; *Guoyu* 3.5–6 ["Zhou yu xia" 周語下]). *Wuyi* 無射 is a musical term: it is the name one of the twelve ancient modes (十二音律).
35. *Chang* 嘗 sacrifices were ancestral sacrifices normally conducted in autumn (but perhaps in spring as well). "Guest" refers here to the diplomats (or rulers) of the neighboring polities who were expected to arrive at King Zhuang's court to express their submission.
36. For this line of analysis, see Yuasa 2017, 97–100. Yuasa avers that the anecdote could be hinting that the casting of the Wuyi bells was a manifestation of King Zhuang's hubris, which caused Chu's ensuing decline.
37. Chen Wei 2007; Ebine 2012; Yuasa 2017.
38. *Zuozhuan*, Xiang 26.6a.
39. Since Chu's rulers assumed the title of kings, their appointees to the position of local governors were normally designated "dukes" (*gong* 公) in an emulation of the Zhou royal custom.
40. *Zuozhuan*, Zhao 8.6.
41. The Shanghai Museum anecdote refers to the major protagonist by his later title, the Duke of Chen, adding his appellative Zihuang, whereas in *Zuozhuan* he appears under the lineage plus personal name as Chuanfeng Xu. The anecdote refers to the Zheng leader Huang Jie as Sir Huang (Huangzi) and locates the military encounter between Chu and Zheng in the place tentatively identified by Chen Wei as Jisui rather than Chengjun. For possible explanations of these discrepancies, see Yuasa 2017, 103.
42. See Durrant, Li, and Schaberg 2016, 1442n434.

43. For a different interpretation of the *Shen gong* anecdote, see Yuasa 2017, 109–11. Krijgsman and Vogt (2019, 484), following Chen Wei (2007), also read the *Shen gong* anecdote as closer to *Zuozhuan* and interpret *zhi* 致 as an abridgment of *zhi si* 致死, translating the sentences as "If I had known that you would become the ruler, then perhaps I would have taken it further." I think it is far-fetched and imposes the *Zuozhuan* narrative on the entirely different type of exchange between the Duke of Chen and King Ling in the *Shen gong* anecdote.
44. See, e.g., Li Feng 2006 (for geography); Li Feng 2008 (for administrative history); Kern 2009 (for cultural history).
45. Falkenhausen 1993a, 146–56. For "auspicious words," see Xu Zhongshu (1936) 1988.
46. Falkenhausen 1993a, 152.
47. See Goldin 2008. There are at least five inscriptions that explicitly mention campaigns against Chu (the Shi Qiang-pan 史墻盤 [CHANT 10175], Zuoce Zeling-gui 乍冊夨令簋 [4300–4301], Guobo-gui 過伯簋 [3907], Hongshu-gui 鴻叔簋 [3950], and Lai-pan 逨盤 [Cook and Goldin 2016, 230–38]), but none refers to the Zhou armies' ultimate defeat. To be sure, it is possible that each of these inscriptions refers to an earlier and more successful campaign of King Zhao against Chu in about 960 BCE, but the silence on the subsequent defeat cannot be accidental.
48. A series of inscriptions by Qin rulers from the eighth to fifth centuries BCE, made on bronze vessels and chime stones, provide a fascinating glimpse into their assertive mind-set and are revealing of Qin's proximity to Zhou ritual culture. See the translation and analysis in Kern 2000, 59–105, and further discussion in Pines 2005–2006, 18–22. The inscriptions on the vessels cast by the sixth century BCE Chu aristocrats discovered in the late 1970s in Xiasi 下寺 cemetery (Xichuan 淅川, Henan) are translated in Falkenhausen 1988, 1076–1116. For these inscriptions as indicative of the aristocrats' excessive self-confidence, see Pines 2002, 173–75. For a general overview of Eastern Zhou bronze inscriptions, see Mattos 1997.
49. The Qin inscriptions are discussed in note 48; for the new information about Wu history, see Qi 2017; for Zhongshan inscriptions and their value, see Wu Xiaolong 2017.
50. See, e.g., Wang Zewen 2002.
51. I modify David W. Pankenier's translation in Cook and Goldin 2016, 263–65 (see there also the introduction to the bells). In addition, I consulted Chen Shuangxin 2000.
52. For designations of rulers in Jin inscriptions, see Wang Shimin 2017, 367–401, especially 377–78, 393–95 (this is a reprint of Wang's articles of 1983 and 2012); see also Han Wei 2010.

53. On this, see Zhu Fenghan 2014.
54. For the style of the bells, see Cook and Goldin 2016, 263. For the expression "Six Armies of the West" (with its unmistakable Western Zhou flavor) and the debates around its meaning, see Zhao Xiaolong 2009.
55. *Zuozhuan*, Xi 28.3h. Some scholars rejected this interpretation of the inscription's date because the tenth day of the fifth month in 632 BCE was not within the first lunar quarter, which is commonly identified as pertaining to "initial auspiciousness" *chu ji* 初吉 (see, e.g., Feng 1997). As noted by Bai Guangqi (1997), the discrepancy simply shows that the erstwhile identification of "initial auspiciousness" with the first lunar quarter is not necessarily correct.
56. See Maspero (1927) 1965, chapter 7.
57. See Falkenhausen 1993b.
58. Mi Jia (Mi 嬭 is a native transcription for 羋, Chu's royal clan name) had an important role in the life of the state of Zeng/Sui after the death of her husband, Marquis Bao. For a preliminary analysis of the inscription on her bells (嬭加編鐘), see Guo Changjiang et al. 2019. One of Mi Jia's betrothal vessels, with the inscription "the king of Chu makes the betrothal gift to Mi Jia, [the wife] of the second-born Sui [ruler]" (楚王媵隨仲嬭加) was plundered around 2010 and already then had attracted considerable scholarly attention (Guo Changjiang et al. 2019, 15n4). Similarly inscribed vessels have been discovered from Mi Jia's tomb (Tomb 169 at Zaoshulin 棗樹林 cemetery), proving her identity—and by inference the fact that Sui and Zeng are two names of a single polity—beyond doubt (see Li Yun 2019). For a very good introduction to the Zeng-Sui debates and to major Zeng discoveries prior to the discovery of Mi Jia vessels, see Venture 2017.
59. The inscription's content was published in the 2014.4 issue of *Jianghan kaogu* (Hubei sheng 2014). The same issue contained several discussions of the inscription by eminent paleographers. Later reconstructions were proposed by the Tsinghua University team (Qinghua daxue chutu wenxian dushuhui 2014) and by Li Xueqin (2015), on whose readings my translation relies. I provide additional notes only in cases in which an alternative reading may considerably alter our understanding of the inscriptions' content.
60. Reading the character as 庀 following Wei Dong 2016b, 62.
61. Most scholars read the name Boshi 伯适 as Bo Kuo 伯括, a reference to Nangong Kuo 南宮括, an important assistant to the Zhou dynastic founders.
62. The last character of this sentence, 啻, has been interpreted by some scholars (e.g., Huang Jinqian 2017b, 79) as standing for 帝, in which case *shangdi* 上帝 would be Lord on High. This reading does not, however, make sense grammatically, because in the sentence "Elder Kuo, Lord on High" the verb would be missing. My reading of the disputed character as *yong* 庸 in the meaning of being enrolled or employed follows Li Xueqin 2015, 18.

63. Following Li Xueqin 2015, 18, I read Nangong 南公 as standing for Nangong 南宫, i.e., Nangong Kuo. It is possible of course that the inscription refers to one of Kuo's offspring, the real founder of the state of Zeng. See more in Wang Zewen 2015, 106–8.
64. The "confluence of the rivers" (汭土) refers to the geographical area of Suizhou (where the statelet of Zeng was located), a place between the Huai River and the basin of the Yangzi and Han Rivers. Xia was the name of the Han River near its entrance into the Yangzi (Wei Dong 2016b, 61–62).
65. Reading the character 譶 as standing for *qi* 戚 (being amicable), as in Qinghua daxue chutu wenxian dushuhui 2014. Huang Jinqian 2017b, 80, proposes reading it as *jiao* 驕 (arrogant), referring to Chu's arrogance, which does not make sense here.
66. Gao Chongwen (2015) reads this phrase literally as referring to the route of Wu's incursion: first westward, along the Huai River line, and then southward into the Nanyang 南陽 Basin and further toward the Chu capital, Ying. For reading 加於楚 as standing for 加亂於楚 (adding turmoil to Chu—i.e., making a military incursion), see Wei Dong 2016b, 62.
67. Reading 誤 as 虞 (here, to be concerned, worried), following Qinghua daxue chutu wenxian dushuhui 2014. An alternative reading would be that the mandate was about to be mistakenly [transmitted to Wu].
68. This tension is analyzed in Khayutina 2019.
69. *Zuozhuan*, Ding 4.3e.
70. Actually, the first real appearance of Chu in the pages of *Zuozhuan* is related to its campaign against Sui in 706 BCE (*Zuozhuan*, Huan 6.2). After this campaign Sui retained its nominal independence but became a Chu satellite. That Sui leaders identified their country's raison d'être as counterbalancing Chu is evident from the inscription on the Mi Jia bells (Guo Changjiang et al. 2019). Interestingly, the fact that the inscription was authored by a Chu princess betrothed to the Sui ruler does not alleviate the anti-Chu sentiments.
71. The Sui leaders imply that only if Wu succeeds in stabilizing its rule over the Chu realm will Sui submit to Wu.
72. *Zuozhuan*, Ding 4.3e. Note that *Xinian* 15 also records King Zhao's fleeing to Sui to escape Wu invaders.
73. *Zuozhuan*, Ding 4.3e.
74. Li Xueqin 2015 proposes to date the inscription at 497 BCE. Even if this dating is incorrect, there are many reasons to date it in the early fifth century BCE (Xu Shaohua 2014, 77–78).
75. Aside from the Mi Jia inscriptions, an earlier piece of evidence for the identity of Zeng and Sui is a halberd head bearing the inscription "Minister of War of Sui" (隨司馬), excavated at Tomb 21 of Wenfengta (Zeng) cemetery during the 2012–2013 excavation season (Venture 2017, 25).

76. This cautious treading among Zhou, Chu, and Wu may be compared with the equally delicate balancing acts by the contemporaneous Cai 蔡 leaders, whose inscriptions were unearthed in the 1950s. See more in Falkenhausen 1988, 1126–47; Wang Zewen 2002, 69–86.
77. See the insightful discussion in Goldin 2017; see also Goldin 2008.
78. For some examples, see Pines 2005a and 2008; Allan 2016.
79. For what appears to be a direct citation, see *Han Feizi* 39:384 ("Nan 難 4") versus *Zuozhuan*, Huan 17.8, and discussion in Pines 2002, 29–30 (more generally, much of the "Nan 4" chapter can be read as *Zuozhuan*'s exegesis). For what appears to be a slight abridgement of *Zuozhuan* or of related materials, compare, e.g., *Han Feizi* 14:107 ("Jian, jie, shi chen" 姦劫弑臣) and *Zuozhuan*, Zhao 1.12 and Xiang 25.2.
80. For example, in chapter 10 ("Shi guo" 十過), *Han Feizi* confuses the death of Lord Huan of Qi and that of King Wuling of Zhao 趙武靈王 (r. 325–299 BCE) (it was the latter, not the former, who was starved to death by his underlings; see *Han Feizi* 10:74). Elsewhere in the same chapter (p. 66), Han Fei confuses Zhi the Elder (Zhi Bo 智伯 or 知伯), named Yao 瑤, who was killed in 453 BCE after the epic struggle with the Zhao lineage, with another Zhi the Elder, who fought the Fan 范 and Zhonghang 中行 lineages in the civil war of 497–470 BCE. The latter was either Yao's grandfather Zhi Li 知躒, or, possibly, Yao's father, Zhi Jia 知甲. The confusion about Zhi Bo is ubiquitous in Warring States–period texts (see, e.g., *Zhanguo ce* 18.4:618 [Zhao 1]).
81. For instance, in one anecdote Confucius's rival in plotting to deprive him of political power suggests distracting "Lord Ai of Lu" (魯哀公) from political matters by presenting him with singing girls (*Han Feizi* 31.51 ["Nei chu shuo xia" 內儲說下]). This is an obvious anachronism: Lord Ai died in 468 BCE, and his posthumous name could not have been known during Confucius's lifetime (recall that Confucius died in 479 BCE). Elsewhere, Han Fei treats Marquis Wen of Wei 魏文侯 (r. 445–396 BCE) and Marquis Su of Zhao 趙肅侯 (r. 349–326 BCE) as contemporaries (*Han Feizi* 22:173; "Shui lin shang" 說林上). The existence of such blatant anachronisms is indicative of the overall neglect of even a semblance of historical accuracy in some—but not all!—of the *Han Feizi* anecdotes.
82. Exceptionally, the text (slip 10) also records teachers and aides of the famous prime minister of the state of Zheng 鄭, Zichan 子產 (d. 522 BCE). This peculiarity, in addition to the text's orthography, which is reminiscent of that of the "Three Jin" area (i.e., the state of Jin and its successors, Wei, Han, and Zhao), caused the Tsinghua team to believe that the text may somehow be related to Zichan (Li Xueqin 2012a, 156).
83. Han Yujiao 2013. Han provides traces of similar lists in received texts (pp. 91–92).

84. See more in Kuroda 2013, 98–99.
85. See, e.g., Durrant, Li, and Schaberg 2016, xxiii–xxv.
86. Jiu 咎 in Jiufan stands for jiu 舅 (maternal uncle). Recall that Hu Yan was a maternal uncle of Lord Wen of Jin.
87. The oddest case is Nangong Kuo, minister to King Wen of Zhou, mentioned in connection with the Sui/Zeng bells (note 61). He is referred to as Nangong Kuo (or Shi), as Bo Shi (i.e., Shi the elder, which is also the reference to Nangong in Marquis Yu of Zeng's inscription), and, possibly, by the third name of Nangong Yao 夭 (see more in Kuroda 2013, 91–92). Cheng Hao (2016), in a pathetic attempt to defend the historicity of *Liang chen*, argues that Nangong Yao was Nangong Kuo's son and the founder of the Zeng polity. Cheng fails to explain why, then, this personage is mentioned among the leading ministers of King Wen, during which time Nangong Kuo's son could not have been a major political figure.
88. For this suggestion, see Yang Mengsheng 2014. For treating *Liang chen* as an ordinary historical text, see, e.g., Guo Li 2015; Cheng Hao 2016; Yang Bo 2019, 160–63.
89. In an insightful discussion, Mark E. Lewis analyzes the rationalization of bronze inscriptions in the "Ji tong" (祭統) chapter of the *Records of Rites* (*Liji* 禮記). In Lewis's view, the text's assertion that the inscription simultaneously "generated honor for the ancestors and the caster" can "offer insights into the ideas that informed a text like the *Zuozhuan*" (forthcoming, chapter 1). This observation surely deserves further exploration.
90. Some scholars have considered the so-called *Annals* from Tomb 11, Shuihudi, as a historical text (Mittag 2003; Shaughnessy 2014). As mentioned in note 10 of the introduction, this text should probably be read as the personal calendar of the tomb occupant rather than as a historical text. The fact that the so-called *Annals* normally record a single event per year and provide details only with regard to the occupant's and his family's life shows that the text was not prepared as a historical work.
91. *Shiji* 15:686.

4. Beyond Sima Qian

1. Du Yu, who reviewed the *Bamboo Annals* shortly after their discovery, was the first to notice that this text demonstrates the incorrectness of Sima Qian's chronology of the Wei 魏 ruling house (*Chunqiu Zuozhuan zhengyi* 60:2187–88). For an overview of chronological inaccuracies in the early to middle Warring States–period sections of *Records of the Historian*, which were corrected thanks to the *Bamboo Annals*, see Yang Kuan 1998, 14–16.

2. Li Feng 2006.
3. *Shiji* 4:143–49.
4. *Guoyu* 1.3–5 ("Zhou yu shang" 周語上).
5. The only important piece of information about Western Zhou history, ignored by Sima Qian, is the letter of Prince Zhao 王子朝 to regional lords, cited in *Zuozhuan*, which states that the regional lords intervened in the royal government before allowing King Xuan to assume power but does not specify the nature of this intervention. *Zuozhuan*, Zhao 26.9.
6. 幽王既亡，有共伯和者攝行天子事，非二相共和也。(*Jin shu* 51:1432).
7. The identification of Gong as a regional polity and Bo as earl was habitual among commentators and is routinely followed by a majority of scholars into the present. The problem of this line of interpretation is that it relies primarily on the allegedly Warring States–period text *Lu Lianzi* 魯連子, cited in the gloss to the *Records of the Historian*. However, as I argue in note 11, the cited passage clearly cannot come from a Warring States–period text but is much later and is not at all reliable. An alternative, and in my mind more plausible, identification of Gong He would be with a noble from within the Zhou royal domain—e.g., Bo Hefu 伯龢父, as discussed in Satō 2017 (see also Shaughnessy 1991, 272–73). However, as demonstrated by Satō and by Su Jianzhou (in Su, Wu, and Lai 2013, 24–28), this identification leaves many questions unresolved.
8. 周厲之難，天子曠絕，而天下皆來謂矣。(*Lüshi chunqiu* 21.1).
9. *Lüshi chunqiu* 14.6; *Zhuangzi* 28:765 ("Rang wang" 讓王). *Lu Lianzi* is cited in Lu Deming's 陸德明 (ca. 550–630) *Jingdian shiwen* 經典釋文 (28:25).
10. *Records of the Historian* mentions that Lord Wu, whose personal name was He 和, rose to power by murdering his elder brother, the crown prince, who was posthumously named Gong the Elder (or the Earl of Gong) 共伯. This conflation of Gong the Elder and his brother He may be Sima Qian's attempt to accommodate the scattered information about Gong He from the Warring States–period literature without properly understanding who he was. Note that the dates of Lord Wu of Wei in *Records of the Historian* rule out the possibility that he could have participated in the events of 841 BCE. For an interesting but somewhat speculative attempt to defend this interpretation while correcting some of Sima Qian's inaccuracies, see Chao Fulin 1992.
11. Zhang Shoujie states, "*Lu Lianzi* says, 'Gongcheng County of Wei Prefecture is the original state of the Zhou Earl of Gong. The Earl of Gong was named He. He was fond of practicing benevolence and righteousness, and the regional lords considered him worthy. King Li of Zhou lacked the Way, and the capital dwellers made troubles; the king fled to Zhi. The regional lords upheld He to make him fulfill the tasks of the Son of Heaven. This was the first year under the reign date *gonghe*'" (衛州共城縣本周共伯之國也。共伯名和，好行仁義，諸侯

賢之。周厲王無道，國人作難，王奔於彘，諸侯奉和以行天子事，號曰'共和'元年。 [*Shiji* 4:144]). The date of this extract can be deduced from its usage of the name Gongcheng County 共城縣: this county was established only in 596 CE. Besides, the very nature of the cited extract is that of a gloss, perhaps related to the short statement in the original *Lu Lianzi*, according to which "Gong Bo later returned to [his] state" (共伯後歸于國; cited from *Jingdian shiwen* 經典釋文 28:25).

12. See the comprehensive summary in Satō 2017.
13. *Hanshu* 20:899.
14. See Zhang Shoujie's gloss in *Shiji* 4:144. For Cui Shu, see *Cui dongbi yishu*, p. 237.
15. For summaries of the debates, see Chao Fulin 1992; Tao Xinghua 2013a; Satō 2017.
16. Note that the editorial team of *Xinian* reads Song 宋 as *zong* 宗 (referring to Gong Bo He's ancestral home). For my disagreement with this interpretation, see *Xinian* 1, note 7.
17. Li Ling 2016, 170.
18. See Tao Xinghua 2013a, 2013b, 2014. For somewhat similar reasoning, see Wang Hongliang 2016. For a more fanciful interpretation of the events, which departs both from *Xinian* and *Records of the Historian* and claims that the single power holder in the aftermath of the overthrow of King Li was the Duke of Shao, see Ma Wenzeng 2018.
19. Li Xueqin 2011b; Niu 2012.
20. Satō 2017, 26n1.
21. Li Feng 2006, 193–278. For earlier studies, see, e.g., Wang Yuzhe 1986; Yoshimoto 1990b; Chao Fulin 1991. See also the summary of these and other studies in Shim 2016, 129–38. Yoshimoto Michimasa updated his account in Yoshimoto 2017.
22. *Guoyu* 10.1 ("Jin yu 晉語 4"); *Zuozhuan*, Xuan 12.2; *Lüshi chunqiu* 22.3:1507 ("Yi si" 疑似).
23. *Guoyu* 1.3–1.10 ("Zhou yu shang"), 7.1 ("Jin yu 1"), 16.1 ("Zheng yu" 鄭語); *Lüshi chunqiu* 22.3:1507.
24. *Zuozhuan*, Zhao 26.9.
25. *Chunqiu Zuozhuan zhengyi* 52:2114.
26. *Chunqiu Zuozhuan zhengyi* 52:2114. Note that this interpretation considers Xie both as a place-name and as a derogatory designation of Yuchen (King of Discord).
27. For "Zheng yu," see *Guoyu* 16.1:475, and more in Chen Minzhen and Pines 2018, 12.
28. Judging from *Xinian* and the *Bamboo Annals*, the more likely designation of this king would be King Hui from Xie, but since some sources refer to him as

King Xie (reading Xie as King Hui's designation rather than as the place-name of his capital), I am intermittently following this convention.
29. Shim Jae-hoon makes strong arguments in favor of identifying this location in the Nanyang 南陽 Basin, to the southeast of the Western Zhou capital; see Shim 2016, 141–45; 2017.
30. Li Xueqin 2011a, 139.
31. For two representative articles that propose these views, see, respectively, Xu Shaohua 2016 and Li Ling 2016.
32. See Wei Dong 2013.
33. Zhu Fenghan 2016.
34. In Su, Wu, and Lai 2013, which collects early debates over this phrase, the summary covers no fewer than twenty-five pages (77–102). The plain reading of the text as dating the relocation to 738 BCE is supported, in addition to the scholars cited by Su and his coeditors, in Yoshimoto 2013, 16n18 (this dating supports Yoshimoto's early study [1990b]); see also Wang Hui 2013a and Shim 2016.
35. See Li Ling 2016; Zhu Fenghan 2016; Xu Shaohua 2016.
36. Sima Qian's endorsement of Lord Wu of Wei may well be related to the tradition in the Mao Commentary of the *Canon of Poems*, which attributes several poems either to Lord Wu directly ("The Guests Are Taking Their Seats" [賓之初筵] and "Grave" [抑]; Mao 220 and 256, respectively) or to his admirers praising his virtues ("Little Bay of the Qi" [淇奧] and "Pole Banners" [干旄]; Mao 55 and 53, respectively). As mentioned in note 10, the discussion of Lord Wu in *Records of the Historian* is highly confused.
37. Cheng Pingshan 2015; for more see also Chen Minzhen and Pines 2018, 20.
38. See additional in Chen Minzhen and Pines 2018, 17–21. In that text we also show that the statement in Kong Yingda's subcommentary cited earlier about the simultaneous rule of two kings in Zhou may be more related to Kong's personal interpretation than to the text of the *Bamboo Annals*. See Li Feng 2006, 349, on this last point.
39. See more in Xu Jianwei 2017, 187–96.
40. *Zuozhuan*, Zhao 26.9.
41. See the gloss in Durrant, Li, and Schaberg 2016, 1662–1663n1083. The possibility that Prince Zhao is indirectly responsible for the abundance of Zhou-related texts among heretofore published Tsinghua University documents cannot be dismissed.
42. In 2019, archaeologists unearthed twenty-nine tombs near the city of Nanyang, Henan (a strategically important area of the state of Chu). Although all the tombs had been plundered, their shape and the remnants of mortuary objects allow a tentative conclusion that they belonged to the members of the Zhou elite who had migrated to the state of Chu. In a preliminary report,

speculation was made that the cemetery may have belonged to followers of Prince Zhao (Gui and Yuan 2019).

43. An area near the Yi River 伊河 in the vicinity of the Zhou eastern capital, Luoyang.
44. *Zuozhuan*, Xi 22.4.
45. See more in Wang He 1984.
46. See, e.g., Liu Guozhong 2013, 178; Wang Hui 2013a, 78n4.
47. *Shiji* 15:686 and 5:179.
48. Pines 2005–2006. For broader engagement with Qin historical records and their reliability, see Yoshimoto 1995 and Fujita 1997 (the latter focuses primarily on Warring States–period Qin records and not on the earliest sections of Qin history).
49. See, e.g., Heather 2010, 1–35.
50. Meng 1936.
51. Fu (1933) 2003.
52. For debates about Qin origins, see Falkenhausen 2008; Liu Yu 2016. The list of the "eastern" traits of Qin culture is based on Zhao Huacheng 2014 and Liang Yun 2017. For the abundance of markedly "eastern" (i.e., Shang-related) indicators in early Qin burials, see Yin Qun 2014; Liang Yun 2017. In light of these studies, Cao Dingyun (2017, 137) plainly argues that "the eastern origins" theory is now "overwhelmingly accepted by the scholarly community." Nonetheless, one should keep in mind Yin Qun's sober caution that archaeological studies are still unable to fully resolve the riddle of Qin's origins (2017, 291).
53. The other is section 5 (discussed in chapter 2). That section, however, is focused on a much shorter time span within the reign of a single Chu king; hence, perhaps, the editors did not feel it important to add the dates. In the case of *Xinian* 3, the absence of a precise chronology is less expected.
54. For Wugeng's numerous names in the early Zhou sources, and for the link between the Luzi Geng 彔子耿 of *Xinian* and Wugeng, see Lu Yihan 2013b.
55. See the discussion in Xing 2013.
56. A possible reconciliation of *Xinian* and *Shiji* is adopting Lu Yihan's (2013c) proposal to distinguish the unnamed "three supervisors" from the rebellious brothers of the Duke of Zhou, who are, after all, not referred to as "supervisors" in *Records of the Historian*.
57. *Mengzi* 6.9.
58. Li Xueqin 2011a, 142n8; see more in Tian 2012, 38–39; Su, Wu, and Lai 2013, 168–72; Zhang Tian'en 2014: 108–9.
59. For recent (2009–2011) discoveries that strengthen the notion of the impact of Shang material culture on Qin burials, see Zhao Huacheng 2014, 70; Zaoqi Qin wenhua lianhe kaogudui 2012. See also the summaries in Liang Yun 2017 and Yin Qun 2017.

60. See Li Xueqin 2011d.
61. Teng Mingyu 2014, 80–82. The evidence for two coexisting cultures comes only from the middle period of the Maojiaping settlement (ca. sixth to fifth centuries BCE), but it is possible that the producers of the so-called Maojiaping B-type pottery occupied the settlement from the beginning, yet their early remnants cannot be found because they practiced different burial customs from those of the Maojiaping A (Zhou-related, probably Qin) settlers.
62. On this point, see Liang Yun 2017, 42.
63. *Shiji* 28:1358.
64. See more in Wang Hongjun 2013.
65. See Mawangdui Hanmu boshu zhengli xiaozu 1983, 32. The editors of the manuscript originally believed that Shangyan refers to Shangyu 商於, a locality in the Dan River 丹水 valley, the southeastern boundary of Qin during the Warring States period (33n19). Note that the parallel statement in the received *Zhanguo ce* version says, "Qin would not depart from [its eastern stronghold,] the Yao Pass" (秦不出殽塞) (*Zhanguo ce* 29.14:1122 [Yan 1]). In light of *Xinian* 3, it is clear that Shangyan in Su Qin's anecdote represents an ancestral locality of the Qin ruling lineage.
66. For such a dismissal of *Xinian*, see, e.g., Li Qingling 2017 (esp. p. 183).
67. Besides, if the chronology of King Ping's relocation to the east in *Xinian* 2, discussed in the preceding, is correct, then "Qin Zhong" should stand for Lord Wen of Qin 秦文公 (r. 765–716 BCE).
68. See Wu's gloss in Su, Wu, and Lai 2013, 184–86.
69. This is the date of the last entry in *Zuozhuan*. Note that its final sentence jumps to 453 BCE.
70. See Pines 2018b.
71. For a brief introduction to the coverage of Yue history, see Milburn 2010, 4–23. To her sources one may add a lengthy quasi-historical piece, *Yue gong qi shi* 越公其事, published in the seventh volume of the Tsinghua manuscripts (Li Xueqin 2017, 115–51). For its comparison with the accounts about Goujian in the Wu and Yue sections of *Discourses of the States*, see Li Shoukui 2017; Yang Bo 2019, 123–29.
72. 四分天下而有之。(*Mozi*, V.19:221 ["Fei gong xia" 非攻下]).
73. See *Shiji* 41:1747.
74. The transfer of the capital to Langye (which can also be transcribed 琅邪, 瑯邪, or 瑯琊) is hinted at in a variety of Han and later texts, in addition to the direct record in the *Current Bamboo Annals*. Although none of these texts is reliable in its own right, and although they disagree about the precise date of relocation, there is currently scholarly consensus that the relocation did take place, probably around 468 BCE (see Ren Huibin 2014; see also Xin 2017, 19–108). For an intriguing, although not necessarily convincing, hypothesis that

the Langye to which Yue moved the capital does not refer to the current eponymous location in southern Shandong but to another location near present-day Lianyungang City 連雲港 (Jiangsu), see Zhang Zhili, Peng, and Liang 2010, and Ma Xueqin 2008, 217–25.

75. Chen Minzhen 2017.
76. The relocation of Yue's capital back to the south, to the former Wu capital, is recorded in the *Bamboo Annals* cited in a gloss to *Shiji* (41:1747). It is partly confirmed by the inscription on the dagger axe of King Chaxu of Yue (Yue Wang Chaxu-*ge* 越王差徐戈) (Xiong 2014).
77. Pines 2018b.
78. Han Qian and Zhao Ji are heads of the Han and Zhao polities; Wei Ji is the future Marquis Wu of Wei 魏武侯 (r. 395–370 BCE); Lord Yi of Yue is King Yi of Yue (越王翳, r. ca. 410–375 BCE).
79. Marquis Dai of Qi is Lord Kang 齊康公 (r. 404–379 BCE), the last ruler of the Jiang 姜 clan in Qi. Marquis Yan of Lu is Lord Mu 魯穆公 (r. ca. 416–383 BCE). The Ji Gate was the southern gate of the Lu capital.
80. *Zizhi tongjian* 1:1–6.
81. *Shiji* 4:158; 15:709; 32:1512; 39:1687; 40:1719; 42:1776; 43:1797; 44:1839; 45:1867. For the confusion in these dates, see the brief summary in Liao Wenyuan 1997, 1–2.
82. The *Bamboo Annals* as cited in *Shui jing zhu* 14:2044 ("Huzi he" 瓠子河). This battle is mentioned in an anecdote told in *Lüshi chunqiu* 15.6:925–26 ("Bu guang" 不廣). The internal turmoil in the Tian house probably followed (or was otherwise related to) the death of one of Tian's leaders, posthumously known as Tian Daozi 田悼子 (for whom see Xiong 2017, 144–46).
83. *Shui jing zhu* 26:2258 ("Wen shui" 汶水).
84. *Lüshi chunqiu* 15.6:887 ("Xia xian" 下賢). The last word in this section is disputed. Most versions imply that Marquis Wen was elevated to the position of "supreme minister" (*shang qing* 上卿), which is not attested in other sources. Yet a few commentators insist that the character *qing* should be amended to *wen* 聞 (renown) and that "supreme renown" refers to the position of a regional lord. See comments collected by Chen Qiyou in *Lüshi chunqiu*, 899–900n61.
85. *Huainanzi* 18.9:730 ("Ren jian xun" 人間訓).
86. Yang Kuan 1998, 315–17.
87. The Three Masters of Jin are the heads of the Wei, Han, and Zhao lineages. The covenant was made between their subordinates and the de facto (but still not de jure) leader of Qi, Chen He (Tian He 田和). This arrangement apparently reflected the fact that the Three Masters of Jin were already acting as heads of independent polities, whose ranks were superior to Chen He's rank; by dispatching their subordinates they emphasized the lowly position of Chen

He, who still acted on behalf of the puppet lord of Qi (Li Xueqin 2011a, 194n12; Ma Weidong 2014).
88. Linqiu 廩丘 was a locus of contention between Qi and Jin; in 405 BCE (one year before the campaign depicted in *Xinian* 22) it was the basis of Ducal Grandson Hui's rebellion (Ma Weidong 2014).
89. For the An campaign, see *Zuozhuan*, Cheng 2.3; see also *Xinian* 14 (where the battlefield is called Miji).
90. The inscription is translated and discussed by Wolfgang Behr in Cook and Goldin 2016, 286–88. My translation incorporates the insights of Chen Minzhen 2015a and Zhang Shuguo 2016.
91. Zhang Shuguo (2016, 194–95) prefers to read the character 找 as *rong* 戎, implying that Piao Qiang became a military commander. Behr (in Cook and Goldin 2016, 288) parses the sentences differently, reading as follows: "Piao Qiang supported his lord, the lineage head of the Han, and stood by him in warfare."
92. The background for this record is not clear. *Xinian* 23 does mention a war between Jin and Qin, but this war occurred in the fourth year of King Sheng of Chu—that is, in 401 BCE, later than the events depicted in the Piao Qiang bell inscription. Some scholars identify Qin as a place-name on the western side of the Ji River, but as Chen Minzhen (2015a, 84) correctly notes, the verb *zheng* 征 normally refers to the invasion of a polity and not of a town.
93. See details in Pines 2018b.
94. Of course, some lapses and problematic revisions of *Zuozhuan* materials in *Records of the Historian* do occur (see examples in Rubin 1966; Nienhauser 2007). These lapses notwithstanding, Sima Qian's treatment of *Zuozhuan* is overwhelmingly reliable.
95. *Shiji* 15:686; Watson 1993, 87.

5. Chu Historiography and Chu Cultural Identity

1. See, e.g., Lewis 1999, 308–17.
2. See, e.g., Cook and Blakeley 1999, 2.
3. This chapter is based largely on Pines 2018a.
4. For King Zhao's campaigns, see Li Feng 2006, 93–94, 327–29. For referring to King Zhao's inglorious defeat in 656 BCE—a full three centuries after its occurrence—as a pretext to attack Chu, see *Zuozhuan*, Xi 4.1.
5. For the poem (Mao 178) and different interpretations of its content, see Cheng and Jiang 1991, 505–11.
6. See the Shang hymn "Yin wu" 殷武 (Mao 305) and the Lu hymn "Bigong" 閟宮 (Mao 300) (Cheng and Jiang 1991, 1040 and 1017, respectively).

7. Cited from the first part of the inscription on the Mi Jia bells, in which Mi Jia speaks on behalf of the Zeng ruling house (Guo Changjiang et al. 2019). Chen Minzhen (personal communication) offers a different, pro-Chu interpretation of this sentence.
8. *Zuozhuan*, Cheng 4.4. For a manipulative misreading of this passage as referring to Chu's racial otherness, see, e.g., Dikötter 1992, 3. This interpretation is patently wrong: in *Zuozhuan*, the term *zulei* 族類 refers exclusively to a lineal descent group and not to one's "race" (see *Zuozhuan*, Xi 10.3, 31.5). The rulers of Chu did not belong to the Zhou royal clan (Ji 姬), but this did not automatically make them ethnically or culturally alien.
9. *Zuozhuan*, Wen 28.3.
10. For Lu's alliance with Chu, see, e.g., *Zuozhuan*, Xi 26.4; for Jin's elimination of the Ji polities, see, e.g., *Zuozhuan*, Xiang 29.11. The complexity of the *Zuozhuan* portrait of Chu generates ongoing scholarly debate. Compare Schaberg 2001, 133–35; Pines 2002, 42–44; Li Wai-yee 2007, 298–330, and my summary of these debates in Pines 2009c, 441–42.
11. *Zhuzi yulei* 93:2153.
12. See *Guoyu* 5.4:186 ("Lu yu xia" 魯語下); 14.12:430 ("Jin yu 8"); 18.7:527 ("Chu yu xia" 楚語下).
13. *Gongyang zhuan*, Zhuang 10:130; Xi 21:241; Zhao 16:540. For the nature and dating of *Gongyang zhuan*, see Gentz 2001 and 2015. For the existence of ranked nobles (*dafu* 大夫) in Chu, see, e.g., the *Annals*' entry in *Chunqiu*, Xi 28.6.
14. *Gongyang zhuan*, Xi 4:203. The alleged ties between southern and northern "barbarians" refer to the simultaneous attacks on the Central States by the northern ethnicities Rong 戎 and Di 狄 and the southern Chu.
15. For Mengzi's denigration of Chu (amid praise of Chu personalities who were attracted by the Central States' culture and were able to transcend their barbarianism), see *Mengzi* 5.4. For a statement that the men of Chu are just "monkeys who were washed and capped" (*mu hou er guan* 沐猴而冠), see *Shiji* 7:315.
16. Goldin 2015, 31.
17. Falkenhausen 2006, 264. For a representative example of this reimagining of Chu, albeit as an alternative to Qin 秦 rather than to Zhou civilization, see the final magnum opus by a major Chu historian, Zhang Zhengming (2007).
18. Xu Shaohua 1999, 21.
19. Falkenhausen 2006, 264.
20. *Mengzi* 5.4. For reaffirmation of this line of analysis, see, e.g., Peng 2014.
21. Such a trajectory would greatly resemble that of Qin, as noted in Falkenhausen 2006, 264; for the case of Qin, see Pines 2004; Shelach and Pines 2006; Pines, Falkenhausen, Shelach, and Yates 2014. For alternative speculations about Chu's cultural trajectory, see, e.g., Yan 2015.

22. Cook and Blakeley 1999, 2.
23. Zhang Zhengming 2007, 8; Peng 2014.
24. Regarding how historians reflected and contributed to the formation of national identities in modern western Europe, see, e.g., Berger, Donovan, and Passmore 1999; for east-central Europe, see Baár 2010.
25. Goldin 2015, 37.
26. The cache of Chu manuscripts from Tomb 1, Guodian 郭店 (Hubei), yielded a single manuscript that can be called an anecdote; namely, *Lu Mugong wen Zisi* 魯穆公問子思 (S. Cook 2012, 1:419–27). An anecdotal text resembling the Wu section of *Discourses of the States* is part of the badly damaged materials from Tomb 36, Shibancun, Cili County (Zhang Chunlong 2004).
27. Note that the manuscripts in the Shanghai Museum collection are unprovenanced; they were allegedly looted from a Warring States–period Chu tomb and subsequently bought by the Shanghai Museum team at the Hong Kong antiquities market. For speculation that the Shanghai materials may have been looted from an elite female tomb, see Allan 2015, 53–55.
28. Allan 2015, 58–59.
29. In two cases (1–2 and 4–5 in table 5.1) two different anecdotes were written in the same manuscript (i.e., the new anecdote started on the same slip on which the previous one had ended). On the other hand, in not a few cases (some of which are specified in the table) later redactors proposed a rearrangement of the slips, merging two previously independent anecdotes into one.
30. Of the nine anecdotes scattered through volumes 6 and 7 of the Tsinghua collection, only one deals with Chu affairs, while the rest focus on Jin (three anecdotes), Zheng (three anecdotes), Qi, and Wu-Yue (one anecdote each).
31. *Zuozhuan*, Xi 27.4. It should be noted that the manuscript appears to be incomplete (Gao Youren 2014); hence it is possible that the original narrative continued into the battle itself.
32. Wei Cide 2013, 17–22.
33. For one example, see Chen Jian (2005) 2013.
34. The document is badly damaged, and the precise identity of the speakers and their audience is contestable. For different interpretations, see Wang Qing 2013 versus Wang Hui 2013b.
35. *Guliang zhuan* 23:687 (Ding 4). For discussion of the historicity of flogging King Ping's corpse, see Cang Linzhong 2013.
36. For the evolution of Wu Zixu's story, see Johnson 1981.
37. See, respectively, S. Cook 2012, 1:463, and Li Xueqin 2012a, 157, slip 7.
38. Luo Dan 2015; Cook and Luo 2017, 75–107. It should be mentioned that in light of the information from the Chu historical manuscript in the Anhui University collection, the mythological content of *Chu ju* requires reinterpretation (see Huang Dekuan 2017, 58–59).

39. For reading this sentence I rely on Chen Minzhen's exegesis (2011).
40. For an alternative translation of this passage, see Cook and Luo 2017, 84.
41. C. Cook 2013; Cook and Luo 2017, 75–76.
42. *Shiji* 40:1689–90. The inadequacy of this information has been fully exposed by the Anhui University Chu historical manuscript (Huang Dekuan 2017, 58–59).
43. Da 2015.
44. Yin Hongbing 2012.
45. Huang Dekuan 2017, 58–59.
46. See C. Cook 2013 for further aspects of Chu-Shang relations in *Chu ju*.
47. See Qiu Feng 2007.
48. The character *xin* 心 is redundant here (see Xu Yuangao's gloss, *Guoyu* 16.1:465).
49. *Guoyu*, 16.1:464–68 ("Zheng yu").
50. Note that Bo 伯, Zhong 仲, Shu 叔, and Ji 季 refer to the order of birth; eventually these terms became a part of the protagonists' personal names.
51. From *Shiji* (40:1694) we know that Boshuang died after six years on throne, and the second brother, Zhongxue, died soon after. Pu, to which Shuxiong fled, was probably located on the southern bank of the Han River.
52. Heaven's support as manifested in elimination of one's domestic rivals is a persistent topic in, e.g., the *Zuozhuan* accounts of the rise of Lord Wen of Jin.
53. Gaoxin 高辛 is another primeval thearch. Chong 重 and Li 黎 (who are sometimes treated as a single person) are attributed with the separation of Heaven and Earth (*Guoyu* 18.1:512–16 ["Chu yu xia"]).
54. Mi is the royal clan of Chu. Note that following the Chu historical manuscript in the Anhui University collection, Li 黎 (who is indeed identified as Zhurong) is the father of Jilian, the Chu progenitor from the *Chu ju* manuscript.
55. Kui 夔 was a small polity in Hubei, eliminated by Chu in 634 BCE because its ruler discontinued sacrifices to the common ancestors of the Mi clan. Yue 越 is a broad designation of southern ethnicities; it does not refer here to the state of Yue, which did not belong to the Mi clan. Xu Yuangao (*Guoyu*, p. 468) reads Kuiyue as a single name, but this is disputable (Qiu Feng 2007). Min usually refers to the dwellers of Fujian; it is not at all clear how they were related to the Mi clan.
56. The Huangchi campaign took place a year before the depicted events; Chu was defeated there by Jin armies. Yiyang was under Han control; it is located to the west of Luoyang. Chu wanted to shift the campaign westward, closer to its major power bases. The location of Chiyan is unknown. *Moao* was a high-ranking military office in the state of Chu.

57. For the Long Wall of Chu, see, in the present volume, the introduction to section 21.
58. Wuyang 武陽 was a newly built Chu fortress near the Yu Pass 榆關 at the intersection of Zheng, Jin, and Song territories. Chu's incursion into Gao occurred in 397 BCE.
59. Luyang 魯陽 was a Chu county, the governor of which bore the title of "duke" (*gong* 公).
60. Possession of the *gui* 珪 tablet marked the highest degree of authority in Chu: the ducal position of an enfeoffed noble (Chen Yingfei 2012, 106). Zhao Si 昭渒 was another important noble, probably a descendant of King Zhao of Chu 楚昭王 (r. 516–489 BCE).
61. For Royal Son Ding and his rebellion, see the notes to *Xinian* 23 in this book.
62. Wei Cide 2013; Cai 2016.
63. *Zuozhuan*, Cheng 12.2.
64. For these conferences, see Kōno 1978 and *Xinian* 18 this book.
65. *Zuozhuan*, Cheng 12.3.
66. For details, see the introduction to *Xinian* 16 in this book.
67. See *Xinian* 18, slip 98.
68. Pines 2010; Allan 2015, 181–262.
69. For the *Rongchengshi* narrative of the Nine Provinces and its comparisons with other variants of this story, see Dorofeeva-Lichtmann 2009 and 2010.
70. 禹乃從漢以南爲名谷五百，從漢以北爲名谷五百。(*Rongchengshi*, slips 27–28). For the original publication of *Rongchengshi*, see Li Ling 2002; immediately after the publication, the slips were rearranged by Chen Jian (2004), whose rearrangement became the foundation of subsequent studies of the text. For details, see Pines 2010 and Allan 2015.
71. Dorofeeva-Lichtmann 2016.
72. *Rongchengshi*, slip 5. For an alternative translation, see Allan 2015, 230. Allan follows Guo Yongbing (2008, 43–79) in identifying the pre-Yao thearch as Youyu Tong 有虞迵.
73. *Rongchengshi*, slips 19–20.
74. For the trope of the monarch's virtue reaching and transforming birds and beasts, see Sterckx 2002, 147–48.
75. Note, however, that these ancestors are given due attention in the Chu historical manuscript in the Anhui University collection (Huang Dekuan 2017, 58–59). Yet, since the manuscript had not been published heretofore, I do not discuss it in this chapter.
76. See *Qu Yuan ji jiaozhu* 485–506 and 282–87. For the Chu poetry, see Kern 2010, 76–86. For a fascinating account of the dialog between Chu poetry and the *Canon of Poems*, see Hunter 2019.
77. This point is most strongly made in Karapet'iants 1988.

78. For the rise, nature, and ideological outlook of Warring States–period *shi*, see Pines 2009b, 115–84.
79. This can be inferred from a comparison between Chu and Qin. In the latter, scattered material and paleographic evidence suggest that a separate identity was being formed among the lower strata during the second half of the Warring States period (Shelach and Pines 2006).
80. See Lewis 2006.
81. Allan 2015, 58–59.
82. Goldin 2015.

Bibliography

Allan, Sarah. 2015. *Buried Ideas: Legends of Abdication and Ideal Government in Recently Discovered Early Chinese Bamboo-Slip Manuscripts*. Albany: State University of New York Press.

———. 2016. *The Heir and the Sage: Dynastic Legend in Early China*. Rev. ed. Albany: State University of New York Press.

Asano Yūichi 淺野裕一. 2011. "Shangbo Chu jian *Wang ju* zhi fuyuan yu jieshi" 上博楚簡《王居》之復原與解釋. Trans. Diao Xiaolong 刁小龍. http://www.gwz.fudan.edu.cn/Web/Show/1685. Accessed November 30, 2018.

———. 2012a. "Qinghua jian *Chu ju* chutan" 清華簡《楚居》初探. *Qinghua jian yanjiu* 清華簡研究 1:242–47.

———. 2012b. "Shisho to shite no Seika kan *Keinen* no seikaku" 史書としての清華簡『繫年』の性格. In *Shutsudo bunken kara mita koshi to juka kyōten* 出土文獻から見た古史と儒家經典, by Asano Yūichi 淺野裕一 and Ozawa Kenji 小澤賢二, 59–104. Tokyo: Kyūko shoin.

Asano Yūichi 浅野裕一 and Ozawa Kenji 小澤賢二. 2013. *Sekkōdai* Saden *shingi kō* 浙江大『左傳』真偽考. Tokyo: Kyūko shoin.

Baár, Monika. 2010. *Historians and Nationalism: East Central Europe in the Nineteenth Century*. Oxford: Oxford University Press.

Bai Guangqi 白光琦. 1997. "Zifan bianzhong de nianfen wenti" 子犯編鐘的年份問題. *Wenwu shijie* 文物世界 2:53.

Berger, Stefan, Mark Donovan, and Kevin Passmore, eds. 1999. *Writing National Histories: Western Europe Since 1800*. London: Routledge.

Boltz, William G. 1990. "Notes on the Textual Relationships between the *Kuo Yu* and the *Tso Chuan*." *Bulletin of the School of Oriental and African Studies* 53, no. 3 (October): 491–502.

Cai Yingying 蔡瑩瑩. 2016. "*Qinghua jian Xinian* Chuguo jinian wu zhang de xushi tese guankui" 《清華簡・繫年》楚國紀年五章的敘事特色管窺. *Chengda zhongwen xuebao* 成大中文學報 55:51–94.

Cang Linzhong 倉林忠. 2013. "Guanyu Wu Zixu youfou dui Chu Pingwang juemu bianshi de bianxi" 關於伍子胥有否對楚平王掘墓鞭尸的辨析. *Mianyang shifan xueyuan xuebao* 綿陽師範學院學報 10:58–64.

Cang Xiuliang 倉修良. 2006. *Zhongguo shixue mingzhu pingjie* 中國史學名著評介. 5 vols. Ji'nan: Shandong jiaoyu chubanshe.

Cao Dingyun 曹定雲. 2017. "Lun Xi Zhou jinwen zhong de Qin di, Qin Yi he Qin ren: 'Ying Qin' qiyuan dongfang de quezheng" 論西周金文中的秦地、秦夷和秦人—"嬴秦"起源東方的確證. In *Huihuang Yongcheng: Quanguo (Fengxiang) Qin wenhua xueshu yantaohui lunwenji* 輝煌雍城：全國（鳳翔）秦文化學術研討會論文集, ed. Zhongguo xian Qin shixuehui 中國先秦史學會 et al., 136–41. Xi'an: San Qin chubanshe.

Chang, Jung-Im. 2012. "Yú 于 and Yū 於: Their Origins, Their Grammaticalization, and the Process of Encroachment of the Former by the Latter from a Historical Perspective." PhD diss., University of Washington.

Chao Fulin 晁福林. 1991. "Lun Pingwang dongqian" 論平王東遷. *Lishi yanjiu* 歷史研究 6:8–23.

———. 1992. "Shi lun 'gonghe xingzheng' ji qi xiangguan wenti" 試論"共和行政"及其相關問題. *Zhongguo shi yanjiu* 中國史研究 2:45–54.

Chao Yuefeng 晁岳佩. 2000. "*Chunqiu* shuo li" 《春秋》說例. *Guji zhengli yanjiu xuekan* 古籍整理研究學刊 1:8–13.

Chen Fengfen 陳佩芬, ed. 2007. *Zhuang Wang ji cheng* 莊王既成 and *Shen gong chen Ling wang* 申公臣靈王. In *Shanghai bowuguan cang Zhanguo Chu zhushu* 上海博物館藏戰國楚竹書, ed. Ma Chengyuan 馬承源, 6:237–52. Shanghai: Shanghai guji chubanshe.

Chen Jian 陳劍. 2004. "Shangbo jian *Rong Cheng shi* de zhujian pinhe yu pianlian wenti xiaoyi" 上博簡《容成氏》的竹簡拼合與編連問題小議. In *Shangbo guan cang Zhanguo Chu zhushu yanjiu xubian* 上博館藏戰國楚竹書研究續編, ed. Shanghai daxue gudai wenming yanjiu zhongxin 上海大學古代文明研究中心 and Qinghua daxue sixiang wenhua yanjiu suo 清華大學思想文化研究所, 327–34. Shanghai: Shanghai shudian.

———. (2005) 2013. "Shangbo zhujian *Zhao wang yu Gongzhi Shui* he *Jianda wang po han* du houji" 上博竹書《昭王與龔之脽》和《柬大王泊旱》讀後記. Reprinted in *Zhanguo zhushu lunji* 戰國竹書論集, 125–33. Shanghai: Shanghai guji chubanshe.

———. 2013. "Jian tan *Xinian* de X he Chujian bufen Y zi dang shedu wei 'jie'" 簡談《繫年》的"𢦏"和楚簡部分"𣌭"字當釋讀為"捷." *Anhui daxue xuebao (zhexue shehui kexue ban)* 安徽大學學報（哲學社會科學版）6:67–70.

Chen Jie 陳絜. 2016. "Qinghua jian *Xinian* di ershi zhang diming buzheng" 清華簡《繫年》第二十章地名補正. In *Qinghua jian* Xinian *yu gushi xintan* 清華簡《繫年》與古史新探, ed. Li Shoukui 李守奎, 107–15. Shanghai: Zhongxi shuju.

Chen Kuang Yu 陳光宇. 2012. "Ni shi jiapu keci zongshu ji qi que wei zhenpin de zhengju" 兒氏家譜刻辭綜述及其確為真品的證據. http://chemsites.chem.rutgers.edu/~kyc/pdf/16chen2016.pdf. Accessed April 4, 2020.

Chen Minzhen 陳民鎮. 2011. "Qinghua jian *Chu ju jishi*" 清華簡《楚居》集釋. http://www.gwz.fudan.edu.cn/Web/Show/1663. Accessed April 4, 2020.

———. 2012. "*Xinian* 'gu zhi' shuo: Qinghua jian *Xinian* xingzhi ji zhuanzuo beijing chuyi" 《繫年》"故志"說：清華簡《繫年》性質及撰作背景芻議. *Handan xueyuan xuebao* 邯鄲學院學報 2:49–57, 100.

———. 2013. "Qi changcheng xinyan: Cong Qinghua jian *Xinian* kan Qi changcheng de ruogan wenti" 齊長城新研——從清華簡《繫年》看齊長城的若干問題. *Zhongguo shi yanjiu* 中國史研究 3:5–19.

———. 2015a. "Piao Qiang zhong yu Qinghua *Xinian* hezheng" 羌鐘與清華《繫年》合證. *Kaogu yu wenwu* 考古與文物 6:82–87.

———. 2015b. "Qinghua jian *Xinian* xuci chutan" 清華簡《繫年》虛詞初探. *Chutu wenxian yuyan yanjiu* 出土文獻語言研究 2:38–59.

———. 2017. "Qinghua jian *Xinian* suo jian 'Shandong shiqi' Yue guo de junshi yu waijiao" 清華簡《繫年》所見"山東時期"越國的軍事與外交. In *Qinghua jian yu Rujia jingdian: Guoji xueshu yantaohui lunwenji* 清華簡與儒家經典國際學術研討會論文集, ed. Jiang Linchang 江林昌 and Sun Jin 孫進, 205–13. Shanghai: Shanghai guji chubanshe.

Chen Minzhen 陳民鎮 and Yuri Pines. 2018. "Where is King Ping? The History and Historiography of the Zhou Dynasty's Eastward Relocation." *Asia Major*, 3rd ser., 31, no. 1:1–27.

Chen Shuangxin 陳雙新. 2000. "Zifan zhongming kaoshi" 子犯鐘銘考釋. *Anhui jiaoyu xueyuan xuebao* 安徽教育學院學報 18, no. 1:35–37.

Chen Wei 陳偉. 2007. "Du *Shanghai liu* tiaoji" 讀《上博六》條記. http://www.bsm.org.cn/show_article.php?id=597. Accessed April 4, 2020.

———, ed. 2009. *Chu di chutu Zhanguo jiance (shisi zhong)* 楚地出土戰國簡冊〔十四種〕. Beijing: Jingji kexue chubanshe.

———. 2012a. "Du Qinghua jian *Xinian* zhaji" 讀清華簡《繫年》札記. *Jianghan kaogu* 江漢考古 3:117–20, 112.

———. 2012b. "Qinghua jian *Chu ju* 'pianshi' gushi xiao kao" 清華簡《楚居》"楩室"故事小考. *Qinghua jian yanjiu* 清華簡研究 1:274–76.

——. 2013. "Qinghua daxue cang zhushu *Xinian* de wenxianxue kaocha" 清華大學藏竹書《繫年》的文獻學考察. *Shilin* 史林 1:43–48.

Chen Weiwu 陳偉武. 2016. "Qinghua jian *Xinian* shouzhang 'yang di' yishi" 清華簡《繫年》首章"央帝"臆釋. In *Qinghua jian* Xinian *yu gushi xintan* 清華簡《繫年》與古史新探, ed. Li Shoukui 李守奎, 82–90. Shanghai: Zhongxi shuju.

Chen Yingdi 陳迎娣. 2013. "*Qinghua daxue cang Zhanguo zhujian (er)* xuci zhengli" 《清華大學藏戰國竹簡（貳）》虛詞整理. http://www.bsm.org.cn/show_article.php?id=1846. Accessed April 4, 2020.

Chen Yingfei 陳穎飛. 2012. "Chu Daowang chuqi de da zhan yu Chu fengjun—Qinghua jian *Xinian* zhaji zhi yi" 楚悼王初期的大戰與楚封君—清華簡《繫年》札記之一. *Wenshi zhishi* 文史知識 5:105–7.

——. 2018. "Qinghua jian *Xinian* mo zhang suo ji Jin Zheng Chu dazhan zaishi" 清華簡《繫年》末章所記晉鄭楚大戰再識. *Handan xueyuan xuebao* 邯鄲學院學報 28, no. 2:16–19.

Chen Yingjie 陳英傑. 2007. "Jinwen zhong 'jun' zi zhi yiyi ji xiangguan wenti tanxi" 金文中"君"字之意義及相關問題探析. *Zhongguo wenzi* 中國文字 33:107–52.

Cheng Hao 程浩. 2016. "You Qinghua jian *Liang chen* lun chudai Zeng Hou 'Nangong Yao'" 由清華簡《良臣》論初代曾侯"南宫夭." *Guanzi xuekan* 管子學刊 1:99–100.

Cheng Junying 程俊英 and Jiang Jianyuan 蔣見元. 1991. *Shijing zhuxi* 詩經注析. Beijing: Zhonghua shuju.

Cheng Pingshan 程平山. 2013. *Zhushu jinian yu chutu wenxian yanjiu zhi yi: Zhushu jinian kao* 竹書紀年與出土文獻研究之一：竹書紀年考. Beijing: Zhonghua shuju.

——. 2015. "Tang Shu Yu zhi Jin Wugong niandai shiji kao" 唐叔虞至晉武公年代事蹟考. *Wen shi* 3:5–23.

Cheng Wei 程薇. 2012a. "Qinghua jian *Xinian* yu Jin fa Zhongshan" 清華簡《繫年》與晉伐中山. *Shenzhen daxue xuebao (renwen shehui kexue ban)* 深圳大學學報（人文社會科學版）2:50–53.

——. 2012b. "Qinghua jian *Xinian* yu Xi Gui shiji" 清華簡《繫年》與息媯事跡. *Wenshi zhishi* 文史知識 4:45–48.

Chunqiu Gongyang zhuan yizhu 春秋公羊傳譯注. 2011. Annot. Liu Shangci 劉尚慈. Beijing: Zhonghua shuju.

Chunqiu Guliang jing zhuan buzhu 春秋穀梁經傳補注. 1996. Annot. Zhong Wenzheng 鍾文烝 [1818–1877]. Coll. Pian Yuqian 駢宇騫 and Hao Shuhui 郝淑慧. Beijing: Zhonghua shuju.

Chunqiu jizhuan zuanli 春秋集傳纂例. N.d. By Lu Chun 陸淳 [d. 805]. e-*Siku quanshu* 四庫全書 edition.

Chunqiu Zuozhuan zhengyi 春秋左傳正義. (1815) 1991. Annot. Du Yu 杜預 [222–285] and Kong Yingda 孔穎達 [574–648]. In *Shisan jing zhushu fu jiaokanji* 十三經注疏附校勘記, comp. Ruan Yuan 阮元 [1764–1849], 2:1697–2188. Beijing: Zhonghua shuju.

Chunqiu Zuozhuan zhu 春秋左傳注. 1990. Annot. Yang Bojun 楊伯峻. Rev. ed. Beijing: Zhonghua shuju.

Cook, Constance A. [Ke Heli 柯鶴立]. 2013. "Chu xianzu de dansheng gushi: Jianlun Shang yu Chu de guanxi" 楚先祖的誕生故事——兼論商與楚的關係. In *Chu jian, Chu wenhua yu xian Qin lishi wenhua guoji xueshu yantaohui lunwenji* 楚簡楚文化與先秦歷史文化國際學術研討會論文集, ed. Luo Yunhuan 羅運環, 134–50. Wuhan: Hubei jiaoyu chubanshe.

Cook, Constance A., and Barry B. Blakeley. 1999. Introduction to *Defining Chu: Image and Reality in Early China*, 1–5. Ed. Constance A. Cook and John S. Major. Honolulu: University of Hawai`i Press.

Cook, Constance A., and Paul R. Goldin. 2016. *A Source Book of Ancient Chinese Bronze Inscriptions*. Berkeley, Calif.: Society for the Study of Early China.

Cook, Constance A., and Luo Xinhui. 2017. *Birth in Ancient China: A Study of Metaphor and Cultural Identity in Pre-imperial China*. Albany: State University of New York Press.

Cook, Constance A., and John S. Major, eds. 1999. *Defining Chu: Image and Reality in Early China*. Honolulu: University of Hawai`i Press.

Cook, Scott. 2012. *The Bamboo Texts of Guodian: A Study and Complete Translation*. Vols. 1 and 2. Ithaca, N.Y.: East Asia Program, Cornell University.

Creel, Herrlee G. 1964. "The Beginnings of Bureaucracy in China: The Origin of the *Hsien*." *Journal of Asian Studies* 23, no. 2:155–84.

———. 1970. *The Origins of Statecraft in China, Volume 1: The Western Chou Empire*. Chicago: University of Chicago Press.

Cui Dongbi yishu 崔東壁遺書. 1983. By Cui Shu 崔述 [1739–1816]. Ed. Gu Jiegang 顧頡剛. Reprint, Shanghai: Shanghai guji chubanshe.

Da Haobo 笪浩波. 2015. "Cong Qinghua jian *Chu ju* kan Chu shi de ruogan wenti" 從清華簡《楚居》看楚史的若干問題. *Zhongguo shi yanjiu* 中國史研究 1:85–87.

Dikötter, Frank. 1992. *The Discourse of Race in Modern China*. Stanford, Calif.: Stanford University Press.

Dong Shan 董珊. 2014. *Jianbo wenxian kaoshi luncong* 簡帛文獻考釋論叢. Shanghai: Shanghai guji chubanshe.

Dorofeeva-Lichtmann, Vera. 2009. "Ritual Practices for Constructing Terrestrial Space (Warring States–Early Han)." In *Early Chinese Religion, Part One: Shang through Han (1250 BC–220 AD)*, ed. John Lagerwey and Marc Kalinowski, 1:629–36. Leiden: Brill

———. 2010. "The *Rong Cheng shi* version of the 'Nine Provinces': Some Parallels with Transmitted Texts." *East Asian Science, Technology and Medicine* 32:13–58.

———. 2016. "The Crucial Role of the Han River in the Chu Conception of Space: Questioning 'No Chu-Related Traits' in the *Rong Cheng shi* Version of the 'Nine Provinces.'" Paper presented at the European Association for Chinese Studies conference, St. Petersburg, Russia, August.

Du Weiyun 杜維運. 2010. *Zhongguo shixue shi* 中國史學史. 3 vols. Beijing: Shangwu.

Du Xinyu 杜新宇. 2015. "Qinghua jian *Xinian* 'Hengtong er gui zhi yu Chu' xiao yi" 清華簡《繫年》"遷 迴而歸之於楚"小議. http://www.gwz.fudan.edu.cn/Web/Show/2707. Accessed April 4, 2020.

Durrant, Stephen W. 1995. *The Cloudy Mirror: Tension and Conflict in the Writings of Sima Qian.* Albany: State University of New York Press.

———. 2019. "The Problem of 'Other Annals' Embedded in *Zuozhuan*." Paper presented at the conference on "Rethinking Early Chinese Historiography," Jerusalem, May 12–16 (forthcoming in the conference volume).

———. 2020. "From 'Scribe' to 'History:' The Keyword *shi* 史." In *Keywords in Chinese Culture*, ed. Li Wai-yee and Yuri Pines, 85–119. Hong Kong: Chinese University of Hong Kong Press.

Durrant, Stephen W., Li Wai-yee, Michael Nylan, and Hans van Ess. 2016. *The Letter to Ren An and Sima Qian's Legacy.* Seattle: University of Washington Press.

Durrant, Stephen W., Li Wai-yee, and David Schaberg. 2016. *Zuo Tradition/Zuozhuan Commentary on the "Spring and Autumn Annals."* Seattle: University of Washington Press.

Ebine Ryōsuke 海老根量介. 2012. "Shangbo jian *Shengong chen Lingwang* jianlun: Tongguo yu *Zuozhuan* bijiao" 上博簡《申公臣靈王》簡論——通過與《左傳》比較. http://www.gwz.fudan.edu.cn/SrcShow.asp?Src_ID=1893. Accessed April 4, 2020.

Elvin, Mark. 2004. *The Retreat of the Elephants: An Environmental History of China.* New Haven, Conn.: Yale University Press.

Eno, Robert. 2009. "Shang State Religion and the Pantheon of the Oracle Texts." In *Early Chinese Religion, Part One: Shang through Han (1250 BC–220 AD)*, ed. John Lagerwey and Marc Kalinowski, 1:41–101. Leiden: Brill.

Falkenhausen, Lothar von. 1988. "Ritual Music in Bronze Age China." PhD diss., Harvard University.

———. 1993a. "Issues in Western Zhou Studies: A Review Article." *Early China* 18:139–226.

———. 1993b. *Suspended Music: Chime-Bells in the Culture of Bronze Age China.* Berkeley: University of California Press.

———. 2006. *Chinese Society in the Age of Confucius (1000–250 B.C.): The Archaeological Evidence.* Los Angeles: Cotsen Institute of Archaeology, University of California, Los Angeles.

———. 2008. "Les origines ethniques des Qin: Perspectives historiques et archéologiques." In *Les soldats de l'éternité: L'armée de Xi'an*, ed. Alain Thote and Lothar von Falkenhausen, 47–54. Paris: Pinacothèque.

Falkenhausen, Lothar von, with Gideon Shelach. 2014. "Introduction: Archaeological Perspectives on the Qin 'Unification' of China." In *Birth of an Empire: The State of Qin Revisited*, ed. Yuri Pines, Lothar von Falkenhausen, Gideon Shelach and Robin D. S. Yates, 37–51. Berkeley: University of California Press.

Fan Changxi 范常喜. 2018. "Qinghua jian *Xinian* 'han ge yu shao' xiaokao" 清華簡《繫年》"鶡骼玉鈔"小考. *Guwenzi yanjiu* 古文字研究 32:361–65.

Fang Shiming 方詩銘. 1991. *Zhongguo lidai jinian biao* 中國歷代紀年表. Shanghai: Shanghai cishu chubanshe.

Fang Shiming 方詩銘 and Wang Xiuling 王修齡, eds. 2005. *Guben Zhushu jinian jizheng* 古本竹書紀年輯證. Shanghai: Shanghai guji chubanshe.

Fang Tao 方韜. 2017. "Cong Qinghua jian *Xinian* kan Xi Ke yu An zhi zhan" 從清華簡《繫年》看郤克與鞌之戰. *Nanjing shifan daxue wenxue yuan xuebao* 南京示範大學文學院學報 2:144–49.

Feng Shi 馮時. 1997. "Chunqiu Zifan bianzhong jinian yanjiu: Jin Chonger guiguo kao" 春秋子犯編鐘紀年研究：晉重耳歸國考. *Wenwu jikan* 文物季刊 4:59–65.

Foster, Christopher J. 2017. "Introduction to the Peking University Han Bamboo Strips: On the Authentication and Study of Purchased Manuscripts." *Early China* 40 (2017): 167–239.

Fu Sinian 傅斯年 (1896–1950). (1933) 2003. "Yi Xia dong xi shuo" 夷夏東西說. Reprinted in *Fu Sinian quanji* 傅斯年全集, ed. Ouyang Zhesheng 歐陽哲生, 3:181–232. Changsha: Hunan jiaoyu chubanshe.

Fujita Katsuhisa 藤田勝久. 1997. *Shiki Sengoku shiryō no kenkyū* 史記戰國史料の研究. Tokyo: Tōkyō daigaku shuppankai.

———. 2013. "*Shiki* no nendaigaku to Seika kan *Sokyo, Keinen*"「史記」の年代學と清華簡「楚居」「繫年」. *Ehime daigaku Hōbun Gakubu ronshū* 愛媛大學法文學部論集 35:1–33.

Gálik, Marián. 2010. "King David (ca. 1037–ca. 967 B.C.) and Duke Wen of Jin (ca. 697–628 B.C.): Two Paradigmatic Rulers from the Hebrew Deuteronomistic and Early Chinese Confucian Historiography." *Asian and African Studies* 19, no. 1:1–25.

Gao Chongwen 高崇文. 2015. "Zeng Hou Yu bianzhong mingwen suo ji Wu fa Chu luxian bianxi: Jianlun Chunqiu shiqi Chu Yingdu diwang" 曾侯與編鐘銘文所記吳伐楚路綫辨析——兼論春秋時期楚郢都地望. *Jianghan kaogu* 江漢考古 3:82–85.

Gao Youren 高佑仁. 2014. "Shangbo jiu *Cheng wang wei Chengpu zhi hang* zici xuanshi" 上博九〈成王為城濮之行〉字詞選釋. *Chengda zhongwen xuebao* 成大中文學報 47:39–74.

Gentz, Joachim. 2001. *Das Gongyang zhuan: Auslegung und Kanonisierung der Frühlings und Herbstannalen (Chunqiu)*. Opera Sinologica 12. Wiesbaden: Harrassowitz.

———. 2005. "The Past as a Messianic Vision: Historical Thought and Strategies of Sacralization in the Early *Gongyang* Tradition." In *Historical Truth, Historical Criticism and Ideology: Chinese Historiography and Historical Culture from a New Comparative Perspective*, ed. Helwig Schmidt-Glintzer, Achim Mittag, and Jörn Rüsen, 227–54. Leiden: Brill.

———. 2015. "Long Live the King! The Ideology of Power between Ritual and Morality in the *Gongyang zhuan* 公羊傳." In *Ideology of Power and Power of Ideology in Early China*, ed. Yuri Pines, Paul R. Goldin, and Martin Kern, 69–117. Leiden: Brill.

———. 2017. "One Heaven, One History, One People: Repositioning the Zhou in Royal Addresses to Subdued Enemies in the 'Duo shi' 多士 and 'Duo fang' 多方 Chapters of the *Shangshu* and in the 'Shang shi' 商誓 Chapter of the *Yi Zhoushu*." In *Origins of Chinese Political Philosophy: Studies in the Composition and Thought of the* Shangshu *(Classic of Documents)*, ed. Martin Kern and Dirk Meyer, 146–92. Leiden: Brill.

Gernet, Jacques. 1982. *A History of Chinese Civilization*. Trans. J. R. Foster. Cambridge: Cambridge University Press.

Goldin, Paul R. 2005. "The Theme of the Primacy of the Situation in Classical Chinese Philosophy and Rhetoric." *Asia Major*, 3rd ser., 18, no. 2:1–25.

———. 2008. "Appeals to History in Early Chinese Philosophy and Rhetoric." *Journal of Chinese Philosophy* 35, no. 1:79–96.

———. 2013. "*Heng xian* and the Problem of Studying Looted Artifacts." *Dao* 13:153–60.

———. 2015. "Representations of Regional Diversity during the Eastern Zhou Dynasty." In *Ideology of Power and Power of Ideology in Early China*, ed. Yuri Pines, Paul R. Goldin, and Martin Kern, 31–48. Leiden: Brill.

———. 2017. "Non-deductive Argumentation in Early Chinese Philosophy." In *Between Philosophy and History: Rhetorical Uses of Anecdotes in Early China*, ed. Paul van Els and Sarah Queen, 41–62. Albany: State University of New York Press.

———. 2020. *The Art of Chinese Philosophy: A History and Interpretation of Eight Classical Texts*. Princeton, N.J.: Princeton University Press.

Goldin, Paul R., and Elisa Levi Sabattini, trans. 2020. *Lu Jia's* New Discourses*: A Political Manifesto from the Early Han Dynasty*. Leiden: Brill.

Grebnev, Georgij [Yegor] A. 2016. "Эволюция Памяти о Чжоуском Завоевании Шан на Примере одного Текста." *Восток (ORIENS)* 4:76–103.

Gu Jiegang 顧頡剛 [1893–1980]. 1988a. *Chunqiu san zhuan ji Guoyu zhi zonghe yanjiu* 春秋三傳及國語之綜合研究, ed. Liu Qiyu 劉起釪 [1917–2012]. Chengdu: Bashu chubanshe.

———. 1988b. *Zhongguo shanggushi yanjiu jiangyi* 中國上古史研究講義. Beijing: Zhonghua shuju.

Gu Jiegang 顧頡剛 [1893–1980] and Liu Qiyu 劉起釪 [1917–2012]. 2005. *Shangshu jiaoshi yilun* 尚書校釋譯論. Beijing: Zhonghua shuju.

Gu lienü zhuan 古列女傳. N.d. Composed by Liu Xiang 劉向 [79–8 BCE]. e-*Siku quanshu* 四庫全書 edition.

Guan Liyan 關立言. 1998. "Chunqiu rishi sanshiqi shi kao" 春秋日食三十七事考. *Shixue yuekan* 史學月刊 2:95–102.

Gui Juan 桂娟 and Yuan Yueming 袁月明. 2019. "Henan Nanyang fajue Dong Zhou guizu muzang qun" 河南南陽發掘東周貴族墓葬群. http://kaogu.cssn.cn/zwb/xccz/201908/t20190828_4963617.shtml. Accessed April 4, 2020.

Guo Changjiang 郭長江, Li Xiaoyang 李曉楊, Fan Guodong 凡國棟, and Chen Hu 陳虎. 2019. "Mi Jia bianzhong mingwen de chubu shidu" 嫡加編鐘銘文的初步釋讀. *Jianghan kaogu* 江漢考古 3:9–19.

Guo Dewei 郭德維. 1999. *Chu du Ji'nancheng fuyuan yanjiu* 楚都紀南城復原研究. Beijing: Wenwu chubanshe.

Guo Li 郭麗. 2015. "Qinghua jian *Liang chen* wenben jiegou yu silu kaolue" 清華簡《良臣》文本結構與思路考略. *Shandong ligong daxue xuebao (shehui kexue ban)* 山東理工大學學報（社會科學版）31, no. 4:48–51.

Guo Yongbing 郭永秉. 2008. *Di xi xin yan: Chu di chutu Zhanguo wenxian zhong de chuanshuo shidai gu diwang xitong yanjiu* 帝系新研：楚地出土戰國文獻中的傳說時代古帝王系統研究. Beijing: Beijing daxue.

———. 2016. "Qinghua jian *Xinian* chaoxie shidai zhi guce: Jian cong wenzi xingti jiaodu kan Zhanguo Chu wenzi quyuxing tezheng xingcheng de fuza guocheng" 清華簡《繫年》抄寫時代之估測——兼從文字形體角度看戰國楚文字區域性特徵形成的複雜過程. *Wen shi* 文史 3:5–42.

———. 2018. "Jinnian chutu Zhanguo wenxian gei gushi chuanshuo yanjiu dailai de ruogan xin zhi yu fansi" 近年出土戰國文獻給古史傳說研究帶來的若干新知與反思. *Chutu wenxian yu guwenzi yanjiu* 出土文獻與古文字研究 7:215–47.

Guodian Chu mu zhujian 郭店楚墓竹簡. 1998. Ed. Jingmenshi bowuguan 荊門市博物館. Beijing: Wenwu chubanshe.

Guoyu jijie 國語集解. 2002. Annot. Xu Yuangao 徐元誥 [1878–1955]. Coll. Wang Shumin 王樹民 and Shen Changyun 沈長雲. Beijing: Zhonghua shuju.

Han Feizi jijie 韓非子集解. 1998. Comp. Wang Xianshen 王先慎 [1859–1922]. Beijing: Zhonghua shuju.

Han Wei 韓巍. 2010. "Xinchu jinwen yu Xi Zhou zhuhou chengwei de zai renshi: Yi Shouyangzhai cangqi wei zhongxin de kaocha" 新出金文與西周諸侯稱謂的再認識——以首陽齋藏器為中心的考察. http://cccp.uchicago.edu/archive/2010FanBronzesConference/2010FanBronzesConference_HanWei.pdf. Accessed April 8, 2020.

Han Yujiao 韓宇嬌. 2013. "Qinghua jian *Liang chen* de xingzhi yu shidai bianxi" 清華簡《良臣》的性質與時代辨析. *Zhongguo gaoxiao shehui kexue* 中國高校社會科學 3:90–93.

Hanshu 漢書. 1997. By Ban Gu 班固 [32–92] et al. Annot. Yan Shigu 顏師古 [581–645]. Beijing: Zhonghua shuju.

Hardy, Grant. 1999. *Worlds of Bronze and Bamboo: Sima Qian's Conquest of History*. New York: Columbia University Press.

He Jin 何晉. 2001. *Zhanguo ce yanjiu* 《戰國策》研究. Beijing: Beijing daxue chubanshe.

He Leshi 何樂士. 2004. *Zuozhuan xuci yanjiu* 《左傳》虛詞研究. Rev. ed. Beijing: Shangwu chubanshe.

Heather, Peter. 2010. *Empires and Barbarians: The Fall of Rome and the Birth of Europe*. Oxford: Oxford University Press.

Henry, Eric. 1999. "'Junzi yue' and 'Zhongni yue' in *Zuozhuan*." *Harvard Journal of Asiatic Studies* 59, no. 1:125–61.

———. 2003. "Anachronisms in *Lüshi chunqiu* and *Shuo yuan*." *Early Medieval China* 1:127–38.

Hu Nianyi 胡念貽. 1987. "*Zuozhuan* de zhenwei he xiezuo shidai kaobian" 《左傳》的真偽和寫作時代考辨. In *Zhongguo gudai wenxue lungao* 中國古代文學論稿, 21–76. Shanghai: Shanghai guji chubanshe.

Hu Pingsheng 胡平生. 1989. "Some Notes on the Organization of the Han Dynasty Bamboo 'Annals' Found at Fuyang." Trans. Deborah Porter. *Early China* 14:1–25.

———. 2010. "Lun jianbo bianwei yu liushi jiandu qiangjiu" 論簡帛辨偽與流失簡牘搶救. *Chutu wenxian yanjiu* 出土文獻研究 9:76–108.

———. 2013. "Fuyang Shuanggudui Han jian *Shuilei zashi* yanjiu" 阜陽雙古堆漢簡〈說類雜事〉研究. In *Chutu cailiao yu xin shiye* 出土材料與新視野, ed. Li Zongkun 李宗焜, 613–67. Taipei: Zhongyang yanjiuyuan.

The Huainanzi: A Guide to the Theory and Practice of Government in Early China. 2010. Trans. and ed. John S. Major, Sarah A. Queen, Andrew Seth Meyer, and Harold D. Roth. New York: Columbia University Press.

Huang Dekuan 黃德寬. 2017. "Anhui daxue cang Zhanguo zhujian gaishu" 安徽大學藏戰國竹簡概述. *Wenwu* 9:54–59.

Huang Jinqian 黃錦前. 2012. "'Xu Zi Tuo' yu 'Xu Gong Tuo': Jian tan Qinghua jian *Xinian* de kekaoxing" "許子佗"與"許公佗"—兼談清華簡《繫年》的可靠性. http://www.bsm.org.cn/show_article.php?id=1756. Accessed April 9, 2020.

———. 2017a. "Cong jinkan Ruoqi shenlun Ruoguo diwang ji Chu mie Ruo de niandai" 從近刊鄀器申論鄀國地望及楚滅鄀的年代. *Zhongguo lishi dili luncong* 中國歷史地理論叢 32, no. 3:115–26.

———. 2017b. "Zeng Hou Yu bianzhong mingwen dushi" 曾侯與編鐘銘文讀釋. *Zhongguo guojia bowuguan guankan* 中國國家博物館館刊 3:76–89.

Huang Ziyong 黃梓勇. 2015. "Lun Qinghua jian *Xinian* de xingzhi" 論清華簡《繫年》的性質. *Qinghua jian yanjiu* 清華簡研究 2:238–51.

Hubei Sheng wenwu kaogu yanjiusuo 湖北省文物考古研究所 and Suizhou Shi bowuguan 隨州市博物馆. 2014. "Suizhou Wenfengta M1 (Zeng Hou Yu mu), M2 fajue jianbao" 隨州文峰塔 M1（曾侯與墓）、M2發掘簡報. *Jianghan kaogu* 江漢考古 4:3–51.

Hunter, Michael. 2017. "Against (Uninformed) Idleness: Situating the Didacticism of 'Wu yi' 無逸." In *Origins of Chinese Political Philosophy: Studies in the Composition and Thought of the* Shangshu *(Classic of Documents)*, ed. Martin Kern and Dirk Meyer, 393–415. Leiden: Brill.

———. 2019. "To Leave or Not to Leave: The *Chu ci* 楚辭 (Verses of Chu) as Response to the *Shi jing* 詩經 (Classic of Odes)." *Early China* 42:111–46.

Jin Yuxiang 金宇祥 2016. "Qinghua jian *Xinian* 'Jing zhi shi' xiangguan wenti chutan" 清華簡《繫年》"頸之師"相關問題初探. *Jianbo* 簡帛 13:91–105.

Jingdian shiwen 經典釋文. n. d. By Lu Deming 陆德明 [ca. 550–630]. e-*Siku quanshu* 四庫全書 edition.

Johnson, David. 1981. "Epic and History in Early China: The Matter of Wu Tzu-Hsü." *Journal of Asian Studies* 40, no. 2 (February): 255–71.

Kang Youwei 康有為 [1859–1927]. 1955. "*Hanshu yiwenzhi* bianwei" 漢書藝文志辨偽. Reprinted in *Guji kaobian congkan* 古籍考辨叢刊, ed. Gu Jiegang 顧頡剛, 605–17. Beijing: Zhonghua shuju.

Karapet'iants, Artemij M. 1988. "Чуньцю и древнекитайский исторический ритуал." In *Этика и ритуал в традиционном Китае*, ed. L. S. Vasil'ev et al., 85–154. Moscow: Nauka.

Ke Yaqin 柯亞琴. 2019. "Longhui He Beiyan di 324 hao mudi chutu Chujian yanjiu gongzuo qude xin jinzhan" 龍會河北岸第324號墓地出土楚簡研究工作取得新進展. http://news.jznews.com.cn/system/2019/12/06/011976783.shtml. Accessed December 9, 2019.

Keightley, David N. 1978. "The *Bamboo Annals* and Shang-Chou Chronology." *Harvard Journal of Asiatic Studies* 38, no. 2: 423–38.

———. 1997. "Shang Oracle-Bone Inscriptions." In *New Sources of Early Chinese History: An Introduction to the Reading of Inscriptions and Manuscripts*, ed. Edward L. Shaughnessy, 15–56. Berkeley: Society for the Study of Early China and the Institute of East Asian Studies, University of California, Berkley.

Kern, Martin. 2000. *The Stele Inscriptions of Ch'in Shih-huang: Text and Ritual in Early Chinese Imperial Representation*. New Haven, Conn.: American Oriental Society.

———. 2009. "Bronze Inscriptions, the *Shijing* and the *Shangshu*: The Evolution of the Ancestral Sacrifice during the Western Zhou." In *Early Chinese Religion, Part One: Shang through Han (1250 BC–220 AD)*, ed. John Lagerwey and Marc Kalinowski, 1:143–200. Leiden: Brill.

———. 2010. "Early Chinese Literature, Beginnings through Western Han." In *The Cambridge History of Chinese Literature, Volume 1: To 1375*, ed. Kang-I Sun Chang and Stephen Owen, 1–115. Cambridge: Cambridge University Press.

———. 2016. "*Shiji* li de 'zuozhe' gainian" 《史記》裡的"作者"概念. In *Shiji xue yu shijie hanxue lunji xubian* 史記學與世界漢學論集續編, ed. Martin Kern and Lee Chi-hsiang 李紀祥, 23–61. Taipei: Tangshan chubanshe.

———. 2018. "Early Chinese Divination and Its Rhetoric." In *Coping with the Future: Theories and Practices of Divination in East Asia*, ed. Michael Lackner, 255–88. Leiden: Brill.

———. 2019. "'Xi Shuai' 蟋蟀 ('Cricket') and Its Consequences: Issues in Early Chinese Poetry and Textual Studies." *Early China* 42:39–74.

Kern, Martin, and Dirk Meyer, eds. 2017. *Origins of Chinese Political Philosophy: Studies in the Composition and Thought of the* Shangshu *(Classic of Documents)*. Leiden: Brill.

Khayutina, Maria. 2019. "Reflections and Uses of the Past in Chinese Bronze Inscriptions from ca. 11th to 5th centuries BC: The Memory of the Conquest of Shang and the First Kings of Zhou." In *Historical Consciousness and the Use of the Past in the Ancient World*, ed. John Baines, Henriette van der Blom, Yi Samuel Chen, and Tim Rood, 157–80. Sheffield, U.K.: Equinox.

Kinney, Anne Behnke, trans. and ed. 2014. *Exemplary Women of Early China: The* Lienü zhuan *of Liu Xiang*. New York: Columbia University Press.

Kominami Ichirō 小南一郎. 1992. "Tenmei to toku" 天命と德. *Tōhō gakuhō* 東方學報 64:1–59.

Kōno Osamu 河野收. 1978. "Chūgoku kodai no aru hibusō heiwa undō" 中國古代の或る非武裝平和運動. *Gunji shigaku* 軍事史學 13:64–74.

Kotera Atsushi 小寺敦. 2016. "Seika kan *Keinen* yakuchū, kaidai" 清華簡『繫年』譯注・解題. *Tōyō bunka kenkyūsho kiyō* 東洋文化研究所紀要 170:31–316.

Krijgsman, Rens, and Paul Nicholas Vogt. 2019. "The One Text in the Many: Separate and Composite Readings of an Early Chinese Historical Manuscript." *Bulletin of the School of Oriental and African Studies* 82, no. 3: 473–92.

Kryukov, Vassili. 1995. "Symbols of Power and Communication in Pre-Confucian China (On the Anthropology of De)." *Bulletin of the School of Oriental and African Studies* 58:314–33.

Kudō Takushi 工藤卓司. 2014. "*Shangbo jiu–Bangren bu cheng* zhaji" 《上博九・邦人不稱》札記. *Zhili xuebao, renwen yu shenghuo yingyong tekan* 致理學報，人文與生活應用特刊 (July): 997–1026.

Kuroda Hidenori 黑田秀教. 2013. "Seika kan *Ryōshin* hattan" 清華簡『良臣』初探. *Chūgoku kenkyū shūkan* 中國研究集刊 56:83–105.

Kurz, Johannes L. 2012. "The Consolidation of Official Historiography during the Early Northern Song Dynasty." *Journal of Asian History* 46, no. 1:13–36.

Lai Guolong 來國龍. 2013. "Qinghua jian *Chu ju* suo jian Chuguo de gongzu yu shixi" 清華簡《楚居》所見楚國的公族與世系. In *Jianbo–jingdian–gushi* 簡帛·經典·古史, ed. Chen Zhi 陳致, 159–64. Shanghai: Shanghai guji chubanshe.

Lan Bixian 蘭碧仙. 2016. "Cong chutu wenxian kan fuci 'nai' de shuncheng yiyanhua" 從出土文獻看副詞"乃"的順承義衍化. *Jimei daxue xuebao (zhe she ban)* 集美大學學報（哲社版）4:127–31.

Lewis, Mark E. 1999. *Writing and Authority in Early China*. Albany: State University of New York Press.

———. 2006. *The Construction of Space in Early China*. Albany: State University of New York Press.

———. Forthcoming. *Honor and Shame in Early China*. Cambridge: Cambridge University Press.

Li Feng. 2006. *Landscape and Power in Early China: The Crisis and Fall of the Western Zhou 1045–771 BC*. Cambridge: Cambridge University Press.

———. 2008. *Bureaucracy and the State in Early China: Governing the Western Zhou*. Cambridge: Cambridge University Press.

Li Huibo 李慧博 and Wu Yaxiong 吳亞雄. 2019. "Hubei Jingzhou faxian zhengui Xi Han jiandu he Zhanguo Chu jian jiju xueshu jiazhi" 湖北荊州發現珍貴西漢簡牘和戰國楚簡極具学術价值. http://culture.people.com.cn/BIG5/n1/2019/0507/c1013-31071897.html. Accessed April 4, 2020.

Li Ling 李零, ed. 2002. *Rong Cheng shi* 容成氏. In *Shanghai bowuguan cang Zhanguo Chu zhushu* 上海博物館藏戰國楚竹書, ed. Ma Chengyuan 馬承源, 2:247–92. Shanghai: Shanghai guji chubanshe.

———. 2004. *Jianbo gushu yu xueshu yuanliu* 簡帛古書與學術源流. Beijing: Sanlian.

———. 2016. "Du jian biji: Qinghua Chu jian *Xinian* di yi zhi si zhang" 讀簡筆記：清華楚簡《繫年》第一至四章. *Jilin daxue shehui kexue xuebao* 吉林大學社會科學學報 56, no. 4:168–76.

Li Meiyan 李美妍 2017. "Lun Qinghua jian *Xinian* zhong chengjie guanxi ci 'nai' he 'yan'" 論清華簡《繫年》中承接關係詞"乃"和"焉." *Chutu wenxian* 出土文獻 11:156–64.

Li Qingling 李清凌. 2017. "Qinghua jian *Xinian* 'shi Qin xianren' xinjie" 清華簡《繫年》"是秦先人"新解. In *Huihuang Yongcheng: Quanguo (Fengxiang) Qin wenhua xueshu yantaohui lunwenji* 輝煌雍城：全國（鳳翔）秦文化學術研討會論文集, ed. Zhongguo xian Qin shixuehui 中國先秦史學會 et al., 181–84. Xi'an: San Qin chubanshe.

Li Rui 李銳. 2013. "You Qinghua jian *Xinian* tan Zhanguo chu Chu shi niandai de wenti" 由清華簡《繫年》談戰國初楚史年代的問題. *Shixueshi yanjiu* 史學史研究 2:100–104.

Li Shoukui 李守奎. 2014a. "Qinghua jian *Xinian* 'moao Yiwei' kaolun" 清華簡《繫年》"莫囂易為"考論. *Zhongyuan wenhua yanjiu* 中原文化研究 2:50–54.

———. 2014b. "Shuo Qinghua jian *Xinian* zhong de zhuangshixing bihua 'yi'" 說清華簡《繫年》中的裝飾性筆畫"一." *Chutu wenxian yanjiu* 出土文獻研究 13:34–46.

———, ed. 2016. *Qinghua jian* Xinian *yu gushi xintan* 清華簡《繫年》與古史新探. Shanghai: Zhongxi shuju.

———. 2017. "*Yue gong qi shi* yu Goujian mie Wu de lishi shishi ji gushi liuchuan" 《越公其事》與句踐滅吳的歷史事實及故事流傳. *Wenwu* 文物 6:75–80.

Li Shoukui 李守奎 and Xiao Pan 肖攀. 2015. *Qinghua jian* Xinian *wenzi kaoshi yu gouxing yanjiu* 清華簡《繫年》文字考釋與構形研究. Shanghai: Zhongxi shuju.

Li Songru 李松儒. 2015. *Qinghua jian* Xinian *jishi* 清華簡《繫年》集釋. Shanghai: Zhongxi shuju.

Li, Wai-yee. 2007. *The Readability of the Past in Early Chinese Historiography*. Cambridge, Mass.: Harvard University Asia Center.

———. 2014. *Women and National Trauma in Late Imperial Chinese Literature*. Cambridge, Mass.: Harvard University Asia Center.

———. 2019. "Inconvenient and Unnecessary Details in *Zuozhuan*." Paper presented at the conference on "Rethinking Early Chinese Historiography," Jerusalem, May 12–16 (forthcoming in the conference volume).

Li Xueqin 李學勤, ed. 2010. *Qinghua daxue cang Zhanguo zhujian* 清華大學藏戰國竹簡. Vol. 1. Shanghai: Zhongxi shuju.

———, ed. 2011a. *Qinghua daxue cang Zhanguo zhujian* 清華大學藏戰國竹簡. Vol. 2. Shanghai: Shanghai wenyi.

———. 2011b. "Qinghua jian *Xinian* ji youguan gushi wenti" 清華簡《繫年》及有關古史問題. *Wenwu* 文物 3:70–74.

———. 2011c. "Qinghua jian *Xinian* 'Nucuo zhi Rong' shi kao" 清華簡《繫年》"奴虘之戎"試考. *Shehui kexue zhanxian* 社會科學戰線 12:27–28.

———. 2011d. "Tan Qinren chu ju 'Zhuwu' de dili weizhi" 談秦人初居"邾吾"的地理位置. *Chutu wenxian* 出土文獻 2:1–5.

———. 2012a. *Qinghua daxue cang Zhanguo zhujian* 清華大學藏戰國竹簡. Vol. 3. Shanghai: Shanghai wenyi.

———. 2012b. "You Qinghua jian *Xinian* lun *Jinian* de tili" 由清華簡《繫年》論《紀年》的體例. *Shenzhen daxue xuebao (renwen shehui kexue ban)* 深圳大學學報（人文社會科學版）2:42–44.

———. 2013. "You Qinghua jian *Xinian* chongshi Mei situ Yi-gui" 由清華簡《繫年》重釋沬司徒疑簋. *Zhongguo gaoxiao shehui kexue* 中國高校社會科學 3:83–85.

———. 2015. "Zhengyue Zeng Hou Yu bianzhong mingwen qianban xiangjie" 正月曾侯與編鐘銘文前半詳解. *Zhongyuan wenhua yanjiu* 中原文化研究 4:16–20.

———, ed. 2016. *Qinghua daxue cang Zhanguo zhujian* 清華大學藏戰國竹簡. Vol. 6. Shanghai: Shanghai wenyi.

———, ed. 2017. *Qinghua daxue cang Zhanguo zhujian* 清華大學藏戰國竹簡. Vol. 7. Shanghai: Shanghai wenyi.

Li Yipi 李一丕. 2014. "Henan Chu changcheng fenbu ji fangyu tixi yanjiu" 河南楚長城分佈及防禦體系研究. *Zhongyuan wenwu* 中原文物 5:44–50, 74.

Li Yun 李韵. 2019. "Suizhou you xian Zenghou mu" 隨州又現曾侯墓. http://kaogu.cssn.cn/zwb/xccz/201908/t20190807_4952646.shtml. Accessed April 4, 2020.

Liang Qichao 梁啟超. (1922) 2000. *Zhongguo lishi yanjiu fa* 中國歷史研究法. Reprint, Shijiazhuang: Hebei jiaoyu chubanshe.

Liang Yun 梁雲. 2017. "Guanyu zaoqi Qin wenhua de kaogu shouhuo ji xiangguan renshi" 關於早期秦文化的考古收穫及相關認識. *Zhongguo shi yanjiu dongtai* 中國史研究動態 4:39–43.

Liao Mingchun 廖名春. 2012. "Qinghua jian *Xinian* guankui" 清華簡《繫年》管窺. *Shenzhen daxue xuebao (renwen shehui kexue ban)* 深圳大學學報（人文社會科學版）3:51–54.

Liao Wenyuan 廖文遠. 1997. *Zhanguo shi xinian jizheng* 戰國史繫年輯證. Chengdu: Bashu shushe.

Liji jijie 禮記集解. 1995. Comp. Sun Xidan 孫希旦 [1736–1784]. Ed. Shen Xiaohuan 沈嘯寰 and Wang Xingxian 王星賢. Beijing: Zhonghua shuju.

Lin Zhipeng 林志鵬. 2008. "Zhanguo zhushu *Bao Shuya yu Xi Peng zhi jian* yizhu" 戰國竹書《鮑叔牙與隰朋之諫》譯注. *Jianbo yanjiu* 簡帛研究 2008:1–18.

Liu Chengqun 劉成群. 2016. *Qinghua jian yu gushi zhenwei* 清華簡于古史甄微. Shanghai: Shanghai guji chubanshe.

Liu Fenglu 劉逢祿 [1776–1829]. 1955. "*Zuoshi chunqiu* kaozheng" 左氏春秋考證. Reprinted in *Guji kaobian congkan* 古籍考辨叢刊, ed. Gu Jiegang 顧頡剛, 561–604. Beijing: Zhonghua shuju.

Liu Guang 劉光. 2017a. "Qinghua jian *Xinian* di ershi zhang suo jian Jin Zhao jinian xin shi" 清華簡《繫年》第二十章所見晉、趙紀年新識. *Chutu wenxian* 出土文獻 11:177–83.

———. 2017b. "Qinghua jian *Xinian* suo jian Wu Zixu zhiguan kao" 清華簡《繫年》所見伍子胥職官考. *Guanzi xuekan* 管子學刊 3:112–18.

———. 2018. "Qinghua jian *Xinian* 'Nanhuai zhi xing' kaoxi" 清華簡《繫年》"南懷之行"考析. *Shixue jikan* 史學集刊 3:110–17.

Liu Guozhong 劉國忠. 2013. "Cong Qinghua jian *Xinian* kan Zhou Pingwang dongqian de xiangguan shishi" 從清華簡《繫年》看周平王東遷的相關史實. In *Jianbo–jingdian–gushi* 簡帛·經典·古史, ed. Chen Zhi 陳致, 173–79. Shanghai: Shanghai guji chubanshe.

———. 2016. *Introduction to the Tsinghua Bamboo-Strip Manuscripts*. Trans. Christopher J. Foster and William N. French. Leiden: Brill.

Liu Jiao 劉嬌. 2018. "Cong xiangguan chutu wenxian kan *Yanzi* de chengshu he liuchuan" 從相關出土文獻看《晏子》的成書和流傳. In *Chutu wenxian yu gudianxue chongjian lunji* 出土文獻與古典學重建論集, ed. Fudan daxue chutu wenxian yu guwenzi yanjiu zhongxin 復旦大學出土文獻與古文字研究中心, 54–91. Shanghai: Zhongxi shuju.

Liu jing aolun 六經奧論. N.d. By Zheng Qiao 鄭樵 [1104–1162]. e-*Siku quanshu* 四庫全書 edition.

Liu Yu 劉宇. 2016. "Qinghua jian *Xinian* yu 'Qin ren dong chu' shuo" 清華簡《繫年》與"秦人東出"說. *Jishou daxue xuebao (shehui kexue ban)* 吉首大學學報（社會科學版）37, no. 12:111–14.

Liu Zhuoyi 劉卓異. 2018. "Zhanguo Weiguo jinian sankao" 戰國衛國紀年三考. *Zhongguo shi yanjiu* 中國史研究 4:195–205.

Lu Yihan 路懿菡. 2013a. "Cong Qinghua jian *Xinian* kan Kangshu de shifeng" 從清華簡《繫年》看康叔的始封. *Xibei daxue xuebao (zhexue shehui kexue ban)* 西北大學學報（哲學社會科學版）4:136–41.

———. 2013b. "Cong Qinghua jian *Xinian* kan 'Wugeng zhi luan'" 從清華簡《繫年》看"武庚之亂." *Qilu xuekan* 齊魯學刊 5:51–52.

———. 2013c. "Cong Qinghua jian *Xinian* kan Zhou chu de 'san jian'" 從清華簡《繫年》看周初的"三監." *Liaoning shifan daxue xuebao (shehui kexue ban)* 遼寧師範大學學報（社會科學版）6:924–28.

Lu Zongyuan 路宗元, ed. 1999. *Qi changcheng* 齊長城. Ji'nan: Shandong youyi chubanshe.

Lunyu yizhu 論語譯注. 1992. Annot. Yang Bojun 楊伯峻. Beijing: Zhonghua shuju.

Luo Dan 羅丹. 2015. "Qinghua jian suo jian Chuguo zaoqi shishi dingbu" 清華簡所見楚國早期史事訂補. *Chu xue luncong* 楚學論叢 4:103–17.

Luo Xinhui 羅新慧. 2012. "Zhoudai tianming guannian de fazhan yu shanbian" 周代天命觀念的發展與嬗變. *Lishi yanjiu* 歷史研究 5:4–18.

———. 2016. "Shi shuo Qinghua jian *Xinian* diyi zhang ji qita pianzhang zhong de 'di'" 試說清華簡《繫年》第一章及其他篇章中的"帝." In *Qinghua jian* Xinian *yu gushi xintan* 清華簡《繫年》與古史新探, ed. Li Shoukui 李守奎, 91–106. Shanghai: Zhongxi shuju.

Luo Yunhuan 羅運環. 2015. "Qinghua jian *Xinian* ticai ji xiangguan wenti xintan" 清華簡《繫年》體裁及相關問題新探. *Hubei shehui kexue* 湖北社會科學 3:193–98.

Lüshi chunqiu xin jiaoshi 呂氏春秋新校釋. 1995. Comp. and annot. Chen Qiyou 陳奇猷. Shanghai: Shanghai guji chubanshe.

Ma Chengyuan 馬承源, ed. 2001–2012. *Shanghai bowuguan cang Zhanguo Chu zhushu* 上海博物館藏戰國楚竹書. Vols. 1–9. Shanghai: Shanghai guji chubanshe.

Ma Nan 馬楠. 2015. *Qinghua jian* Xinian *jizheng* 清華簡《繫年》輯證. Shanghai: Zhongxi shudian.

Ma Weidong 馬衛東. 2014. "Qinghua jian *Xinian* San Jin fa Qi kao" 清華簡《繫年》三晉伐齊考. *Jinyang xuekan* 晉陽學刊 1:16–22.

Ma Wenzeng 馬文增. 2018. "Qinghua jian *Xinian* shouzhang xinyan: Jianji 'guoren baodong,' 'gonghe xingzheng' wenti" 清華簡《繫年》首章新研──兼及"國人暴動"、"共和 行政"問題. *Yindu xuekan* 殷都學刊 2:26–29.

Ma Xueqin 馬雪芹. 2008. *Gu Yueguo xingshuai bianqian yanjiu* 古越國興衰變遷研究. Jinan: Qi-Lu shushe.

Maspero, Henri. (1927) 1965. *La Chine antique*. Reprint, Paris: Presses universitaires de France.

Masubuchi Tatsuo 増淵龍夫. 1993. "Shuo Chunqiu shidai de xian" 說春秋時代的縣, trans. Suo Jieran 索介然. In *Riben xuezhe yanjiu Zhongguo shi lunzhu xuanyi* 日本學者研究中國史論著選譯, ed. Liu Junwen 劉俊文, 3:189–213. Beijing: Zhonghua shuju.

Mattos, Gilbert L. 1997. "Eastern Zhou Bronze Inscriptions." In *New Sources of Early Chinese History: An Introduction to Reading Inscriptions and Manuscripts*, ed. Edward L. Shaughnessy, 85–124. Berkeley: Society for the Study of Early China and the Institute of East Asian Studies, University of California, Berkeley.

Mawangdui Hanmu boshu zhengli xiaozu 馬王堆漢墓帛書整理小組, ed. 1976. *Mawangdui Hanmu boshu: Zhanguo zonghengjia shu* 馬王堆漢墓帛書：戰國縱橫家書. Beijing: Wenwu.

——. 1983. *Mawangdui Hanmu boshu (san)* 馬王堆漢墓帛書（叁）. Beijing: Wenwu.

Meng Wentong 蒙文通 (1894–1968). 1936. "Qin wei Rong zu kao" 秦為戎族考. *Yu gong* 禹貢 6, no. 7:17–20.

Mengzi yizhu 孟子譯注. 1992. Annot. Yang Bojun 楊伯峻. Beijing: Zhonghua shuju.

Milburn, Olivia. trans. 2010. *The Glory of Yue: An Annotated Translation of the* Yuejue shu. Sinica Leidensia 93. Leiden: Brill.

——. 2016. "The *Xinian*: An Ancient Historical Text from the Qinghua University Collection of Bamboo Books." *Early China* 39:53–109.

Mittag, Achim. 2003. "The Qin *Bamboo Annals* of Shuihudi: A Random Note from the Perspective of Chinese Historiography." *Monumenta Serica* 51:543–70.

Mizuno Taku 水野卓. 2017. "Ōi no keishō kara mita Shū no tōsen: Seika kan *Keinen* o tegakari to shite" 王位の継承から見た周の東遷──清華簡『繫年』を手がかりとして. In *Kandoku ga kaku Chūgoku kodai no seiji to shakai* 簡牘が描く中国古代の政治と社会, ed. Fujita Katsuhisa 藤田勝久 and Sekio Shirō 關尾史郎, 29–50. Tokyo: Kyūko shoin.

Mozi jiaozhu 墨子校注. 1994. Comp. and annot. Wu Yujiang 吳毓江 [1898–1977]. Beijing: Zhonghua shuju.

Nienhauser, William H., Jr. 2007. "For Want of a Hand: A Note on the 'Hereditary House of Jin' and Sima Qian's 'Chunqiu.'" *Journal of the American Oriental Society* 127, no. 3:229–47.

Niu Pengtao 牛鵬濤. 2012. "Qinghua jian *Xinian* yu tongqi mingwen huzheng er ze" 清華簡《繫年》與銅器銘文互證二則. *Shenzhen daxue xuebao (renwen shehui kexue ban)* 深圳大學學報（人文社會科學版）29, no. 2:47–49.

———. 2013. "Qinghua jian *Chu ju* yu 'qian Ying yu Ruo' kaobian" 清華簡《楚居》與"遷郢於鄀"考辨. *Shenzhen daxue xuebao (renwen shehui kexue ban)* 深圳大學學報（人文社會科學版）30, no. 6:72–75.

Nivison, David S. 2009. *The Riddle of the Bamboo Annals.* Taipei: Airiti.

Nivison, David S., and Edward L. Shaughnessy. 2000. "The Jin Hou Su Bells Inscription and Its Implications for the Chronology of Early China." *Early China* 25:29–48.

Ōnishi Katsuya 大西克也. 2017. "Qinghua jian *Xinian* wei Chujian shuo: Cong Chuwang shihao yongzi tantao" 清華簡《繫年》為楚簡說—從楚王諡號用字探討. In *Yuanyuan liuchang: Hanzi guoji xueshu yantaohui ji AEARU di san jie Hanzi wenhua yantaohui lunwenji* 源遠流長：漢字國際學術研討會暨 AEARU 第三屆漢字文化研討會論文集, ed. Yang Rongxiang 楊榮祥 and Hu Chirui 胡敕瑞, 36–45. Beijing: Beijing daxue chubanshe.

Peng Fengwen 彭豐文. 2014. "Cong Manyi dao Huaxia: Xian Qin Chu ren de zuyuan jiyi yu minzu rentong" 從蠻夷到華夏：先秦楚人的族源記憶與民族認同. *Zhongguo bianjiang minzu yanjiu* 中國邊疆民族研究 7:214–23.

Petersen, Jens Østergård. 2019. "The Zhejiang Daxue *Zuozhuan* Manuscript." https://independent.academia.edu/PetersenJens. Accessed April 4, 2020.

Pi Xirui 皮錫瑞 [1850–1908]. (1907) 1998. *Jingxue tonglun* 經學通論. Reprint, Beijing: Zhonghua shuju.

Pines, Yuri. 2002. *Foundations of Confucian Thought: Intellectual Life in the Chunqiu Period, 722–453 B.C.E.* Honolulu: University of Hawai`i Press.

———. 2003. "History as a Guide to the Netherworld: Rethinking the *Chunqiu shiyu.*" *Journal of Chinese Religions* 31:101–26.

———. 2004. "The Question of Interpretation: Qin History in Light of New Epigraphic Sources." *Early China* 29:1–44.

———. 2005a. "Disputers of Abdication: Zhanguo Egalitarianism and the Sovereign's Power." *T'oung Pao* 91, no. 4/5:243–300.

———. 2005b. "Speeches and the Question of Authenticity in Ancient Chinese Historical Records." In *Historical Truth, Historical Criticism, and Ideology: Chinese Historiography and Historical Culture from a New Comparative Perspective,* ed. Helwig Schmidt-Glintzer, Achim Mittag, and Jörn Rüsen, 195–224. Leiden: Brill.

———. 2005–2006. "Biases and Their Sources: Qin History in the *Shiji.*" *Oriens Extremus* 45:10–34.

———. 2008. "To Rebel Is Justified? The Image of Zhouxin and Legitimacy of Rebellion in Chinese Political Tradition." *Oriens Extremus* 47:1–24.

———. 2009a. "Chinese History Writing between the Sacred and the Secular." In *Early Chinese Religion, Part One: Shang through Han (1250 BC–220 AD),* ed. John Lagerwey and Marc Kalinowski, 1:315–40. Leiden: Brill.

———. 2009b. *Envisioning Eternal Empire: Chinese Political Thought of the Warring States Era.* Honolulu: University of Hawai`i Press.

———. 2009c. "Rethinking the Origins of Chinese Historiography: The *Zuo Zhuan* Revisited" (Review Article). *Journal of Chinese Studies* 49:431–44.

———. 2010. "Political Mythology and Dynastic Legitimacy in the *Rong Cheng shi* Manuscript." *Bulletin of the School of Oriental and African Studies* 73, no. 3:503–29.

———. 2013. "Reassessing Textual Sources for Pre-imperial Qin History." In Синологи мира к юбилею Станислава Кучеры: Собрание трудов, ed. Sergej Dmitriev and Maxim Korolkov, 236–63. Moscow: Institut Vostokovedeniia RAN.

———. 2014. "Zhou History and Historiography: Introducing the Bamboo *Xinian*." *T'oung Pao* 100, no. 4/5: 287–324.

———. 2016. "Cong *Xinian* xuci de yongfa chongshen qi wenben de kekaoxing—jian chutan *Xinian* yuanshi ziliao de laiyuan" 從《繫年》虛詞的用法重審其文本的可靠性—兼初探《繫年》原始資料的來源. In *Qinghua jian* Xinian *yu gushi xintan* 清華簡《繫年》與古史新探, ed. Li Shoukui 李守奎, 236–54. Shanghai: Zhongxi shuju.

———. 2017a. "History without Anecdotes: Between the *Zuozhuan* and the *Xinian* Manuscript." In *Between Philosophy and History: Rhetorical Uses of Anecdotes in Early China*, ed. Paul van Els and Sarah Queen, 263–99. Albany: State University of New York Press.

———. 2017b. "A Toiling Monarch? The 'Wu yi' 無逸 Chapter Revisited." In *Origins of Chinese Political Philosophy: Studies in the Composition and Thought of the* Shangshu *(Classic of Documents)*, ed. Martin Kern and Dirk Meyer, 360–92. Leiden: Brill.

———. 2018a. "Chu Identity as Seen from Its Manuscripts: A Reevaluation." *Journal of Chinese History* 2, no. 1:1–26.

———. 2018b. "The Earliest 'Great Wall?' Long Wall of Qi Revisited." *Journal of the American Oriental Society* 138, no. 4:743–61.

Pines, Yuri, with Lothar von Falkenhausen, Gideon Shelach, and Robin D. S. Yates. 2014. "General Introduction: Qin History Revisited." In *Birth of an Empire: The State of Qin Revisited*, ed. Yuri Pines, Lothar von Falkenhausen, Gideon Shelach, and Robin D. S. Yates, 1–36. Berkeley: University of California Press.

Pu Maozuo 濮茅左, ed. 2007. *Jing Gong nüe* 競公瘧. In *Shanghai bowuguan cang Zhanguo Chu zhushu* 上海博物館藏戰國楚竹書, ed. Ma Chengyuan 馬承源, 6:157–91. Shanghai: Shanghai guji chubanshe.

Puett, Michael J. 2001. *The Ambivalence of Creation: Debates Concerning Innovation and Artifice in Early China*. Stanford, Calif.: Stanford University Press.

Qi Minshuai 亓民帥. 2017. "Suzhou bowuguan cang Wu wang Yumo jian mingwen yu Yuji, Yumo shishi" 蘇州博物館藏吳王餘眛劍銘文與餘祭、餘眛史事. *Qingtongqi yu jinwen* 青銅器與金文 1:598–606.

Qian Xuantong 錢玄同 [1887–1939] (1931) 1963. "*Zuoshi Chunqiu kaozheng* shu hou" 左氏春秋考證書後. In *Gushi bian* 古史辨, ed. Gu Jiegang 顧頡剛, 5:1–21. Reprint, Hong Kong: Taiping shuju.

Qiao Zhizhong 喬治忠. 2016. "*Zuozhuan, Guoyu* bei Liu Xin cuanluan de yixiang tiezheng: Lishi niandaixue Liu Tan zhi shuo shenlun" 《左傳》《國語》被劉歆竄亂的一項鐵證—歷史年代學劉坦之說申論. *Beijing shifan daxue xuebao (shehui kexue ban)* 北京師範大學學報（社會科學版）3:68–78.

Qin jiandu heji shiwen zhushi xiuding ben 秦簡牘合集釋文注釋修訂本. 2016. Ed. Chen Wei 陳偉 et al. 4 vols. Wuhan: Jing Chu wenku bianzuan chuban weiyuanhui and Wuhan daxue chubanshe.

Qinghua daxue chutu wenxian dushuhui 清華大學出土文獻讀書會. 2014. "Zeng Hou Yu bianzhong mingwen bushi" 曾侯與編鐘銘文補釋. http://www.ctwx.tsinghua.edu.cn/publish/cetrp/6841/20141013090038578527324/zenghouyu.pdf. Accessed April 4, 2020.

Qiu Feng 邱鋒. 2007. "Lun *Guoyu–Zheng yu* chansheng de diyu he shidai" 論《國語·鄭語》產生的地域和時代. *Gansu shehui kexue* 甘肅社會科學 2:124–25, 138.

———. 2013. "*Zhushu jinian* yu Jin Tang jian de shixue" 《竹書紀年》與晉唐間的史學. *Shixue shi yanjiu* 史學史研究 1:24–32.

Qiu Xigui 裘錫圭. 2016. "Shuo Houma mengshu 'biangai Ran ji Huan bi bushou ergong'" 說侯馬盟書"邊改助及奐俾不守二宮." In *Qinghua jian* Xinian *yu gushi xintan* 清華簡《繫年》與古史新探, ed. Li Shoukui 李守奎, 6–18. Shanghai: Zhongxi shuju.

Qu Yuan ji jiaozhu 屈原集校注. 1996. Prepared by Jin Kaicheng 金開誠, Dong Hongli 董洪利, and Gao Luming 高路明. Beijing: Zhonghua shuju.

Ren Huibin 任會斌. 2014. "Yue qiandu Langye shijian chukao" 越遷都琅琊時間初考. *Nanfang wenwu* 南方文物 4:117–20.

Ren Xianghong 任相宏. 2005. "Qi changcheng yuantou jianzhi kao" 齊長城源頭建置考. In *Dongfang kaogu* 東方考古, ed. Luan Fengshi 欒豐實, 1:263–75. Beijing: Kexue chubanshe.

Richter, Matthias L. 2013. *The Embodied Text: Establishing Textual Identity in Early Chinese Manuscripts*. Leiden: Brill.

Rubin, Vitalij A. 1966. "Как Сыма Цянь изображал период Чуньцю." *Народы Азии и Африки* 2:66–76.

Satō Shin'ya 佐藤信弥. 2017. "Rekishi hyōka to shite no Kyōhakuwa" 歴史評価としての共伯和. *Chūgoku kodaishi ronsō* 中國古代史論叢 9:1–30.

Schaberg, David. 2001. *A Patterned Past: Form and Thought in Early Chinese Historiography*. Cambridge Mass.: Harvard University Asia Center.

———. 2011. "Chinese History and Philosophy." In *The Oxford History of Historical Writing, Volume 1: Beginnings to AD 600*, ed. Andrew Feldherr and Grant Hardy, 394–414. Oxford: Oxford University Press.

———. 2013. "Functionary Speech: On the Work of *shi* 使 and *shi* 史." In *Facing the Monarch: Modes of Advice in the Early Chinese Court*, ed. Garret P. S. Olberding, 19–41. Cambridge, Mass.: Harvard University Asia Center.

Selbitschka, Armin. 2018. "'I Write Therefore I Am': Scribes, Literacy, and Identity in Early China." *Harvard Journal of Asiatic Studies* 78, no. 2:413–76.

Shangshu jinguwen zhushu 尚書今古文注疏. (1815) 1998. Comp. Sun Xingyan 孫星衍 [1753–1818]. Proofread by Sheng Dongling 盛冬鈴 and Chen Kang 陳抗. Beijing: Zhonghua shuju.

Shaughnessy, Edward L. 1991. *Sources of Western Zhou History: Inscribed Bronze Vessels*. Berkeley: University of California Press.

———. 1997. *Before Confucius: Studies in the Creation of the Chinese Classics*. Albany: State University of New York Press.

———. 2006. *Rewriting Early Chinese Texts*. Albany: State University of New York Press.

———. 2007. "The Writing of a Late Western Zhou Bronze Inscription." *Asiatische Studien/Études asiatiques* 61, no. 3:845–77.

———. 2014. "The Qin *Biannian ji* 編年記 and the Beginnings of Historical Writing in China." In *Beyond the First Emperor's Mausoleum: New Perspectives on Qin Art*, ed. Liu Yang, 115–36. Minneapolis: Minneapolis Institute of Arts.

Shelach, Gideon, and Yuri Pines. 2006. "Secondary State Formation and the Development of Local Identity: Change and Continuity in the State of Qin (770–221 B.C.)." In *Archaeology of Asia*, ed. Miriam T. Stark, 202–30. Malden, Mass.: Blackwell.

Shen Guangming 沈光明 and Yi Shasha 易莎莎. 2017. "Qinghua jian *Chu ju* yanjiu zongshu" 清華簡《楚居》研究綜述. *Keji chuangye yuekan* 科技創業月刊 7:59–61.

Shen Jianhua 沈建華. 2016. "*Xinian* 'yu Nucuo zhi Rong' yu buci 'si feng fang' xiangguan dili" 《繫年》"御奴虘之戎"與卜辭"四封方"相關地理. In *Qinghua jian* Xinian *yu gushi xintan* 清華簡《繫年》與古史新探, ed. Li Shoukui 李守奎, 64–71. Shanghai: Zhongxi shuju.

Shen Yucheng 沈玉成 and Liu Ning 劉寧. 1992. *Chunqiu Zuozhuan xueshi gao* 春秋左傳學史稿. Nanjing: Jiangsu guji chubanshe.

Shi ben bazhong 世本八種. 2008. Annot. Song Zhong 宋衷 [fl. 200]. Comp. Qin Jiamo 秦嘉謨 [fl. 1812–1818]. Beijing: Zhonghua shuju.

Shiji 史記. 1997. By Sima Qian 司馬遷 [ca. 145–90 BCE] et al. Annot. Zhang Shoujie 張守節, Sima Zhen 司馬貞, and Pei Yin 裴駰. Beijing: Zhonghua shuju.

Shim Jae-hoon. 1997. "The 'Jinhou Su *bianzhong*' Inscription and Its Significance." *Early China* 22:43–75.

———. 2016. "Dui chuanshi wenxian de xin tiaozhan: Qinghua jian *Xinian* suo ji Zhou dongqian shishi kao" 對傳世文獻的新挑戰：清華簡《繫年》所記周東遷史

事考. In *Qinghua jian* Xinian *yu gushi xintan* 清華簡《繫年》與古史新探, ed. Li Shoukui 李守奎, 128–59. Shanghai: Zhongxi shuju.

———. 2017. "The Eastward Relocation of the Zhou Royal House in the *Xinian* Manuscript: Chronological and Geographical Aspects." *Archiv Orientální* 85:67–98.

Shou Bin 守彬. 2011. "Cong Qinghua jian *Chu ju* tan 'x Ying'" 從清華簡《楚居》談"x郢." *Chu wenhua yanjiu lunji* 楚文化研究論集 10:94–100.

Škrabal, Ondřej. 2014. "Nově objevený rukopis *Xìnián* a jeho význam pro studium nejstarších čínských dějin." *Nový orient* 3:10–29.

———. 2019. "Writing before Inscribing: On the Use of Manuscripts in the Production of Western Zhou Bronze Inscriptions." *Early China* 42:273–332.

Song Huaqiang 宋華強. 2010. *Xincai Geling Chujian chutan* 新蔡葛陵楚簡初探. Wuhan: Wuhan daxue chubanshe.

Staack, Thies. 2015. "Identifying Codicological Sub-units in Bamboo Manuscripts: Verso Lines Revisited." *Manuscript Cultures* 8:157–86.

Sterckx, Roel. 2002. *The Animal and the Daemon in Early China*. Albany: State University of New York Press.

Su Jianzhou 蘇建洲. 2012. "*Qinghua daxue cang Zhanguo zhujian (er)-Xinian* kaoshi si ze"《清華大學藏戰國竹簡（貳）·繫年》考釋四則. *Jianbo* 簡帛 7:65–78.

———. 2014. "Ye lun Qinghua jian *Xinian* 'moao Yiwei'" 也論清華簡《繫年》"莫囂易為." *Zhonghua wenhua yanjiu* 中華文化研究 5:115–21.

Su Jianzhou 蘇建洲, Wu Wenwen 吳雯雯, and Lai Yixuan 賴怡璇, eds. 2013. *Qinghua er* Xinian *jijie* 清華二《繫年》集解. Taipei: Wanjuan lou.

Sun Feiyan 孫飛燕. 2012. "Shitan *Xinian* zhong Juemo zhi hui yu Jin Wu fa Chu de jinian" 試談《繫年》中厥貉之會與晉吳伐楚的紀年. http://www.gwz.fudan.edu.cn/Web/Show/1810. Accessed April 6, 2020.

Taniguchi Mitsuru 谷口滿. 2011. "Shi lun Qinghua jian *Chu ju* duiyu Chuguo lishi dili yanjiu de yingxiang" 試論清華簡《楚居》對於楚國歷史地理研究的影響. Trans. Chen Wei 陳偉. *Chu wenhua yanjiu lunji* 楚文化研究論集 10:23–30.

Tao Xinghua 陶興華. 2013a. "Cong Qinghua jian *Xinian* kan 'gonghe' yu 'Gong He xingzheng'" 從清華簡《繫年》看"共和"與"共和行政." *Gudai wenming* 古代文明 2:57–62.

———. 2013b. "Shezheng weibi bian cheng wang, dangguo weibi shi jianye: Cong chutu wenxian kan Gong Bo He shezheng cheng wang wenti" 攝政未必便稱王，當國未必是僭越——從出土文獻看共伯和攝政稱王問題. *Xibei shida xuebao (shehui kexue ban)* 西北師大學報（社會科學版）5:40–45.

———. 2014. "Xi Zhou 'Gong' di suo zai yu Gong Bo He 'ru wei sangong' kao" 西周"共"地所在與共伯和"入為三公"考. *Lishi dili* 歷史地理 29:82–93.

Teng Mingyu. 2014. "From Vassal State to Empire: An Archaeological Examination of Qin Culture." Trans. Susanna Lam. In *Birth of Empire: The State of Qin*

Revisited, ed. Yuri Pines, Lothar von Falkenhausen, Gideon Shelach, and Robin D. S. Yates, 71–112. Berkeley: University of California Press.

Tian Xudong 田旭東. 2012. "Qinghua jian *Xinian* yu Qin ren xiqian xintan" 清華簡《繫年》與秦人西遷新探. *Qin Han yanjiu* 秦漢研究 6:36–41.

Twitchett, Denis C. 1992. *The Writing of Official History Under the T'ang*. Cambridge: Cambridge University Press.

Van Auken, Newell Ann. 2007. "Could 'Subtle Words' Have Conveyed 'Praise and Blame'? The Implications of Formal Regularity and Variation in *Spring and Autumn* (*Chūn qiū*) Records." *Early China* 31:47–111.

———. 2014. "*Spring and Autumn* Use of *Jí* 及 and Its Interpretation in the *Gōngyáng* and *Gǔliáng* Commentaries." In *Studies in Chinese and Sino-Tibetan Linguistics: Dialect, Phonology, Transcription, and Text*, ed. Richard VanNess Simmons and Newell Ann Van Auken, 429–56. Taipei: Institute of Linguistics, Academia Sinica.

———. 2016a. *The Commentarial Transformation of the Spring and Autumn*. Albany: State University of New York Press.

———. 2016b. "Judgments of the Gentleman: A New Analysis of the Place of *junzi* Comments in *Zuozhuan* Composition History." *Monumenta Serica* 64, no. 2:277–302.

van Els, Paul. 2017. "Old Stories No Longer Told: The End of the Anecdotes Tradition of Early China." In *Between Philosophy and History: Rhetorical Uses of Anecdotes in Early China*, ed. Paul van Els and Sarah Queen, 331–56. Albany: State University of New York Press.

van Els, Paul, and Sarah Queen, eds. 2017. *Between Philosophy and History: Rhetorical Uses of Anecdotes in Early China*. Albany: State University of New York Press.

van Ess, Hans. 1994. "The Old Text/New Text Controversy: Has the 20th Century Got It Wrong?" *T'oung Pao* 80:146–70.

———. 2014. *Politik und Geschichtsschreibung im alten China: Pan-ma i-tung*. Wiesbaden: Harrassowitz.

Vankeerberghen, Griet. 2005–2006. "Choosing Balance: Weighing (*quan* 權) as a Metaphor for Action in Early Chinese Texts." *Early China* 30:47–89.

Venture, Olivier [Feng Yicheng 風儀誠]. 2007. "Zhanguo liang Han 'yu,' 'yu' er zi de yongfa yu gushu de chuanxie xiguan" 戰國兩漢"于"、"於"二字的用法與古書的傳寫習慣. *Jianbo* 簡帛 2:81–95.

———. 2017. "Zeng: The Rediscovery of a Forgotten Regional State." In *China across the Centuries: Papers from a Lecture Series in Budapest*, ed. Gábor Kósa, 1–32. Budapest: Department of East Asian Studies, Eötvös Loránd University.

Vogelsang, Kai. 2002. "Inscriptions and Proclamations: On the Authenticity of the '*gao*' Chapters in the *Book of Documents*." *Bulletin of the Museum of Far Eastern Antiquities* 74:138–209.

———. 2003/2004. "The Scribes' Genealogy." *Oriens Extremus* 44:1–9.

———. 2007. *Geschichte als Problem: Entstehung, Formen und Funktionen von Geschichtsschreibung im alten China*. Lun Wen: Studien zur Geistesgeschichte und Literatur in China 9. Wiesbaden: Harrassowitz.

Waley, Arthur, trans. 1996. *The Book of Songs: The Ancient Chinese Classic of Poetry*. Edited with additional translations by Joseph R. Allen. New York: Grove Press.

Wang He 王和. 1984. "Lun *Zuozhuan* yuyan" 論《左傳》預言. *Shixue yuekan* 史學月刊 6:13–18.

———. 2011. "*Zuozhuan* zhong houren fuyi de gezhong chengfen"《左傳》中後人附益的各種成分. *Beijing shifan daxue xuebao (shehui kexue ban)* 北京師範大學學報（社會科學版）1:82–95.

Wang Hongjun 王洪軍. 2013. "Qinghua jian *Xinian* yu Shaohao 'Xi qian' zhi mi" 清華簡《繫年》與少皡"西遷"之謎. *Beifang luncong* 北方論叢 1:57–62.

Wang Hongliang 王紅亮. 2016. "You Qinghua jian *Xinian* lun 'gonghe xingzheng' de xiangguan wenti" 由清華簡《繫年》論"共和行政"的相關問題. *Shixueshi yanjiu* 史學史研究 3:91–99.

Wang Hui 王暉. 2013a. "Chunqiu zaoqi Zhou wangshi wangwei shixi bianju kaoyi: Jianshuo Qinghua jian *Xinian* 'Zhou wu wang jiu nian'" 春秋早期周王室王位世襲變局考異——兼說清華簡《繫年》"周無王九年." *Renwen zazhi* 人文雜志 5:75–81.

———. 2013b. "Chu zhushu *Wu ming* zhuilian pianpai xin kao" 楚竹書《吳命》綴連編排新考. *Zhongyuan wenhua yanjiu* 中原文化研究 2:60–65.

———. 2016. "Ye tan Qinghua jian *Xinian* 'xiang Xi Rong' de shidu" 也談清華簡《繫年》"降西戎"的釋讀. In *Qinghua jian* Xinian *yu gushi xintan* 清華簡《繫年》與古史新探, ed. Li Shoukui 李守奎, 487–93. Shanghai: Zhongxi shuju.

Wang Qing 王青. 2013. "'Ming' yu 'yu': Shangbo jian *Wu ming* bushi; Jianlun 'ming' de wenti wenti" "命"與"語"：上博簡《吳命》補釋——兼論"命"的文體問題. *Shixue jikan* 史學集刊 7:47–55.

Wang Shimin 王叔民. 2017. *Kaoguxue shi yu Shang Zhou tongqi yanjiu* 考古學史與商周銅器研究. Beijing: Shehui kexue wenxian chubanshe.

Wang Yongbo 王永波 and Wang Yunpeng 王雲鵬. 2013. "Qi changcheng de renzi xing buju yu jianzhi niandai" 齊長城的人字形布局與建制年代. *Guanzi xuekan* 管子學刊 2:33–39, 64.

Wang Yuzhe 王玉哲. 1986. "Zhou Pingwang dongqian nai bi Qin fei bi Quanrong shuo" 周平王東遷乃避秦非避犬戎說. *Tianjin shehui kexue* 天津社會科學 3:49–52.

Wang Zewen 王澤文. 2002. "Chunqiu shiqi de jinian tongqi mingwen yu *Zuozhuan* de duizhao yanjiu" 春秋時期的紀年銅器銘文與《左傳》的對照研究. PhD diss., Zhongguo shehui kexueyuan.

———. 2015. "Wenfengta M1 chutu Zeng Hou Yu zhongming de chubu yanjiu" 文峰塔 M 1 出土曾侯與鐘銘的初步研究. *Jianghan kaogu* 江漢考古 6:106–10.

Wang Zhengdong 王政冬. 2014. "You Qinghua jian *Xinian* dingzheng Zhaoguo shixi" 由清華簡《繫年》訂正趙國世系. http://www.gwz.fudan.edu.cn/Web/Show/2246. Accessed April 4, 2020.

Watson, Burton, trans. 1989. *The Tso Chuan: Selections from China's Oldest Narrative History*. New York: Columbia University Press.

———, trans. 1993. *Records of the Grand Historian, Volume 3: Qin Dynasty*. Hong Kong: Chinese University of Hong Kong.

Wei Cide 魏慈德. 2013. "*Qinghua jian* Xinian yu *Zuozhuan* zhong de Chu shi yitong" 《清華簡·繫年》與《左傳》中的楚史異同. *Donghua Hanxue* 東華漢學 17:1–48.

———. 2016. "*Xinian* de jianbei xingzhi tanjiu ji qi jishi guandian yu *Zuozhuan* yitong liju" 《繫年》的簡背形制探究及其記事觀點與《左傳》異同例舉. In *Qinghua jian* Xinian *yu gushi xintan* 清華簡《繫年》與古史新探, ed. Li Shoukui 李守奎, 329–40. Shanghai: Zhongxi shuju.

Wei Dong 魏棟. 2013. "Qinghua jian *Xinian* 'Zhou wang wang jiu nian' ji liang Zhou zhiji xiangguan wenti xintan" 清華簡《繫年》「周亡王九年」及兩周之際相關問題新探. In *Chu jian Chu wenhua yu xian Qin lishi wenhua guoji xueshu yantaohui lunwenji* 楚簡楚文化與先秦歷史文化國際學術研討會論文集, ed. Luo Yunhuan 羅運環, 109–21. Wuhan: Hubei jiaoyu chubanshe.

———. 2016a. "Qinghua jian *Xinian* yu Xu qian Rongcheng shi fawei" 清華簡《繫年》與許遷容城事發微. *Chutu wenxian* 出土文獻 8:90–96.

———. 2016b. "Suizhou Wenfengta Zenghou Yu mu A zu bianzhong mingwen yishi" 隨州文峰塔曾侯與墓 A 組編鐘銘文拾遺. *Zhongguo guojia bowuguan guankan* 中國國家博物館館刊 9:58–64.

———. 2018. "Qinghua jian *Xinian* 'Chu Wen wang yi qi yu Hanyang' xilun" 清華簡《繫年》「楚文王以啟于漢陽」析論. *Rao Zongyi guoxueyuan yuankan* 饒宗頤國學院院刊 5:87–112.

Williams, Crispin. 2012–2013. "Dating the Houma Covenant Texts: The Significance of Recent Findings from the Wenxian Covenant Texts." *Early China* 35–36: 247–75.

Wong, Young-tsu. 2010. *Beyond Confucian China: The Rival Discourses of Kang Youwei and Zhang Binglin*. London: Routledge.

Wu, Xiaolong. 2017. *Material Culture, Power, and Identity in Ancient China*. Cambridge: Cambridge University Press.

Wu Xueru [Wu Hsueh-ju] 巫雪如. 2019. "Cong ruogan zici yongfa tan Qinghua jian *Xinian* de zuozhe jiqi wenben goucheng" 從若干字詞用法談清華簡《繫年》的作者及其文本構成. *Qinghua xuebao* 清華學報, n. s., 49, no. 2:187–227.

Xiaohu 小狐. 2012. "Du *Xinian* yizha" 讀《繫年》臆札. http://www.gwz.fudan.edu.cn/Web/Show/1766. Accessed April 4, 2020.

Xia-Shang-Zhou duandai gongcheng zhuanjia zu 夏商周斷代工程專家組. 2000. *Xia-Shang-Zhou duandai gongcheng 1996–2000 nian jieduan chengguo baogao: Jianben*

夏商周斷代工程1996–2000年階段成果報告：簡本. Beijing: Shijie tushu chuban gongsi.

Xin Deyong 辛德勇. 2017. *Xin Deyong shuo Zhongguo lishi dili: Yanmo de guowang* 辛德勇說中國歷史地理：湮沒的過往. Shenyang: Wanjuan.

Xin jiben Huan Tan Xin lun 新輯本桓譚新論. 2009. Coll. Zhu Qianzhi 朱謙之. Beijing: Zhonghua shuju.

Xin lun. See *Xin jiben Huan Tan Xin lun*.

Xing Wen 邢文. 2013. "Qinghua jian *Jinteng* yu sanjian" 清華簡《金縢》與三監. *Shenzhen daxue xuebao (renwen shehui kexue ban)* 深圳大學學報（人文社會科學版）1:68–71.

Xiong Xianpin 熊賢品. 2014. "*Yuewang Chaxu-ge* mingwen yu Yueguo xidu 'Gusu' bulun"《越王差徐戈》銘文與越國徙都"姑蘇"補論. *Suzhou jiaoyu xueyuan xuebao* 蘇州教育學院學報 31, no. 6:6–12.

———. 2017. *Zhanguo wangnian wenti yanjiu* 戰國王年問題研究. Beijing: Zhongguo shehui kexue chubanshe.

———. 2018. "Zhanguo shiqi Wei jun shixi kao" 戰國時期衛君世襲考. *Zhongguo shi yanjiu* 中國史研究 4:181–94.

Xu Jianwei 徐建委. 2017. *Wenben geming: Liu Xiang, "Hanshu-yiwenzhi" yu zaoqi wenben yanjiu* 文本革命：劉向、《漢書·藝文志》與早期文本研究. Beijing: Zhongguo shehui kexue chubanshe.

Xu Shaohua 徐少華. 1999. "Chu Culture: An Archaeological Overview." In *Defining Chu: Image and Reality in Ancient China*, ed. Constance A. Cook and John S. Major, 21–32. Honolulu: University of Hawai`i Press.

———. 2005. "Cong Shu Jiang-fu xi gu Shenguo lishi yu wenhua de youguan wenti" 從叔姜簠析古申國歷史與文化的有關問題. *Wenwu* 文物 3:66–68, 80.

———. 2011. "Chunqiu Chu Shengong xulie shubu" 春秋楚申公序列疏補. *Chu wenhua yanjiu lunji* 楚文化研究論集 10:215–25.

———. 2014. "Lun Suizhou Wenfengta yi hao mu de niandai jiqi xueshu jiazhi" 論隨州文峰塔一號墓的年代及其學術價值. *Jianghan kaogu* 江漢考古 4:76–84.

———. 2016. "Qinghua jian *Xinian* 'Zhou wu wang jiu nian' qianyi" 清華簡《繫年》"周無王九年"淺議. *Jilin Daxue shehui kexue xuebao* 吉林大學社會科學學報 56, no. 4:183–87.

Xu Zhaochang 許兆昌 and Qi Dandan 齊丹丹. 2012. "Shilun Qinghua jian *Xinian* de bianzuan tedian" 試論清華簡《繫年》的編纂特點. *Gudai wenming* 古代文明 6:60–66.

Xu Zhongshu 徐仲舒. (1936) 1988. "Jinwen guci shili" 金文嘏辭釋例. Reprinted in *Xu Zhongshu lishi lunwen xuanji* 徐仲舒歷史論文選輯, 502–64. Beijing: Zhonghua shuju.

Xunzi jijie 荀子集解. 1992. Annot. Wang Xianqian 王先謙 [1842–1917]. Ed. Shen Xiaohuan 沈嘯寰 and Wang Xingxian 王星賢. Beijing: Zhonghua shuju.

Yan Deliang 閆德亮. 2015. "Churen de Huaxia guan jiqi shenhua lunlue" 楚人的華夏觀及其神話論略. *Jiangxi shehui kexue* 江西社會科學 1:119–25.

Yang Bo 楊博. 2019. *Zhanguo Chu zhushu shixue jiazhi tanyan* 戰國楚竹書史學價值探研. Shanghai: Shanghai guji chubanshe.

Yang Kuan 楊寬. 1998. *Zhanguo shi* 戰國史. Rev. ed. Shanghai: Renmin chubanshe.

Yang Mengsheng 楊蒙生. 2014. "Qinghua jian (san) *Liang chen* pian guanjian" 清華簡(叁)《良臣》篇管見. *Shenzhen daxue xuebao (renwen shehui kexue ban)* 深圳大學學報(人文社會科學版) 31, no. 2:59–61.

Yanzi chunqiu yizhu 晏子春秋譯注. 1996. Annot. and ed. Chen Tao 陳濤. Tianjin: Tianjin guji chubanshe.

Yates, Robin D. S. 1979. "The Mohists on Warfare: Technology, Technique, and Justification." In "Studies in Classical Chinese Thought," ed. Henry Rosemont Jr. and Benjamin I. Schwartz, special issue, *Journal of the American Academy of Religion*, 47, no. 3:549–603.

———. 2011. "Soldiers, Scribes, and Women: Literacy among the Lower Orders in Early China." In *Writing and Literacy in Early China*, ed. Li Feng and David Prager Banner, 339–69. Seattle: University of Washington Press.

Yin Hongbing 尹弘兵. 2012. "Cong *Chuju* kan Jilian yu Xuexiong de guanxi" 從《楚居》看季連與穴熊的關係. http://www.bsm.org.cn/show_article.php?id=1711. Accessed April 4, 2020.

Yin Qun 印群. 2014. "Lun Dabuzi shan Qin gong lingyuan de renxun: Jian tan Ying Qin xianren xiqian de diwang" 論大堡子山秦公陵園的人殉──兼談嬴秦先人西遷之地望. *Fudan xuebao (shehui kexue ban)* 復旦學報(社會科學版) 6:80–87.

———. 2017. "Jinnian lai guanyu Qin ren zuyuan de kaogu yanjiu" 近年來關於秦人族源的考古研究. In *Huihuang Yongcheng: Quanguo (Fengxiang) Qin wenhua xueshu yantaohui lunwenji* 輝煌雍城：全國(鳳翔)秦文化學術研討會論文集, ed. Zhongguo xian Qin shixuehui 中國先秦史學會 et al., 289–92. Xi'an: San Qin chubanshe.

Yoshimoto Michimasa 吉本道雅. 1990a. "*Shunjū jigo kō*" 《春秋事語》考. *Sen'oku hakubutsukan kiyō* 泉屋博物館紀要 6:37–52.

———. 1990b. "Shūshitsu tōsen kō" 周室東遷考. *Tōyō gakuhō* 東洋學報 71, no. 3-4:33–56.

———. 1991. "Saden tangen josetsu" 左傳探源說序. *Tōhōgaku* 東方學 81:16–27.

———. 1995. "Shin shi kenkyū josetsu" 秦史研究序說. *Shirin* 史林 78, no. 3:34–67.

———. 2013. "Seika kan keinen kō" 清華簡繫年考. *Kyōto daigaku bungakubu kenkyū kiyō* 京都大學文學部研究紀要 52:1–94.

———. 2017. "Shūshitsu tōsen saikō" 周室東遷再考. *Kyōto daigaku bungakubu kenkyū kiyō* 京都大學文學部研究紀要 56:1–58.

Yuan Jinping 袁金平. 2016. "You Qinghua jian *Xinian* 'Zi Xinshou' tan Xian Qin renming guan 'zi' zhi li" 由清華簡《繫年》"子颦壽"談先秦人名冠"子"之例. In *Qinghua jian* Xinian *yu gushi xintan* 清華簡《繫年》與古史新探, ed. Li Shoukui 李守奎, 215–26. Shanghai: Zhongxi shuju.

Yuasa Kunihiro 湯淺邦弘. 2017. *Zhujian xue: Zhongguo gudai sixiang de tanjiu* 竹簡學—中國古代思想的探究. Trans. Bai Yutian 白雨田. Shanghai: Dongfang chubanshe.

Zaoqi Qin wenhua lianhe kaogudui 早期秦文化聯合考古隊. 2012. "Gansu Qingshui Liya yizhi kaogu fajue huode zhongda tupo" 甘肅清水李崖遺址考古發掘獲得重大突破. *Zhongguo wenwu bao* 中國文物報 8 (January 20). http://big5.cntv.cn/gate/big5/kejiao.cntv.cn/20120202/100142.shtml. Accessed April 4, 2020.

Zhang Chongyi 張崇依. 2017. "Cong *Chunqiu Zuoshi zhuan* kan Qinghua jian *Xinian* suo yong shiliao: Yi Xia Ji shishi weili" 從《春秋左氏傳》看清華簡《繫年》所用史料——以夏姬史事為例. *Yindu xuekan* 殷都學刊 2:54–58.

Zhang Chunlong 張春龍. 2004. "Cili Chujian gaishu" 慈利楚簡概述. In *Xinchu jianbo yanjiu* 新出簡帛研究, ed. Ai Lan 艾蘭 [Sarah Allan] and Xing Wen 邢文, 4–11. Beijing: Wenwu.

Zhang Handong 張漢東. 1988. "*Zuozhuan* jiqi xiang *Chunqiu* xue de yanbian"《左傳》及其向《春秋》學的演變. *Zhongguoshi yanjiu* 中國史研究 4:154–62.

Zhang, Hanmo. 2018. *Authorship and Text-Making in Early China*. Boston: De Gruyter.

Zhang Huaitong 張懷通. 2013. *Yizhou shu xin yan* 《逸周書》新研. Beijing: Zhonghua shuju.

Zhang Shuguo 張樹國. 2016. "*Piao Qiang zhong* ming yu Chu zhushu *Xinian* suo ji Zhanguo chunian shishi kaolun"《驫羌鐘》銘與楚竹書《繫年》所記戰國初年史實考論. *Zhonghua wenshi luncong* 中華文史論叢 2:191–218.

Zhang Shuo 張碩 and Xiao Yang 肖洋. 2013. "Cong *Chu ju* kan Chu Zhaowang shidai Chuguo ducheng de qianxi" 從《楚居》看楚昭王時代楚國都城的遷徙. In *Chu jian Chu wenhua yu xian Qin lishi wenhua guoji xueshu yantaohui lunwenji* 楚簡楚文化與先秦歷史文化國際學術研討會論文集, ed. Luo Yunhuan 羅運環, 72–93. Wuhan: Hubei jiaoyu chubanshe.

Zhang Tian'en 張天恩. 2014. "Qinghua jian *Xinian* (san) yu Qin chu shishi luexi" 清華簡《繫年（三）》與秦楚史事略析. *Kaogu yu wenwu* 考古與文物 2:107–9.

Zhang Yiren 張以仁. 1962. "Lun *Guoyu* yu *Zuozhuan* de guanxi" 論國語與左傳的關系. *Zhongyang yanjiuyuan lishi yuyan yanjiusuo jikan* 中央研究院歷史語言研究所季刊 33:233–86.

———. 1963. "Cong wenfa, yuhui de chayi zheng *Guoyu*, *Zuozhuan* ershu fei yiren suo zuo" 從文法、語匯的差異證國語、左傳二書非一人所作. *Zhongyang yanjiuyuan lishi yuyan yanjiusuo jikan* 中央研究院歷史語言研究所季刊 34, no. 1:333–66.

Zhang Yujin 張玉金. 2011. *Chutu Zhanguo wenxian xuci yanjiu* 出土戰國文獻虛詞研究. Beijing: Renmin chubanshe.

Zhang Zhengming 張正明. 2007. *Qin yu Chu* 秦與楚. Wuhan: Huazhong shifan daxue chubanshe.

Zhang Zhili 張志立, Peng Yun 彭雲, and Liang Yong 梁涌. 2010. "Yuewang Goujian qiandu Langye kaogu diaocha zongshu" 越王勾踐遷都琅琊考古調查綜述. In *Xin shiye xia de Zhong-wai guanxi shi* 新視野下的中外關係史, ed. Zhongguo zhongwai lianxi shi xuehui 中國中外關係史學會 et al., 436–51. Lanzhou: Gansu renmin chubanshe.

Zhao Boxiong 趙伯雄. 1999. "*Zuozhuan* wu jing zhi zhuan kao"《左傳》無經之傳考. *Wen shi* 文史 49, no. 4:23–39.

———. 2004. *Chunqiu xue shi* 春秋學史. Ji'nan: Shandong jiaoyu chubanshe.

Zhao Daming 趙大明. 2007. *Zuozhuan jieci yanjiu*《左傳》介詞研究. Beijing: Shoudu shifan daxue chubanshe.

Zhao Guangxian 趙光賢. 1982. "*Zuozhuan* bianzhuan kao"《左傳》編撰考. *Zhongguo lishi wenxian yanjiu jikan* 中國歷史文獻研究季刊 1:135–53, 2:45–58.

Zhao Huacheng. 2014. "New Explorations of Early Qin Culture." In *Birth of an Empire: The State of Qin Revisited*, ed. Yuri Pines, Lothar von Falkenhausen, Gideon Shelach, and Robin D. S. Yates, 53–70. Berkeley: University of California Press.

Zhao Ping'an 趙平安. 2011. "*Chu ju* de xingzhi, zuozhe ji xiezuo niandai"《楚居》的性質、作者及寫作年代. *Qinghua daxue xuebao (zhexue shehui kexue ban)* 清華大學學報（哲學社會科學版）. 4:29–33.

———. 2012. "*Chu ju* 'Wei Ying' kao"《楚居》"為郢"考. *Zhongguo shi yanjiu* 中國史研究 4:5–10.

Zhao Shengqun 趙生群. 2000. *Chunqiu jing zhuan yanjiu*《春秋》經傳研究. Shanghai: Shanghai guji chubanshe.

Zhao Xiaolong 趙曉龍. 2009. "Zifan bianzhong mingwen 'Xi zhi liu shi' shijie" 子犯編鐘銘文"西之六師"試解. *Xinan jiaotong daxue xuebao (shehui kexue ban)* 西南交通大學學報(社會科學版) 10, no. 1:97–99.

Zheng Wei 鄭威. 2012. *Chuguo fengjun yanjiu* 楚國封君研究. Wuhan: Hubei jiaoyu chubanshe.

———. 2017. *Chutu wenxian yu Chu Qin Han lishi dili yanjiu* 出土文獻與楚秦漢歷史地理研究. Beijing: Kexue chubanshe.

Zhu Fenghan 朱鳳瀚. 2014. "Guanyu Xi Zhou fengguo junzhu chengwei de ji dian renshi" 關於西周封國君主稱謂的幾點認識. In *Liang Zhou fengguo lunheng: Shaanxi sheng Hancheng chutu Ruiguo wenwu ji Zhoudai fengguo kaoguxue yanjiu guoji xueshu yantaohui lunwenji* 兩周封國論衡：陝西韓城出土芮國文物暨周代封國考古學研究國際學術研討會論文集, ed. Shaanxi sheng kaogu yanjiuyuan 陝西省考古研究院 and Shanghai bowuguan 上海博物館, 272–85. Shanghai: Shanghai guji chubanshe.

———. 2016. "Qinghua jian *Xinian* 'Zhou wu wang jiu nian' zaiyi" 清華簡《繫年》"周無王九年"再議. *Jilin daxue shehui kexue xuebao* 吉林大學社會科學學報 56, no. 4:177–82.

Zhu Qixiang 朱歧祥. 2014. "You 'yu, yu' yongzi pinggu Qinghua jian (er) *Xinian*: Jian tan 'mou zhi mou' de yongfa" 由「于、於」用字評估清華簡（貳）《繫年》——兼談「某之某」的用法. *Guwenzi yanjiu* 古文字研究 30:381–86.

Zhuzi yulei 朱子語類. (N.d.) 1986. By Zhu Xi 朱熹 [1130–1200]. Comp. Li Jingde 黎靖德 [13th century]. Coll. Wang Xingxian 王星賢. Beijing: Zhonghua shuju.

Ziju 子居. 2011. "Qinghua jian *Chu ju* jiexi" 清華簡《楚居》解析. Originally available at http://www.confucius2000.com; currently retrievable at http://www.xianqin.tk. Accessed April 4, 2020.

———. 2012. Comments on *Xinian*. Originally available at http://www.confucius2000.com; currently retrievable at http://www.xianqin.tk. Accessed April 4, 2020.

Zizhi tongjian 資治通鑑. 1992. By Sima Guang 司馬光 (1019–1086). Annotated by Hu Sanxing 胡三省 (1230–1302). Beijing: Zhonghua shuju.

Zuozhuan. See *Chunqiu Zuozhuan zhu*.

Index

Page references to place names on the maps appear in boldface.

Allan, Sarah, 127–28, 147
An 鞌 battle, 589 BCE, **xiii**, 118, 196, 199n11, 271n89. See also Miji battle
anecdotes, 2–4, 22, 37, 39, 64–65, 67–68, 73–80, 88–90, 93, 96–97, 101, 106, 111, 113, 126, 146, 244n10, 258n25, 258nn28–29, 259n33, 260n43, 269n65; and Chu historiography, 127–34, 141, 144, 147, 273n26, 273nn29–30; in *Discourses of the States,* 34, 244n8; in *Han Feizi,* 263n81; in *Lüshi chunqiu* 270n82; in *Stratagems of the Warring States,* 35–36; and *Xinian,* 49, 52, 60
Anhui University bamboo slips, 43, 68, 135, 245n11, 273n38, 274n42, 274n54, 275n75
annalistic writings. See chronicles
Annals (*Biannian ji 編年記) from Shuihudi Tomb 11, 244n10, 264n90
aristocracy, x, 22, 33, 61, 69, 81, 94, 146, 246n19, 256n5, 257n13, 260n48, 271n3

assemblies (*hui* 會), 22, 84, 114, 138, 159n18, 168n14, 190n1, 192, 215, 193nn2–3, 195n3, 217n8, 218n15, 219n16, 221n4, 255n48
  in section 2, 158
  in section 4, 166
  in section 12, 193
  in section 14, 197
  in section 16, 207
  in section 17, 211
  in section 20, 224–25

Bamboo Annals (*Zhushu jinian* 竹書紀年), 4, 37, 39, 94–99, 102–4, 106, 113–14, 116–17, 120, 152, 156, 158n2, 159n10, 167nn8–9, 220n2, 223, 232, 240n18, 243n5, 244n9, 251n4, 252n6, 264n1, 266n28, 267n38, 270n76, 270n82; *Current Bamboo Annals* 244n9, 269n74
Ban Gu 班固 (32–92 CE), 2
**Bang ren bu cheng* 邦人不稱 manuscript, 131

[307]

Bao Si 褒姒 (d. 771 BCE), 97, 101–3, 155, 158n6
　in section 2, 157
Bao Shuya yu Xi Peng zhi jian 鮑叔牙與隰朋之諫 manuscript, 258n28
Baoshan, Jingmen 荊門包山 (Hubei), Tomb 2, 135, 145–46
"barbarians" (*yi* 夷 or *yidi* 夷狄), 125–26, 272nn14–15. *See also* Di 狄; Rong 戎; "savages"; Yi 夷
Bi 邲, battle, 597 BCE, **xii–xiii**, 75, 129, 131, 194, 204n9, 259n33
biblioclasm, Qin, 213 BCE, 64, 67, 94, 95, 120
Biographies of Exemplary Women (*Lienü zhuan* 列女傳), 52, 203n3, 254n36
Bo Hefu 伯龢父, Zhou noble, 265n7
Bo Pi 伯嚭 (d. ca. 473 BCE), Wu official, 57, 205n19
Bo Zhouli 伯州梨 (d. 540 BCE), Chu official, 77
Boju 柏舉 battle, 506 BCE, **xii**, 57, 204, 205n20
Bopan 伯盤 (or Bofu 伯服), son of King You of Zhou (d. 771 BCE), 101–3, 155–56
　in section 2, 157
Bozhou 亳州 (Anhui), 257n14
bronze inscriptions, 4–6, 16, 68, 80–88, 91, 96, 113, 118–20, 124, 234, 191n8, 222n8, 264n89. *See also* Guobo-*gui*; Hongshu-*gui*; Jin Hou Su-*bianzhong*; Lai-*pan*; Mi Jia-*bianzhong*; Shi Qiang-*pan*; Yue Wang Chaxu-*ge*; Zeng Hou Yu-*bianzhong*; Zifan-*bianzhong*; Zuoce Zeling-*gui*

Cai 蔡, state of, later Chu county, **xii–xiv**, 49–52, 169–70, 190n1, 217n9, 220, 221n3, 222n8–10, 254n34, 263n76
　in section 5, 170
　in section 7, 179
　in section 18, 216
　in section 19, 221
Cai Zhao 蔡朝 (aka Sir Cai 蔡子) (fl. 590 BCE), Qi official, 198n8
　in section 14, 197
Caishu Du 蔡叔度 (d. ca. 1040 BCE), son of King Wen of Zhou, 110, 163n2
calendars, 25, 82–84, 86, 107, 250n78; personal (*shiri* 視日), 244n10, 264n90
Canon of Documents (*Shujing* 書經 or *Shangshu* 尚書), 2, 14–16, 37, 45, 121, 243n6, 246n12; "Declaration to Kang" ("Kang gao" 康誥), 15, 167n6; "Decree to Marquis Wen" ("Wen hou zhi ming" 文侯之命), 159n10; "Do not be idle" ("Wu yi" 無逸), 15; "Many officers" ("Duo shi" 多士), 15, 245n5; "Many regions" ("Duo fang" 多方), 15
Canon of Poems (*Shijing* 詩經), 14–15, 37, 45, 96, 120, 123, 153n3, 246n16, 267n36, 275n76
Cao 曹, state of, **xii–xiii**, 168n10, 176n13, 179n4, 198n1, 211n1, 254n41
　in section 4, 166
　in section 7, 179
Cao 曹 (Wei 衛 capital location), **xii–xiii**, 168n10
"capital dwellers" (*guo ren* 國人), 96, 191n11, 265n11
chang 嘗 sacrifices, 75, 259n35
Changling 長陵, Chu locality, 240n16
　in section 23, 237–38
Chen 陳, state of, later Chu county, **xii–xiv**, 41, 50–51, 55, 57, 59, 78, 138, 188, 192, 201, 220, 172nn9–10, 190n1, 190n3, 203n6, 221n3, 226n9, 241n22
　in section 5, 170–71
　in section 7, 179
　in section 15, 203
　in section 18, 216
　in section 19, 221
　in section 23, 238

Chen 陳 lineage. *See* Tian lineage
Chen Fengfen 陳佩芬, 77
★*Chen gong zhi bing* 陳公治兵 manuscript, 130
Chen Hao 陳澔, Qi official, 63, 118, 234n9, 241n23
   in section 22, 233
   in section 23, 238
Chen He 陳和 (aka Tian He 田和, aka Lord Tai of Qi 齊太公, d. 384 BCE), 118, 231, 234n9, 270n87
   in section 22, 233
Chen Jimu 陳疾目, Qi military commander, 63
   in section 23, 238
Chen Jing (?) Ziniu 陳釐子牛, Qi leader, 234n8
   in section 22, 233
Chen Minzhen 陳民鎮, 45, 105, 114, 159n11, 257n16, 271n92, 272n7
Chen Wei 陳偉, 77, 212n6, 259n41, 260n43
★*Cheng wang wei Chengpu zhi xing* 成王為城濮之行 manuscript, 130
Chengjun 城麇, Zheng town, 77–78, 259n41
Chengpu 城濮 battle, 632 BCE, **xiii**, 83, 130–31, 171n6, 178, 180n6, 247n1
   in section 7, 179
Chengzhou 成周, Zhou eastern capital, **xii–xiv**, 103, 109, 163n6
   in section 2, 157
   in section 3, 162
   See also Luoyang 洛陽
Chinese University of Hong Kong bamboo slips, 43
Chiyan 赤岸, Jin location, 137, 230n8, 274n56
   in section 21, 228
Chong 重 and Li 黎 (or Chongli), mythical figure(s), 136, 274n53
Chong'er 重耳. *See* Lord Wen of Jin

chronicles (court annals), 2–4, 16, 18, 22, 29, 47, 61–62, 92, 94, 117, 145, 232, 234n11, 248nn47–48, 251n5. *See also* Spring and Autumns Annals
Chu 楚, state of, **xi–xiv**, 4, 6, 38, 106–7, 114, 151, 166n1, 191n13, 193n2, 195n1, 238n3, 239n7, 258n20, 260n48, 274n46; administration in, x, 177n16, 190n5, 191n8, 204n9, 208n2, 221n1, 229n4, 240n21, 275n59; ancestors of, 69, 134–36, 142, 144–46, 274nn54–55, 275n75; anecdotes of, 74–80, 127–34, 273n30; capitals of, 69–72, 256n10; cultural identity of, 122–27, 132–34, 144–47, 272n8, 272nn14, 15, 17; domestic turmoil in, 42, 131, 137, 218n10, 241n22, 252n10, 257n13; expansion of, 49–52, 131–32, 138, 156, 160n21, 169–70, 171n6, 172n10, 178, 179n1, 188–89, 193n3, 194, 217nn8–9, 218n17, 220, 222nn9–10, 229n5, 257n12, 262n70; in *Discourses of the States*, 125–26, 135–36; historiography in, 6, 22, 29, 31, 42, 47, 61–63, 68–69, 72, 77–80, 85, 88, 112, 122–47, 232, 234n11, 241n24, 244–45n11, 254n34, 255n52, 255n54, 273n38, 275n75; and Jin, 52–54, 62, 82–84, 114, 117, 120, 173–74, 176n12, 178, 180n6, 192, 193n6, 195nn3–4, 195n6, 198n1, 206–7, 208nn4–6, 209nn7–8, 210, 211n2, 212n3, 214–15, 218n13, 218n15, 219n17, 221n4, 223, 227–28, 229–30n7, 230n8, 239n8, 235–36, 274n56; and Qi, 63, 196, 199n10, 231–32, 252n9; and Qin, 57, 59, 181, 204n8, 205n21, 222nn6–7, 231, 238n4, 276n79; in *Spring and Autumn Annals*, 21; and Wu, 32, 54–59, 76, 86–88, 114, 133, 200–2, 204n15, 205n18, 205nn20–23, 214–15, 218n14, 220, 221n5, 222n8, 257nn15–17, 262n66, 263n76; in

INDEX [309]

Chu 楚, state of (*continued*)
    Xinian, 38–47, 49–52, 54–59, 61–67, 137–41, 252n7, 245n21; and Yue, 114, 223, 231, 240n18; and Zhou, 81, 86, 106–7, 123–24, 260n47, 263n76, 267n42; in *Zuozhuan*, 31, 124, 138–41, 272n8, 272n10
        in section 2, 158
        in section 5, 170–71
        in section 6, 175
        in section 7, 179
        in section 8, 182
        in section 11, 189
        in section 12, 193
        in section 13, 194
        in section 15, 202–3
        in section 16, 207–8
        in section 18, 216–17
        in section 19, 221
        in section 20, 225
        in section 21, 228
        in section 23, 237–38
★*Chu ju* 楚居 (Chu Dwellings) manuscript, 4, 68–74, 91–92, 134–36, 141, 144, 253n27, 256n2–3, 256n5–7, 256n10, 257n15, 257n18–19, 273n38, 274n46, 274n54
Chu Songs (*Chuci* 楚辭), 145
Chuanfeng Xu 穿封戍, appellative Zihuang 子皇, Duke of Chu dependency of Chen 陳公, 76–79, 259n41
Chuci. See *Chu* Songs
Chunqiu 春秋. See *Spring and Autumns Annals*
★*Chunqiu shiyu* 春秋事語 manuscript, 244n10
Chunyu fields 淳于田, Qi location, 199n13
    in section 14, 197
Chuqiu (Chu Hill) 楚丘 (Wei 衛 capital location), **xii–xiii**, 168nn13–14
    in section 4, 165

commemoration, 3, 12, 14, 16, 246n11
Comprehensive Mirror to Aid the Government (*Zizhi tongjian* 資治通鑑), 116, 251n6
concealment (*hui* 諱), 21, 42, 66, 71, 81, 137, 217n7, 247n44
Confucius (Kongzi 孔子, 551–479 BCE), 17–27, 32, 90, 128, 246n24–25, 248n58, 263n81
covenants (*meng* 盟), 19, 21–22, 28, 47, 55, 61–62, 84, 87, 114–15, 118, 139–41, 180n9, 195nn4–6, 206, 208n6, 217n6, 218–19n15, 226n11, 231, 234n9, 270n87
    in section 7, 179
    in section 13, 194
    in section 16, 208
    in section 18, 216
    in section 20, 225
    in section 22, 233
Cui Shu 崔述 (1739–1816), 99
Cui Zhu 崔杼 (d. 546 BCE), Qi leader, 213n12
    in section 17, 211

Daliang 大梁 (Wei 魏 capital), **xiv**, 229n5, 238n3
Dan River 丹水, 269n65
Dan Zhu 啖助 (724–770), 31, 248n54, 250n75
Daozi 悼子 (aka Zhuozi 卓子) (d. 651 BCE), Jin prince, 53–54, 175–76n8, 270n82
    in section 6, 174
de 德 (moral virtue, charisma, *mana*). See virtue
Di 狄, ethnic group (also designation for "barbarians"), **xi**, **xiii**, 53, 124, 165, 167n7–9, 168n13–14, 175n7, 209n7, 272n14
    in section 4, 166
    in section 6, 174
Di Pei 翟茷, 139
    in section 16, 207–8

Diqiu (Di Hill) 帝丘 (Wei 衛 capital location), **xii–xiv**, 168n14
  in section 4, 166
Discourses of the States (*Guoyu* 國語), 3, 34–35, 39, 45, 53, 56, 65, 73, 81, 93, 113, 154n6, 154n9, 158n7, 159n10, 176n8, 199n14, 201, 204n7, 226n9, 226n12, 244n7, 249n64, 250nn79–81, 253n27; Chu image in, 125–26, 135; Western Zhou history in, 96–97, 101, 103, 152, 156; "Wu yu" 吳語 section, 244n10, 269n71, 273n26; "Zheng yu" 鄭語 section, 103, 135, 158n8; and *Zuo zhuan*, 34–35, 58, 83, 244n8, 250n80
Dong Hu 董狐, Jin scribe, 22, 248n47
Dorofeeva-Lichtmann, Vera, 142
Dou Jiao 鬬椒 (d. 605 BCE), Chu official, 257n13
Dou Ke 鬬克 (aka Ziyi 子儀, Duke of Shen 申公, d. 613 BCE), Chu official, 176n15, 177n16, 183n8
  in section 6, 175
  in section 8, 182
Du Yu 杜預 (222–285), 26, 102, 249n61, 249n67, 251n4, 264n1
Duandao 斷道, Jin location, **xiii**, 198n1, 198n7
  in section 14, 197
Du'ao 堵敖. *See* King Du'ao of Chu
Ducal Grandson Hui 公孫會, Qi leader, 116, 118, 234n10, 271n88
Ducal Son Chong'er 公子重耳. *See* Lord Wen of Jin
Ducal Son Guisheng 公子歸生 (aka Zijia 子家) of Zheng, 130–31
Ducal Son Ying 公子嬰, ruler of Zheng (r. 693–680 BCE), 160n19
Ducal Son Yong 公子雍 of Jin (fl. 615 BCE), 186, 187n2
  in section 9, 185
  in section 10, 186

Ducal Son Yong 公子雍 of Qi (fl. 633 BCE), 179n1
Ducal Son Zhengshu 公子徵舒. *See* Zhengshu
Duke of Bai 白公 (Chu) (d. 479 BCE), 71
Duke of Luyang 魯陽公 (Chu), 137–38, 239n12, 240n21, 275n59
  in section 23, 237–38
Duke of Shao 召公 (eleventh century BCE), 91, 96, 98, 100, 152, 266n18
Duke of Song, Tian 宋公田. *See* Lord Xiu of Song
Duke of Teng, Shejian 滕公涉潤 (Yue official?), 240n18
  in section 23, 238
Duke of Xú 徐公, 217n8
  in section 18, 216
Duke of Zhou 周公 (d. 1035 BCE), 14–15, 96, 98, 100, 110, 152, 163n2, 167n6, 245n5, 268n56
  in section 4, 166
Dun 頓, polity, later Chu dependency, **xii**, 51, 172n9
  in section 5, 171
Duo Jiao 鐸椒 (fl. 340 BCE), tutor of Chu prince, 252n6. *See also Subtleties of Mr. Duo* (鐸氏微)
Durrant, Stephen, 7, 23

Earl of Zheng, Tai 鄭伯駘. *See* Lord Xu of Zheng 鄭繻公
Eastern Sea (Yellow Sea) 東海, 212n6
  in section 17, 211
Ebine Ryōsuke 海老根量介, 77
Emperor Gao of Han 漢高祖 (r. 202–195 BCE), 248n57

Fan 氾 River, **xii–xiv**, 208n1, 239n14
  in section 16, 207
  in section 23, 237
Fancheng 樊城 (Hubei), 257n11

Fangcheng 方城, Chu defensive line, **xii–xiv**, 51–52, 137, 171–72nn7–8, 212n3, 215, 218nn13–14, 228, 229n1, 230n9
    in section 5, 171
    in section 7, 179
    in section 17, 211
    in section 18, 216–17
    See also Long Wall of Chu
Fei Wuji 費無極, 56, 204n16
    in section 15, 203
Feilian 飛廉, Qin ancestor, 109–10, 112, 161, 163n4
    in section 3, 162
Fen 汾 River, **xi–xiv**
Five Thearchs (*wu di* 五帝), 245n3
Fu Sinian 傅斯年 (1896–1950), 108
Fu Yu 鮒余, Jin official, 239n10
    in section 23, 237
Fugai 夫槩. *See* Royal Son Chen of Wu 吳王子晨

Gangu 甘谷 County (Gansu), 111, 161
Gansu 甘肅 Province, 109, 111, 161
ganzhi 干支 dates. *See* sexagenary cycle
Gao 郜, location in Shandong, **xiv**, 137, 240n18, 275n58
    in section 23, 238
Gao Gu 高固 (early sixth century BCE), Qi official, 198n3
    in section 14, 197
Gao Hou 高厚 (d. 554 BCE), Qi official, 211n1, 212n4
    in section 17, 211
Gao Qumi 高渠弥 (aka Qumi of Gao) (d. 694 BCE), Zheng leader, 160n17
    in section 2, 158
Gao Shiqi 高士奇 (1645–1704), 32, 39
Gaoxin 高辛, primeval thearch, 136, 274n53
Geling, Xincai 新蔡葛陵 (Henan), Tomb 1, 135, 145–46, 272n9, 275n17

Gentz, Joachim, 246n12, 247n33
Gernet, Jacques (1921–2018), 248n56
The Glory of Yue (*Yuejue shu* 越絕書), 113
Gongyang Commentary (*Gongyang zhuan* 公羊傳), 18, 20, 24, 125, 198n4, 246n24–25, 247n33, 253n22, 272n13
Goldin, Paul R., 44, 127, 248n57
Gong 龔, locality (in Shandong?), 226n11
    in section 20, 225
Gong Bo He 共伯和, 98–100, 152, 154nn7–8, 265n7, 265n10, 266n11, 266n16
    in section 1, 153
Gongcheng County 共城縣 (sixth century), 265n11
gonghe 共和 ("Joint Harmony" years, 841–828 BCE), 97–100, 106, 152, 265n11
Gu 穀, locality between Lu and Qi, **xiii–xiv**, 114, 179n1, 226n13
    in section 7, 179
    in section 20, 225
Gu Jiegang 顧頡剛 (1893–1980), 24
Guanshu Xian 管叔鮮 (d. ca. 1040 BCE), son of King Wen of Zhou, 110, 163n2
gui 珪 tablet, status symbol (Chu), 138, 240n21, 275n60
    in section 23, 238
Guiling 桂陵, Jin locality, **xiv**, 236, 239n8
    in section 23, 237
Guliang Commentary (*Guliang zhuan* 穀梁傳), 20, 24, 133, 198n4, 246n25, 247n33, 253n22
Guo 虢, state of, 28, 102–3, 157, 158n2, 158n9
    in section 2, 157
Guo 虢, locality (Zheng), **xii–xiv**
    in section 18, 216
    in section 20, 224
Guo Yongbing 郭永秉, 43, 153n4, 275n72
Guobo-*gui* 過伯簋 inscription, 260n47

Guodian 郭店 (Hubei), Tomb 1, 133, 273n26

Guoyu. See *Discourses of the States*

Han 漢 dynasty (206/202 BCE–220 CE), 24, 43, 74, 113, 121–22, 198n6, 246n26, 258n28, 269n74

Han 漢 River, **xi–xiv**, 71, 76, 85–87, 160n21, 172n7, 257n11, 257n16, 262n64, 274n51
  in section 2, 158

Han 韓, aristocratic lineage and state, **xiv**, 113, 116–20, 227, 231–32, 230n8, 234n9, 236, 240n15, 230n20, 263n82, 270n87, 271n91, 274n56

Han 韓 (Hanyuan 韓原), battle of, 176n10
  in section 6, 174

Han Fei 韓非 (d. 233 BCE) and *Han Feizi* 韓非子, 73, 89, 113, 240n15, 263n80

Han Qian 韓虔. See Marquis Jing of Han 韓景侯

Han Qizhang 韓啓章 (aka Han Wuzi 韓武子), head of the would-be Han polity (d. 409 BCE), 229n6
  in section 21, 228

Han Qu 韓取. See Marquis Lie of Han 韓烈侯

Hanshu 漢書. See *History of the Former Han Dynasty*

Heaven, 13–15, 65, 87–88, 101, 109, 136, 141, 143, 151, 153n4, 274nn52–53
  in section 1, 152
  in section 3, 162
  See also Mandate of Heaven

Heiyao 黑要 (d. 584 BCE), Chu official, 55–56, 204nn10–11
  in section 15, 202

Hengyong 衡雍, Jin (Zhou) location, **xiii**, 180n9
  in section 7, 179

Hequ 河曲, Jin location, **xiii**, 187n3
  in section 10, 186

Heyong 河雍, Zheng location, 55, 204n9
  in section 15, 202

histories, local, 25–26, 29, 31, 60, 62–64, 69, 73–76, 79–80, 82, 84, 92–94, 108, 127, 145–47, 276n24

historiography, 33, 190; Chinese imperial, 1–2; Chinese pre-imperial, 1–7, 11–17, 21–23, 27, 33–36, 62, 65, 68, 73–74, 80–82, 91–95, 145–46; in Chu, 38, 42, 124, 142, 144; and cultural identities, 122–23, 127; European, modern, 273n24; Greek, 144; Jewish, 144; and ritual, 11, 21. See also anecdotes; bronze inscriptions; chronicles

History of the Former Han Dynasty (*Hanshu* 漢書), 99, 246n26

Hong Kong antiquity market, 6, 37, 43–44, 48

Hongshu-*gui* 鴻叔簋 inscription, 260n47

Hu 扈, Zheng locality, 192, 193n2, 193n6
  in section 12, 193

Hu 胡 polity, **xii**, 220, 221n4, 222n8
  in section 19, 221

Hu Sanxing 胡三省 (1264–1302), 171n2

Hu Yan 狐偃 (appellative Zifan 子犯) (fl. 650–630 BCE), 82–84, 91, 264n86, 179n4, 180n8

Hua 滑, polity, **xiii**, 30, 182n5
  in section 8, 182

Hua Yuan 華元 (aka Huasun Yuan 華孫元) (fl. 610–570 BCE), Song official, 139, 188, 190n2, 191n10, 191n13, 208n5
  in section 11, 189
  in section 16, 208

Hua Yushi 華御事 (fl. 620 BCE), Song official, 188, 190n2

Huai 淮 River, **xi–xiv**, 13, 76, 86, 138, 169–70, 188, 204n15, 205n21, 220, 222n9, 235, 240n16, 257n17, 262n64, 262n66

Huainanzi 淮南子, 117, 120
Huan Tan 桓譚 (ca. 20 BCE–56 CE), 20
Huang Jie 皇頡 (aka Sir Huang, Huangzi 黃子) (fl. 545 BCE), Zheng official, 77, 259n41
Huangchi 黃池, location between Song and Zheng, **xiii–xiv**, 137, 227, 274n56, 226n9, 229n5, 229n7
  in section 20, 225
  in section 21, 228
Huangzi 皇子 (fl. 400 BCE), Zheng official, 77–78
  in section 23, 206
Huaxia 華夏 ("Chinese") 83. *See also* Xia (cultural entity)
Hundred Schools of Thought, 3, 93
Huoshu Chu 霍叔處, son of King Wen of Zhou, 110, 163n2
Huozhou 霍州, 154n6

identities, cultural, 122–23, 127, 144; in Europe, 147, 273n24; of Chu, 7, 123, 126–28, 132–34, 138, 141, 145–47; of Qin, 272n21, 276n79

Japan, 38, 119, 154, 243n1
Ji 姬 clan, 49, 85, 87, 124, 169–70, 272n8, 272n10
Ji 汲 Commandery, Henan, 4, 102. *See also* *Bamboo Annals*
Ji 濟 River, **xi–xiv**, 114, 224, 179n1, 225n3, 226n13, 229n5, 271n92
  in section 20, 225
Ji (state) 紀, 27, 199n12
Ji 季 (Jisun 季孫) lineage, Lu, 32, 90
Ji Kangzi 季康子 (d. 468 BCE), 90
Ji Wenzi 季文子 (d. 568 BCE), 90
★*Jian da wang po han* 柬大王泊旱 manuscript, 129, 258n29
Jia'ao 郟敖. *See* King Jia'ao of Chu
Jianyang 建陽, Qi location, 115, 234n4
  in section 22, 233

Jiang 絳, Jin's capital, **xii–xiii,** 212n10
  in section 17, 211
Jiang 姜 clan, 118, 231, 270n79
Jiantu 踐土 covenant, 632 BCE, **xiii**, 84, 180n9
  in section 7, 179
Jilian 季連, Chu primordial ancestor, 69, 134–35, 274n54
Jin 津, Chu locality, 240n16
  in section 23, 237
Jin 晉 state of, **xi–xiv**, 16, 22, 30–31, 49, 67, 82–84, 106, 156, 263n82, 245n14, 250n11, 252n4, 253nn8–9, 254n6, 257n2, 258nn1–2, 263n9, 264n1, 264n7, 265n9, 267n16; and Chu, 54, 62–63, 75–76, 83–84, 124, 137–41, 171n6, 173–74, 176n12, 178, 179n1, 180n6, 192, 195nn3–5, 204n9, 206–7, 208nn5–6, 209nn7–8, 210, 212n3, 214–15, 218nn13–15, 219n17, 220, 221n4, 227–28, 229n5, 229–30n7, 230n9, 235–36, 239n8, 240n16, 240n18, 274n56; dissolution of (403 BCE), 5, 113, 116–20, 229n6, 231–32, 234n9, 240n20, 270n87; history writing in, 60, 64, 107, 126, 128, 131, 248n47, 251n4, 255n52, 260n32, 273n30; and Qi, 61, 114–19, 196, 199nn9–11, 199n13, 210, 212nn4–5, 212n11, 212–13n12, 214–16, 223–24, 231–32, 234nn9–10, 271n88; and Qin, 107, 173–74, 176n13, 176n15, 180n8, 181, 182n1, 184, 186, 187n1, 187n3, 209n7, 238n4, 271n92; and Wu, 54, 56, 114–15, 200, 204n14, 215, 218n14, 223, 226n9; in *Xinian*, 38–48, 52–54, 60, 65–66, 137–41, 151, 252n7; and Yue, 114–15, 223–24, 201–2
  in section 2, 157
  in section 6, 174–75
  in section 7, 179
  in section 8, 182
  in section 9, 185

in section 10, 186
in section 12, 193
in section 13, 194
in section 14, 197
in section 15, 203
in section 16, 207–8
in section 17, 211
in section 18, 216–17
in section 20, 224–25
in section 21, 228
in section 22, 233
in section 23, 237–38
Jin Hou Su-*bianzhong* 晉侯穌編鐘 inscription, 16, 30, 81
Ji'nan City 紀南城, site of the Chu capital, 71–72, 258n22, 259n11
Jing Gong nüe 競公瘧 manuscript, 258n28
Jing Jia 景賈 (aka Jia of Jing 景之賈) (d. 400 BCE), Chu noble
in section 23, 237
Jinsai County (Anhui) 金寨縣, 257n16
Jing River 涇, **xiii**, 139, 209n7
in section 16, 208
Jinyin 菫陰, Jin locality, **xiii**, 187n1
in section 10, 186
Jiong (泂 or 熒) Marsh, 167n8
jishi benmo. See "topical arrangement" style
Jixun 季紃 (fl. ca. 770 BCE), Chu leader, 136
Ju Dam 淏梁, Jin locality, 212n4
in section 17, 211
Juemo 厥貉, Song (?) locality, **xii**, 190n1
in section 11, 189
Juling 郘陵, Qi locality, 115
in section 22, 233
★*Jun ren zhe he bi an zai* 君人者何必安哉 manuscript, 130

Kang Hill 康丘, 165, 167n6
in section 4, 166
Kang Youwei 康有爲 (1859–1927), 24, 248n55, 249n59, 250n79

Kangshu Feng 康叔封 (aka Weishu Feng 衛叔封), son of King Wen of Zhou and the founder of Wei 衛 polity, 159, 167n6
in section 4, 166
Kern, Martin, 246n12
King Cheng of Chu 楚成王 (r. 672–626 BCE), 51, 52, 171n6, 172n9, 176n12, 180n6, 256n10
in section 5, 171
in section 7, 179
King Cheng of Zhou 周成王 (r. ca. 1042–1021 BCE), 109, 161
in section 3, 162
in section 4, 166
King Dao of Chu 楚悼王 (aka King Daozhe 悼哲) (r. ca. 400–381 BCE), 42–43, 64, 69, 205, 229n2, 239n5, 255n54
in section 23, 237
King Du'ao of Chu 楚王堵敖 (r. 675–672 BCE), 51–52, 171n6
in section 5, 171
King from Xie. *See* King Hui of Xie
King Fuchai of Wu 吳王夫差 (r. 495–473 BCE), 133
in section 20, 225
King Gong of Chu 楚恭王 (r. 590–560 BCE), 56, 70, 138–39
in section 15, 202
in section 16, 207–8
King Goujian of Yue 越王句踐 (r. 496–464 BCE), 113–14, 223, 226n12, 269n71
in section 20, 225
King Helu of Wu 吳王闔閭 (r. 514–496 BCE), 57, 70, 205nn22–23, 257n17
in section 15, 203
in section 20, 225
King Hui of Chu 楚惠王 (aka King Xianhui 獻惠) (r. 489–432 BCE), 130, 222n9
in section 19, 221

King Hui of Xie 攜惠王 (aka King Xie, King from Xie 攜王) (r. 770–750 BCE), 101–6, 156, 158–59n10, 266n28
    in section 2, 157
King Hui of Zhou 周惠王 (r. 676–652 BCE)
    in section 4, 166
King Jia'ao of Chu 楚王郟敖 (aka Child King 孺子王 or Heir Child King 嗣子王) (r. 544–541 BCE), 70, 76, 78, 217n5, 217n7, 257n14
    in section 18, 216
King Jian of Chu 楚簡王 (aka King Jianda 柬大) (r. ca. 431–405 BCE), 129, 131, 229n2, 259n29
    in section 21, 228
King Jing of Zhou 周景王 (r. 544–520 BCE), 259n34
King Kang of Chu 楚康王 (r. 559–545 BCE), 70
    in section 18, 216
King Li of Zhou 周厲王 (r. ca. 877–842 BCE), 96–99, 152, 154n6, 265n11, 266n18
    in section 1, 152
King Ling of Chu 楚靈王 (r. 540–529 BCE), 33, 42, 56, 70, 76–79, 124, 129–30, 132–33, 141, 207, 214, 217n7, 218n10, 220, 221n3, 252n10, 257n14–15, 260n43
    in section 15, 203
    in section 18, 216
    in section 19, 221
King Maohu of the Red Di, 赤翟王 茆胡
    in section 4, 166
King Mu of Chu 楚穆王 (r. 625–614 BCE), 70, 188, 190n1, 256n10
    in section 11, 189
King Ping of Chu 楚平王 (aka King Jingping 景平, named Qiji 棄疾) (r. 528–516 BCE), 56, 70, 129, 132–33, 204n17, 218n10, 221n3, 273n35
    in section 15, 203
    in section 18, 216
    in section 19, 221
King Ping of Zhou 周平王 (named Yijiu 宜臼) (r. 770/741–720 BCE), 100–7, 109, 155–56, 158n5, 158–59n10, 269n67
    in section 2, 157
    in section 3, 162
King Sheng of Chu 楚聲王 (aka King Shenghuan 聲桓) (r. 404–401 BCE), 61, 229n2, 233n1, 235–36, 239n5, 239n11, 271n92
    in section 22, 233
    in section 23, 237
King Shoumeng of Wu 吳王壽夢 (r. 585–561 BCE)
    in section 20, 224–25
King Weilie of Zhou 周威烈王 (r. 425–402 BCE), 116, 119, 232
King Wen of Chu 楚文王 (r. 689–675 BCE), 49–52, 159n21, 169–70, 171nn5–6, 172n10, 190n5, 254n36, 257n11
    in section 2, 158
    in section 5, 170–71
King Wen of Zhou 周文王 (d. 1047 BCE), 14–15, 20, 86, 264n87
King Wu of Chu 楚武王 (r. 740–690 BCE), 69, 71–72, 245n21
King Wu of Zhou 周武王 (d. 1042 BCE), 14, 86, 91, 109–10, 151, 153nn3–4, 162, 163n2
    in section 1, 152
    in section 3, 162
King Wuling of Zhao 趙武靈王 (r. 325–299 BCE), 263n80
King Xiang of Wei 魏襄王 (r. 318–296 BCE), 4

King Xiang of Zhou 周襄王 (r. 651–619
  BCE), 83, 165, 170n15, 180n9, 247n44
  in section 7, 179
King Xie. *See* King Hui of Xie
King Xuan of Zhou 周宣王 (r. 827–782
  BCE), 97, 99, 123, 151–52, 154n9,
  265n5
  in section 1, 153
King Yi of Yue 越王翳 (aka Lord Yi of
  Yue 越公翳) (r. ca. 410–375 BCE),
  114–15, 233n3, 270n78
  in section 22, 233
King You of Zhou 周幽王 (r. 781–771
  BCE), 97–98, 101–5, 155–56, 158n7
  in section 2, 157
King Zhao of Chu 楚昭王 (r. 515–489
  BCE), 57, 70, 72, 76, 86–87, 129–30,
  132–33, 205n21, 214, 219n17, 222n9,
  240n21, 257nn16–17, 262n72, 275n60
  in section 15, 203
  in section 18, 216–17
  in section 19, 221
King Zhao of Zhou 周昭王 (r. ca.
  975–957 BCE), 123, 260n47, 271n4
King Zhuang of Chu 楚莊王 (r. 613–591
  BCE), 55–56, 70–71, 75–76, 124,
  129–31, 133, 138, 188–89, 191n9,
  195n1, 259nn35–36
  in section 11, 189
  in section 12, 193
  in section 13, 194
  in section 15, 202
King Zhuju of Yue 越王朱句 (aka Lord
  Zhuju of Yue 越公朱句) (r. ca.
  447–411 BCE), 114, 226n12
  in section 20, 225
Kong Yingda 孔穎達 (574–648), 102, 155,
  158n2, 267n38
Kui 夔, statelet, 136, 256n10, 274n55

Lai 賴, polity, **xii**, 217n8
  in section 18, 216

Lai-*pan* 逨盤 inscription, 260n47
Langye 琅琊 (or Langya), Yue capital,
  xiv, 114, 269n74
Laotong 老僮, Chu primordial ancestor,
  135
Lewis, Mark E., 264n89
Li 厲, locality between Chu and Zheng,
  192, 193n3, 255n48
  in section 12, 193
Li Feng, 96, 100
Li Ji 驪姬, concubine of Lord Xian of
  Jin, 53–54, 65, 174nn4–5, 175n8,
  254n39
  in section 6, 174
Li Ke 里克 (or Ke of Li 里之克) (d. 650
  BCE), Jin noble, 53–54, 175n8
  in section 6, 174
Li Ling 李零, 100
Li Meiyan 李美妍, 46, 253n27
Li Rui 李銳, x, 227, 230n9
Li Wai-yee 李惠儀, 7, 23
Li Xueqin 李學勤 (1933–2019), 39, 59,
  104, 111, 205n21, 251n5, 261n59,
  262n74
Liang 梁, polity, later Qin dependency,
  xiii, 53, 175n7
  in section 6, 174
Liang 梁, Chu locality, **xiv**, 239n13
★*Liang chen* 良臣 (Good ministers)
  manuscript, 90–91, 133, 264nn87–88
Liang Qichao 梁啟超 (1873–1929), 1
Lianyungang City 連雲港 (Jiangsu),
  270n74
Lienü zhuan. *See Biographies of Exemplary
  Women*
Liji 禮記. *See Records of the Rites*
★*Ling wang sui Shen* 靈王遂申 manuscript,
  130
Linqiu 廩丘, Qi settlement, **xiv**, 116, 118,
  234n10, 271n88
  in section 22, 233
Linquan County 臨泉縣 (Anhui), 259n33

Linzi 臨淄, Qi capital, **xiii–xiv**, 199n13
Liu Fenglu 劉逢祿 (1776–1829), 247n38, 248n59
Liu Xiang 劉向 (79–8 BCE), 35, 250n83, 260n3
Liu Xin 劉歆 (46 BCE–23 CE), 23–24, 26, 249n64, 249n67, 250n79
Liya 李崖 site, Qingshui 清水 County (Gansu), 111
Long Wall of Chu, **xiv**, 137, 227–28, 230n9, 275n57
    in section 21, 228. *See also* Fangcheng
Long Wall of Qi, **xiv**, 113–14, 117–19, 224, 226nn13–14, 234n4, 234n7
    in section 20, 225
    in section 22, 233
Longhui River 龍會河, Jingzhou (Hubei), Chu cemetery, 68, 245n11
looted manuscripts, 6, 42–44, 67, 82, 123, 126–27, 142, 245n11, 252n16, 273n27
Lord-on-High (Shangdi 上帝), 65, 151–52, 153nn3–4, 261n62
    in section 1, 152
Lord Ai of Lu 魯哀公 (r. 494–468 BCE), 90, 263n81
Lord Ai of Qin 秦哀公 (aka Lord Yi 畢公) (r. 536–500 BCE), 222n6
    in section 19, 221
Lord Cheng of Wei 衛成公 (r. 634–600 BCE)
    in section 4, 166
Lord Cheng of Jin 晉成公 (r. 606–600 BCE), 182, 193n2, 193n6
    in section 12, 193
Lord Dai of Wei 衛戴公 (r. 660 BCE), 167n11
    in section 4, 166
Lord Dao of Jin 晉悼公 (r. 573–558 BCE)
    in section 20, 224

Lord Dao of Song 宋悼公 (r. 421–404 BCE), 227, 229n2
    in section 21, 228
    in section 22, 233
Lord Daowu of Pingye 平夜悼武君 (d. 395 BCE), Chu enfeoffed noble, 63, 138, 240n17
    in section 23, 238
Lord Ding of Jin 晉定公 (aka Lord Jian 簡公) (r. 511–475 BCE), 218n11, 225n8
    in section 18, 216
    in section 20, 224–25
Lord Huai of Jin 晉懷公 (r. 637 BCE), 176nn11,13,14
    in section 6, 174–75
Lord Huan of Qi 齊桓公 (r. 685–643 BCE), 168n13, 252n9, 258n28, 263n80
    in section 4, 166
Lord Huan of Lu 魯桓公 (r. 711–694 BCE), 247n29
Lord Huan of Zheng 鄭桓公 (r. 806–770 BCE), 135
Lord Huanding of Yangcheng 陽城桓定君 (d. 395 BCE), Chu enfeoffed noble, 138
    in section 23, 237–38
Lord Hui of Jin 晉惠公 (named Yiwu 夷吾) (r. 650–637 BCE), 53, 176nn5–6
    in section 6, 174–75
Lord Hui of Lu 魯惠公 (r. 768–723 BCE), 19, 28–29
Lord Jian of Jin 晉簡公. *See* Lord Ding of Jin
Lord Jing of Jin 晉敬公 (r. 451–434 BCE), 114
    in section 20, 225
Lord Jing of Jin 晉景公 (r. 599–581 BCE), 138–39
    in section 14, 197
    in section 16, 207–8
    in section 20, 224

Lord Kang of Qi 齊康公 (aka Marquis of Qi, Dai 齊侯貸) (r. 404–379 BCE), 61, 115, 117–18, 231, 234nn5,11, 270n79
　in section 22, 233
Lord Kang of Qin 秦康公 (r. 620–609 BCE), 186
　in section 10, 186
Lord Li of Jin 晉厲公 (r. 580–574 BCE), 139–40, 207, 209n9
　in section 16, 208
Lord Li of Zheng 鄭厲公 (r. 700–697 and 679–673 BCE), 159–60n16
　in section 2, 158
Lord Lie of Jin 晉烈公 (aka the Duke of Jin, Zhi 晉公止) (r. 415–389 BCE), 61, 82–83, 116–19, 232, 233n1
　in section 22, 233
Lord Ling of Cai 蔡靈公 (r. 542–531 BCE), 217n9
　in section 18, 216
Lord Ling of Chen 陳靈公 (r. 613–599 BCE), 55, 58, 201, 204n7
　in section 15, 202
Lord Ling of Jin 晉靈公 (named Gao 高 or Yigao 夷皋) (r. 620–607 BCE), 22, 184, 185n1, 185n6
　in section 9, 185
　in section 10, 186
Lord Ling of Zheng 鄭靈公 (r. 605 BCE), 131
Lord Mu of Lu 魯穆公 (aka Marquis of Lu, Yan 魯侯衍 or Xian 顯) (r. ca. 416–383 BCE), 61, 115, 118, 231, 234n5, 234n11, 270n79
　in section 22, 233
Lord Mu of Qin 秦穆公 (r. 659–621 BCE), 53, 173, 181, 176n13, 182n1
　in section 6, 173–74
　in section 8, 182
Lord Mu of Zheng 鄭穆公 (r. 627–606 BCE), 55
　in section 15, 202

Lord Ping of Jin 晉平公 (aka Lord Zhuangping 莊平公) (r. 557–532 BCE), 210
　in section 17, 211
　in section 18, 216
Lord Qing of Jin 晉頃公 (r. 525–512 BCE), 214
　in section 18, 216
Lord Qing of Qi 齊頃公 (r. 598–582 BCE), 196, 198n4, 199n14
　in section 14, 197
Lord Shi 君奭. See Duke of Shao
Lord of Xǔ, Tuo 許公佗 (fl. 510 BCE), 215, 218n12
　in section 18, 216
Lord Wen of Wei 衛文公 (aka Ducal Son Qifang 公子启方) (r. 659–635 BCE), 168n13
　in section 4, 166
Lord Wen of Guo 虢文公 (fl. 789 BCE), 152
Lord Wen of Jin 晉文公 (aka Ducal Son Chong'er 公子重耳) (r. 636–628 BCE), 32, 52–54, 65, 83–84, 91, 173, 175n6, 176nn11–15, 178, 179n2, 179n4, 180n8, 181, 183n6, 196, 247n44, 254n41, 264n86, 274n52
　in section 6, 174–75
　in section 7, 179
　in section 8, 182
Lord Wen of Qin 秦文公 (r. 765–716 BCE), 269n67
Lord Wu of Wei 衛武公 (r. 812–758 BCE), 98, 101, 104–5, 265n10, 267n36
Lord Wu of Zheng 鄭武公 (r. 770–744 BCE), 101, 105, 156
　in section 2, 158
Lord Xian of Jin 晉獻公 (r. 676–651 BCE), 53, 173, 175n5, 254n39
　in section 6, 174

Lord Xian of Qin 秦獻公 (r. 384–362 BCE), 249n65
Lord Xiang of Jin 晉襄公 (r. 627–621 BCE), 181, 184, 185n6
 in section 8, 182
 in section 9, 185
Lord Xiang of Qi 齊襄公 (r. 697–686 BCE)
 in section 2, 158
Lord Xiang of Qin 秦襄公 (r. 777–766 BCE), 101, 104–05, 111–12, 163n7
Lord Xiang of Zheng 鄭襄公 (r. 604–587 BCE), 193n4
 in section 12, 193
Lord Xiao of Qin 秦孝公 (r. 361–338 BCE), 249n65
Lord Xiu of Song 宋休公 (aka Duke of Song, Tian 宋公田) (r. ca. 403–385 BCE), 61, 115, 118, 234n11
 in section 22, 233
 in section 23, 237
Lord Xu of Zheng 鄭繻公 (aka Earl of Zheng, Tai 鄭伯駘) (r. ca. 422–396 BCE), 61, 118, 234n11
 in section 22, 233
 in section 23, 237
Lord Yi of Qin 秦異公. *See* Lord Ai of Qin
Lord Yi of Wei 衛懿公 (aka Marquis You 幽侯) (r. 668–660 BCE), 167n9
 in section 4, 166
Lord Yi of Yue 越公翳. *See* King Yi of Yue
Lord Yin of Lu 魯隱公 (r. 722–712 BCE), 19, 28–29, 247n29
Lord You of Jin 晉幽公 (r. 433–416 BCE), 114
 in section 20, 225
Lord Zhao of Jin 晉昭公 (r. 531–526 BCE), 214
 in section 18, 216
Lord Zhao of Lu 魯昭公 (r. 541–510 BCE), 21, 30, 249n73, 265n1

Lord Zhao of Zheng 鄭昭公 (r. 696–695 BCE), 159–60n16
 in section 2, 158
Lord Zhuang of Qi 齊莊公 (r. 553–548 BCE) 210, 212nn8,9,11,12
 in section 17, 211
Lord Zhuang of Zheng 鄭莊公 (r. 743–701 BCE)
 in section 2, 157
Lord Zhuangping of Liang 梁莊平君 (fl. 398 BCE), Chu enfeoffed noble
 in section 23, 237
Lord Zhuju of Yue 越公朱句. *See* King Zhuju of Yue
Lu 魯, state of **xi–xiv**, 42, 59, 64, 90, 110, 115, 118, 123–24, 128, 163n4, 179n1, 180, 198n1, 199n10, 199n13, 211n1, 226n13, 231–32, 233n1, 234n5, 240n18, 249n73, 270n79, 271n6; and *Spring and Autumn Annals,* 2, 11, 17, 19–23, 61–62, 92, 126, 145, 252n10, 255n52; and *Zuozhuan,* 28–29, 31–32, 107, 126, 145
 in section 14, 197
 in section 22, 233
Lu Deming 陸德明 (ca. 550–630), 265n9
Lu Jia 陸賈 (ca. 228–ca. 140 BCE), 248n57
Lu Lianzi 魯連子, 98, 154n8, 265n7, 265n9, 265n11
Lu Mu Gong wen Zisi 魯穆公問子思 (Lord Mu of Lu asked Zisi), manuscript, 273n26
Luan Ying 欒盈 (d. 550 BCE), Jin leader, 210, 212nn7–11
 in section 17, 211
Luo 洛 River, **xi–xiv**, 219n17, 257n12
 in section 18, 217
Luoyang 洛陽, 97, 100–101, 103–4, 119, 156, 166n3, 180n9, 219n17, 230n8, 268n43, 274n56
 in section 2, 158

in section 4, 166
  See also Luoyi; Chengzhou
Luoyi 洛邑, 247n3
  in section 4, 166
  See also Luoyang 洛阳
Luoyin 洛陰, Jin locality, **xiv**, 238n4
  in section 23, 237
Luyang 魯陽, Chu county, **xiv**, 239n12, 275n59
Lü Xiang 呂相 (fl. 570s BCE), Jin official, 67, 256n59
Lüshi chunqiu 呂氏春秋, 52, 73, 98, 101, 117–18, 120, 153n5, 158n10, 232, 270n82

Man 蠻, ethnic group (also: referent to "savages"), **xi**, 178, 180n6, 219n17
  in section 7, 179
Mandate, Heaven's (*tian ming* 天命), 13–15, 65, 86, 88, 151, 245n5, 246n9
Maojiaping 毛家坪 site, Gangu 甘谷 County (Gansu), 111, 269n61
Marquis Ai of Cai 蔡哀侯 (r. 694–675 BCE), 49–51, 169–70, 171nn4–5
  in section 5, 170
Marquis Bao of Zeng 曾侯寶 (dates unknown), 85, 261n58
Marquis Jing of Han 韓景侯 (aka Han Qian 韓虔) (r. 408–400 BCE), 119, 233n3, 270n78
  in section 22, 233
Marquis Lie of Han 韓烈侯 (aka Han Qu 韓取) (r. 399–387 BCE), 240n20
  in section 23, 238
Marquis Lie of Zhao 趙烈侯 (aka Zhao Ji 趙籍) (r. 408–387 BCE), 115, 233n3, 270n78
  in section 22, 233
Marquis Ling of Cai 蔡靈侯. *See* Lord Ling of Cai
Marquis of [Western] Shen 申侯 (fl. 780–770 BCE), 101–102

Marquis of Wei, Qian 衛侯虔 (ruled ca. 404 BCE, reign dates and posthumous name unclear), 28, 61, 118–19
  in section 22, 233
Marquis Su of Zhao 趙肅侯 (r. 349–326 BCE), 263n81
Marquis Wen of Jin 晉文侯 (r. 780–746 or 770–736 BCE), 101–5, 156, 158–59n10, 270n84
  in section 2, 157
Marquis Wen of Wei 魏文侯 (aka Wei Si 魏斯) (r. 445–396 BCE), 117–18, 137, 229n6, 232, 233n3, 234n6, 240n20, 263n81
  in section 21, 225
  in section 22, 233
Marquis Wu of Wei 魏武侯 (aka Wei Ji 魏擊) (r. 395–370 BCE), 115, 137, 233n3, 234n6, 240n20, 270n78
  in section 22, 233
  in section 23, 238
Marquis Xian of Zhao 趙獻侯 (aka Zhao Huan 趙浣) (r. 423–409 BCE), 137, 233n6
  in section 21, 225
Marquis Yi of Zeng 曾侯乙 (d. 433 BCE), 85
Marquis You of Wei 衛幽侯. *See* Lord Yi of Wei
Marquis Yu of Zeng 曾侯與 (fl. 500 BCE), 85–88, 264n87
Marquis Zhao of Cai 蔡昭侯 (r. 518–491 BCE), 222n9–10
  in section 19, 221
Maspero, Henri (1883–1945), 248n56
Mawangdui 馬王堆, Changsha 長沙 (Hunan), Tomb 3, 111, 244n10
Meng Wentong 蒙文通 (1894–1968), 108
Mengzhu 孟渚 Marsh, 190n3
  in section 11, 189

Mengzi 孟子 (ca. 380–304 BCE) and *Mengzi*, 17–18, 62, 110, 125–26, 246n4, 255n52, 272n15
Mi 芈 clan, 135–36, 261n58, 274nn54–55
Mi Jia 嬭加, wife of Marquis Bao of Zeng, 85, 261n58, 272n7
Mi Jia-*bianzhong* 嬭加編鐘 inscription, 261n58, 262n70, 262n75, 272n7
Mie 蔑, Zheng locality, 239n14
    in section 23, 237
Miji 靡笄, battle location (Qi; see also An), **xiii**, 196, 199n11
    in section 14, 197
Min 緡, Song locality, **xiii**, 179n1
    in section 7, 179
Ming 命 manuscript, 130
Mozi 墨子 (ca. 460–390 BCE) and *Mozi*, 113–14, 116, 196, 239n12, 253n23, 253n27
Muling Pass 穆陵關 (Qi), **xiv**, 234n7

naming patterns, ix–x, 61–62, 90, 255n51, 255nn53–54, 274n50
Nangong Kuo 南宮括 (fl. eleventh century BCE), 86, 261n61, 262n63, 264n87
Nanguo Yan 南郭偃 (aka Sir Nanguo 南郭子) (fl. 590 BCE), Qi official 198n8
    in section 14, 197
Nanyang 南陽 basin, 159n13, 171–72n7, 230n9, 262n66, 267n29
National Palace Museum in Taipei, 82
Ni 兒 lineage (Shang), 245n6
Nie 聶, location between Song and Zheng, 63, 241n25
    in section 23, 238
Nine Provinces (*jiu zhou* 九州), 142, 275n69
"noble man," comments by in *Zuo zhuan*, 3, 24–27, 32, 51–53, 244n7, 248n58, 254n35

oracle-bone inscriptions, 12, 46
Ōnishi Katsuya 大西克也, 239n5
Pangeng 盤庚, Shang king, 134–36
Pankenier, David W., 260n51
Peking (Beijing) University bamboo slips, 43
Pi 疲 (fl. 420 BCE), Song leader, 229n3
    in section 21, 228
Pi Xirui 皮錫瑞 (1850–1908), 247n38
Piao Qiang (or Biao Qiang) 驫羌 bells, 113, 119–20, 224, 232, 271n92
★*Ping wang wen Zheng Shou* 平王問鄭壽 manuscript, 129
★*Ping wang yu Wangzi Mu* 平王與王子木 manuscript, 129
Pingye 平夜, Chu locality, **xiv**, 240n17
Pingyin 平陰, Qi locality and site of campaigns (555, 430, 404 BCE), **xiii–xiv**, 119, 210, 212n5
    in section 17, 211
Poverty and Success are a Matter of Timing (*Qiong da yi shi* 窮達以時) manuscript, 133
Prince Wei 王子圍. See King Ling of Chu
Prince Zhao of Zhou 王子朝 (d. 505 BCE), 29–31, 101, 106–7, 120, 265n5, 267n41–42
Pu Pond 莆池, 198n7
    in section 14, 197

Qi 齊, state of, **xi, xiii–xiv**, 21–22, 31–32, 41–42, 52, 56, 61, 63–64, 114–19, 122, 124, 126, 128, 168n13, 176n13, 179n1, 179n4, 191n9, 196, 198n3, 198n7–8, 199n9, 210, 215–16, 223–24, 228, 231–32, 235–36, 240n22, 252n9, 258n28, 270n79, 270n87–88, 273n30
    in section 4, 166
    in section 6, 174

 in section 7, 179
 in section 11, 189
 in section 14, 197
 in section 15, 202
 in section 17, 211
 in section 18, 217
 in section 20, 225
 in section 22, 233
 in section 23, 238
Qĭ 杞, state of, 211n1
Qin 秦, state of, **xi, xiii–xiv**, 26, 40, 42, 45, 67, 81, 122, 146, 163n7, 221n1, 249n65, 252n8, 253n23, 258n20, 260nn48–49, 268n48, 269n61, 269n65, 272n21; and Chu, 42, 55–59, 183n8, 204n8, 205nn21–22, 222nn6–7, 238n4, 255n45, 272n17; dynastic legend of, 108–12, 161–62; ethnic origins of, 108–9, 268n52, 268n59; and Jin, 40, 52–54, 67, 107, 139–41, 173, 175n7, 176n9, 176n11, 176n13, 176n15, 179n3, 180n8, 181, 182n1, 182nn4–5, 183n6, 184, 186, 187nn1–3, 206–7, 209n7, 235–36, 271n92; in *Records of the Historian*, 96, 106, 108, 110, 112, 246nn7–8
 in section 3, 162
 in section 6, 174–75
 in section 7, 179
 in section 8, 182
 in section 9, 185
 in section 10, 186
 in section 15, 202
 in section 16, 208
 in section 19, 221
 in section 23, 237
Qin 秦, imperial dynasty (221–207 BCE), 64, 67, 94–95, 255n56. *See also* biblioclasm
Qin Zhong 秦仲 (d. 822 BCE), Qin ruler, 109, 112, 246n7, 269n67
 in section 3, 162

Qing Feng 慶封 (d. 538 BCE), Qi leader, 217n8
Qiong da yi shi. See *Poverty and Success are a Matter of Timing*
Qu Jian 屈建 (appellative Zimu 子木) (d. 545 BCE), Chu leader, 217n4
 in section 18, 216
Qu Wuchen 屈巫臣 (aka Qu Wu 屈巫) (fl. 596–580 BCE), Duke of Shen 申公, Chu official, later Jin official, 54–56, 58–59, 200–1, 204n8, 204n11, 204n14
 in section 15, 202
 in section 20, 224
Qufu 曲阜, Lu capital, **xii–xiv**, 110, 163n4
Quwo 曲沃, Jin city, **xiii**, 212n10
 in section 17, 211

Records of the Historian (*Shiji* 史記), 4–6, 34, 81, 94–121, 125–26, 135, 154n8, 155–56, 162, 163n4, 163n7, 171n6, 180n6, 222n9, 227, 229n2, 234n11, 239n11, 258n20, 264n1, 265n7, 265n10, 266n18, 267n36, 268n56, 271n94. *See also* Sima Qian
Records of the Rites (*Liji* 禮記), 264n89
Red Di 赤狄. *See* Di 狄
Remainder of Zhou Documents (*Yizhoushu* 逸周書) 2, 16; "Shi fu" 世俘 ("The great capture"), 16
Ren 任, location between Song and Lu, **xiv**, 233n1
 in section 22, 233
Romance of the Three Kingdoms (*Sanguo yanyi* 三國演義), 24
Rong 戎, ethnic group (also designation for "barbarians"), **xi, xiii**, 84, 97, 108–9, 124, 151–52, 155, 161, 163n5, 178, 180n6, 180n8, 272n14; Jiang Rong 姜戎, 154n9; Quanrong 犬戎, 101; Rong of Luhun 陸渾之戎 107

INDEX   [323]

Rong 戎, ethnic group (*continued*)
   in section 1, 153
   in section 2 (Western Rong 西戎), 157
   in section 3 (Nucuo(?) Rong 奴虘戎), 162
   in section 7, 179
Rongcheng 容城, locality near Chu, temporary capital of Xǔ, **xii–xiii**, 215, 218n12–13
   in section 18, 216
Rongchengshi 容成氏 manuscript, 142–44, 146, 275n69–70
Roots of Generations (*Shi ben* 世本), 13, 69, 106, 245n6, 256n2
Royal Son Chen 王子晨 of Chu (fl. 580 BCE), 139, 208n4–5
   in section 16, 208
Royal Son Chen 王子晨 of Wu (fl. 506 BCE), 57, 205n22
   in section 15, 203
Royal Son Ding of Chu 楚王子定 (fl. 400 BCE), 138, 236, 275n61, 239n11, 241n22
   in section 23, 237–38
Royal Son Jueyou 王子蹶由 of Wu (fl. 530s BCE), 56, 204n15
   in section 15, 203
Royal Son Pi of Chu 楚王子罷 (fl. 580 BCE), 139
   in section 16, 208
Ru 汝 River, **xi–xiv**, 51–52, 169, 172n8, 172n10, 215, 218n13, 239n12–13, 240n17
   in section 5, 171
   in section 18, 216
Ruo 鄀 (Lower Ruo 下鄀), polity, then Chu dependency, **xii–xiii**, 54, 71, 176n15, 257n18, 258n21–22; Upper Ruo (上鄀), temporary location of Chu capital, **xii**, 71, 257n18, 258nn21–22
   in section 6, 175

Ruo'ao 若敖 lineage, Chu, 70–71, 257n13

"savages" (*manyi* 蠻夷 or *yi* 夷) 123–25, 136. *See also* "barbarians"; Di; Rong; Yi
Schaberg, David, 7, 23, 60, 66, 73, 80, 93, 261n9
Scribe Bo 史伯 (Zhou) (fl. 770 BCE), 135, 158n8
scribes (*shi* 史), 18, 21–22, 29–31, 54, 60, 62–64, 66, 72, 74, 91–93, 126, 137, 142, 146, 151, 232, 239n5, 246n19
sexagenary (*ganzhi* 干支) cycle, 35, 63, 241n24, 255n55
Shandong 山東 Province, 16, 110, 114, 161, 223, 163n4, 199n13, 234n4, 240n18, 249n69, 270n74
Shang 商 (aka Yin 殷) dynasty (ca. 1600–1046 BCE), x, 3, 12–16, 46, 65, 86, 108–11, 123, 135–36, 144, 151, 153n3, 161–62, 163nn2–4, 165, 166n3, 167n4, 167n6, 245nn4–6, 246n16, 257n12, 268n52, 268n59, 271n6
   in section 1, 152
   in section 3, 162
   in section 4, 166
Shangdi 上帝. *See* Lord-on-High
Shanghai Museum bamboo slips, 43, 74–75, 77, 127–33, 142, 258n28–29, 259n41, 273n27
Shanghe 商蓋 or Shangyan 商奄 (商閹), Shang settlement, 109–11, 161, 163n4, 269n65
   in section 3, 162
Shangmi 商密, capital of Lower Ruo, **xii–xiii**, 54, 176n15
   in section 6, 175
Shangqiu (Shang Hill) 商丘, Song capital, **xii–xiv**, 190n1, 190n3
Shanxi 山西 Province, 82, 97, 154n6, 226n11
Shao Kong 少孔. *See* Xia Ji 夏姬

Shao'e 少鄂, locality to which King Ping of Zhou fled, 103, 159n13
  in section 2, 157
Shaohao 少皞, primordial thearch, 111
Shaoling 召陵, location of 506 BCE assembly, **xii–xiii**, 215, 218n15, 219n16, 221n4
  in section 18, 216
She 葉, temporary capital of Xǔ, **xii–xiii**, 211n2, 212n3, 218n13
  in section 17, 211
Shen 莘, Cai locality, 50, 171n3
  in section 5, 170
Shěn 沈, Chu county, 75, 259n33
Shen 申 (Western Shen) Western Zhou-period polity, 101–102, 155, 158n4, 244n7
  in section 2, 157
Shen 申, polity and Chu county, **xii–xiv**, 54, 172n10, 175, 176n15, 177n16, 188, 190n5, 191n8, 217n8
  in section 18, 216
Shen 申 lineage, Chu, 190n5
Shen Baoxu 申包胥 (fl. 505 BCE), Chu official, 59, 191n5, 204n8, 222n6, 255n45
*Shen gong chen Ling wang 申公臣靈王 manuscript, 75–79, 129, 259n41, 260n43
Shen Wuwei 申無畏 (aka Shen Zhou 申舟 or Shen Elder Wuwei 申伯無畏) (d. 595 BCE), Chu official, 188–89, 190n5, 191n7–10
  in section 11, 189
Shen Zhou 申舟. See Shen Wuwei 申無畏
Shensheng 申生 (aka Lord Gong 共君) (d. 656 BCE), Jin crown prince, 53, 254n39, 175nn5–6
  in section 6, 174
shi 士, "men of service," 146, 275n78
shi 史, meaning of, 12, 18, 66, 245n2, 255n58. See also scribes

Shi ben. See Roots of Generations
Shi Hui 士會 (aka Sui Hui 隨會) (fl. 630–590 BCE), Jin official, 185n5, 187n2, 198n1
  in section 9, 185
  in section 10, 186
  in section 14, 197
Shi Qiang-pan 史墻盤 inscription, 260n47
Shi Xie 士燮 (aka Wenzi Xie 文子燮 or Shi Wenzi 士文子) (d. 574 BCE), 139
  in section 16, 208
Shibancun 石板村, Cili 慈利 County (Hunan), Tomb 36, 244n10, 273n26
Shiji. 史記. See Records of the Historian
Shijing. See Canon of Poems
Shou Bin 守彬, 71, 258n20
Shouzhi 首止, **xiii–xiv**, 160n17
  in section 2, 158
Shuanggudui 雙古堆, Fuyang 阜陽 (Anhui), Tomb 1, 244n10
Shuhou, the Duke of Shen 申公叔侯 (fl. 630s), Chu official, 188, 179n1, 190n5
  in section 11, 189
Shuihudi 睡虎地, Yunmeng 雲夢 (Hubei), Tomb 11, 244n10, 264n90
Shujing. See Canon of Documents
Shun 舜, legendary thearch, 90, 108
Shuzi Gong 舒子共 (d. 400 BCE), Chu noble
  in section 23, 237
Si 泗 River, **xi–xiv**, 179n1
Sima Biao 司馬彪 (d. 306), 154n8
Sima Guang 司馬光 (1019–1086), 116. See also Comprehensive Mirror to Aid the Government (Zizhi tongjian 資治通鑑)
Sima Qian 司馬遷 (ca. 145–90 BCE), 1–2, 4, 6, 13, 24, 34, 94–122, 126, 152, 156, 180n6, 228, 235, 238n1, 243n3, 245n6, 250n79, 255n57, 264n1, 265n5, 265n10, 267n36, 271n94. See also Records of the Historian

Sima Tan 司馬談 (d. 110 BCE), 94
Song, prime minister of Yue 越令尹宋 (fl. 441 BCE), 114, 226n11
  in section 20, 225
Song 宋, state of, **xi–xiv**, 19, 28, 31, 41, 64, 99, 139, 154n8, 176n13, 179n1, 179n4, 188, 190n1, 190n3, 191nn9–11, 191n13, 211n1, 227, 229n3, 229n5, 233n1, 235, 238n3, 239n6, 240n18, 241n25, 249n73, 266n16, 275n58
  in section 1, 153
  in section 6, 174
  in section 7, 179
  in section 11, 189
  in section 16, 208
  in section 18, 216
  in section 21, 228
Spring and Autumn (Chunqiu 春秋, 770–453 BCE) period, x, 5, 17–18, 20, 23, 25, 33–38, 59–60, 68, 74, 78, 82, 88, 90–93, 113, 124, 126, 146, 173, 178, 248n54, 256n10, 258n22
Spring and Autumn Annals (*Chunqiu* 春秋), 2–3, 11, 17–23, 29, 32, 39, 45, 49–50, 59, 92, 125–26, 137, 140, 145, 171n4, 185n1, 193n6, 198n1, 205n18, 211n1, 215, 218n12, 218–19n15, 219n16, 221n4, 225n7, 226n13, 232, 243n6, 246nn24–25, 247n27, 252n10, 255n52; and Confucius, 17–18, 21–22; "rules of recording" (*shu fa* 書法), 21–22, 61–62, 247nn43–44, 248n46; and *Zuo zhuan*, 24–26, 28, 167n11, 247n38, 249n67, 249n70, 254n34
Springs and Autumns of Master Yan (*Yanzi chunqiu* 晏子春秋), 93
Springs and Autumns of Sire Lü. See *Lüshi chunqiu*
Springs and Autumns of Wu and Yue (*Wu Yue chunqiu* 吳越春秋), 113

Stratagems of the Warring States (*Zhanguo ce* 戰國策), 35, 39, 73, 113, 126, 250n83, 269n65
Su Jianzhou 蘇建洲, 191n8, 195n4, 227, 239n5, 240n16
Su Qin 蘇秦 (d. ca. 284 BCE), 111, 269n65
Subtleties of Mr. Duo (*Duoshi wei* 鐸氏微) 251–52n6
Sui 隨, state of (Chu dependency), **xii**, 57, 85–88, 124, 171n6, 205n21, 261n58, 262n70–72, 262n75, 264n87
  in section 15, 203
  See also Zeng 曾
Sui Hui 隨會. See Shi Hui
Suizhou 隨州 (Hubei), 85, 193n3, 205n21, 262n64
Sunshu Ao 孫叔敖 (fl. 600 BCE), Chu official, 259n33
Suzhou 蘇州 (Jiangsu), 114, 274n6

Taijia 太甲, Shang king, 257n12
Tan 郯, statelet, 114
Tang 唐 polity, **xii**, 220, 222n7
  in section 19, 221
Tang Center for Early China, 252n16
Taniguchi Mitsuru 谷口滿, 69, 258n20
Teng 滕, statelet, and Yue county, **xiv**, 114, 240n18
  in section 23, 238
Tian 田 (Chen 陳) lineage, Qi, 32, 115, 270n82, 234nn8–10, 240–41n22
Tian Daozi 田悼子 (d. 404 BCE?), 270n82
"topical arrangement" (*jishi benmo* 紀事本末) style, 32, 39, 251n6
True Monarch (*wangzhe* 王者), 125
Tsinghua (Qinghua) University, vii, 4, 37, 43, 48, 68–69, 72, 74, 90, 110, 112, 127, 133, 251n3, 251n5, 253n18, 253n21, 253n27, 256n3, 261n59, 263n82, 267n41, 269n71, 273n30, 153n4, 183n8

Tulin 徒棶(林), hunting location between Song and Chen, 190n3
  in section 11, 189

"unicorn" (*lin* 麟), 20, 246n25

virtue (*de* 德), 14, 136, 178–79, 246n9, 267n36, 275n74

★*Wang ju* 王居 manuscript, 130
Wangshan, Jiangling 江陵望山 (Hubei), Tomb 1, 135, 145–46
Warring States (Zhanguo 戰國) period (453–221 BCE), 3, 6, 12–13, 18, 33–37, 46–48, 67–69, 85, 88–91, 93–96, 98, 102, 106, 108, 111–22, 125–26, 136, 146–47, 153n4, 159n11, 159n14, 168n13–14, 232, 248n54, 253n23, 253n30–31, 254n42, 255n56, 258n22, 263n80, 264n1, 265n7, 265n10, 268n48, 269n65, 273n27, 275n78, 276n79
Watson, Burton (1925–2017), 250–51n85
"weighing" (*quan* 權), 20, 247n35
Wei 衛, state of, **xi–xiv**, 28–29, 40, 61, 64, 96, 98–99, 101, 154n8, 165, 166n1, 167n6, 167nn8–10, 168n13–14, 176n13, 178, 179n4, 198n1, 198n7, 199n10, 199n13, 211n1, 212n11, 219n19, 234n11, 254n41
  in section 4, 166
  in section 6, 175
  in section 7, 179
Wei 魏, lineage and state, **xiv**, 113, 116–20, 227, 229n5, 231–32, 234n9, 236, 238nn3–4, 240n20, 249n65, 263n82, 270n87
Wei Ji 魏擊. *See* Marquis Wu of Wei
Wei 潤 River, **xi, xiii–xiv**, 159n14, 176n9, 238n4
Wei 濰 River, 212n6
Wei Si 魏斯. *See* Marquis Wen of Wei

Wen 溫, settlement, **xiii**, 247n44, 180n9
Wen 汶 River, 199n13
Wenfengta 文峰塔 cemetery, Suizhou Municipality 隨州 (Hubei), 85, 262n75
Western Shen 西申. *See* Shen, Western
Western Zhou 西周 period (ca. 1046–771 BCE), x, 3, 11, 12–17, 38, 40, 47–48, 64, 80, 84–85, 95–100, 103–9, 112, 120, 123–24, 126, 135, 151, 154n9, 155–56, 158n13, 161, 163n7, 246n12, 246n19, 252n7, 261n54, 265n5, 267n29
Wu 吳, state of, **xi–xiii**, 21, 32, 41–42, 54–60, 66, 71, 76, 81, 86–88, 113–15, 124, 128–29, 132–33, 200–2, 204n8, 204nn14–15, 205nn18–19, 205nn21–23, 214–15, 217n8, 218nn14–15, 220, 221nn4–5, 222nn7–8, 223, 225n7, 226nn9–10, 255n45, 257n15–17, 260n49, 262n66–67, 262n71–72, 263n76, 269n71, 270n76, 273n26, 273n30
  in section 15, 202–3
  in section 18, 216
  in section 19, 221
  in section 20, 224–25
Wu Ji 伍雞 (or Ji of Wu 伍之雞), legendary personality, 56–57, 59, 64, 92, 201, 204n17, 205n18
  in section 15, 203
Wu ming 吳命 manuscript, 133
Wu Yue chunqiu. *See Springs and Autumns of Wu and Yue*
Wu Yun 伍員. *See* Wu Zixu
Wu Zixu 伍子胥 (aka Wu Yun 伍員) (d. 484 BCE), Chu fugitive and Wu official, 56–59, 64, 92, 133, 144, 200–201, 203n1, 204nn16–17, 205n19, 205n23, 254n42, 273n36
  in section 15, 203

INDEX [327]

Wu She 伍奢 (d. 522 BCE), Chu official, 56–57, 204nn16–17
  in section 15, 203
Wuchang 武昌 (part of Wuhan, Hubei), 257n16
Wugeng 武庚 (aka Luzi Geng 祿子耿 or Sheng 聖) (d. ca. 1041 BCE), son of King Zhouxin of Shang, 109–10, 161, 268n54, 163nn2–3
  in section 3, 162
Wulu 五鹿, location in Wei 衛 (later Jin), **xiii**, 179–80n4
  in section 7, 179
Wuyang 武陽 fortress, **xiv**, 63, 137, 235–36, 238n3, 241n23, 241n25, 275n58
  in section 23, 237–38

xi 夕 sacrifice, Chu, 69, 256n6
Xi 析, locality in Lower Ruo, later Xǔ capital, **xii–xiii**, 176n15
Xi 息, state of, later Chu county, **xii**, 49–52, 102, 169–70, 171n1, 171n5, 172n10, 254n34
  in section 5, 170–71
Xi Gui 息媯 (fl. 680s to 660s BCE), wife of the Xi ruler, later of King Wen of Chu, 49–52, 171n5, 254n36
  in section 5, 170–71
Xi Ke 郤克 (aka Ke of Ju or Ju Ke 駒克) (d. 587 BCE), 196, 198n1–2, 198n5, 199n10–11, 199n14
  in section 14, 197
Xia 夏 dynasty 13, 15, 159, 167n4, 245n5, 246n16
  in section 4, 166
Xia 夏 calendar, 83
Xia 夏, cultural entity, 124
Xia 夏 River. *See* Han River
Xia Ji 夏姬 (aka Shao Kong), femme fatale from Chen, 55–56, 58, 64–65, 201, 203n3, 203n6, 204n7, 204nn10–11, 254n43
  in section 15, 202
Xiasi 下寺 cemetery (Xichuan 淅川, Henan) 260n48
Xian 汧 (岷?) River, in the state of Qi, 234n7
  in section 22, 233
Xian Spring 鹹泉, Wei 衛 locality
  in section 18, 217
Xian Gao 弦高 (fl. 630 BCE), Zheng merchant 182n4
  in section 8, 182
Xian Mie 先蔑 (fl. 630 BCE), Jin official, 185n4, 187n2
  in section 9, 185
  in section 10, 186
Xiang the Elder 襄老 (d. 597 BCE), Chu official, 55, 204n9
  in section 15, 202
Xiangping 襄平, Qi locality, 115, 226n14
  in section 20, 225
Xianyu 鮮虞, ethnic group, 219n16. *See also* Zhongshan
Xiao Tongshu Zi 蕭同叔子 (d. after 589 BCE), mother of Lord Qing of Qi, 198n4
Xieyong 洩庸 (fl. 490 BCE), Wu official
  in section 19, 221
Xin, Grand Steward of Zheng 鄭太宰欣, 240n15
  in section 23, 237
Xin You 辛有 (fl. 740 BCE), Zhou official, 107
Xinian 繫年 ("String of years" or "Linked years") manuscript, 4–7, 32, 37–67, 72, 74, 91–92, 95–97, 151–241 (translation), 251n3, 253n30, 255n44, 255n48, 255n51, 255n54, 256n6, 262n72, 266n28, 271n92; audience of, 65–67; authenticity of, 43–48, 253n18; and Chu, 39, 42,

45–46, 66, 137–42, 144, 252n7;
dating of, 42–43, 252n13; and Jin,
39, 45–46, 137–42, 252n7, 254n41;
and Qi, 252n9; and Qin, 108–12,
268n53, 269n65; sources of, 39, 42,
45–49, 59–65, 76, 254n34; structure
of, 38–43, 251nn5–6; Warring
States-period history in, 114–20;
Western Zhou history in, 97–100,
103–6; and *Zuozhuan*, 48–60, 64–65

Xintian 新田, Jin capital, **xii–xiv**, 212n10

Xinzheng 新鄭, Zheng capital, **xii–xiv**, 239n14

Xiqi 奚齊 (d. 651 BCE), Jin prince, 53–54
  in section 6, 174

Xú 徐, state of, **xii–xiii**, 217n8
  in section 18, 216

Xǔ 許, state of, **xii–xiii**, 102, 210, 211n2, 212n3, 215, 218nn12–13
  in section 17, 211
  in section 18, 216

Xu Shaohua 徐少華, 126

Xun Linfu 荀林父 (aka Zhonghang Linfu 中行林父) (d. ca. 593 BCE), Jin leader, 195n2
  in section 13, 194

Yan 鄢, Chu city, **xii–xiv**, 256n10, 258n21

Yan 鄢 (Yanling 鄢陵) battle, 575 BCE and locality in Zheng, **xii–xiii**, 19, 139, 140–41, 207, 209n8
  in section 16, 208

Yan 燕, state of, 111

Yan Ruo 晏弱 (aka Sir Yan 晏子) (d. 556 BCE), Qi official, 198n8, 199n9
  in section 14, 197

Yan Shigu 顏師古 (581–645), 99

Yan Ying 晏嬰 (d. 500 BCE), 198n8, 258n28. See also *Springs-and-Autumns of Master Yan*

Yang Wei 陽爲 (fl. 420 BCE), Chu military leader, 137, 229n4, 230n9
  in section 21, 228

Yangcheng 陽城, Chu County, **xiv**, 239n6

Yangzi River (Changjiang 長江), **xi–xii**, 76, 86, 123, 258n22, 262n64

Yanzi chunqiu. See *Springs-and-Autumns of Master Yan*

Yao 堯, primeval thearch, 90, 143, 275n72

Yao 崤, battle of (627 BCE), **xiii**, 180n8, 183nn6–7
  in section 8, 182

Yellow River 黃河 (aka the River 河), **xi–xiv**, 13, 71, 188, 235, 158n14, 175n7, 176n9, 180n9, 187n1, 195n3, 198nn6–7, 211n11, 211–12n12, 219n17, 238n4, 239n8, 257n12
  in section 4, 166
  in section 6, 174
  in section 13, 194
  in section 17, 211

Yellow Thearch (Huangdi 皇帝), 90, 153n4

Yi 夷, ethnic group, **xi**, 86, 125, 178, 180n6; Eastern Yi 東夷, 108; Yi of Su (Su Yi 蘇夷), 16
  in section 7, 179

Yi 夷, polity in Shandong, 27, 249n69

Yi 伊 River, **xii–xiv**, 268n43, 267n17
  in section 18, 217

Yi 沂, battle of (505 BCE), **xii**, 57, 205n21
  in section 15, 203

Yi, Duke of Yun 鄖公儀. See Zhong Yi 鍾儀

Yi Yin 伊尹, Shang minister, 257n12

Yicheng 宜城 (Hubei), 71, 256n10, 257n18

Yin Qun 印群, 268n52

Ying 郢, Chu capital, **xii**, 57, 69–72, 76, 86, 133, 145, 200, 205n23, 215, 257n17, 258nn20–22, 262n66
  in section 15, 203
  in section 23, 237
ying 郢 designation of residences of Chu kings (x+ *ying* 郢), 70–72, 256–57nn10–11, 257n16, 258n20–21
Ying 嬴 clan, 108
Ying 潁, River, **xi–xiv**, 169, 172n9
Yiyang 宜陽, Jin (Han 韓) locality, **xiv**, 137, 230n8, 274n56
  in section 21, 228
Yizhoushu See *Remainder of Zhou Documents*
Yong 雍, Qin capital, **xiii–xiv**, 176n9
Yongqiu 雍丘 (Yong Hill), location between Song and Zheng, **xiv**, 199, 229n5
  in section 21, 228
Yoshimoto Michimasa 吉本道雅, 159n12, 252n13, 266n21
You 鼬, Song locality
  in section 22, 233
Yu 禹, legendary thearch, 108, 142–43
Yu Pass 榆關, between Zheng and Song, **xiv**, 235–36, 238n3, 241n25, 275n58
  in section 23, 237
Yuasa Kunihiro 湯淺邦弘, 75, 77, 259n32, 259n36
Yue 越, state of, **xi–xii**, **xiv**, 5, 21, 41, 55, 113–16, 118–19, 124, 136, 223–24, 226n9, 226nn11–12, 231, 235, 240n18, 269n71, 270n74, 270n76, 273n30, 274n55
  in section 20, 225
  in section 22, 233
Yue gong qi shi 越公其事 manuscript, 205n18, 269n71
Yue Wang Chaxu-*ge* 越王差徐戈 inscription, 270n76
Yuejue shu. See *Glory of Yue*

Yuelu Academy (Changsha, Hunan) bamboo slips, 43
Yun 鄖, Chu county, **xii**, 208n2
Zangsun Xu 臧孫許 (d. 587 BCE), Lu official
  in section 14, 197
Zeng 曾 polity, 85–88, 124, 205n21, 261n58, 262n63–64, 262n75, 264n87, 272n7. *See also* Sui
Zeng 繒 polity, 101, 154, 158n7
  in section 2, 157
Zeng Hou Yu-*bianzhong* 曾侯與編鐘 inscription, 82, 85–88, 261n59
Zhai Zhong 祭仲 (fl. 730–697 BCE), Zheng official, 160n16
Zhanguo ce. See *Stratagems of the Warring States*
★*Zhanguo zonghengjia shu* 戰國縱橫家書 manuscript, 111, 244n10
Zhang Shoujie 張守節 (fl. 725–735), 98–99, 154n8, 265n11
Zhao 趙, lineage and state, **xiv**, 113, 116–20, 226n11, 227, 231–32, 234nn9–10, 263n80, 263n82, 270n78, 270n87
Zhao Dun 趙盾 (d. 601 BCE), 22, 184
Zhao Gou 趙狗 (aka Muzi of Xinzhi 新稚穆子) (fl. 430 BCE), Jin official, 114, 226n12
  in section 20, 225
Zhao Huanzi 趙桓子 (d. 424 BCE), head of Zhao patrimony, 114, 226n11
  in section 20, 228
Zhao Ping'an 趙平安, 72, 256n3, 256n10
Zhao Si 昭竢 (aka Si of Zhao 昭之竢) (d. 395 BCE), Chu leader, 138, 240n21, 275n60
  in section 23, 238
★*Zhao wang hui shi* 昭王毀室 manuscript, 129
★*Zhao wang yu Gong zhi Shui* 昭王與龔之脽 manuscript, 129

Zhao Wenzi 趙文子 (d. 541 BCE), Jin leader
  in section 18, 216
Zhao Xiangzi 趙襄子 (d. ca. 442 BCE), head of Zhao patrimony, 226n11
Zhao Zhan 趙旃 (fl. 590s BCE), Jin military leader, 195nn5–6
  in section 13, 194
Zhaoge 朝歌 (Wei 衛 capital location, then Jin stronghold), **xii–xiii**, 212n11
  in section 17, 211
Zhejiang University bamboo slips, 43–44, 252n17
Zheng 鄭, state of, **xi–xiv**, 19, 28–29, 31, 40–41, 64, 77, 106, 128, 131, 135, 138–41, 156, 176n13, 180n6, 180n9, 182n1, 182n4, 181, 188, 190n1, 192–93, 193n2, 193n4, 193n6, 194, 195n1, 206–7, 209n8, 211n1–2, 215, 218n13, 219n19, 227, 229n5, 229–30n7, 235–36, 238n3, 240nn14–15, 241n25, 259n41, 263n82, 273n30, 275n58
  in section 2, 158
  in section 6, 175
  in section 7, 179
  in section 8, 182
  in section 12, 193
  in section 13, 194
  in section 16, 207–8
  in section 22, 233
  in section 23, 237–38
Zheng Qiao 鄭樵 (1104–1162), 248n54
Zheng Wei 鄭威, 239n12, 240n21
*Zheng Zijia sang 鄭子家喪 manuscript, 130
Zhengshu 徵舒 (d. 598 BCE), Chen leader, 55, 58, 201, 203n6, 204n7
  in section 15, 202
Zhi 郅, settlement, 97, 99, 154n6, 265n11
  in section 1, 152
Zhi Bo 智伯 or 知伯 (d. 453 BCE), Jin leader, 113, 263n80

Zhong Yi 鍾儀, Duke of Yun 鄖公 (fl. 580s BCE), Chu noble, 139, 208nn4–5
  in section 16, 207
Zhongshan 中山, state of, **xiii**, 81, 215, 260n49, 219n16
  in section 18, 216. See also Xianyu
Zhòu 紂. See Zhouxin
Zhou dynasty (ca. 1046–255 BCE), cultural realm and royal domain, **xi–xiv**, 2–4, 7, 13–14, 18, 20–21, 48, 50n1, 61, 65–66, 80–81, 83–90, 108–10, 116–20, 121–28, 131, 133, 136–37, 142, 145–47, 150–51, 154n9, 159nn12–14, 161–62, 163n1, 163n7, 165, 166n3, 167nn4–5, 174, 176n15, 178–79, 180n9, 182n4, 218n15, 222n8, 223, 232, 234n11, 235, 239n11, 246n7, 246n16, 247n44, 248n48, 259n39, 260nn47–48, 261n61, 263n76, 265n5, 265n7, 265n11, 267n38, 267nn41–42, 268n54, 272n8, 272n17; Eastern Zhou (770–255 BCE), 5, 45–46, 62, 64, 68, 73–74, 81–82, 91–92, 97, 120, 127, 260n48; turmoil in, 29–31, 96–107, 155–56; in *Xinian*, 38–40, 42, 45, 60, 251n4
  in section 1, 152–53
  in section 2, 157
  in section 3, 162
  in section 4, 166
  in section 20, 233. See also Duke of Zhou; Ji clan; Son of Heaven; Western Zhou
Zhoulai 州來, locality between Chu and Wu, later Cai capital, **xii–xiii**, 57
  in section 15, 203
  in section 19, 221
Zhouxin 紂辛 (Zhòu 紂) (d. ca. 1046 BCE), last Shang king, 13, 110, 144, 151, 163n4, 246n8
Zhu 邾, polity, 28, 198n1, 211n1

Zhu Xi 朱熹 (1130–1200), 124, 247n38, 248n59

Zhuang Wang ji cheng 莊王既成 manuscript, 74–75, 129, 259n33

Zhuangzi 莊子, 98, 154n8

Zhuanxu 顓頊, legendary thearch, 108, 135, 142

Zhufang 朱方, Wu locality, **xii**, 266n8
   in section 18, 192

Zhuozi 卓子. See Daozi 悼子

Zhurong 祝融, Chu primordial ancestor, 135–36, 142, 274n54

Zhushu jinian. See *Bamboo Annals*

Zhuyu 朱圉 settlement (Qin), 109, 111, 161
   in section 3, 162

Zi Meishou 子眉壽 (aka Ducal Son Wei 公子亹 or Ziwei 子亹) (d. 695 BCE), Zheng leader, 160n17
   in section 2, 158

Zichan 子產 (d. 522 BCE), Zheng leader, 263n82

Zichi 子池 (fl. 400 BCE), Zheng military commander
   in section 23, 237

Zichong 子重 (d. 570 BCE), Chu prime minister, 138
   in section 16, 207

Zifengzi 子封子 (fl. 400 BCE), Zheng military commander
   in section 23, 237

Zifan 子反 (d. 575 BCE), Chu prince and military commander, 56, 204n11
   in section 15, 202

Zifan 子犯. See Hu Yan 狐偃

Zifan-bianzhong 子犯編鐘 inscription, 82–84, 253n9

Zigao 子高, Duke of She 葉公 (Chu official, aka Shen Zhuliang 沈諸梁) (ca. 550–470 BCE), 130

Zigui 秭歸 (Hubei), 256n10

Zihu 子虎 (fl. 505 BCE), Qin military commander
   in section 19, 221

Zihuang 子皇, Duke of Chen. See Chuanfeng Xu 穿封戌

Zijing, the governor of Shěn 沈尹子桱, Chu official, 75–76

Ziju 子居 (scholar's pen name), 59, 180n9, 218n13

Zima 子馬 (fl. 400 BCE), Zheng military commander
   in section 23, 237

Zimu 子木. See Qu Jian

Zipu 子蒲 (fl. 505 BCE), Qin military commander
   in section 19, 221

Ziqi 子期 (d. 479 BCE), Chu prime minister, 72, 87

Ziyang 子陽 (d. 398 BCE), Zheng leader, 240n15
   in section 23, 237

Ziyi (aka Yi 儀), Duke of Shen 申公子儀, Chu official. See Dou Ke

Ziyi 子儀 manuscript, 254n8

Ziyu 子玉 (aka Cheng Dechen 成得臣) (d. 632 BCE), Chu official, 124, 130–31, 180n6
   in section 7, 179

Zizhi tongjian. See *Comprehensive Mirror to Aid the Government*

Zuo Qiuming 左丘明, putative author of *Zuozhuan*, 24, 250n79

Zuo Tradition or *Zuo Commentary* (*Zuozhuan* 左傳), ix, 2–7, 11, 18, 23–36, 38–39, 44–45, 47, 66–68, 71–73, 90–91, 94, 95, 97, 102, 105–7, 113, 120, 144, 146, 155, 159–226, 239n7, 241n25, 243n6, 248nn54–56, 248n59, 249n71, 250nn78–80, 250n85, 252n9, 253n30, 254n36, 255n53, 256n59, 263n79, 264n89, 265n5, 269n69, 274n52; and anecdotes, 22,

60, 74, 76–79, 258n27; and bronze inscriptions, 81–89; and Chu, 66, 76–79, 124–26, 131, 138–41, 255n45, 262n70, 272n8, 272n10; dating of, 23–27, 249nn67–68; and *Discourses of the States*, 34–35, 58, 83, 244n8, 250n80; and *Records of the Historian*, 271n94; sources of, 27–34, 248n54, 250n75, 254n34; and *Spring and Autumn Annals*, 23–26, 28, 167n11, 246n25, 247n38, 249n67, 249n70, 254n34; and *Xinian*, 48–60, 64–65, 160–61, 164, 167, 171, 173–91, 194, 196, 254n41, 255n48. *See also* Du Yu; "noble man"; Zuo Qiuming

Zuozhuan. See *Zuo Tradition*

Zuoce Zeling-*gui* 乍冊夨令簋 inscription, 260n47

GPSR Authorized Representative: Easy Access System Europe, Mustamäe tee
50, 10621 Tallinn, Estonia, gpsr.requests@easproject.com

www.ingramcontent.com/pod-product-compliance
Lightning Source LLC
Chambersburg PA
CBHW021353290426
44108CB00010B/218